ALCOHOL AND THE ADULT BRAIN

The research literature on the impact of alcohol on the brain has seen a rapid expansion in recent years. *Alcohol and the Adult Brain* presents an up-to-date overview of some of the issues relevant to understanding and working with people with cognitive impairment as a result of chronic alcohol use.

One issue causing barriers to effective treatment and care is the stigma associated with alcohol dependence, resulting in the belief that difficulties associated with alcohol-related brain damage (ARBD) are 'self-inflicted'. Cognitive changes resulting from alcohol excess and poor nutrition can directly affect an individual's ability to motivate themselves, make decisions and make the informed choices that underlie behavior change. Attitudes held by professionals, reinforced by societal norms, that a person is 'choosing to drink' and 'not motivated to engage with treatment', in combination with the often subtle cognitive deficits associated with ARBD, can result in a lack of timely intervention, with enormous personal, social and economic cost.

The chapters in this book set ARBD in a social and cultural context, provide discussion of the difficulties in definition and diagnosis, and outline the structural brain changes and neuropsychological deficits associated with chronic alcohol use. The book provides an overview of recent research on ARBD, including impairments associated with Wernicke-Korsakoff Syndrome, and discusses up-to-date recommendations for managing and working with this complex and varied disorder.

Alcohol and the Adult Brain will be essential for students and researchers working with ARBD and for practitioners in a range of health, social care and voluntary settings.

Jenny Svanberg is the Consultant Clinical Psychologist at Forth Valley Substance Misuse Service, Scotland, UK, and was previously Principal Clinical Psychologist at the ARBD Service, Glasgow, UK.

Adrienne Withall is a Senior Lecturer and Senior Research Fellow at the School of Public Health and Community Medicine within the University of New South Wales and a clinician within Aged Care Psychiatry at the Prince of Wales Hospital, Sydney, Australia.

Brian Draper is a Professor (Conjoint) at the School of Psychiatry, University of New South Wales, Sydney, and the Director of the Academic Department for Old Age Psychiatry at the Prince of Wales Hospital, Randwick, Australia.

Stephen Bowden is a Professor in the School of Psychological Sciences, University of Melbourne, and Consultant Neuropsychologist at St Vincent's Hospital, Melbourne, Australia.

Current Issues in Neuropsychology

Series Editor: Jon Evans
Gartnavel Royal Hospital, Glasgow, UK

Current Issues in Neuropsychology is a series of edited books that reflect the state-of-the-art areas of current and emerging interest in the psychological study of brain damage, behavior and cognition.

Each volume is tightly focused on a particular topic, with chapters contributed by international experts. The editors of individual volumes are leading figures in their areas and provide an introductory overview of the field.

Each book will reflect an issue, area of uncertainty or controversy, with contributors providing a range of views on the central topic. Examples include the question of whether technology can enhance, support or replace impaired cognition, and how best to understand, assess and manage alcohol related brain damage.

Published titles in the series

Assistive Technology for Cognition
Edited by Brian O'Neill and Alex Gillespie

Alcohol and the Adult Brain
Jenny Svanberg, Adrienne Withall, Brian Draper and Stephen Bowden

ALCOHOL AND THE ADULT BRAIN

Edited by Jenny Svanberg, Adrienne Withall, Brian Draper and Stephen Bowden

ψ Psychology Press

Taylor & Francis Group

LONDON AND NEW YORK

First published 2015
by Psychology Press
27 Church Road, Hove, East Sussex BN3 2FA

and by Psychology Press
711 Third Avenue, New York, NY 10017

Psychology Press is an imprint of the Taylor & Francis Group, an informa business

© 2015 Jenny Svanberg, Adrienne Withall, Brian Draper and Stephen Bowden

The right of the editors to be identified as the authors of the editorial material,
and of the authors for their individual chapters, has been asserted in accordance
with sections 77 and 78 of the Copyright, Designs and Patents Act 1988.

British Library Cataloguing in Publication Data
A catalogue record for this book is available from the British Library

Library of Congress Cataloging-in-Publication Data
Alcohol and the adult brain / edited by Jenny Svanberg, Adrienne Withall,
Brian Draper and Stephen Bowden.
p. ; cm.
Includes bibliographical references and index.
I. Svanberg, Jenny, editor. II. Withall, Adrienne, editor. III. Draper, Brian, editor.
IV. Bowden, Stephen, 1955- , editor.
[DNLM: 1. Alcohol-Induced Disorders, Nervous System–chemically induced.
2. Cognition Disorders–epidemiology. 3. Alcohol Drinking–adverse effects.
WM 274]
RC565
616.86'1–dc23
2014027256

ISBN: 978-1-84872-307-8 (hbk)
ISBN: 978-1-84872-308-5 (pbk)
ISBN: 978-1-315-74292-2 (ebk)

Typeset in Bembo
by Deer Park Productions

Printed and bound in Great Britain by
TJ International Ltd, Padstow, Cornwall

CONTENTS

CONTRIBUTORS

Hélène Beaunieux, Université de Caen Neuropsychologie cognitive et neuro-anatomie fonctionnelle de la mémoire humaine, Université de Caen Basse-Normandie, Unité de recherché, France

Adrian Bonner, The Salvation Army, London, UK; and School of Applied Social Science, University of Stirling, UK

Stephen Bowden, Melbourne School of Psychological Sciences, University of Melbourne, Australia

Breda Cullen, Institute of Health and Wellbeing, University of Glasgow, UK

Apo Demirkol, Drug and Alcohol Services, South Eastern Sydney Local Health District, Australia, and School of Public Health and Community Medicine, UNSW, Australia

Brian Draper, School of Psychiatry, UNSW Australia, Australia; and Academic Department for Old Age Psychiatry, Euroa Centre, Prince of Wales Hospital, Australia

Francis Eustache, Université de Caen Neuropsychologie cognitive et neuroanat-omie fonctionnelle de la mémoire humaine, Université de Caen Basse-Normandie, France

Matti Hillbom, Department of Neurology, University of Oulu, Finland

John Hopkins, Koropiko Mental Health Services for Older People, Counties Manukau District Health Board, Middlemore Hospital, New Zealand

Carly Johnco, Centre for Emotional Health, Department of Psychology, Macquarie University, Australia

Nicholas Lintzeris, Drug and Alcohol Services, South East Sydney Local Health District, Australia, and Discipline of Addiction Medicine, University of Sydney, Australia

Fraser Morrison, Addictions Psychology Service, UK

Chris Perkins, Selwyn Centre for Ageing and Spirituality, The Selwyn Foundation, New Zealand

Anne-Lise Pitel, Université de Caen Neuropsychologie cognitive et neuroanatomie fonctionnelle de la mémoire humaine, Université de Caen Basse-Normandie, France

Nicole Ridley, Dementia Collaborative Research Centre, School of Psychiatry Faculty of Medicine, Australia

Lisa Savage, Developmental Exposure Alcohol Research Center, Binghamton University, State University of New York, USA

Simon Scalzo, Melbourne School of Psychological Sciences, University of Melbourne, Australia

Samaneh Shafiee, School of Public Health and Community Medicine, Faculty of Medicine, Samuels Building, Australia

Jenny Svanberg, Forth Valley Substance Misuse Service, NHS Forth Valley and Forth Valley Alcohol and Drug Partnership, Stirling Community Hospital, UK

Ken Wilson, Institute of Psychology, Health and Society, University of Liverpool, St Catherine's Hospital, UK

Adrienne Withall, School of Public Health and Community Medicine, Faculty of Medicine, UNSW, Australia

ACKNOWLEDGEMENTS

Table 2.1 is reproduced from *Neurologic Clinics*, 28, Kumar, N. Neurologic presentations of nutritional deficiencies, p107-170, Copyright (2010), with permission from Elsevier.

Figures 2.1 and 2.2 are reproduced from Zuccoli, G., Santa Cruz, D., Bertolini, M., Rovira, A., Gallucci, M., Carollo, C., and Pipitone, N. MR imaging findings in 56 patients with Wernicke encephalopathy: Nonalcoholics may differ from alcoholics. *American Journal of Neuroradiology*, 30, p171-176, copyright (2009) by American Society of Neuroradiology.

Figures 8.1 and 8.2 are reproduced from Pitel, A.-L., Chételat, G., Le Berre, A. P., Desgranges, B., Eustache, F., and Beaunieux, H. Macrostructural abnormalities in Korsakoff syndrome compared with uncomplicated alcoholism. *Neurology*, 78(17), 1330–1333, with permission from Wolters Kluwer Health.

Figure 8.6 is reproduced from Le Berre, A. P., Rauchs, G., La Joie, R., Mézenge, F., Boudehent, C., Vabret, F., Segobin, S., Viader, F., Allain, P., Eustache, F., Pitel, A-L., and Beaunieux, H. Impaired decision-making and brain shrinkage in alcoholism. European Psychiatry: *The Journal of the Association of European Psychiatrists*, 29(3), 125–133. Copyright © 2014 Elsevier Masson SAS. All rights reserved.

Figures 8.7 is reproduced from Le Berre, A. P., Rauchs, G., La Joie, R., Segobin, S., Mézenge, F., Boudehent, C., Vabret, F., Viader, F., Eustache, F., Pitel, A-L., and Beaunieux, H. Readiness to change and brain damage in patients with chronic alcoholism. *Psychiatry Research*, 213(3), 202–209. Copyright © 2013 Elsevier Masson SAS. All rights reserved.

Table 10.1 is reprinted from *Law, Ethics and Psychiatry*, 25, Hazelton, L., Sterns, G. L., Chisholm, T. Decision making capacity and alcohol abuse: clinical and ethical considerations in personal care choices. 130–135, © (2003), with permission from Elsevier.

The service model described within Chapter 12 is published in the College Report, CR185, 'Alcohol and brain damage in adults, with reference to high-risk groups' (Royal College of Psychiatrists, 2014), and is reprinted here with the kind permission of the Royal College of Psychiatrists, UK.

1

INTRODUCTION

Jenny Svanberg

Alcohol use is common in our society and has been described as the most harmful of the main substances of abuse, when physical, psychological and social harms to the individual and society are considered (Nutt, King and Phillips, 2010). A sizeable proportion of people who drink alcohol to harmful levels experience changes in the structure and functioning of the brain, although some of these changes are reversible in abstinence. "Alcohol-related brain damage" (ARBD) is the umbrella term for the spectrum of neurocognitive changes resulting from long-term excessive alcohol use, particularly in the context of thiamine deficiency. The last decade has seen a rapid expansion in research designed to understand and support people with ARBD. However, there continue to be debates over how to define and diagnose disorders such as Wernicke's Encephalopathy (WE), Korsakoff's Syndrome (KS) and alcohol-related dementia (ARD), with corresponding questions around assessment and treatment. These debates reflect the heterogeneity of this population, which spans mild, pervasive cognitive deficits that can occur early in ARBD to potentially severe and variable cognitive impairments associated with Wernicke-Korsakoff Syndrome (WKS). In a majority of those that develop ARBD, impairments will be to some extent reversible in abstinence, highlighting the need to recognize and treat ARBD as early as possible in order to prevent long-term health and social consequences.

Within this book, we recognize WE and KS as acute and chronic stages of WKS, and highlight that both stages can present with heterogeneity of neurological and neuropsychological symptoms. We set out the evidence that shows that ARD is best understood as chronic WKS, and argue that this offers a wider range of options for treatment. The term "alcohol-related brain damage" has become widely used as it reflects the heterogeneity of neurocognitive impairments caused by alcohol excess, and has been described as a pragmatic solution to address the complexity and dual diagnoses common within this group (Royal College of Psychiatrists, 2014).

ARBD can be understood as a form of acquired brain injury in which damage is caused by an external factor, but may be the only one in which the cause of injury is specified in its title (Scottish Executive, 2004). Arguably, this contributes to the considerable stigma that exists around this group, leading at times to a form of "therapeutic nihilism", where professionals feel that they are unable to intervene effectively or influence longstanding gains. This group also endures the view that their difficulties are "self-inflicted", adding to marginalization and providing barriers to effective treatment and care. In the context of ARBD, attitudes and beliefs around a person "choosing to drink" and "lacking motivation to engage with treatment", in combination with the often subtle cognitive deficits seen early in ARBD, deficits which directly impact on the person's ability to motivate and maintain behavioral change, can result in a lack of timely intervention for this preventable condition, with enormous personal, social and economic costs (Mental Welfare Commission for Scotland, 2006).

Within this book, we hope to challenge some of these attitudes, and aim to present some of the key issues relevant to understanding and working with people with ARBD. We begin in Chapter 2 with an overview of WKS. Simon Scalzo, Stephen Bowden and Matti Hillbom highlight that WE and KS can be seen as acute and chronic phases of WKS with a common underlying neuropathology, complicated by the heterogeneity within both the acute and chronic phases. The authors address problems of diagnosis, and argue that the term "alcohol-related dementia" can be seen as a misdiagnosis of severe WKS, which can result in inadequate or inappropriate treatment and therefore poorer prognosis. The chapter outlines approaches to assessment designed to minimize misdiagnosis, and describes the guidance on prevention and treatment of WKS, covered from different perspectives in later chapters.

In Chapter 3, Nicole Ridley and Brian Draper describe the epidemiology of ARBD, recognizing the difficulties in obtaining accurate epidemiological data when there has been a historical lack of consensus in diagnostic criteria and classification of ARBD. The authors therefore consider international data on alcohol consumption and alcohol-use disorders. Carly Johnco and Brian Draper then place ARBD in a cultural context in Chapter 4, looking at some of the social and cultural factors influencing alcohol consumption and excess, and the risk factors associated with ARBD.

When considering a whole-life perspective on the development of cognitive changes as a result of prolonged alcohol excess, it should be immediately apparent that comorbidity and heterogeneity are likely to be the norm rather than the exception. From the genetic factors or adverse early life experiences that may predispose someone to alcohol dependence, to the physical, psychiatric, neurological and societal consequences of chronic alcohol excess, the complexity of ARBD requires individually designed, multidisciplinary assessment and treatment approaches. In Chapter 5, Apo Demirkol and Nicholas Lintzeris consider comorbidities and consequences of alcohol-use disorders and ARBD, presenting an update of the literature on treatment approaches for concurrent alcohol use, mental health problems and cognitive impairments.

One of the recent advances in the field has been the emergence of a new cohort of older adults who are more likely to use alcohol and other substances to excess. Adrienne Withall and Samaneh Shafiee address this in Chapter 6, which calls for new models of care to respond to this group, who often have additional general health issues and may be uncomfortable in an addiction setting that is more suited to younger clients, but may also be excluded from memory clinics as a result of alcohol use. Issues around assessment and management of this group are presented, and the authors again highlight the need for integrated systems of care.

There remain questions over the underlying pathology of ARBD and its relation to neuropsychological functioning. Chapters 7, by Lisa Savage, and 8, by Hélène Beaunieux, Francis Eustache and Anne-Lise Pitel, address the neuropathological and behavioral changes associated with chronic alcohol use and dependence, drawing on animal models, post-mortem studies and in-vivo imaging studies to specify the structural changes to focal brain regions and the resulting behavioral changes. The authors in this section emphasize recent research into the alcohol-influenced disruption of reward and motivational brain networks, outlining the trap of ARBD: focal brain damage that directly affects the areas of the brain associated with recognizing the need to make behavioral changes, making those changes and maintaining new patterns of behavior. These chapters also illustrate the resilience and adaptability of those with ARBD, describing the mechanisms of recovery and compensation that can occur in abstinence.

The last chapters of the book provide more detail on prevention, assessment and rehabilitation of ARBD. Adrian Bonner, in Chapter 9, describes the nutritional issues and deficiencies associated with alcohol use, which are key in the development of WKS, and considers nutritional interventions that may mitigate cognitive decline.

Chapter 10 covers issues around cognitive screening and neuropsychological assessment with this population, considering questions such as when it may be appropriate to offer neuropsychological assessment to individuals continuing to use alcohol (Svanberg, Morrison and Cullen, 2015). The chapter provides a structure for assessment, and gives guidance on how neuropsychological assessment can be used to support assessment of decision-making capacity where necessary. This latter issue is addressed in detail in Chapter 11, by Chris Perkins and John Hopkins, which describes the ethical and legal issues that are vital to consider with this population. The authors provide a compassionate summary of the ethical dilemmas inherent in finding a balance between autonomy and protection. This is all the more difficult for this population for whom alcohol use may begin as a conscious and informed choice, but through subtle cognitive changes may be robbed of the ability to make and act on the decision to stop drinking. Ironically, in these cases, earlier use of legislation may be the least restrictive option to enable assertive treatment, prevent further deterioration and promote self-determination to the greatest degree.

The final chapter provides an overview of the psychosocial rehabilitation of people with ARBD, from diagnosis to longer-term management, drawing together the earlier chapters and reflecting recent recommendations made by a group of medical associations in the UK (Royal College of Psychiatrists, 2014; Wilson, 2015).

The chapter outlines a successful service model embedded in an evidence base that draws on the cognitive and psychosocial rehabilitation literature, describing the considerable benefits of a flexible, staged framework for managing ARBD. The author emphasizes that timely and appropriate care involving abstinence, nutritional support and assertive follow-up can provide an optimal environment to enhance recovery from ARBD, and points out that although specialist services can be cost effective in preventing hospital admissions and improving individual outcomes, all services can provide an element of prevention and early treatment.

We hope that a number of particular themes stand out within this book. First, that ARBD is preventable, and that some level of recovery is possible for a majority, even for those with severe cognitive impairments as a result of alcohol excess. Second, that the historically narrow diagnostic criteria for WKS have resulted in under-diagnosis, with enormous costs to individuals, families and society. A broader recognition of the heterogeneity of cognitive impairments within ARBD, and at both the acute WE and chronic KS stages of WKS, will allow better targeting of appropriate treatment for both cognitive impairment and alcohol-use disorders. Third, that people with ARBD can present with complex needs which impact on multiple levels of their functioning and ability to participate in their lives. Considering treatment from the point of view of these needs rather than their aetiology may reduce the stigma around this population, and emphasizes the need to draw on expertise from multiple disciplines and at multiple tiers of health and social care, as well as within the community. Neuropsychology has a key role to play at every stage of the journey experienced by people with ARBD, from supporting earlier recognition and assessment of specific cognitive impairments to using assessment feedback to explain difficulties in functioning and influencing the design of multidisciplinary rehabilitation packages for individuals to maximize their independence and participation in their lives.

References

Mental Welfare Commission for Scotland. (2006). *Investigation into the care and treatment of Mr H*. Edinburgh: MWCScot. Available at http://www.mwcscot.org.uk/media/51999/Mr_H_Inquiry.pdf. Accessed 8 July 2014.

Nutt, D. J., King, L. A. and Phillips, L. D. (2010). Drug harms in the UK: a multicriterion decision analysis. *Lancet*, 376, 1558–65.

Royal College of Psychiatrists. (2014). *Alcohol and brain damage in adults, with reference to high-risk groups*. College Report CR185. Available at http://www.rcpsych.ac.uk/files/pdfversion/CR185.pdf. Accessed 8 July 2014.

Scottish Executive. (2004). *A Fuller Life: Report of the Expert Group on Alcohol Related Brain Damage*. Stirling: Dementia Services Development Centre.

Svanberg, J., Morrison, F. and Cullen, B. (2015). Neuropsychological assessment of alcohol-related cognitive impairment. In J. Svanberg, A. Withall, B. Draper and S. Bowden (eds), *Alcohol and the Adult Brain*. Hove: Psychology Press.

Wilson, K. (2015). The clinical rehabilitation of people with alcohol-related brain damage. In J. Svanberg, A. Withall, B. Draper and S. Bowden (eds), *Alcohol and the Adult Brain*. Hove: Psychology Press.

2

WERNICKE-KORSAKOFF SYNDROME

Simon Scalzo, Stephen Bowden and Matti Hillbom

A syndrome resulting from thiamine deficiency was described in ancient China as Jiao Qi disease, now known as Beriberi, but in the late 1880s Carl Wernicke and Sergei Korsakoff independently described the different aspects of the syndrome still carrying their names (Fan, 2004; Victor, Adams and Collins, 1989; Wernicke, 1881). Vitamins were discovered at the beginning of the 20th century and thiamine deficiency was not shown to be the primary reason for Wernicke-Korsakoff Syndrome (WKS) until the middle of the 20th century (for review see Victor, Adams and Collins, 1971). WKS is a frequent cause of cognitive impairment among those with alcohol-use disorders (DSM-5 Codes 305.00 or 309.90 (American Psychiatric Association, 2013) or ICD-10 Codes 10.1 harmful use of alcohol, or 10.2 dependence on alcohol (World Health Organization, 2010)) and the most important preventable and treatable vitamin deficiency syndrome still frequently seen worldwide. This chapter provides an overview of the conditions leading to WKS and its prevalence, and addresses difficulties encountered in prevention, diagnosis and management of the disease.

Throughout this review, the unified term of "Wernicke-Korsakoff Syndrome" (WKS) will be used to refer to the neuropathological condition caused by thiamine deficiency, although the term "Korsakoff's Syndrome" (KS) is sometimes used to describe clinical amnesias due to other aetiologies. However, we would recommend that the term "Korsakoff's Syndrome" be restricted to description of cases of cognitive impairment caused by thiamine deficiency, the chronic or recovering phase of WKS, in line with Korsakoff's original descriptions and the usage recommended by Victor (1994; Victor, Adams and Collins, 1989). Aspects of these alternative definitions will be discussed below. Nevertheless, to preserve accuracy in citing previous authors' work, the separate terms of "Wernicke's Encephalopathy" (WE) and KS will be used as synonyms for the acute and chronic phases of WKS, respectively.

Conditions leading to Wernicke-Korsakoff Syndrome

The cornerstone in the prevention of WKS is to consider the conditions that predispose to thiamine deficiency. This is particularly important because the onset of the disease is often insidious. Signs and symptoms are often slight or mild and easily missed.

Thiamine is a water-soluble vitamin absorbed from the intestines. Much remains to be understood regarding the role of thiamine in metabolism. About half of the thiamine in the body is stored in the muscles and liver, and thiamine functions as a coenzyme in the metabolism of carbohydrates, lipids and branched-chain amino acids (Hoyumpa, 1980). A healthy adult eating an average diet needs about 0.66mg thiamine per 1,000kcal per day (Hoyumpa, 1980). The requirement may be tripled during pregnancy. High caloric and carbohydrate intakes increase the daily demand for thiamine due to the great role of thiamine in carbohydrate metabolism. Major reasons for thiamine deficiency are poor absorption of thiamine, lack of thiamine in ingested food and thiamine depletion from body stores if alcohol or fat are primary energy sources (Hoyumpa, 1980). Among those who eat carbohydrate-containing food the deficiency state may develop within approximately three weeks after total cessation of thiamine supply and WE may manifest as an acute confusional syndrome with nystagmus, and ataxia leading to coma (Bergin and Harvey, 1992; Hillbom et al., 1999). Three weeks is a very short precipitating period when compared with the development of deficiencies due to other vitamins. The period of time required to develop thiamine deficiency may even be less than three weeks if the stores are poor when intake is totally stopped. Thiamine deficiency also develops rapidly if associated with severe prolonged vomiting.

Table 2.1 shows the variety of clinical situations that may predispose to thiamine deficiency, whether through increased thiamine requirements, or nutritional risk factors (Kumar, 2010). As can be inferred, WKS can be seen among patients treated in medical, surgical, pediatric, geriatric, oncologic, neurologic, obstetric and psychiatric departments, as well as in intensive care units.

In other words, any condition or disease that can compromise nutritional status can be considered a risk factor for thiamine deficiency and subsequent WKS (Galvin et al., 2010; Ogershok et al., 2002; Sechi and Serra, 2007). In western countries, patients with WKS most commonly experience thiamine deficiency indirectly as a consequence of alcohol-use disorders (Harper et al., 1995; Rolland and Truswell, 1998). Excessive alcohol intake acts to deplete thiamine stores by i) reducing dietary intake of thiamine, with alcoholic beverage intake sometimes replacing many meals, ii) providing energy thus decreasing metabolic requirements for thiamine; and so iii) reducing thiamine storage and utilization (Heap et al., 2002; Price, 1985; Rees and Gowing, 2013; Sechi and Serra, 2007). The nutritional aspects of excess alcohol use are covered further elsewhere in this volume (Bonner, 2015).

Although it is commonly assumed that the KS phase of WKS is rare or nonexistent when WKS is associated with nutritional deficiency but not alcohol, this view stems from inadequate appreciation of the long-term course of WKS not associated with alcohol-use disorders or inattention to clinical symptoms, particularly

TABLE 2.1 Conditions or settings reported to be associated with thiamine deficiency (adapted from Kumar, 2010)

Increased requirements
- Children, pregnancy, lactation, vigorous exercise
- Critically ill
- Hyperthyroidism
- Malignancy, chemotherapy (e.g., erbulozole, ifosfamide), bone marrow transplantation
- Systemic infection, prolonged febrile illness

Marginal nutritional status (decreased intake or decreased absorption or increased losses)
- Acquired Immuno-Deficiency Syndrome (AIDS)
- Alcoholism
- Anorexia nervosa, dieting, starvation, hunger strike, food refusal, dietary neglect in the elderly
- Commercial dietary formula, slimming diets, food fads
- Decreased absorption caused by excess use of antacids
- Diet: polished rice, foods containing thiaminase or antithiamine compounds
- Dietary supplements with herbal preparations
- Gastrointestinal surgery (including bariatric surgery)
- Inactivation of thiamine in food by excessive cooking of thiaminase-containing foods
- Inadequate supplementation in parenteral or enteral nutrition
- Thiamine loss related to loop diuretics therapy
- Magnesium deficiency
- Persistent vomiting (pancreatitis, migraine attacks, hyperemesis gravidarum) or diarrhea
- Renal failure, hemodialysis, peritoneal dialysis
- Severe gastrointestinal or liver or pancreatic disease
- Tolazamide, high-dose nitroglycerine infusion (ethyl alcohol and propylene glycol on thiamine metabolism)
- High glucose intake
- Intravenous glucose administration
- Refeeding after prolonged starvation

mental status, in non-alcohol-related cases. A systematic review of 120 years of case reports of WKS not related to alcohol shows that severe cognitive impairment, including KS, is a common outcome in cases not related to alcohol, as is the full spectrum of signs of WKS (Scalzo *et al.*, 2015).

It is important to note, however, that thiamine deficiency does not always lead to WE (or WKS), so a genetic risk factor has been hypothesized (Nixon, 1984; Ridley and Draper, 2015; Thomson, Guerrini and Marshall, 2012). Support for a genetic component or risk factor can be found in the results of a Scottish-based study of various GABA gene clusters in 108, mostly male (84 per cent) alcohol-dependent individuals (Loh *et al.*, 1999). However, other genetic association studies have produced less clear results and further research is required to identify genetic risk factors for WE (Guerrini *et al.*, 2005; Guerrini, Thomson and Gurling, 2009; Matsushita *et al.*, 2000; McCool *et al.*, 1993). For further discussion of the genetics of WE and alcohol-related brain damage, see Ridley and Draper (2015).

Clinical diagnosis of the WE phase of WKS

In 1881, Carl Wernicke first described the encephalopathy that now bears his name. In his original article, he provided detailed descriptions of the clinical presentation and pathology of the disease (Wernicke, 1881, as translated in Thomson *et al.*, 2008a). These initial observations have proved enduring, including the initial description of the "classic triad" of diagnostic signs. The classic triad, as currently conceived, consists of (i) oculomotor abnormalities, namely ophthalmoplegia and nystagmus, (ii) cerebellar dysfunction, especially gait ataxia, and (iii) altered mental state, ranging from subtle cognitive impairment to a global confusional state or coma (Caine *et al.*, 1997; Galvin *et al.*, 2010; Thomson *et al.*, 2008a).

However, we now know that the diagnosis of WE is often missed in life and only made at post-mortem examination (Harper, 1983; Naidoo, Bramdev and Cooper, 1991; Torvik, Lindboe and Rogde, 1982). In a recent review, Galvin and colleagues (2010) combined the data from 11 autopsy studies for which clinical examination data were also available. The combined sample totalled 256 cases of WE. Of these cases, 24 per cent had a history of an oculomotor abnormality, 25 per cent a cerebellar sign, including ataxia and gait disturbance, 23 per cent had memory impairment of varying severity and 53 per cent had an "altered mental state". Overall, only 8 per cent of autopsied cases had a clinical history of the full classic clinical triad, demonstrating the very low sensitivity of the triad as an indicator of Wernicke-Korsakoff neuropathology.

Brew (1986) investigated whether altering the diagnostic criteria of WE would lead to a reduced rate of missed diagnosis and a clinically derived incidence figure better approximating of the incidence figures obtained from comparable autopsy studies. Brew found that only 0.4 per cent of medical admissions to the emergency department of a large hospital in Camperdown, NSW, Australia, had the full triad of WE, when the triad was defined as confusion plus ataxia plus ophthalmoplegia, or 0.7 per cent if defined as confusion plus ataxia plus ophthalmoplegia or nystagmus. However, if the diagnostic criteria of WE were revised to be at least two of confusion, ataxia, and ophthalmoplegia or nystagmus, in the absence of other causes, then the prevalence among emergency admissions of WE taken together with cases of KS was 2 per cent, much closer to the prevalence figures reported from autopsy studies in Australia (Brew, 1986; Harper, 1983; Harper *et al.*, 1989).

Similarly, Caine and colleagues (Caine *et al.*, 1997) investigated the effect of relaxing diagnostic criteria on the sensitivity to diagnosis in light of the reported high rates of missed diagnosis revealed by autopsy studies. Unlike Brew (1986), however, Caine and colleagues investigated a sample with a known history of chronic alcohol abuse, and diagnosis of WE was confirmed by post-mortem examination. Caine and colleagues revised the diagnostic criteria of WE to be any two of the following four signs occurring in the context of chronic alcohol abuse: 1) dietary deficiencies, 2) any oculomotor abnormalities, 3) cerebellar dysfunction, such as ataxia or gait unsteadiness, and 4) altered mental state or mild memory impairment. Retrospective application of their revised operational criteria to 106 cases, each with an autopsy report and a history of chronic alcohol abuse (defined as daily consumption of ethanol above 80 grams for most of adult life), showed that WE could be diagnosed with high sensitivity and specificity on clinical grounds. Of the 40 cases with autopsy-confirmed diagnosis of WE or WKS pathology, 34 (85 per cent) were retrospectively diagnosed as having WE or WKS using the revised criteria, as opposed to only nine (23 per cent) that would have been diagnosed if all signs of the classic triad were required. The revised criteria have been adopted as European guidelines for the diagnosis of WE (or acute WKS) (Galvin et al., 2010).

Thomson and colleagues (2008b) have also noted that too much emphasis has been placed on the classic clinical triad of acute WE at the expense of other key signs often indicative of the disease. They reported that early signs and symptoms of thiamine deficiency include loss of appetite, nausea or vomiting, fatigue, weakness, apathy, giddiness, diplopia, insomnia, anxiety, difficulty in concentration and loss of memory. They note that recognition of these early signs in at-risk individuals can assist instigation of early administration of effective treatment in the form of parenteral thiamine (Thomson et al., 2008b).

Even so, the diagnosis of WE is still regarded as difficult. Some of the warning signs and symptoms of thiamine deficiency, such as fatigue, irritability, depressed mood and abdominal discomfort do not differentiate thiamine deficiency from conditions of other aetiology. Further difficulty is encountered when neurological signs are subtle or confused or masked by intoxication, head injury, coma, or other significant illness (Feeney and Connor, 2008; Ferguson, Soryal and Pentland, 1997; Harper, 1983; Rufa et al., 2011). Until neuroimaging and measures of physiological thiamine concentrations become more sensitive and rapidly available, WE remains a challenging clinical diagnosis and the level of suspicion for the disease should be high (Sechi and Serra, 2007). Conditions which lead to thiamine deficiency, such as continuous heavy drinking of alcohol, malnutrition, poor or questionable diet, or prolonged vomiting due to any cause, should always raise suspicion.

Clinical diagnosis of the KS phase of WKS

As shown elsewhere in this volume (Savage, 2015), the neuropathology of the acute (WE) and chronic (KS) phases of WKS are indistinguishable, apart from recency of onset and severity of disease (Torvik, Lindboe and Rogde, 1982). The variable severity of WKS neuropathology is an aspect that has received insufficient attention (Savage, 2015; Torvik, Lindboe and Rogde, 1982). As noted, it makes most sense to regard WE and KS as different phases of the same pathological condition (Bowden, 1990; Torvik, 1991; Victor, 1994; Zahr, Kaufman and Harper, 2011). Nevertheless, many clinicians will be concerned to identify patients in the chronic or post-acute phase of the disease, a clinical diagnosis considered in this section.

In the largest study of its type, Victor and colleagues (1989) observed that KS was preceded by a global confusional state in 80 per cent of cases. For the remaining 20 per cent of observed cases, confusion did not mask cognitive impairment, and

KS was evident from the very first examination. Victor and colleagues also noted that the neurological signs of WE are often evident in patients diagnosed with KS, although frequently overlooked. Based on their clinical observations, Victor and colleagues described chronic KS as a primarily amnestic disorder, affecting both the ability to recall aspects of or whole events which occurred months or years prior to disease onset (retrograde amnesia) and the ability to learn new information (anterograde amnesia). Type and severity of memory impairment was variable between patients, and was variable even within individuals on the same memory subtests over time (Talland, 1960a; Talland and Ekdahl, 1959; Victor, Adams and Collins, 1989; Victor, Talland and Adams, 1959).

However, it is imperative to note that these early and extensive psychological studies examined only a subset of patients with "typical" KS. In their first paper, Victor and colleagues noted that "the group of patients … represented about two-thirds of a larger sample of patients with Korsakoff's psychosis from which they were selected for being less damaged in their general cognitive functioning" (Victor, Talland and Collins, 1959, p. 530). The selection strategy was repeated for many subsequent studies (Talland, 1958, 1959, 1960a, 1960b; Talland and Ekdahl, 1959). In other words, a proportion of patients with KS had more severe or extensive cognitive impairment, but these patients were excluded from this study and many other studies because of a research focus on the selective amnesia (Bowden, 1990). Even within the selective sample, Victor, Talland and colleagues drew attention to the widespread cognitive deficits beyond memory dysfunction seen in KS.

The often repeated definition of KS specifies memory impairment out of proportion to relatively intact general intelligence and other cognitive abilities (Kopelman *et al.*, 2009; Oscar-Berman, 2012; Sechi and Serra, 2007; Victor, Adams and Collins, 1989). Ironically, the research focus on selective amnesia became the diagnostic criterion for psychometric identification of the KS phase of WKS (Butters and Cermak, 1980), although Victor subsequently strongly emphasized the selective and unrepresentative nature of this narrow definition (Victor, 1994).

According to the recently superseded DSM-IV-TR (American Psychiatric Association, 2000), any individual with significant memory impairment plus significant cognitive impairment would meet criteria for dementia, therefore being excluded from a diagnosis of Alcohol-Induced Persisting Amnestic Disorder due to thiamine deficiency (synonym of KS). In the recently published DSM-5 (American Psychiatric Association, 2013), presence of dementia is no longer listed as an exclusion criterion, and general cognitive dysfunction is specifically mentioned as a frequent occurrence in Alcohol-Induced Neurocognitive Disorder. However, the new nomenclature does not shed any light on the aetiological relationship or pathological contributions of thiamine deficiency and alcohol neurotoxicity. In the DSM-5, all references to WKS and KS only describe memory impairment and confabulation as common features, failing to mention the potential for milder impairment or recovery, on the one hand, and more pervasive cognitive impairment, including dementia, on the other hand (Bowden, 1990, 2010; Torvik, Lindboe and Rogde, 1982; Victor, 1994).

An excellent example of the variable severity and pervasive nature of cognitive impairment associated with chronic WKS is provided by Pitel and colleagues (Pitel *et al.*, 2011). While seeking to control for alcohol-use history, including lifetime intake of alcohol, Pitel and colleagues found that participants with a history of alcohol-use disorder and with one of the neurological signs of WKS (see previous section) demonstrated greater cognitive deficits than patients with no neurological signs. Patients with two neurological signs were more impaired than those with one sign or no signs, across a wide range of cognitive abilities, including intelligence, memory, visuo-constructional ability, processing speed and upper limb motor skills. The study by Pitel and colleagues illustrates that if patients with WKS are selected on the basis of neurological signs of WKS, rather than by particular neuropsychological profile, and cognitive function is examined in a comprehensive fashion, then patients with chronic WKS show a wide range of cognitive impairments of variable severity. These aspects of WKS have been highlighted previously but continue to be under-appreciated by many clinicians (Bowden, 1990; Torvik, 1991; Torvik, Lindboe and Rogde, 1982; Victor, 1994).

The wide spectrum or variability in cognitive expression of WKS is illustrated in another recent study of patients with chronic KS. Fujiwara *et al.* (2008) reported a sample of 20 patients with chronic KS residing in specialized nursing homes. These patients performed significantly more poorly than a control group on almost all tests of cognitive function. Performance was relatively stable across two assessments administered two years apart. The patients with chronic KS performed most poorly on tests of memory, but also showed other deficits including indicators of general intellectual function.

In a recent, consecutive case series Scalzo and Bowden (2015) reported psychometric profiles in five patients with WKS diagnosed on neurological grounds and all of whom had histories of alcohol-use disorders. Three of the five patients displayed the classic triad of eye signs, ataxia and cognitive impairment, the other two cases displayed an initial confusion with either ataxia or eye signs, so all patients qualified for a diagnosis of WE according to the European guidelines (Galvin *et al.*, 2010). Patients were assessed when medically stable on intelligence index and memory index scores, being the contemporary versions of the conventional "IQ versus MQ" contrast recommended for diagnosis of KS for many years because it was assumed that a 20–30 point discrepancy, in favor of intelligence, was the "hallmark" of the chronic KS phase of WKS (Butters and Cermak, 1980; Kopelman *et al.*, 2009; Lough, 2012). However, this discrepancy criterion has been criticized as lacking diagnostic sensitivity (Bowden, 1990; Victor, 1994). The average intelligence versus memory index difference in the sample of five cases was 12 points in favor of the intelligence index, but the difference was not statistically significant and the discrepancy range was from −14 to 36, larger positive differences favoring intelligence. Such is the momentum of the "IQ versus MQ" discrepancy that there are few cases of chronic WKS reported in the literature who show cognitive profiles other than the marked IQ versus MQ discrepancy. However, cases with other cognitive profiles clearly constitute a substantial portion of patients diagnosed on neurological grounds with chronic WKS (or the KS phase), excluded from many clinical or cognitive neuropsychological studies because they did not meet the discrepancy criterion (Bowden, 1990; Torvik, Lindboe and Rogde, 1982; Victor, 1994). The case outlined in Table 2.2 outlines some of the different presentations of WKS as it evolves from acute to chronic stages.

This case illustrates several important but not well-recognized aspects of WKS evolving from an acute presentation of WE into a chronic KS followed by gradual recovery enabling resumption of independent living. The thiamine treatment protocol was that in favor in the respective centres at the time of admission, and reflects the considerable variation in practice in the absence of evidence-based guidelines (Day et al., 2013). The patient displayed the classic triad of WKS, namely eye signs, ataxia and cognitive impairment on acute admission and the post-acute phase was marked by a severe clinical amnesia qualifying for a diagnosis of KS. Disabled and unable to care for himself, he initially resided in supported accommodation for almost two years, but by the end of that period had recovered cognitive function sufficiently to enable him to resume independent living. The cognitive recovery was substantiated by significant recovery of verbal memory skills over a three-year post-admission interval, however, the patient himself volunteered that he had not fully recovered and that he could not work in the way he had prior to onset of heavy drinking and the episode of WKS. If seen without knowledge of the episode of severe, acute WE or the post-acute KS, he could easily have been misdiagnosed as a mild alcohol-related dementia but instead should be regarded as variant WKS having experienced a common course, namely, a severe episode of WKS with acute presentation and partial recovery over several years (Victor, 1994; Victor et al, 1989).

Improving diagnostic sensitivity to the variability of WKS, both acute and chronic

The divergence in understanding of WKS in acute and chronic variants, depending on the selection criteria used to identify the condition, illustrates the dangers in relying on diagnostic criteria that are unduly narrow. When diagnosed on the basis of the severe, selective amnesia (Butters and Cermak, 1980), chronic WKS appears to be rare. However, as reviewed above, the early studies that used this diagnostic criterion acknowledged that a substantial portion of patients with WKS were excluded from consideration. If a broader clinical diagnostic criterion is used – for example, some flexible combination of the components of the classic triad (see WE section above), then estimates of the clinical prevalence of WKS increase substantially. Finally, if post-mortem diagnosis of WKS neuropathology is the criterion, then prevalence estimates increase dramatically again, indicating that WKS is a common condition (see section below on prevalence).

As noted above, Caine and colleagues (1997) sought to revise the clinical criteria for recognition of WE in cases confirmed with post-mortem examination. These revised

TABLE 2.2 Case study: recovery from severe Wernicke-Korsakoff Syndrome

ZB was a 34-year-old male, qualified tradesperson when admitted to a tertiary medical centre with an acute episode of WE following prolonged severe alcohol abuse and oesophagitis of recent onset. On admission he was observed to be suffering disorientation to time, place and person, nystagmus, ataxia, peripheral neuropathy, vomiting, melaena and a tender hepatomegaly. No confabulation was noted and no other significant illness was observed. CT showed marked cerebral and cerebellar atrophy. He was treated with 100mg intramuscular thiamine daily for two weeks, then oral multivitamins. He was transferred after five days to a specialist alcohol rehabilitation facility. Re-examination by a physician after transfer confirmed the disorientation and stable signs of WE.

Four weeks after transfer, in the context of a stable medical condition and clinically obvious severe amnesia, he was administered a brief cognitive assessment. At this time he was still disoriented to time, place and person, needing close supervision in daily living skills, in particular to avoid getting lost if he left the ward. At this assessment he obtained Wechsler Intelligence (short-form) scaled scores in the range of 4 to 7 (standardized mean = 10 and SD = 3: patient's scores approximately one to two standard deviations below the reference group mean at the second to 16th percentile). He obtained a Wechsler Memory Scale Auditory-Verbal Memory Index of 56 (standardized mean = 100 and SD = 15: patient's scores approximately 3 standard deviations below the reference group mean and well below the first percentile) and was diagnosed with KS.

He underwent a prolonged period of rehabilitation in supported accommodation, remaining abstinent, and gradually regaining independent living skills. Twenty months after initial admission, in the context of conspicuously improving cognitive status, he commenced taking day leave and travelling independently around his city of residence to attend to personal affairs. He was discharged from supported accommodation approximately 22 months after initial admission and moved into a small apartment, remaining abstinent.

He was reassessed for his cognitive abilities on an out-patient visit approximately three years after initial admission and obtained Wechsler Intelligence Index scores in the range of 84 to 90 (standardized mean = 100 and SD = 15: patient's scores ranging from approximately 1 standard deviation below the reference group mean to 0.33 standard deviation below the mean, at the 14th to 25th percentile). At reassessment he also obtained a Wechsler Memory Scale Auditory-Verbal Memory Index score of 89 (standardized mean = 100 and SD = 15: patient's score approximately 0.33 standard deviations below the reference group mean at the 23rd percentile) with a 95 per cent confidence between 80 and 102 Index points (centered on the predicted true score of 91). These results indicate substantial objective improvement in memory over the three years since initial admission. Other anterograde memory scores were in the same range. At this time he was working part time in his previous trade.

At this last assessment, ZB reflected that when he was first admitted, his mind was "warped, I couldn't think straight about anything. [Before admission] my memory was bad, I'd wake up in the morning and I'd have a desperate scramble to find a drink, I couldn't remember where I had hidden it so my mates would not drink it if I passed out first. … It took me about six months to start recovering, to start being able to think straight again. It is good being able to wake up in the morning and remember where you are and what you did the day before, just the little things, like what you had for tea."

De-identified case report approved by the relevant Hospital Research and Ethics Committee.

criteria, like previous methods to lower the threshold for detection of WKS reviewed above, were shown to greatly improve the sensitivity and specificity of diagnosis. However, several important issues remain to be addressed. One issue is that Caine and colleagues' criteria are explicitly addressed to diagnosis of the acute WE phase of WKS, and might be interpreted as not applying to the KS phase. However, Caine and colleagues included cases of chronic illness and chronic pathology in their study. Therefore, it may be that Caine and colleagues' criteria apply equally well to patients with WKS in the chronic or KS phase of the illness, illustrating the variable nature of neurological and cognitive effects of chronic WKS, perhaps just as variable as in the acute phase (Reuler, Girard and Cooney, 1985; Sechi and Serra, 2007; Victor, 1994). In addition, the prospective and retrospective post-mortem studies of WKS show that many patients are diagnosed with a clinical dementia, not selective amnesia, prior to death (Lishman, 1998; Torvik, Lindboe and Rogde, 1982; Victor, 1994). Therefore, while not specific to WKS, diagnostic sensitivity may be improved by considering cases of clinical dementia as possible WKS, particularly if associated with a known or possible history of alcohol-use disorders or nutritional deficiency (Ambrose, Bowden and Whelan, 2001; Ridley and Draper, 2015; Torvik, Lindboe and Rogde, 1982; Victor, 1994). Since treatment with high-dose thiamine is safe (see below), WKS as an underlying cause of dementia, especially "alcohol-related" dementia, should be considered more often.

The symptomatic presentation of WKS as alcohol-related dementia and potential for long-term recovery with improved health and nutrition has been reviewed in detail elsewhere but is still not well appreciated (Bowden, 1990, 2010; Victor, 1994; Zahr et al., 2011). In an autopsy study of 8,735 cases, Torvik and colleagues (1982) examined the brains of 713 cases with a known alcohol-use disorder. Despite the large sample, Torvik and colleagues failed to detect a single instance of a patient labeled "alcohol-related dementia" in life, which could not be accounted for by WKS pathology or less commonly another dementia not due to alcohol, such as Alzheimer's or vascular dementia. Further, upon retrospective analysis of the clinical records of 20 cases with inactive (chronic) pathology of WE, only five cases were reported to have a clinical amnesia, the others were reported to have exhibited more generalized cognitive impairment. Torvik and colleagues concluded that WE was the primary pathology underlying all reported cases of alcohol-related dementia.

Dementia in the context of severe alcohol-use disorders remains a major cause of dementia after Alzheimer's disease and vascular dementia, particularly among sufferers with early-onset, before 65 years of age (Draper et al., 2011; Harvey, Skelton-Robinson and Rossor, 2003; McMurtray et al., 2006; Ridley and Draper, 2015; Sampson, Warren and Rossor, 2004). A recent and large Australian study revealed that patients admitted to hospital with a diagnosis indicative of a cognitive impairment or a dementia-type presentation due to alcohol tended to be younger than all other dementia patients admitted during the same time frame (Draper et al., 2011). In their study, which had a minimum age threshold of 50 years, Draper and colleagues found that over half of the patients labeled as having an alcohol-related dementia were under the age of 65 compared to only 3.7 per cent of all dementia patients, the latter inclusive of the patients with dementia secondary to excessive alcohol consumption.

MRI and blood thiamine assay in the diagnosis of WKS

MRI is the method of choice to visualize brain lesions in WKS. Frequently radiologists are the first to suggest the diagnosis. Symmetrical lesions in the thalami, mammillary bodies, tectal plate and periaqueductal area suggest WKS (Figure 2.1), but also atypical lesions (Figure 2.2) located in the cerebellum, vermis, cranial nerve nuclei, red nuclei, dentate nuclei, caudate nuclei, splenium and cerebral cortex may be seen (Zuccoli and Pipitone, 2009). Diffusion-weighted imaging (DWI) could be the best MRI method for the diagnosis and follow-up studies.

The widely cited figures for the effectiveness of identifying WE (or acute WKS) on neuroimaging (e.g., Donnino *et al.*, 2007; Galvin *et al.*, 2010; Sullivan and Pfefferbaum, 2009) were originally reported by Antunez *et al.* (1998). Antunez and colleagues investigated the sensitivity and specificity of CT and MR imaging for the diagnosis of WE using three groups matched for age and gender. The groups consisted of 15 patients with acute WE, and comparison groups comprising 15 chronic

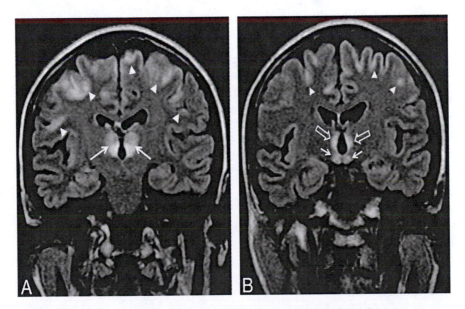

FIGURE 2.1 MRI findings in Wernicke's disease (A) Signal–intensity alterations with different intensity patterns are seen in the thalami (arrows). Diffuse signal–intensity alterations of the frontal cortex (arrowheads) are present. (B) Note signal–intensity alterations in the mammillary bodies (arrows), periventricular region of the third ventricle (empty arrows) and brain cortex (arrowheads).
Source: Zuccoli *et al.* (2009). © American Society of Neuroradiology.

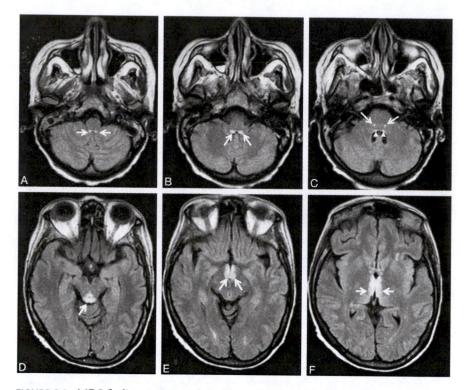

FIGURE 2.2 MRI findings in Wernicke's disease (A) The hypoglossal nuclei show symmetric high-signal-intensity alterations (arrows). (B) The medial vestibular nuclei show symmetric hyperintense lesions (arrows). (C) Symmetric high-signal-intensity alterations in the facial nuclei (arrows) are detected. Subtle signal-intensity alterations in the abducens nuclei are seen (arrowheads). (D) The tectum of the midbrain and the periaqueductal gray matter shows signal-intensity alterations (arrow). (E) The mammillary bodies (arrows) show signal-intensity alterations. (F) Note signal-intensity alterations (arrows) of the medial thalami and periventricular region of the third ventricle. *Source*: Zuccoli *et al.* (2009). © American Society of Neuroradiology.

alcohol-dependent patients without WE, neurological abnormalities or other overt comorbidity, and 15 healthy controls. Diagnosis of WE was based on clinical signs and confirmed by response to thiamine treatment and measures of erythrocyte transketolase activity in the blood before thiamine treatment. CT and MRI scans were coded blind to patients' clinical presentation. Sensitivity of CT to detect acute WE was 13 per cent. Sensitivity of MRI for the diagnosis of acute WE was 53 per cent with a specificity of 93 per cent. It was concluded that MRI is a useful tool for the diagnosis of WE, but that a negative MRI does not rule out the diagnosis.

Similarly, Lough (2012) reviewed case reports of WE published between 2001 and 2011. Most of the cases (81 per cent) reviewed by Lough had no known history of chronic alcohol abuse. In a re-evaluation of the data published in Lough's review for the purposes of this chapter, it was found that of 48 cases with MRI data available,

40 (83 per cent) showed lesions often implicated in WE (lesions in at least one of the following: mammillary bodies, periaqueductal gray matter, hypothalamus, around the third ventricle, midbrain, or inferior colliculi). A further two cases (4 per cent) had MRI abnormalities solely within the basal ganglia, and six (13 per cent) reportedly had MRI results indicative of a normal brain. A further four cases had results of a CT scan reported without additional MRI, in three cases the CT scan was suggestive of a normal brain, and in the remaining case, abnormalities were seen only within the basal ganglia. While lesions typically seen in WE were common in the cases reviewed by Lough, it was unclear as to what proportion of scans were actually diagnostic of WE.

Also, while neuroimaging of chronic WKS is often useful, the distinction between chronic Korsakoff patients and asymptomatic patients with alcohol-related brain changes is at times unclear on scans, and the neuroimaging of chronic WKS can be presumed to have imperfect sensitivity, just as reported for acute WKS (Antunez *et al.*, 1998; Blansjaar *et al.*, 1992; Jung, Chanraud and Sullivan, 2012; Sullivan and Pfefferbaum, 2009). Despite the acute and chronic phases of WKS each having distinguishing features on imaging corresponding to duration of disease (Sullivan and Pfefferbaum, 2009), WE and KS are two stages of the one disease process, much of the neuropathological underpinnings are shared and post-mortem examination of brain tissue cannot distinguish those with versus those without clinical history of memory impairment (Caine *et al.*, 1997; Harris *et al.*, 2008; Jauhar and Montaldi, 2000; Victor, Adams and Collins, 1989).

Others have also concluded that normal or elevated levels of thiamine on blood tests should not exclude the diagnosis of WE (Kono *et al.*, 2009; Lough, 2012; Ma and Truswell, 1995; Rolland and Truswell, 1998; Wood, Currie and Breen, 1986). Accuracy may also be dependent on type of measure (Rooprai *et al.*, 1996; Tallaksen, Bohmer and Bell, 1992), with a recent review suggesting that high-performance liquid chromatography (HPLC) has replaced erythrocyte transketolase assay as the recommended laboratory test for thiamine deficiency (Galvin *et al.*, 2010).

To conclude, despite advances in neuroimaging and measures of circulating thiamine, these technologies have substantial diagnostic limitations and the most efficient method for early diagnosis of WKS remains careful clinical observation and consideration of risk factors relating to malnutrition (Sechi and Serra, 2007; Thomson *et al.*, 2002). If the diagnosis of WKS is suspected, all possible diagnostic facilities should be used to verify the diagnosis, including repetitive MRI scanning.

Guidelines for neuropsychological assessment of patients suspected of chronic WKS

In view of the high rate of missed diagnosis of WKS, particularly in chronic variants, a reconsideration of the approach to cognitive assessment is needed. The accumulation of evidence suggests that use of the "IQ versus MQ" discrepancy (Butters and Cermak, 1980; Kopelman *et al.*, 2009; Lough, 2012) has low diagnostic sensitivity, between 3 per cent and 40 per cent approximately (Bowden, 1990; Bowden and

Ritter, 2005; Scalzo and Bowden, 2015). Instead, cognitive assessment of patients known or suspected to be in the stable, chronic WKS or post-acute WE phase (these two diagnostic categories used as synonyms) should be assessed without prejudice to the cognitive presentation. In particular, just as the classic triad of neurological signs has low sensitivity to acute WE (Galvin et al., 2010), so too, the 20 point plus IQ versus MQ discrepancy *should not be used* to diagnose chronic WKS or KS, *to the exclusion* of patients who do not show the discrepancy. Clinicians who only make the diagnosis in patients who satisfy the discrepancy criterion will miss many patients with chronic WKS because of the limited diagnostic sensitivity of the discrepancy criterion (Bowden, 1990). Some patients may satisfy the discrepancy criterion, others will show dementia of highly variable severity as well as variable patterns of impairment across assessed abilities (Scalzo and Bowden, 2015). Other patients will recover relatively quickly and may appear unimpaired at long-term follow-up. The aim of the cognitive ability assessment should be to identify functional needs and capacities, rather than categorical classification which risks missing cognitive and other psychological needs in patients with variant cognitive presentations.

We recommend careful assessment of cognitive abilities, using any well-normed and validated cognitive battery that covers the core ability factors described by the Cattell–Horn–Carroll (CHC) model of cognitive function (McGrew, 2009). These abilities include acquired knowledge (Gc), fluid intelligence (Gf), working memory (Gsm), processing speed (Gspeed) and long-term retrieval (Glr) (McGrew, 2009). These abilities account for most of the reliable variance in diverse neuropsychological batteries and the CHC model of cognition guides theoretical justification of most contemporary intelligence tests (Bowden, 2013; Kaufman, 2013).

Prevalence of Wernicke-Korsakoff Syndrome at post-mortem

Post-mortem prevalence of WKS is important because so much misunderstanding regarding WKS has arisen as a result of the extreme discrepancy between the clinical prevalence, historically thought to be low, versus the post-mortem prevalence, which shows that WKS is common and frequently not diagnosed in life.

Galvin and colleagues (2010) combined the data from 20 studies of consecutive autopsies. In the combined data, mean prevalence of WKS neuropathology was 1.3 per cent ($N = 39,783$). Among people with a history of alcohol-use disorders mean prevalence was much higher at 9.3 per cent ($N = 1,850$). Galvin and colleagues also reported a mean prevalence of 1.3 per cent in people without a history of alcohol-use disorders, however, this figure may overestimate prevalence because all but one of these non-alcohol-related case series used targeted sampling (Bertrand et al., 2009; Bleggi-Torres et al., 2000; Boldorini et al., 1992).

In an approach similar to that taken by Galvin and colleagues (2010), a list of consecutive autopsy studies with prevalence data available has been summarized in Table 2.3. The samples included in Table 2.3 are similar to those reviewed by Galvin et al., except that more recent figures are used for the Cleveland sample than were used by Galvin et al. (Victor, Adams and Collins, 1971; Victor and Laureno,

1978), and the Austrian study of Jellinger (1976) included by Galvin *et al.* is not included in Table 2.3 because the minimum age in Jellinger's study was 55 years, thus less representative of the adult population. Also, unlike Galvin *et al.*, Table 2.3 does not include studies that restricted examination to specific clinical conditions, whether alcohol-related or not.

As can be seen in Table 2.3, autopsy studies of the mid-late 20th century in Australia, Brazil, Europe and the USA reveal that the mean prevalence of WKS neuropathology is approximately 1.4 per cent ($N = 40,783$), a figure only slightly higher than that reported by Galvin and colleagues. Approximately three-quarters (77 per cent) of positive cases had chronic WKS pathology, whereas only 23 per cent had solely acute lesions. A diagnosis of WKS was suspected during life in only 17 per cent of cases with WKS neuropathology. Males with WKS neuropathology outnumbered women (a male to female ratio of 2.6:1), but this gender ratio may reflect male preponderance for alcohol-use disorders (Lindboe and Løberg, 1988; Torvik, Lindboe and Rogde, 1982; Victor and Laureno, 1978). The great majority of cases had history of alcohol-use disorders, with only 5 per cent of cases identified as not having history of alcohol-use disorders. The most common age at death for cases with WKS neuropathology was in the sixth and seventh decades. However, many of the cases included in these autopsy studies did not die directly of WKS, and because WKS pathology was chronic or longstanding in the majority of cases, it may be assumed that WKS is typically acquired before the age of 50.

Most recent data also suggest that prevalence of WKS is especially high among the population with alcohol-use disorders, some studies reporting prevalence greater than 10 per cent in alcohol-dependent samples (Galvin *et al.*, 2010; Harper *et al.*, 1998; Ridley and Draper, 2015). It should be noted, however, that of the autopsy studies reviewed in Table 2.3 the most recent case material was obtained in 1997, approximately 17 years ago. So, while prevalence appears to be "generally high" (Thomson *et al.*, 2002), recent prevalence data are lacking. Nevertheless, in this compilation of the most representative sampling, approximately 83 per cent of individuals with WKS pathology did not receive a clinical diagnosis of WKS during life.

Prevention of WKS

Apart from strategies to reduce the issue of problem drinking in broader society, such as those outlined by the NHS in the UK (Royal College of Physicians, 2001), other prevention strategies have been proposed to reduce the rate of WKS specifically. One approach is to increase thiamine intake of an entire population via fortification of food or alcoholic beverages with thiamine. For example, thiamine enrichment of bread flour has been associated with a significant reduction in the prevalence of WKS in Australia, although it was unclear whether the enrichment was the causal factor in the reduction (Harper *et al.*, 1998) or whether improved medical education has led to improved treatment.

However, in a study published 20 years after the mandatory fortification of bread flour with thiamine in Australia, Rees and Gowing (2013) found blood thiamine

TABLE 2.3 Prevalence and characteristics of WKS from published autopsy studies

Source	Country	Time of data collection	Total number of autopsies	Total number with WKS pathology	Number with WKS suspected during life (%)	Acute pathology (%)	Chronic pathology (%)	Acute on chronic (%)	Male (%)	Female (%)	Alcohol Hx (%) / No alcohol Hx (%) / Unknown Hx (%)	Age characteristics of WKS
Harper, 1983[a]	Australia (Perth, WA)	1973–81	4,677	131 (2.8%)	26 (20%)	22 (17%)	86 (66%)	23 (18%)	98 (75%)	33 (25%)	118 (90%) / 1 (0.76%) / 12 (9%)[f]	Peak age of incidence: 50–9yo (41%) (Minimum 12yo)
Harper et al., 1989	Australia (Sydney, NSW)	Not reported	285	6 (2.1%)					5 (83%)	1 (17%)	4 (67%) / 0 (0%) / 2 (33%)	Age range 44–61yo (Minimum 15yo)
Harper et al., 1998	Australia (NSW)	1996–7	2,212	25 (1.1%)	4 (16%)				23 (92%)	2 (8%)	16 (64%) / 2 (8%) / 7 (28%)	Mean age of death 55yo (Minimum 15yo)
Lana-Peixoto et al., 1992	Brazil	1978–90	1,655	36 (2.2%)	0 of 11 with coma							
Harper et al., 1995[b]	France	1989–94	256	1 (0.4%)					0 (0%)	1 (100%)	1 (100%) / 0 (0%) / 0 (0%)	63yo (Minimum 18yo)
Hauw et al., 1988	France	1952–83	8,200	111 (1.4%)								
Riethdorf et al., 1991[c]	Germany	1983–6	2,372	14 (0.6%)								

Study	Country	Years	Total sample	Positive cases	Active WKS							Age
Torvik et al., 1982[a]	Norway (Oslo)	1975–9	8,735	75 (0.9%)[c]	1 of 22 with active WKS	19 (27%)	48 (69%)	3 (4%)	56 (80%)	14 (20%)	70 (93%) / 0 (0%) / 5 (7%)	Mean: 59–64yo
Lindboe and Loberg, 1988, 1989	Norway (Oslo)	1983–7	6,964	52 (0.7%)	4 of 18 with active WKS	18 (35%)	34 (65%)		36 (69%)	16 (31%)	40 (77%) / 12 (23%) / 0 (0%)	Mean (active): 57–61yo; Mean (inactive): 66–80yo
Vege et al., 1991	Norway (Oslo)	1988	279	4 (1.4%)	1	1 (25%)	3 (75%)				3 (75%) / 1 (25%) / 0 (0%)	Range 59–82 (Minimum 20yo)
Cravioto et al., 1961	USA (New York)	1957–60	1,600	28 (1.8%)					18 (64%)	10 (36%)	27 (96%) / 1 (4%) / 0 (0%)	32–82 M = 54 (Tot sample included children) (Minimum 18yo)
Victor and Laureno, 1978[d]	USA (Cleveland)	1963–76	3,548	77 (2.2%)					46 (60%)	31 (40%)		(Minimum 18yo)
Total	12 samples 6 countries	1952–97	40,783	560 (1.4%)	36 of 211 (17%)	60 (23%)	171 (67%)	26 (10%)	282 (72%)	108 (28%)	279 (87%) / 17 (5%) / 26 (8%)	Most common age at death approx 50s to mid-60s

[a] Supersedes Harper, 1979.

[b] Case material obtained consecutively and some via random selection.

[c] Riethdorf, Warzok and Schwesinger, 1991 – Data taken from Galvin et al. 2010 and an English version of the abstract available on PubMed.

[d] Supersedes Victor et al., 1971, 1989.

[e] Torvik et al. (1982) re-examined all cases with a history of alcohol-use disorders as well as non-alcohol-related cases with a diagnosis of Wernicke's Encephalopathy already recorded. Therefore the total prevalence reported may have missed an unknown number of positive cases without a history of an alcohol use disorder. Torvik and colleagues themselves noted that without systematic inspection, diagnosis of WKS may be missed.

[f] Of the 12 cases with unknown alcohol use history, most had signs of alcoholism.

levels to be significantly lower in a group of 100 alcohol–dependent patients newly admitted for alcohol withdrawal compared to healthy controls. Patients were not recruited for the study if presented with severe withdrawal symptoms. The study suggests that subclinical thiamine deficiency in the alcohol–dependent population is still common, and alcohol–dependent people remain at risk of thiamine deficiency syndromes despite the fortification of bread flour with thiamine. Based on patient interviews, the authors attributed the low thiamine levels to poor diet.

Another strategy for the prevention of WKS is to target at-risk individuals with prophylactic thiamine treatment (e.g., Guerrini and Mundt-Leach, 2012; Rees and Gowing, 2013; Talbot, 2011; Thomson, Marshall and Bell, 2013). Since a very high percentage of individuals with WKS have a previous history of chronic alcohol abuse, the most obvious target population would be those with alcohol-use disorders. Other groups recommended to be targeted for prophylactic treatment include patients with complications following bariatric surgery, malnourished patients receiving glucose or parenteral feeding, patients undergoing surgery for gastrointestinal disease and others at risk of malnutrition (Aasheim, 2008; Francini-Pesenti *et al.*, 2009; Galvin *et al.*, 2010; Rufa *et al.*, 2011). Concurrent administration of thiamine with glucose is recommended for hypoglycemic patients (Schabelman and Kuo, 2012). Parenteral thiamine appears to be the recommended option for prophylaxis, rather than oral supplementation, due to impaired thiamine absorption in at-risk individuals, combined with the body's inability to absorb high doses of thiamine delivered orally and concerns regarding patient compliance (Galvin *et al.*, 2010; Thomson *et al.*, 2002; Thomson and Marshall, 2006). Poor absorption may last for several weeks after abstinence from alcohol and is compromised by the presence of liver cirrhosis, a common complication of alcohol dependence (Hoyumpa, 1980).

Although parenteral thiamine is regarded as an inexpensive, safe and effective prophylactic treatment, research regarding the route, dose, frequency and duration of treatment is limited (Day *et al.*, 2013; Guerrini and Mundt-Leach, 2012; Rees and Gowing, 2013; Thomson and Cook, 1997). Authors of a Scottish study suggested that treatment of alcohol-dependent patients with prophylactic thiamine infusions may not be occurring often enough, especially when signs of WKS are masked by intoxication or other incidental disease (Ferguson *et al.*, 1997). A recent review from the UK suggests that prophylactic treatment of individuals at risk of WKS remains inconsistent and inadequate (Thomson, Marshall and Bell, 2013). The most recent Cochrane review (Day *et al.*, 2013) found only a single published randomized controlled trial relevant to prophylactic treatment of WKS in people with an alcohol-use disorder. Accordingly, the conclusion of the Cochrane review was that insufficient empirical research exists to guide formal recommendations and guidelines.

Finally, some of the clinical signs of acute WKS, such as confusion, ataxia and varying levels of impaired consciousness are difficult or impossible to differentiate from intoxication (Thomson *et al.*, 2002). Accordingly, any intoxicated patient may be at risk of thiamine deficiency and should be treated with thiamine, as well as those individuals showing evidence of alcohol-use disorders who present with hypoglycemia (Thomson *et al.*, 2002). Presumptive diagnosis and treatment without waiting for assessment of the sober patient can prevent progression of WKS, and is recommended for all patients suspected of thiamine deficiency, irrespective of alcohol-use status (Galvin *et al.*, 2010; Thomson *et al.*, 2002).

Treatment of symptomatic WKS

For many years, recommended treatment for clinical WKS has been parenteral thiamine, although response can be variable (de Wardener and Lennox, 1947; Thomson and Cook, 1997; Victor, Adams and Collins, 1989). It is also indicated for other syndromes caused by thiamine deficiency such as neuropathy with or without high-output congestive heart failure, vomiting associated with lactic acidosis and abdominal pain and Marchiafava-Bignami Syndrome. Current practice views parenteral thiamine as safe and effective treatment of acute WE and for the prevention of chronic KS (Galvin *et al.*, 2010; Strain and Kling, 2010; Thomson *et al.*, 2002; Wrenn, Murphy and Slovis, 1989). However, dose, frequency, route and length of treatment have never been optimally determined via randomized controlled trials and, as a consequence, treatment protocols vary widely (Day *et al.*, 2013; Donnino *et al.*, 2007; Hope, Cook and Thomson, 1999; Ramayya and Jauhar, 1997).

Key points from published guidelines for treatment of WKS are summarized below (Galvin *et al.*, 2010; Sechi and Serra, 2007; Thomson *et al.*, 2002):

i. Patients with or suspected of WE or WKS should be treated promptly with thiamine.
ii. The treatment should be started immediately after obtaining a blood sample for thiamine assay, and should be continued as long as improvement is observable. A normal diet should be instituted immediately after the first dose of thiamine.
iii. Intravenous administration of thiamine may be the optimal route, although this has not been empirically determined. Intravenous thiamine has been recommended to be infused slowly with normal saline. Intramuscular injection also appears to be effective, but may become painful when administering high doses of thiamine. Oral thiamine supplementation may be ineffective or suboptimal due to poor metabolism and absorption of thiamine in at-risk and alcohol-dependent patients.
iv. Due to the limited half-life of free thiamine in the blood, two or three daily doses of thiamine may be more beneficial than a single daily dose.
v. Optimal dosage has not been determined (Day *et al.*, 2013).
vi. Due to the small risk of anaphylaxis associated with any parenteral administration, appropriate facilities for resuscitation should be available during thiamine treatment. Galvin and colleagues (2010) state that absence of such facilities should not delay treatment. Thomson and colleagues (2002), however, recommend that resuscitation facilities must be available at time of treatment.

Clinical improvement of signs and symptoms of acute WKS may be observed within a few days or even within a few hours after instituting the treatment, but total recovery may take several weeks or even months. While parenteral thiamine can lead to dramatic resolution of acute symptoms, response to thiamine treatment of the chronic, cognitive component of WKS can be slow or not apparent in the short term (Freund, 1973; Kopelman et al., 2009; Victor, Adams and Collins, 1989). Cognitive status should be regularly monitored to allow any change to be detected (Ridley, Draper and Withall, 2013). Prompt diagnosis and prevention of WKS is the best course of treatment (Pitkin and Savage, 2001; Rufa et al., 2011; Sechi and Serra, 2007). The diagnosis, if only presumptive, should be established as early as possible to allow for the best possible outcome. As noted in previous sections, WKS remains a difficult diagnosis that is often missed (Feeney and Connor, 2008; Harper, 1983). To conclude, while more research is required to determine optimal treatment protocols, it is perhaps more important to focus research on enhancing detection and timeliness of diagnosis.

Conclusion

WKS is a relatively common disorder with a variable spectrum of clinical manifestations, both in acute and chronic variants. Despite considerable attention over the last two to three decades, it is likely that the majority of cases of WKS still are not accurately diagnosed in life and, as a consequence, do not receive adequate treatment with thiamine. While the variable clinical presentation of the acute variant of WKS, namely WE, has received considerable attention, the logical implication, and the abundant evidence, does not seem to be well appreciated that if the acute phase is highly variable then the chronic KS phase may be highly variable also. It is difficult to resist the conclusion that many clinicians continue, wrongly, to think of WKS, particularly in chronic variants, as rare and readily diagnosed on the basis of the severe, selective amnesia. The common presentation of WKS as a dementia-like impairment of variable severity, and the prospects for recovery from chronic variants, do not appear to be well understood. Of particular concern is the paucity of data on effective thiamine dosing to treat acute and chronic variants.

References

Aasheim, E. T. (2008). Wernicke encephalopathy after bariatric surgery: a systematic review. *Annals of Surgery*, 248, 714–20.

Ambrose, M. L., Bowden, S. C. and Whelan, G. (2001). Thiamine treatment and working memory function of alcohol-dependent people: preliminary findings. *Alcoholism: Clinical and Experimental Research*, 25, 112–16.

American Psychiatric Association. (2000). *Diagnostic and Statistical Manual of Mental Disorders* (4th edn, text rev.). Washington DC: APA.

American Psychiatric Association. (2013). *Diagnostic and Statistical Manual of Mental Disorders* (5th edn). Arlington, VA: APA.

Antunez, E., Estruch, R., Cardenal, C., Nicolas, J. M., Fernandez-Sola, J. and Urbano-Marquez, A. (1998). Usefulness of CT and MR imaging in the diagnosis of acute Wernicke's encephalopathy. *American Journal of Roentgenology*, 171, 1131–7.

Bergin, P. S. and Harvey, P. (1992). Wernicke's encephalopathy and central pontine myelinolysis associated with hyperemsesis gravidarum. *British Medical Journal*, 305, 517–18.

Bertrand, A., Brandel, J. P., Grignon, Y., Sazdovitch, V., Seilhean, D., Faucheux, B., Privat, J., Brault, L., Vital, A., Uro-Coste, E., Pluot, M., Chapon, F., Maurage, C. A., Letournel, F., Vespignani, H., Place, G., Degos, C. F., Peoc'h, K., Haïk, S. and Hauw, J. J. (2009). Wernicke encephalopathy and Creutzfeldt-Jakob disease. *Journal of Neurology*, 256, 904–9.

Blansjaar, B. A., Vielvoye, G. J., Van Dijk, J. G. and Rijnders, R. J. P. (1992). Similar brain lesions in alcoholics and Korsakoff patients: MRI, psychometric and clinical findings. *Clinical Neurology and Neurosurgery*, 94, 197–203.

Bleggi-Torres, L. F., de Medeiros, B. C., Werner, B., Neto, J. Z., Loddo, G., Pasquini, R. and de Medeiros, C. R. (2000). Neuropathological findings after bone marrow transplantation: an autopsy study of 180 cases. *Bone Marrow Transplant*, 25, 301–7.

Boldorini, R., Vago, L., Lechi, A., Tedeschi, F. and Trabattoni, G. R. (1992). Wernicke's encephalopathy: occurrence and pathological aspects in a series of 400 AIDS patients. *Acta bio-medica de L'Ateneo parmense*, 63, 43–9.

Bonner, A. (2015). Alcohol, ageing and cognitive function: a nutritional perspective. In J. Svanberg, A. Withall, B. Draper and S. Bowden (eds), *Alcohol and the Adult Brain*. Hove: Psychology Press.

Bowden, S. C. (1990). Separating cognitive impairment in neurologically asymptomatic alcoholism from Wernicke-Korsakoff syndrome: is the neuropsychological distinction justified? *Psychological Bulletin*, 107, 355–66.

Bowden, S. C. (2010). Alcohol related dementia and Wernicke-Korsakoff syndrome. In D. Ames, A. Burns and J. O'Brien (eds), *Dementia* (4th edn, pp. 722–9). London: Edward Arnold.

Bowden, S. C. (2013). Theoretical convergence in assessment of cognition. *Journal of Psychoeducational Assessment*, 31, 148–56.

Bowden, S. C. and Ritter, A. J. (2005). Alcohol-related dementia and the clinical spectrum of Wernicke-Korsakoff syndrome. In A. Burns, J. O'Brien and D. Ames (eds), *Dementia* (3rd edn). London: Hodder Arnold.

Brew, B. J. (1986). Diagnosis of Wernicke's encephalopathy. *Australian and New Zealand Journal of Medicine*, 16, 676–8.

Butters, N. and Cermak, L. S. (1980). *Alcoholic Korsakoff's syndrome: an information-processing approach to amnesia*. London: Academic Press.

Caine, D., Halliday, G. M., Kril, J. J. and Harper, C. G. (1997). Operational criteria for the classification of chronic alcoholics: identification of Wernicke's encephalopathy. *Journal of Neurology, Neurosurgery, and Psychiatry*, 62, 51–60.

Cravioto, H., Korein, J. and Silberman, J. (1961). Wernicke's encephalopathy: a clinical and pathological study of 28 autopsied cases. *Archives of Neurology*, 4, 510–19.

Day, E., Bentham, P. W., Callaghan, R., Kuruvilla, T. and George, S. (2013). Thiamine for prevention and treatment of Wernicke-Korsakoff Syndrome in people who abuse alcohol. *Cochrane Database of Systematic Reviews*, Issue 7.

de Wardener, H. E. and Lennox, B. (1947). Cerebral beriberi (Wernicke's encephalopathy): review of 52 cases in a Singapore prisoner-of-war hospital. *Lancet*, 249, 11–17.

Donnino, M. W., Vega, J., Miller, J. and Walsh, M. (2007). Myths and misconceptions of Wernicke's encephalopathy: what every emergency physician should know. *Annals of Emergency Medicine*, 50, 715–21.

Draper, B., Karmel, R., Gibson, D., Peut, A. and Anderson, P. (2011). Alcohol-related cognitive impairment in New South Wales hospital patients aged 50 years and over. *Australian and New Zealand Journal of Psychiatry*, 45, 985–92.

Fan, K. W. (2004). Jiao Qi disease in Medieval China. *The American Journal of Chinese Medicine*, 32, 999–1011.

Feeney, G. F. X. and Connor, J. P. (2008). Wernicke-Korsakoff syndrome (WKS) in Australia: no room for complacency. *Drug and Alcohol Review*, 27, 388–92.

Ferguson, R. K., Soryal, I. N. and Pentland, B. (1997). Thiamine deficiency in head injury: a missed insult? *Alcohol and Alcoholism*, 32, 493–500.

Francini-Pesenti, F., Brocadello, F., Manara, R., Santelli, L., Laroni, A. and Caregaro, L. (2009). Wernicke's syndrome during parenteral feeding: not an unusual complication. *Nutrition*, 25, 142–6.

Freund, G. (1973). Chronic central nervous system toxicity of alcohol. *Annual Review of Pharmacology*, 13, 217–27.

Fujiwara, E., Brand, M., Borsutzky, S., Steingass, H.-P. and Markowitsch, H. J. (2008). Cognitive performance of detoxified alcoholic Korsakoff syndrome patients remains stable over two years. *Journal of Clinical and Experimental Neuropsychology*, 30, 576–87.

Galvin, R., Bråthen, G., Ivashynka, A., Hillbom, M., Tanasescu, R. and Leone, M. A. (2010). EFNS guidelines for diagnosis, therapy and prevention of Wernicke encephalopathy. *European Journal of Neurology*, 17, 1408–18.

Guerrini, I. and Mundt-Leach, R. (2012). Preventing long-term brain damage in alcohol-dependent patients. *Nursing Standard*, 27, 43–6.

Guerrini, I., Thomson, A. D., Cook, C. C., McQuillin, A., Sharma, V., Kopelman, M., Reynolds, M., Jauhar, P., Harper, C. and Gurling, H. M. (2005). Direct genomic PCR sequencing of the high affinity thiamine transporter (SLC19A2) gene identifies three genetic variants in Wernicke Korsakoff syndrome (WKS). *American Journal of Medical Genetics. Part B, Neuropsychiatric Genetics*, 137B, 17–19.

Guerrini, I., Thomson, A. D. and Gurling, H. M. (2009). Molecular genetics of alcohol-related brain damage. *Alcohol and Alcoholism*, 44, 166–70.

Harper, C. G. (1983). The incidence of Wernicke's encephalopathy in Australia: a neuropathological study of 131 cases. *Journal of Neurology, Neurosurgery, and Psychiatry*, 46, 593–8.

Harper, C. G., Gold, J., Rodriguez, M. and Perdices, M. (1989). The prevalence of the Wernicke-Korsakoff syndrome in Sydney, Australia: a prospective necropsy study. *Journal of Neurology, Neurosurgery, and Psychiatry*, 52, 282–5.

Harper, C., Fornes, P., Duyckaerts, C., Lecomte, D. and Hauw, J. J. (1995). An international perspective on the prevalence of the Wernicke-Korsakoff syndrome. *Metabolic Brain Disease*, 10, 17–24.

Harper, C. G., Sheedy, D. L., Lara, A. I., Garrick, T. M., Hilton, J. M. and Raisanen, J. (1998). Prevalence of Wernicke-Korsakoff syndrome in Australia: has thiamine fortification made a difference? *Medical Journal of Australia*, 168, 542–5.

Harris, J., Chimelli, L., Kril, J. and Ray, D. (2008). Nutritional deficiencies, metabolic disorders and toxins affecting the nervous system. In S. Love, D. N. Louis and D. W. Ellison (eds), *Greenfield's Neuropathology* (8th edn, vol. 1, pp. 676–731). London: Hodder Arnold.

Harvey, R. J., Skelton-Robinson, M. and Rossor, M. N. (2003). The prevalence and causes of dementia in people under the age of 65 years. *Journal of Neurology, Neurosurgery, and Psychiatry*, 74, 1206–9.

Hauw, J. J., De Baecque, C., Hausser-Hauw, C. and Serdaru, M. (1988). Chromatolysis in alcoholic encephalopathies. *Brain*, 111, 843–57.

Heap, L. C., Pratt, O. E., Ward, R. J., Waller, S., Thomson, A. D., Shaw, G. K. and Peters, T. J. (2002). Individual susceptibility to Wernicke-Korsakoff syndrome and alcoholism-induced cognitive deficit: impaired thiamine utilization found in alcoholics and alcohol abusers. *Psychiatric Genetics*, 12(4), 217–24.

Hillbom, M., Pyhtinen, J., Pylvänen, V. and Sotaniemi, K. (1999). Pregnant, vomiting, and coma. *Lancet*, 353, 1584.

Hope, L. C., Cook, C. C. H. and Thomson, A. D. (1999). A survey of the current clinical practice of psychiatrists and accident and emergency specialists in the United Kingdom concerning vitamin supplementation for chronic alcohol misusers. *Alcohol and Alcoholism*, 34, 862–7.

Hoyumpa, A. M. (1980). Mechanisms of thiamin deficiency in chronic alcoholism. *American Journal of Clinical Nutrition*, 33, 2750–61.

Jauhar, P. and Montaldi, D. (2000). Wernicke-Korsakoff syndrome and the use of brain imaging. *Alcohol and Alcoholism Supplement*, 35, 21–3.

Jellinger, K. (1976). Neuropathological aspects of dementias resulting from abnormal blood and cerebrospinal fluid dynamics. *Acta Neurologica Belgica*, 76, 83–102.

Jung, Y. C., Chanraud, S. and Sullivan, E. V. (2012). Neuroimaging of Wernicke's encephalopathy and Korsakoff's syndrome. *Neuropsychological Review*, 22, 170–80.

Kaufman, A. S. (2013). Intelligent testing with Wechsler's fourth editions: perspectives on the Weiss *et al.* studies and the eight commentaries. *Journal of Psychoeducational Assessment*, 31, 224–34.

Kono, S., Miyajima, H., Yoshida, K., Togawa, A., Shirakawa, K. and Suzuki, H. (2009). Mutations in a thiamine-transporter gene and Wernicke's-like encephalopathy. *New England Journal of Medicine*, 360, 1792–4.

Kopelman, M. D., Thomson, A. D., Guerrini, I. and Marshall, E. J. (2009). The Korsakoff syndrome: clinical aspects, psychology and treatment. *Alcohol and Alcoholism*, 44, 148–54.

Kumar, N. (2010). Neurologic presentations of nutritional deficiencies. *Neurologic Clinics*, 28, 107–70.

Lana-Peixoto, M. A., Dos Santos, 'E. C. and Pittella, J. E. (1992). Coma and death in unrecognized Wernicke's encephalopathy: an autopsy study. *Arquivos de Neuro-psiquiatria*, 50, 329–33.

Lindboe, C. F. and Løberg, E. M. (1988). The frequency of brain lesions in alcoholics: Comparison between the 5-year periods 1975–1979 and 1983–1987. *Journal of the Neurological Sciences*, 88, 107–13.

Lindboe, C. F. and Løberg, E. M. (1989). Wernicke's encephalopathy in non-alcoholics: an autopsy study. *Journal of the Neurological Sciences*, 90, 125–9.

Lishman, W. A. (1998). *Organic Psychiatry: The Psychological Consequences of Cerebral Disorder* (3rd edn). Carlton: Blackwell Science.

Loh, E. W., Smith, I., Murray, R., McLaughlin, M., McNulty, S. and Ball, D. (1999). Association between variants at the GABAAbeta2, GABAAalpha6 and GABAAgamma2 gene cluster and alcohol dependence in a Scottish population. *Molecular Psychiatry*, 4, 539–44.

Lough, M. E. (2012). Wernicke's encephalopathy: expanding the diagnostic toolbox. *Neuropsychological Review*, 22, 181–94.

Ma, J. J. and Truswell, A. S. (1995). Wernicke-Korsakoff syndrome in Sydney hospitals: before and after thiamine enrichment of flour. *Medical Journal of Australia*, 163, 531–4.

Matsushita, S., Kato, M., Muramatsu, T. and Higuchi, S. (2000). Alcohol and aldehyde dehydrogenase genotypes in Korsakoff syndrome. *Alcoholism: Clinical and Experimental Research*, 24, 337–40.

McCool, B. A., Plonk, S. G., Martin, P. R. and Singleton, C. K. (1993). Cloning of human transketolase cDNAs and comparison of the nucleotide sequence of the coding region in Wernicke-Korsakoff and non-Wernicke-Korsakoff individuals. *Journal of Biological Chemistry*, 268, 1397–404.

McGrew, K. S. (2009). CHC theory and the human cognitive abilities project: standing on the shoulders of the giants of psychometric intelligence research. *Intelligence*, 37, 1–10.

McMurtray, A., Clark, D. G., Christine, D. and Mendez, M. F. (2006). Early-onset dementia: frequency and causes compared to late-onset dementia. *Dementia and Geriatric Cognitive Disorders*, 21, 59–64.

Naidoo, D. P., Bramdev, A. and Cooper, K. (1991). Wernicke's encephalopathy and alcohol-related disease. *Postgraduate Medical Journal*, 67, 978–81.

Nixon, P. F. (1984). Is there a genetic component to the pathogenesis of the Wernicke-Korsakoff syndrome? *Alcohol and Alcoholism*, 19, 219–21.

Ogershok, P. R., Rahman, A., Nestor, S. and Brick, J. (2002). Wernicke encephalopathy in nonalcoholic patients. *The American Journal of the Medical Sciences*, 323, 107–11.

Oscar-Berman, M. (2012). Function and dysfunction of prefrontal brain circuitry in alcoholic Korsakoff's syndrome. *Neuropsychological Review*, 22, 154–69.

Pitel, A. L., Zahr, N. M., Jackson, K., Sassoon, S. A. and Rosenbloom, M. J. (2011). Signs of preclinical Wernicke's encephalopathy and thiamine levels as predictors of neuropsychological deficits in alcoholism without Korsakoff's syndrome. *Neuropsychopharmacology*, 36, 580–8.

Pitkin, S. R. and Savage, L. M. (2001). Aging potentiates the acute and chronic neurological symptoms of pyrithiamine-induced thiamine deficiency in the rodent. *Behavioural Brain Research*, 119, 167–77.

Price, J. (1985). The Wernicke-Korsakoff syndrome in Queensland, Australia: antecedents and prevention. *Alcohol and Alcoholism*, 20, 233–42.

Ramayya, A. and Jauhar, P. (1997). Increasing incidence of Korsakoff's psychosis in the east end of Glasgow. *Alcohol and Alcoholism*, 32, 281–5.

Rees, E. and Gowing, L. R. (2013). Supplementary thiamine is still important in alcohol dependence. *Alcohol and Alcoholism*, 48, 88–92.

Reuler, J. B., Girard, D. E. and Cooney, T. G. (1985). Wernicke's encephalopathy. *New England Journal of Medicine*, 312, 1035–9.

Ridley, N. J. and Draper, B. (2015). Alcohol-related dementia and brain damage: a focus on epidemiology. In J. Svanberg, A. Withall, B. Draper and S. Bowden (eds), *Alcohol and the Adult Brain*. Hove: Psychology Press.

Ridley, N. J., Draper, B. and Withall, A. (2013). Alcohol-related dementia: an update of the evidence. *Alzheimer's Research and Therapy*, 5.

Riethdorf, L., Warzok, R. and Schwesinger, G. (1991). Die alkoholenzephalopathien im Obduktionsgut. *Zentralblatt für Pathologie*, 137, 48–56.

Rolland, S. and Truswell, A. S. (1998). Wernicke-Korsakoff syndrome in Sydney hospitals after 6 years of thiamin enrichment of bread. *Public Health Nutrition*, 1, 117–22.

Rooprai, H. K., Pratt, O. E., Shaw, G. K. and Thomson, A. D. (1996). Thiamine pyrophosphate effect and normalized erythrocyte transketolase activity ratio in Wernicke-Korsakoff patients and acute alcoholics undergoing detoxification. *Alcohol and Alcoholism*, 31, 493–501.

Royal College of Physicians. (2001). *Alcohol: Can the NHS Afford It? Recommendations for a Coherent Alcohol Strategy for Hospitals*. London: Royal College of Physicians of London.

Rufa, A., Rosini, F., Cerase, A., Giannini, F., Pretegiani, E., Buccoliero, R., Dotti, M. T. and Federico, A. (2011). Wernicke encephalopathy after gastrointestinal surgery for cancer: causes of diagnostic failure or delay. *International Journal of Neuroscience*, 121, 201–8.

Sampson, E. L., Warren, J. D. and Rossor, M. N. (2004). Young onset dementia. *Postgraduate Medical Journal*, 80, 125–39.

Savage, L. M. (2015). Alcohol-related brain damage and neuropathology. In J. Svanberg, A. Withall, B. Draper and S. Bowden (eds), *Alcohol and the Adult Brain*. Hove: Psychology Press.

Scalzo, S. J. and Bowden, S. C. (2015) Wernicke-Korsakoff syndrome without selective amnesia: a case series. Manuscript submitted for publication.

Scalzo, S. J., Bowden, S. C., Ambrose, M. L., Whelan, G. and Cook, M. J. (2015). Wernicke-Korsakoff syndrome not related to alcohol use: a systematic review. Manuscript submitted for publication.

Schabelman, E. and Kuo, D. (2012). Glucose before thiamine for Wernicke encephalopathy: a literature review. *The Journal of Emergency Medicine*, 42, 488–94.

Sechi, G. and Serra, A. (2007). Wernicke's encephalopathy: new clinical settings and recent advances in diagnosis and management. *The Lancet Neurology*, 6, 442–55.

Strain, J. and Kling, C. (2010). Thiamine dosing for Wernicke's encephalopathy in alcoholics: is traditional dosing inadequate? *South Dakota Medicine*, 63, 316–17.

Sullivan, E. V. and Pfefferbaum, A. (2009). Neuroimaging of the Wernicke-Korsakoff syndrome. *Alcohol and Alcoholism*, 44, 155–65.

Talbot, P. A. (2011). Timing of efficacy of thiamine in Wernicke's disease in alcoholics at risk. *Journal of Correctional Health Care*, 17, 46–50.

Tallaksen, C. M., Bohmer, T. and Bell, H. (1992). Blood and serum thiamin and thiamin phosphate esters concentrations in patients with alcohol dependence syndrome before and after thiamin treatment. *Alcoholism: Clinical and Experimental Research*, 16, 320–5.

Talland, G. A. (1958). Psychological studies of Korsakoff's psychosis. II. Perceptual functions. *The Journal of Nervous and Mental Disease*, 127, 197–219.

Talland, G. A. (1959). Psychological studies of Korsakoff's psychosis. III. Concept formation. *The Journal of Nervous and Mental Disease*, 128, 214–26.

Talland, G. A. (1960a). Psychological studies of Korsakoff's psychosis. VI. Memory and learning. *The Journal of Nervous and Mental Disease*, 130, 366–85.

Talland, G. A. (1960b). Psychological studies of Korsakoff's psychosis: V. Spontaneity and activity rate. *The Journal of Nervous and Mental Disease*, 130, 16–25.

Talland, G. A. and Ekdahl, M. (1959). Psychological studies of Korsakoff's psychosis: IV. The rate and mode of forgetting narrative material. *The Journal of Nervous and Mental Disease*, 129, 391–404.

Thomson, A. D. and Cook, C. C. H. (1997). Parenteral thiamine and Wernicke's encephalopathy: the balance of risks and perception of concern. *Alcohol and Alcoholism*, 32, 207–9.

Thomson, A. D., Cook, C. C. H., Guerrini, I., Sheedy, D., Harper, C. G. and Marshall, E. J. (2008a). Wernicke's encephalopathy revisited. Translation of the case history section of the original manuscript by Carl Wernicke 'Lehrbuch der Gehirnkrankheiten fur Aerzte and Studirende' (1881) with a commentary. *Alcohol and Alcoholism*, 43, 174–9.

Thomson, A. D., Cook, C. C. H., Guerrini, I., Sheedy, D., Harper, C. G. and Marshall, E. J. (2008b). Wernicke's encephalopathy: 'Plus ca change, plus c'est la meme chose'. *Alcohol and Alcoholism*, 43, 180–6.

Thomson, A. D., Cook, C. C. H., Touquet, R. and Henry, J. A. (2002). The Royal College of Physicians report on alcohol: guidelines for managing Wernicke's encephalopathy in the accident and emergency department. *Alcohol and Alcoholism*, 37, 513–21.

Thomson, A. D., Guerrini, I. and Marshall, E. J. (2012). The evolution and treatment of Korsakoff's syndrome: out of sight, out of mind? *Neuropsychological Review*, 22, 81–92.

Thomson, A. D. and Marshall, E. J. (2006). The treatment of patients at risk of developing Wernicke's encephalopathy in the community. *Alcohol and Alcoholism*, 41, 159–67.

Thomson, A. D., Marshall, E. J. and Bell, D. (2013). Time to act on the inadequate management of Wernicke's encephalopathy in the UK. *Alcohol and Alcoholism*, 48, 4–8.

Torvik, A. (1991). Wernicke's encephalopathy: prevalence and clinical spectrum. *Alcohol and Alcoholism Supplement*, 1, 381–4.

Torvik, A., Lindboe, C. F. and Rogde, S. (1982). Brain lesions in alcoholics: a neuropathological study with clinical correlations. *Journal of the Neurological Sciences*, 56, 233–48.

Vege, A., Sund, S. and Lindboe, C. F. (1991). Wernicke's encephalopathy in an autopsy material obtained over a one-year period. *APMIS: Acta Pathologica, Microbiologica, et Immunologica Scandinavica*, 99, 755–8.

Victor, M. (1994). Alcoholic dementia. *Canadian Journal of Neurological Sciences*, 21, 88–9.

Victor, M., Adams, R. D. and Collins, G. H. (1971). *The Wernicke-Korsakoff Syndrome: A Clinical and Pathological Study of 245 Patients, 82 with Post-Mortem Examinations*. Philadelphia: F. A. Davis Co.

Victor, M., Adams, R. D. and Collins, G. H. (1989). *The Wernicke-Korsakoff Syndrome and Related Neurologic Disorders due to Alcoholism and Malnutrition* (2nd edn). Philadelphia: F. A. Davis Co.

Victor, M. and Laureno, R. (1978). Neurologic complications of alcohol abuse: epidemiologic aspects. *Advances in Neurology*, 19, 603–17.

Victor, M., Talland, G. A. and Adams, R. D. (1959). Psychological studies of Korsakoff's psychosis. I. General intellectual functions. *The Journal of Nervous and Mental Disease*, 128, 528–37.

Wernicke, C. (1881). Lehrbuch der Gehirnkrankheiten fur Aerzte und Studirende. *Theodor Fischer, Kassel*, 2, 229–42.

Wood, B., Currie, J. and Breen, K. (1986). Wernicke's encephalopathy in a metropolitan hospital: a prospective study of incidence, characteristics and outcome. *Medical Journal of Australia*, 144, 12–16.

World Health Organization. (2010). International Classification of Diseases (ICD). Available from: http://www.who.int/classifications/icd/en/

Wrenn, K. D., Murphy, F. and Slovis, C. M. (1989). A toxicity study of parenteral thiamine hydrochloride. *Annals of Emergency Medicine*, 18, 867–70.

Zahr, N. M., Kaufman, K. L. and Harper, C. G. (2011). Clinical and pathological features of alcohol-related brain damage. *Nature Reviews. Neurology*, 7, 284–94.

Zuccoli, G. and Pipitone, N. (2009). Neuroimaging findings in acute Wernicke's encephalopathy: review of the literature. *American Journal of Roentgenology*, 192, 501–8.

Zuccoli, G., Santa Cruz, D., Bertolini, M., Rovira, A., Gallucci, M., Carollo, C. and Pipitone, N. (2009). MR imaging findings in 56 patients with Wernicke encephalopathy: nonalcoholics may differ from alcoholics. *American Journal of Neuroradiology*, 30, 171–6.

3

ALCOHOL-RELATED DEMENTIA AND BRAIN DAMAGE

A focus on epidemiology

Nicole Ridley and Brian Draper

Alcohol consumption is a risk factor for development of disease and injury, including permanent physical and cognitive impairment. Industrialization of production and globalization of marketing over the last century has increased availability of alcohol and the potential for associated harms, including health and social problems (Rehm *et al.*, 2009). Despite this, up-to-date data on the epidemiology of alcohol-related brain damage (ARBD) – including disorders such as alcohol-related dementia (ARD) and Wernicke-Korsakoff Syndrome (WKS) – are scarce. In the World Health Organization's most recent global status report on alcohol and health (World Health Organization [WHO], 2011), for instance, neuropsychiatric disorders are identified as a significant contributor to the disease burden of alcohol; however, no specific mention of alcohol-related brain injury is made, let alone any examination of prevalence and incidence rates across countries.

One factor that significantly relates to development of alcohol-related brain injury – and has been more widely documented than rates of ARBD – is patterns of alcohol consumption within a country or region. This includes both volume of alcohol consumption and frequency of drinking, such as heavy or binge episodes; these patterns differ significantly between countries (Peltzer, Davids and Njuho, 2011). Notably, while the world's highest levels of alcohol consumption are found in the developed world, this does not always translate into high rates of alcohol-related problems and high-risk drinking (WHO, 2011). Western European countries, for example, have, in general, high-levels of consumption but low alcohol-related mortality rates, reflecting a pattern of regular but moderate drinking occasions. Alternatively, Eastern European countries, South American and southern African countries have higher rates of heavy episodic drinking and the potential for more acute alcohol-related injury (WHO, 2011). While the relationship between economic status, alcohol consumption and disease burden is complex, the lower economic development of a country and socio-economic status of the individual generally translates to greater health problems related to alcohol. In all regions worldwide men consume more alcohol than women, although the exact ratio varies; women in high-income countries typically make up a larger proportion of the drinking population than those from low-income countries (Rehm *et al.*, 2009). A large percentage (around half) of the world's population abstain from drinking alcohol; abstention rates are low in high-income, high-consumption countries, and higher in North African and South Asian countries with large Muslim populations (WHO, 2011).

The prevalence of substance-use disorders is one marker used to measure the extent of alcohol-related harm within a country and examine change in drinking habits over time. Harmful alcohol use/abuse and alcohol dependence are the key diagnostic categories of alcohol-use disorders (AUDs), with abuse referring to maladaptive drinking patterns that cause impairment/distress, and dependence referring to a typically more chronic state involving increased tolerance and withdrawal upon cessation of drinking (International Statistical Classification of Diseases and Related Health Problems [ICD-10]; WHO, 1992; American Psychiatric Association, 1994). Among the 30 ICD-10 codes that relate to alcohol use, AUDs are the most significant cause of disease and injury relating to alcohol consumption, and while they are responsible for less mortality than physical diseases, they have a pronounced and prolonged impact on disability over the lifespan (WHO, 2011). Early estimates of AUD rates in population groups were confounded by methodological differences between studies, including variations in sampling methods, locations and diagnostic criteria (Hasin *et al.*, 2007). Rehm and colleagues (2009) attempted to address some of these limitations by restricting their review to only those studies that used established diagnostic criteria and set diagnostic instruments: 37 in total. In 2004, the total prevalence of AUDs worldwide was estimated as 3.6 per cent, with men having significantly higher rates than women (6.3 vs 0.9 per cent). The Eastern European region had the highest rates of AUD (10.9 per cent), while the eastern Mediterranean region reported the lowest (0.3 per cent). European and American regions also had relatively high overall rates of AUDs (5.2 to 5.5 per cent; Rehm *et al.*, 2009).

Most recent World Health Organization data suggest that adult per capita consumption of alcohol has remained generally stable in most geographic regions since 1990, with the exception of the African and South-East Asia regions, where consumption has increased (WHO, 2011). Increases in consumption in some specific regions – such as Scotland, where per capita consumption of alcohol has doubled since 1990 – may be masked by this regional evaluation (McCabe, 2011). Per capita alcohol consumption in England, for instance, increased by 60 per cent between 1970 and 2007 (Kopelman *et al.*, 2009); however, in Australia there appears to have been a recent slight drop in per capita alcohol consumption between 2006 and 2011 (10.6 to 10.0 litres per person; Australian Bureau of Statistics, 2013). Hazardous and harmful drinking patterns such as binge drinking in young populations seem to be on the rise in most regions; 80 per cent of the 82 countries involved in the survey by the WHO demonstrated an increase in drinking among 18–25-year-olds over a five-year period (WHO, 2011). Other evidence points to an increase in risky levels of drinking in high-income countries. In the USA, binge-drinking episodes (five or more alcoholic beverages on one occasion) per person per year increased by 35 per cent between 1995 and 2001 (Naimi et al., 2003). Men accounted for 81 per cent of these episodes and although rates of binge drinking were highest in those aged 18–25 years, over two-thirds of binge-drinking episodes occurred among those aged 26 years or older. A comparison of AUD rates in the USA between 1992 and 2002 also indicated an increase in 12-month alcohol abuse in both sexes over this time (3.0 to 4.7 per cent) despite decreasing rates of alcohol dependence (Grant et al., 2004). Australian surveys also suggest an increase in risky levels of alcohol consumption from 1995 to 2005 (8 to 13 per cent; Australian Institute of Health and Welfare [AIHW], 2006) and an increase in hazardous drinking rates was also observed in South Africa between 2005 and 2008 (a rise of 6.2 to 9.0 per cent; Peltzer et al., 2011).

While comparisons between these studies are limited by different interpretations of hazardous use and differences in survey design, general trends include higher rates of substance misuse among males and an age trend, with rates of misuse peaking in young adults and declining with age, although continued heavy drinking in men in middle age has been documented in a number of European studies (Peltzer et al., 2011; Teesson et al., 2006). Convergence of male and female rates of abuse over the last decade, with rising rates of alcohol abuse in females, was also documented (Grant et al., 2004; Peltzer et al., 2011), in line with reports of an increase in women's rates of drinking over the last decade in high-income countries (Grucza et al., 2009). Other data also present some evidence for higher amounts of alcohol consumption in the middle aged and elderly than ever before in middle- to high-income countries. Historically, an age effect has been observed on drinking rates, with people drinking less as they age. However, recent data suggests that this decline is slower now compared to earlier cohorts; British data suggests that the 45–64 age group are drinking more than older people before them (Grucza et al., 2009; McCabe, 2011; Moore et al., 2005; Nadkarni et al., 2011). Studies in the UK, Finland, Brazil and America estimate around 2 to 9 per cent of older people are drinking at levels that could be harmful, and rates of AUD in the elderly have been suggested to afflict 1 to 3 per cent of individuals over 65, based on American data (Blazer and Wu, 2011; Caputo et al., 2012; Lopes et al., 2010; McCabe, 2011; Nadkarni et al., 2011; Platt, Sloan and Costanzo, 2010). Some authors suggest that diagnosis of AUDs in the elderly is underestimated, particularly given that standardized questionnaires used to evaluate AUD prevalence may not account for reduced tolerance to alcohol in the elderly (Caputo et al., 2012). Indeed, one US review study has warned of a "silent epidemic of alcohol abuse in older people" (Nadkarni et al., 2011). Further research into the drinking characteristics of this age group, including examination of cohort effects and trends over time, is warranted given reliance on cross-sectional data and corresponding lack of current available longitudinal data (Platt et al., 2010; Withall and Shafiee, 2015). In the context of a rapidly ageing global population that will see the number of people aged 65 years and over increase from nearly 579 million (8.2 per cent) in 2013 to a projected 1.45 billion (15.6 per cent) by 2050, the potential for a marked increase in rates of ARBD is perhaps unprecedented (Central Intelligence Agency, 2013; United Nations Department of Economic and Social Affairs, 2001).

The epidemiology of alcohol-related dementia (ARD)

The presence of a dementia secondary to excessive or prolonged alcohol misuse has long been recognized by principal diagnostic systems. Alcohol-induced persisting dementia in the DSM-IV (American Psychiatric Association, 1994) has now been updated to recognize the heterogeneity of alcohol-related cognitive impairment, with DSM-5 describing either major or mild alcohol-induced neurocognitive disorders (American Psychiatric Association, 2013). Alcohol-induced dementia is also included in the ICD-10 (WHO, 1992). However, there remains limited representative data on the prevalence of ARD. The reasons for this are several. First, there has been debate as to the very nature of such a disorder – that is, whether the existence of a dementia due to the neurotoxic effects of alcohol in isolation is a valid entity in and of itself, or whether the dementia syndrome more accurately represents a combination of causative factors, such as nutritional (e.g., thiamine) deficiencies, head injuries and liver disease (Smith and Atkinson, 1995, Moriyama et al., 2006). The lack of an established gold standard for diagnosis has meant that diagnostic systems have depended upon largely vague and subjective criteria, which are difficult to apply on a practical level and rely upon clinical opinion. Second, dementia research in the last two decades has largely concentrated on neurodegenerative syndromes such as Alzheimer's disease and, in many cases, studies have neglected to examine the presence of ARD or examine drinking variables in population groups (Oslin et al., 1998; Ritchie and Villebrun, 2008). The World Health Organization's release on Dementia and Health (2012), for example, focuses on the predominant dementia syndromes; however, no mention is made of alcohol-related disorders. Third, the course of ARD may fluctuate (i.e., individuals may stabilize or improve), which also complicates consistency of diagnosis and comparison of rates longitudinally. One recent study of young-onset dementia diagnosed in Danish hospitals found that ARD was being over-diagnosed by clinicians in acute hospitals (Salem et al., 2012). This debate is considered further in Chapter 2 of this volume (Scalzo, Bowden and Hillbom, 2015).

Early epidemiological studies did not examine the prevalence of ARD as a distinct disorder per se but instead attempted to correlate heavy use of alcohol and the presence of a global dementia (Ritchie and Villebrun, 2008). Older studies found an association between heavy use of alcohol and cognitive disorders. In the US Epidemiologic Catchment Area study, those over the age of 65 with a cognitive disorder had a 1.5 times higher prevalence of a lifetime history of alcohol abuse or dependence than those without (George et al., 1991). The Liverpool Longitudinal Study in the UK (Saunders et al., 1991) also found dementia was 4.6 times more likely in subjects with a history of excessive drinking. Note that, in the latter study, dementia was not explained by current drinking habits but related to heavy drinking in earlier years, suggesting that cross-sectional analyses of current alcohol consumption and cognitive functioning may be insufficient when considering the relationship of alcohol consumption to cognitive outcomes. More recent studies have continued to promote a link between heavy alcohol use and increased dementia risk. In a community-based sample of individuals aged 60 or over in Brazil, heavy alcohol use was associated with higher cognitive and functional impairment compared to mild to moderate alcohol use (Lopes et al., 2010). A prospective study conducted over three years in the USA also demonstrated higher odds of dementia for those with heavier alcohol consumption (Mukamal et al., 2003). More recent studies have attempted to distinguish between dementia subtypes, with the majority focusing on the outcomes of light to moderate alcohol consumption on specific dementia syndromes (such as the possible protective effect on Alzheimer's disease; Anstey, Mack and Cherbuin, 2009).

Of the studies that have specifically investigated ARD syndromes in population groups, prevalence rates vary substantially. This is not surprising given the differences between studies in age inclusions, locations, recruitment methods and classification systems used. An early Canadian study by Carlen and colleagues (Carlen et al., 1994) determined that 24 per cent of cognitively impaired residents of long-term facilities in a Canadian sample suffered from ARD. The authors established their own criteria for a diagnosis of ARD, and only a quarter of those to whom they assigned a diagnosis of ARD had a prior diagnosis of ARD listed in the medical records, which may suggest that cases had been missed previously or reflect differences in diagnostic approaches. In their review of a dementia registry in a Veterans Medical Centre in America, Smith and Atkinson (1993) identified 10 per cent that had a diagnosis of alcohol-related dementia; they also noted that another 11 per cent of patients diagnosed with possible Alzheimer's disease had histories of "heavy alcohol use" and shared many of the neurological, cognitive and prognostic features of patients with ARD. Rains and Ditzler (1993) found that ARD represented 13 per cent of all dementias of patients that had presented for out-patient geriatric assessment (1985–90) in an American sample; an additional 9 per cent of the total sample also gave a current or past history of hazardous or problematic consumption that was not considered in their diagnosis. Oslin and Cary (2003) also reported rates of ARD as 10 per cent of total dementias (based on their own criteria) in a nursing home sample. In each of these studies rates of ARD were gathered from populations disproportionately high in cognitive impairment, and do not represent true population estimates; however, the difficulty with differentiating alcohol-related cognitive impairment from other dementia syndromes, or impairment related to other medical problems or trauma, is clear.

Other studies have examined prevalence rates of ARD while comparing degenerative and non-degenerative forms of dementia. Clarfield (1988) pooled data from 32 studies of dementia assessment and found that 4.2 per cent of cases were due to ARD. In a retrospective medical file review of out-patients of a neurology unit in Brazil spanning ten years (1991–2001; Takada et al., 2003), only 1.1 per cent of patients with a dementia diagnosis had a diagnosis of "alcoholic dementia", while another 1.1 per cent had diagnoses of WKS. Bello and Schultz (2011), in their later (1999–2009) review of the records of a neurology unit in Brazil in the decade following, reported a higher prevalence than the previous study of dementia due to alcohol use (5.7 per cent) with an increased overall prevalence of "reversible" dementia diagnoses. Given the similarities between studies, this may indicate an increase in rates of non-degenerative dementia syndromes; however, minor methodological differences between studies (such as the exclusion of patients with vascular dementia from the latter study) may also account for rate differences. In both studies, patients with aetiologies of potentially reversible dementias, including ARD, were on average younger than those with progressive dementia syndromes. An earlier review of medical records in an English health district (1990–4) also found that alcohol-related dementia was more common in the younger group than in patients over 70 (22.2 vs 12.0 per cent); in total ARD made up 16.2 per cent of non-degenerative, non-vascular causes (Knopman et al., 2006). Despite the wide range in prevalence rates between studies, a general pattern of younger age of onset of ARD groups compared to other dementia syndromes is noteworthy. The age effect was again demonstrated in an Australian analysis of hospital admissions of 20,000 dementia patients who were at least 50 years old; ARD made up 1.4 per cent with a diagnosed dementia, but 22 per cent of dementia patients under 65 (Draper et al., 2011).

Early or young-onset dementia (YOD) population studies have increased in number over the last decade and many have included ARD rates in their estimates. Differences in methods of recruitment, reporting of rates and diagnostic systems complicate comparisons. In a Danish study which examined consecutive patients of a memory clinic over four years (Elberling et al., 2002), ARD approached 10 per cent of total YOD cases; again the number of patients with ARD were significantly higher in the under 60 age group compared to elderly patients referred to the same memory clinic. Other memory clinic samples from English (McMurtray et al., 2006) and French (Picard et al., 2011) populations identified rates of ARD from total YOD cases as 5.0 and 9.4 per cent, respectively. Similar rates of ARD (5.4 per cent) were found in an Australian prospective study of young patients (<65) referred with suspected dementia to an out-patient clinic (Panegyres and Frencham, 2007); and also in a Brazilian study, which conducted retrospective medical file reviews of patients of a cognitive clinic (5.0 per cent of early-onset dementia cases; Fujihara et al., 2004). These studies were generally based on very small sample sizes; however, they reflect a general pattern of prevalence rates of ARD within the range of 5 to 10 per cent of YOD populations.

Population-based studies that have included ARD in their analyses have been limited; in the context of YOD research, this may be due to the impracticality of collecting population-based prevalence figures due to the rarity of many conditions. One exception was Harvey, Skelton-Robinson and Rossor (2003), who conducted a large-scale survey of YOD cases in a catchment area in London. ARD represented 10 per cent of YOD cases with an estimated prevalence rate of 6.6 cases per 100,000 people at risk; it was the fourth most common cause of dementia in this group after

Alzheimer's disease, vascular and fronto-temporal dementias. Renvoize and col-leagues (Renvoize, Hanson and Dale, 2011) reported higher rates than this in their survey of YOD cases identified in a northern English district (10.9/100,000); they note that the large contribution of ARD was not unexpected given that this area had the highest recorded alcohol-related death rates in England between 1998 and 2004. Interestingly, Australian pilot data (Withall *et al.* 2014) of YOD cases within the eastern Sydney region, reported considerably higher rates of ARD (16.3 per 100,000 population aged 30–64; 33.1 per population aged 45-64); ARD was the most common primary diagnosis of identified cases (18.4 per cent of cases). These high rates were somewhat surprising given that Australia's alcohol consumption has been relatively stable over the last two decades. However, as many were identified in acute hospital admissions, the possibility of over-diagnosis of ARD by clinicians who are not dementia specialists, as found in Denmark (Salem *et al.*, 2012), must be considered. Of concern, hazardous and harmful alcohol consumption remains over-represented among Emergency Department presentations (Feeney and Connor, 2008) and risky and binge-drinking rates appear to be on the rise (AIHW, 2006).

The epidemiology of Wernicke-Korsakoff Syndrome

Apart from ARD, Korsakoff's Syndrome (KS) is the other main cognitive disorder related to alcohol consumption that has been examined in the literature.

The syndrome was first documented by Sergei Korsakoff, who described a syndrome of prominent memory disturbance in "not less than 30" cases of chronic alcohol abuse as well as 16 patients in whom alcohol had not played a role. Neurological signs including prodromal confusion, opthalmoplegia, nystagmus and ataxia were also prominent (Kopelman *et al.*, 2009). It is now well known that KS can result from thiamine deficiency and, more specifically, untreated Wernicke's Encephalopathy (WE). WE is an acute neurological disorder historically character-ized by a clinical triad of oculomotor abnormalities, cerebellar dysfunction and altered mental state, and pathologically by neuronal loss and haemorrhagic lesions in the paraventricular and periaqueductal gray matter (Isenberg-Grzeda, Kutner and Nicolson, 2012; Kril and Harper, 2012). If untreated, the acute WE may progress to chronic KS, which appears to be related to additional damage to diencephalic and hippocampal circuitry (Harper, 2009). Given the close relationship between WE and KS and the fact that they share similar pathological substrates, it is commonly referred to as the Wernicke-Korsakoff Syndrome. Not all individuals with WE show the triad of neurological symptoms, and progression to the severe amnesic syndrome documented in KS may occur without these classic clinical signs (Sullivan and Pfefferbaum, 2009). While WE can occur in a number of clinical settings such as in malnutrition, following gastrointestinal surgical procedures and long-term parenteral feeding, individuals with AUDs are at high risk of thiamine deficiency because of poor diet associated with their lifestyle and because alcohol compromises thiamine absorption (Zahr, Kaufman and Harper, 2011). Notably, KS is rarely seen in those without a history of alcoholism (Kril and Harper, 2012). Reasons suggested for this include exacerbation of thiamine deficiency with alcohol consumption or that thiamine deficiency in non-alcohol-dependent populations tends to take the form of a single and acute episode, which may be more readily identified and treated than in chronic cases, such as in AUDs, where subclinical episodes of thiamine deficiency can occur (Sechi and Serra, 2007).

Korsakoff's syndrome has been recognized by key diagnostic systems. In the DSM-5 (American Psychiatric Association, 2013), KS is described as "persistent alcohol-induced amnestic-confabulatory major neurocognitive disorder" and memory disturbance is the key diagnostic feature. ICD-10 (WHO, 1992) criteria for "alcohol-induced amnesic syndrome" detail impairment of recent memory and disturbance of time sense in the absence of impaired immediate recall or generalized cognitive impairment. There has been much variation in how these criteria have been operationalized in empirical research: inclusion criteria for Korsakoff patients have included a specific discrepancy between intellectual and memory abilities (Bowden, 1990) or that a minimal number of WE symptoms must occur for diagnosis (Joyce and Robbins, 1991). However, recent evidence suggests that the KS may actually be more heterogeneous in nature than originally thought, with a range of intellectual abilities affected and added impairment in executive abilities (Jacobson, Acker and Lishman, 1990; Van Oort and Kessels, 2009). Therefore studies that have used more restrictive criteria may have captured only a refined "pure" subset of the Korsakoff population that is not representative of the broader clinical group or, in epidemiological research, an accurate reflection of population prevalence (Bowden, 2010).

Epidemiological studies that have examined the prevalence and incidence of KS in population groups have been limited and most are now many years out of date. A survey undertaken of health care services by Blansjaar and colleagues (Blansjaar, Horjus and Nijhuis, 1987) in the Hague found a prevalence of 4.8 per 10,000 inhabitants; male patients made up two-thirds of the group with a mean age of 60 years; 75 per cent of patients had been hospitalized for several years. While limitations of the study included that the authors relied on hospital diagnoses and that patients with mild symptoms or living at home were not included, it is notable that they report an increase of more than six fold in admittance of patients with KS in the previous 13 years in Dutch general hospitals, which they speculate may relate to an increase of 237 per cent in alcohol consumption in the Netherlands between 1960 and 1983 (Blansjaar, Horjus and Nijhuis, 1987).

A rise in incidence of KS rates was also reported in Glasgow, Scotland, in the early 1990s. Ramayya and Jauhar (1997) conducted a retrospective analysis of all admissions between 1990 and 1995 in a population of 160,000, with data revealing a rise of incidence from 12.5 per million in 1990 to 18.3 per million in 1995. These figures may even represent an underestimate of Korsakoff cases, given that diagnosis in the study was according to "classical criteria" for KS. WE preceded KS in only 14.8 per cent of cases. A more recent review by Smith and Flanigan (2000) of Scottish national hospital database figures (1970–95) also reported a sustained increase in rates of KS as a discharge diagnosis and as a diagnosis in hospital residents over the past three decades. In Scotland the per capita consumption of alcohol has doubled since 1990 (McCabe, 2011), which has also been accompanied by a dramatic increase in alcohol-related morbidity, particularly liver cirrhosis, for both men and women. However, there appear to be other factors at play, as increases in morbidity are not seen in other parts of the UK despite similar rises in consumption levels. One likely contribution is poor diet, with alcohol-related morbidity and brain damage more prevalent in areas of socio-economic deprivation (MacRae and Cox, 2003).

The prevalence and incidence of WE has been more extensively documented than the outcome syndrome of KS. The mismatch between prevalence of WE lesions on autopsy and appearance on clinical presentation is apparent; the classic triad of signs (confusion, ataxia and opthalmoplegia) occurs in only around 10 to 20 per cent of cases (Harper, Giles and Finlay-Jones, 1986; Thomson, Marshall and Bell, 2013). The review by Galvin and colleagues (Galvin *et al.*, 2010) of studies with cases of WE diagnosed post-mortem suggests that WE was suspected during life in only about one-third of alcohol-dependent and 6 per cent of non-alcohol-dependent patients. In an attempt to improve diagnostic sensitivity, Caine and colleagues (1997) conducted a retrospective analysis of the clinical history of individuals with alcohol dependence diagnosed with WE post-mortem. They proposed new operational criteria for diagnosis of WE, which included presence of two of the following four criteria: (1) history of dietary deficiencies, (2) oculomotor abnormalities, (3) cerebellar dysfunction and (4) either an altered mental state or mild memory impairment. The use of these operational criteria considerably increased diagnostic sensitivity in Caine's review (22 to 85 per cent) and more recent evidence supports the utility of these criteria in identifying individuals at risk for neurological and neuropsychological complications (Pitel *et al.*, 2011). Recent guidelines by the European Federation of Neurological Societies (Galvin *et al.*, 2010) promote the use of Caine's criteria in clinical practice; however, they are yet to be widely implemented in clinical settings. Despite this movement towards better identification practices, there remains no universal consensus on the best treatment protocol for patients at risk, including dose, frequency and route of administration of thiamine (Day *et al.*, 2013).

In necropsy studies representative of the general population in developed countries, around 1.5 per cent of brains show the pathological lesions of WE, with a range of 0 to 2.8 per cent (UK 0.5 per cent; mainland Europe 0.1 to 1.3 per cent; USA 0 to 1 per cent; Australia 1.1 to 2.8 per cent; Harper *et al.*, 1995; Thomson, Guerrini and Marshall, 2012). These figures may include cases of WE from non-alcohol-dependent aetiologies; however, in developed countries up to 90 per cent of WE cases are alcohol-related (Dumitrescu *et al.*, 2011). In individuals with a history of alcoholism, WE pathology at post-mortem is much more frequent; in their series of post-mortem examinations, Torvik, Lindboe and Rogde (1982) found 70 cases of WE from 561 individuals with known alcohol histories: a prevalence of 12.5 per cent. Harper and colleagues (1998) also found a prevalence of WKS of 19 per cent in an Australian forensic population who had a history suggestive of alcohol problems. More recent data of WE necropsy rates are lacking; this is likely related to the dramatic decrease in the number of post-mortems carried out in hospitals in the western world (Thomson and Marshall, 2006). Similarly, longitudinal series investigating WE rates post-mortem across cohorts – thus allowing comparison of rates across time – are lacking. The exception has been examinations by Harper and colleagues (Harper et al., 1998), who reported a decline in prevalence rates of WKS in Australia through comparison of autopsy studies in Western Australia (Harper, 1983) and Sydney (Harper et al., 1998). Prevalence rates of WKS in the 1997–8 analyses were 1.1 per cent compared to the 4.7 per cent observed in the earlier period (1973–81); the authors speculate that this may relate to general improvement of health in the general public in Australia, or a result of introduction of the supplementation of bread with thiamine in Australia since 1991. Notably, the rate still remained higher than most other western countries.

Alcohol-related brain damage and new nosological approaches

While historically cognitive disorders related to alcohol consumption have been dichotomized into either ARD or WKS, in the past decade a trend towards use of the term "alcohol-related brain damage" (ARBD) or "alcohol-related cognitive impairment" (ARCI) has been observed. Supporters suggest that this more inclusive approach reflects the similar aetiologies of ARD and WKS, illustrating a spectrum of cognitive impairment resulting from the effects of thiamine deficiency in combination with alcohol neurotoxicity, and that it is preferential for clinical use as it better accounts for the heterogeneity of presentations in alcohol-related conditions. In the UK, for instance, the term ARBD has generally superseded use of KS/ARD in clinical practice and its use has been incorporated into health policy and research (Jauhar and Smith, 2009). An overall rise in general hospital admissions in Scotland from ARBD between 1997 and 2005 has been observed: 254 to 472 patients in the years, respectively (Jahuar and Smith, 2009), and increasing efforts to identify and address the needs of this population have been implemented (McCabe, 2011). A survey of the Glasgow homeless hostel population estimated that 21 per cent showed evidence of some degree of ARBD (Gilchrist and Morrison, 2005). It is likely that the term "alcohol-related brain damage" or similar all-inclusive terminology will enjoy greater utility in future epidemiological research, given that the recently released DSM-5 has adopted the categories of major and minor "neurocognitive disorder due to substance disorder" to replace the use of ARD and WKS terminology (American Psychiatric Association, 2013).

Factors in the expression of alcohol-related brain damage

As not all individuals that are alcohol-dependent develop lasting cognitive impairment, it is critical to examine what factors influence progression to ARBD. Females are suggested to have heightened vulnerability to the effects of alcohol when compared to males; however, the evidence is not yet conclusive. In Victor's case series analysis, the ratio of male to female KS cases was 1.7:1, lower than concurrent ratios of alcohol dependency (3–4:1; Victor, Adams and Collins, 1989). A similar low ratio (1.5:1) was found by Ramayya and Jauhar (1997) in their Scottish sample. This could suggest that women are particularly vulnerable to the effects of alcohol and/or thiamine deficiency, although this has not been a universal finding. Harper (1979) and Torvik, Lindboe and Rogde (1982) reported ratios of 3:1 and 4:1, respectively; more compatible with population estimates of AUDs. However, more recent data does point to an influence of gender. In a magnetic resonance imaging study, females who drank heavily were found to have a disproportionate reduction in frontal gray matter than males with a comparative history of alcohol use (Mason *et al.*, 2005), while in a longitudinal study of detoxified KS patients, better outcome occurred more frequently in men than women (Fujiwara *et al.*, 2008). These findings need further clarification, taking into account the respective impact of drinking amounts: women typically have reduced tolerance to alcohol compared to men due to differences in body composition and metabolism (e.g., lower quantities of the enzyme dehydrogenase, which breaks down alcohol in the stomach; Baraona *et al.*, 2006).

Nutritional status is a clear factor in risk for ARBD. The prevalence of thiamine deficiency in a population influences the prevalence of WE; however, the susceptibility to develop WKS in the presence of thiamine deficiency is influenced by less well-known genetic and environmental factors (Dumitrescu *et al.*, 2011). A correlation between per capita consumption of alcohol and prevalence of WE has not been found (Harper *et al.*, 1995). This may be due to the influence of national thiamine supplementation programs in some countries and not others; changes in patterns of drinking including rates of binge drinking and improved early treatment options (Thomson and Marshall, 2006). Genetic defects may also impact the ability of an individual to cope with borderline thiamine deficient states and resistance to adequate treatment (Dumitrescu *et al.*, 2011). These defects may include mutation of the X-linked thiamine transketolase-like 1 gene or the gene that encodes for human thiamine transporter 1 – SLCA19. Genetic variants of the enzymes involved in ethanol metabolism may also predispose to WE (Sechi and Serra, 2007). Furthermore, APOE ε4 carrier status, a known genetic risk factor for development of Alzheimer's disease, may modify the effect of alcohol on risk of dementia. The protective effects of light to moderate alcohol consumption against dementia and cognitive decline are more likely in the absence of an APOE ε4 allele. The response to thiamine deficiency may also be population specific: Asians are more likely to develop a cardiovascular (wet) Beriberi, while Europeans tend to develop features of polyneuropathy and WE (Sechi and Serra, 2007).

Education may also serve as a protective factor in the expression of ARBD. Lower levels of education predicted less improvement in verbal ability in individuals who entered addiction treatments (Bates, Labouvie and Voelbel, 2002). Higher premorbid education was also associated with better outcome in KS patients who remained detoxified over two years (Fujiwara *et al.*, 2008). In an analysis of the clinical presentation of WE in those with alcohol dependence, individuals with a higher education were less likely to display signs of WE than individuals with lower education levels, which, given no group differences on measures of age, sex, lifetime alcohol intake or length of sobriety, may suggest a protective effect of education on

ARBD (Pitel *et al.*, 2011). It is unclear whether education is a protective factor or whether low pre-morbid intelligence is a risk for both cognitive impairment and poor educational attainment (Bates, Bowden and Barry, 2002).

What remains uncertain is the influence of drinking patterns, length and severity, on later development of cognitive impairment. The differing aspects of drinking patterns, including binges and withdrawal patterns, as well as difficulty gathering an accurate self-report, have complicated attempts to link drinking levels to later cognitive impairment. The criteria proposed by Oslin and colleagues (1998) imply that a five-year history of 35 standard drinks a week for men and 28 for women is sufficient to risk development of ARD; however, this requires further validation. In groups of alcohol-dependent females who had recently ceased drinking, length of sobriety before testing did not correlate significantly with performance on any tests; lifetime alcohol consumption, however, was associated with global cognitive functioning and information processing tasks (Rosenbloom *et al.*, 2005). Mason and colleagues (2005) found that both current and lifetime alcohol consumption were associated with neurological damage on MR imaging; gray matter volume loss was correlated with current drinking severity and also with monthly average lifetime alcohol consumption. A recent meta-analysis by Stavro, Pelletier and Potvin (2012) on the effects of abstinence on cognitive function in individuals with alcohol abuse/dependence reported that duration of abstinence was significantly associated with cognitive recovery; notably, criteria for the investigation excluded those with diagnoses of WKS or ARD.

In the longitudinal follow-up of KS patients by Fujiwara and colleagues (2008), improved outcome was associated with fewer past detoxifications; this is compatible with other studies that relate number of previous withdrawals to lower cognitive performance (Duka *et al.*, 2003). It is thought that drinking patterns of repeated binges and withdrawals may enhance neuronal injury through increased vulnerability of receptors to glutamate-induced excitotoxicity – this is particularly relevant to consider given increased reported rates of hazardous and binge drinking in western countries (Brust, 2010). Age may also be a significant factor in impact of drinking levels and recovery of function; animal studies have indicated that the adolescent brain is more vulnerable to the effects of binge drinking compared to the adult, and that a younger age of onset of AUDs may be associated with greater cognitive deficits and degree of neurological damage (Hermens *et al.*, 2013). Greater recovery of function may be seen with younger age; older drinkers are less likely to recover their normal levels of function, even with abstinence. The DSM-5 reports that substance-induced major or mild neurocognitive disorders are most likely to become persistent in individuals who continue abuse of substances past the age of 50 years, potentially due to a combination of lessened neural plasticity and beginning of other age-related changes (American Psychiatric Association, 2013).

Summary

Attempts to examine the epidemiology of alcohol-related cognitive disorders over the past few decades are confounded by differences in nosological and methodological approaches to research. Changing patterns of drinking in western countries – including a rise in hazardous drinking episodes, rising rates of abuse in females and longer periods of drinking in the middle aged and elderly – will likely be reflected in the changing profile of alcohol-related cognitive disorders in the near future. However, at present we have limited current representative data on the prevalence of these disorders. ARD has been reported to represent, on average, 5 to 15 per cent of total dementia cases, depending on the population from which data was gathered, and appears to have an earlier age of onset than other dementia syndromes. An accurate estimate of rates of WKS has been limited by poor clinical identification rates and we have insufficient current autopsy evidence to determine whether rates identified on autopsy have changed over time. Factors such as nutritional status, regional health patterns and individual characteristics (including education, age and genetic vulnerability) likely influence progression to alcohol-induced brain damage, as do length and patterns of drinking. Time will tell whether the introduction of more inclusive terminology by the DSM-5 (American Psychiatric Association, 2013) will address these nosological issues and allow a more comprehensive and accurate evaluation of the epidemiology of alcohol-related cognitive disorders.

References

American Psychiatric Association. (1994). *Diagnostic and Statistical Manual of Mental Disorders* (4th edn). Washington DC: APA.

American Psychiatric Association. (2013). *Diagnostic and Statistical Manual of Mental Disorders* (5th edn). Arlington, VA: American Psychiatric.

Anstey, K. J., Mack, H. A. and Cherbuin, N. (2009). Alcohol consumption as a risk factor for dementia and cognitive decline: meta-analysis of prospective studies. *The American Journal of Geriatric Psychiatry*, 17(7), 542–55.

Australian Bureau of Statistics (2013). *Apparent Consumption of Alcohol, Australia, 2011–12.* Canberra, Australia: ABS.

Australian Institute of Health and Welfare (AIHW; 2006). *Australia's Health 2006.* Canberra, Australia: AIHW.

Baraona, E., Abittan, C. S., Dohmen, K., Moretti, M., Pozzato, G., Chayes, C. Q., Schaefer, C. and Lieber, C. S. (2006). Gender differences in pharmacokinetics of alcohol. *Alcoholism: Clinical and Experimental Research*, 25(4), 502–7.

Bates, M. E., Bowden, S. C. and Barry, D. (2002). Neurocognitive impairment associated with alcohol use disorders: implications for treatment. *Experimental and Clinical Psychopharmacology*, 10(3), 193–212.

Bates, M. E., Labouvie, E. W. and Voelbel, G. T. (2002). Individual differences in latent neuropsychological abilities at addictions treatment entry. *Psychology of Addictive Behaviors*, 16, 35–46.

Bello, B. M. E. and Schultz, R. R. (2011). Prevalence of treatable and reversible dementias: a study in a dementia outpatient clinic. *Dementia e Neuropsychologia*, 5(1), 44–7.

Blansjaar, B. A, Horjus, M. C. and Nijhuis, H. G. (1987). Prevalence of the Korsakoff syndrome in The Hague, The Netherlands. *Acta Psychiatrica Scandinavica*, 75(6), 604–7.

Blazer, D. G. and Wu, L.T. (2011). The epidemiology of alcohol use disorders and subthreshold dependence in a middle-aged and elderly community sample. *The American Journal of Geriatric Psychiatry*, 19(8), 685–94.

Bowden, S. C. (1990). Seperating cognitive impairment in neurologically asymptomatic alcoholism from Wernicke-Korsakoff Syndrome: is the neuropsychological distinction justified? *Psychological Bulletin*, 107(3), 355–66.

Bowden, S. C. (2010). Alcohol-related dementia and Wernicke-Korsakoff Syndrome. In *Dementia*, 4th edn. Ed. D. Ames, A. Burns and J. O'Brien. London: Edward Arnold, 730–7.

Brust, J. C. M. (2010). Ethanol and cognition: indirect effects, neurotoxicity and neuroprotection: a review. *International Journal of Environmental Research and Public Health*, 7, 1540–7.

Caine, D., Halliday, G. M., Kril, J. J. and Harper, C. G. (1997). Operational criteria for the classification of chronic alcoholics: identification of Wernicke's encephalopathy. *Journal of Neurology, Neurosurgery, and Psychiatry*, 62(1), 51–60.

Caputo, F., Vignoli, T., Leggio, L., Addolorato, G., Zoli, G. and Bernardi, M. (2012). Alcohol use disorders in the elderly: a brief overview from epidemiology to treatment options. *Experimental Gerontology*, 47(6), 411–6.

Carlen, P. K., McAndres, M. P., Weiss, R. T., Dongier, M., Hill, J. M., Menzano, E., Farcnik, K., Abarbanel, J. and Eastood, M. R. (1994). Alcohol-related dementia in the intitutionalised elderly, *Alcoholism: Clinical and Experimental Research*, 18(6).

Central Intelligence Agency. (2013). *The World Factbook*. Retrieved 16 September 2012, from https://www.cia.gov/library/publications/the-world-factbook/geos/xx.html

Clarfield, A. M. (1988). The reversible dementias: do they reverse? *Annals of Internal Medicine*, 109, 476–86.

Day, E., Bentham, P. W., Callaghan, R., Kuruvilla, T. and George, S. (2013). Thiamine for prevention and treatment of Wernicke-Korsakoff Syndrome in people who abuse alcohol. *Cochrane Database of Systematic Reviews*, 7, 1–20.

Draper, B., Karmel, R., Gibson, D., Peut, A. and Anderson, P. (2011). Alcohol-related cognitive impairment in New South Wales hospital patients aged 50 years and over. *Australian and New Zealand Journal of Psychiatry*, 45(11), 985–92.

Duka, T., Townshend, J. M., Collier, K. and Stephens, D. N. (2003). Impairment in cognitive functions after multiple detoxifications in alcoholic inpatients. *Alcoholism, Clinical and Experimental Research*, 27, 1563–72.

Dumitrescu, L., Simionescu, O., Oprisan, A., Luca, D., Gitman, A., Ticmeanu, M. and Tanasescu, R. (2011). Update on Wernicke's: considerations on epidemiology. *Romanian Journal of Neurology/Revista Romana de Neurologie*, 10(4), 172–8.

Elberling, T. V., Stokholm, J., Høgh, P. and Waldemar, G. (2002). Diagnostic profile of young and middle-aged memory clinic patients. *Neurology*, 59(8), 1259–62.

Feeney, G. F. X. and Connor, J. P. (2008). Wernicke-Korsakoff syndrome (WKS) in Australia: no room for complacency. *Drug and Alcohol Review*, 27(4), 388–92.

Fujihara, S., Brucki, S. M. D., Rocha, M. S. G., Carvalho, A. A. and Piccolo, A. C. (2004). Prevalence of presenile dementia in a tertiary outpatient clinic. *Arquivos de neuro-psiquiatria*, 62(3A), 592–5.

Fujiwara, E., Brand, M., Borsutzky, S., Steingass, H. P. and Markowitsch, H. J. (2008). Cognitive performance of detoxified alcoholic Korsakoff syndrome patients remains stable over two years. *Journal of Clinical and Experimental Neuropsychology*, 30(5), 576–87.

Galvin, R., Bråthen, G., Ivashynka, A, Hillbom, M., Tanasescu, R. and Leone, M. A. (2010). EFNS guidelines for diagnosis, therapy and prevention of Wernicke encephalopathy. *European Journal of Neurology: The Official Journal of the European Federation of Neurological Societies*, 17(12), 1408–18.

George, L. K., Landerman, R., Blazer, D. G. and Anthony, J. C. (1991). Cognitive impairment. In L. N. Robins and D. A. Regier (eds), *Psychiatric Disorders in America: The Epidemiologic Catchment Area Study*. New York: Free Press.

Gilchrist, G. and Morrison, D. S. (2005). Prevalence of alcohol related brain damage among homeless hostel dwellers in Glasgow. *European Journal of Public Health*, 15(6), 587–8.

Grant, B. F., Dawson, D. A., Stinson, F. S., Chou, S. P., Dufour, M. C. and Pickering, M. S. (2004). The 12-month prevalence and trends in DSM – IV Alcohol abuse and dependence. *Drug and Alcohol Dependence*, 74(3), 223–34.

Grucza, R. A., Norberg, K., Bucholz, K. K. and Bierut, L. J. (2009). Correspondence between secular changes. *Alcoholism: Clinical and Experimental Research*, 32(8), 1493–501.

Harper, C. G. (1979). Wernicke's encephalopathy: a more common disease than realised. A neuropathological study of 51 cases. *Journal of Neurology, Neurosurgery and Psychiatry*, 42, 226–31.

Harper, C. (1983). The incidence of Wernicke's encephalopathy in Australia: a neuropathological study of 131 cases. *Journal of Neurology, Neurosurgery and Psychiatry*, 46, 593–8.

Harper, C. (2009). The neuropathology of alcohol-related brain damage. *Alcohol and Alcoholism*, 44(2), 136–40.

Harper, C., Fornes, P., Duyckaerts, C., Lecomte, D. and Hauw, J. J. (1995). An international perspective on the prevalence of the Wernicke-Korsakoff syndrome. *Metabolic Brain Disease*, 10(1), 17–24.

Harper, C. G., Giles, M. and Finlay-Jones, R. (1986). Clinical signs in the Wernicke-Korsakoff complex: a retrospective analysis of 131 cases diagnosed at necropsy. *Journal of Neurology, Neurosurgery, and Psychiatry*, 49(4), 341–5.

Harper, C. G., Sheedy, D. L., Lara, A. I., Garrick, T. M., Hilton, J. M. and Raisanen, J. (1998). Prevalence of Wernicke-Kosrakoff syndrome in Australia: has thiamine fortification made a difference? *Medical Journal of Australia*, 168(11), 542–5.

Harvey, R. J., Skelton-Robinson, M. and Rossor, M. N. (2003). The prevalence and causes of dementia in people under the age of 65 years. *Journal of Neurology, Neurosurgery and Psychiatry*, 74, 1206–9.

Hasin, D., Stinson, F., Elizabeth, O. and Grant, B. (2007). Prevalence, correlates, disability and comorbidity of DSM-IV alcohol abuse and dependence in the United States. *Archives of General Psychiatry*, 64(7), 830–42.

Hermens, D. F., Lagopoulos, J., Tobias-Webb, J., De Regt, T., Dore, G., Juckes, L., Latt, N. and Hickie, I. B. (2013). Pathways to alcohol-induced brain impairment in young people: a review. *Cortex*, 49, 3–17.

Isenberg-Grzeda, E., Kutner, H. E. and Nicolson, S. E. (2012). Wernicke-Korsakoff-syndrome: under-recognized and under-treated. *Psychosomatics*, 53(6), 507–16.

Jacobson, R. R., Acker, C. F. and Lishman, W. A. (1990). Patterns of neuropsychological deficit in alcoholic Korsakoff's Syndrome. *Psychological Medicine*, 20, 321–34.

Jauhar, S. and Smith, I. D. (2009). Alcohol-related brain damage: not a silent epidemic. *British Journal of Psychiatry*, 194, 287–8.

Joyce, E. M. and Robbins, T. W. (1991). Frontal lobe function in Korsakoff and non-Korsakoff alcoholics: planning and spatial working memory. *Neuropsychologia*, 19(8), 709–23.

Knopman, D. S., Petersen, R. C., Cha, R. H., Edland, S. D. and Rocca, W. A. (2006). Incidence and causes of nondenerative non-vascular dementia: a population-based study. *Archives of Neurology*, 63, 218–21.

Kopelman, M. D., Thomson, A. D., Guerrini, I. and Marshall, E. J. (2009). The Korsakoff syndrome: clinical aspects, psychology and treatment. *Alcohol and Alcoholism*, 44(2), 148–54.

Kril, J. J. and Harper, C. G. (2012). Neuroanatomy and neuropathology associated with Korsakoff's syndrome. *Neuropsychology Review*, 22(2), 72–80.

Lopes, M. A., Furtado, E. F., Ferrioli, E., Litvoc, J. and Bottino, C. M. D. C. (2010). Prevalence of alcohol-related problems in an elderly population and their association with cognitive impairment and dementia. *Alcoholism: Clinical and Experimental Research*, 34(4), 726–33.

MacRae, R. and Cox, S. (2003). *Meeting the Needs of People with Alcohol Related Brain Damage: A Literature Review on the Existing and Recommended Service Provision and Models of Care.* University of Stirling, Stirling: Dementia Services Development Centre.

Mason, G. F., Bendszus, M., Meyerhoff, D. J., Hetherington, H. P., Schweinsburg, B., Ross, B. D., Taylor, M. J. and Krysal, J. H. (2005). Magnetic resonance spectroscopic studies of alcoholism: from heavy drinking to alcohol dependence and back again. *Alcoholism: Clinical and Experimental Research*, 29(1), 150–8.

McCabe, L. F. (2011). Alcohol, ageing and dementia: a Scottish perspective. *Dementia*, 10(2), 149–63.

McMurtray, A., Clark, D. G., Christine, D. and Mendez, M. F. (2006). Early-onset dementia: frequency and causes compared to late-onset dementia. *Dementia and Geriatric Cognitive Disorders*, 21(2), 59–64.

Moore, A., Gould, R., Reuben, D. B., Greendale, G. A., Carter, M. K., Zhou, K. and Karlamangla, A. (2005). Longitudinal patterns and predictors of alcohol consumption in the United States. *American Journal of Public Health*, 95(3).

Moriyama, Y., Mimura, M., Kato, M. and Kashima, H. (2006). Primary alcoholic dementia and alcohol-related dementia. *Psychogeriatrics*, 6(3), 114–18.

Mukamal, K. J., Kuller, L. H., Fitzpatrick, A. L., Longstreth, W. T., Mittleman, M. A. and Siscovick, D. S. (2003). Prospective study of alcohol consumption and risk of dementia in older adults. *JAMA (Journal of the American Medical Association)*, 289(11), 1405–13.

Nadkarni, A., Acosta, D., Rodriguez, G., Prince, M. and Ferri, C. P. (2011). The psychological impact of heavy drinking among the elderly on their co-residents: the 10/66 group population based survey in the Dominican Republic. *Drug and Alcohol Dependence*, 114(1), 82–6.

Naimi, T. S., Brewer, R. D., Mokdad, A., Denny, C., Serdula, M. K. and Marks, J. S. (2003). Binge drinking among US adults. *JAMA (Journal of the American Medical Association)*, 289(1), 70–5.

Oslin, D. W. and Cary, M. S. (2003), Alcohol-related dementia: validation of diagnostic criteria. *American Journal of Geriatric Psychiatry*, 11(4), 441–7.

Oslin, D., Atkinson, R. M., Smith, D. M. and Hendrie, H. (1998). Alcohol-related dementia: proposed clinical criteria. *International Journal of Geriatric Psychiatry*, 13, 203–12.

Panegyres, P. K. and Frencham, K. (2007). Course and causes of suspected dementia in young adults: a longitudinal study. *American Journal of Alzheimer's Disease and Other Dementias*, 22(1), 48–56.

Peltzer, K., Davids, A. and Njuho, P. (2011). Alcohol use and problem drinking in South Africa: findings from a national population-based survey. *African Journal of Psychiatry*, 14(1), 30–7.

Picard, C., Pasquier, F., Martinaud, O., Hannequin, D. and Godefroy, O. (2011). Early onset dementia: characteristics in a large cohort from academic memory clinics. *Alzheimer Disease and Associated Disorders*, 25(3), 203–5.

Pitel, A. L., Zahr, N. M., Jackson, K., Sassoon, S. A, Rosenbloom, M. J., Pfefferbaum, A. and Sullivan, E. V. (2011). Signs of preclinical Wernicke's encephalopathy and thiamine levels as predictors of neuropsychological deficits in alcoholism without Korsakoff's syndrome. *Neuropsychopharmacology*, 36(3), 580–8.

Platt, A., Sloan, F. A. and Costanzo, P. (2010). Alcohol-consumption trajectories and associated characteristics among adults older than age 50. *Journal of Studies on Alcohol and Drugs*, 71(2), 169–79.

Ramayya, A. and Jauhar, P. (1997). Increasing incidence of Korsakoff's psychosis in the East End of Glasgow. *Alcohol and Alcoholism*, 32(3), 281–5.

Rains, V. S. and Ditzler, T. F. (1993). Alcohol use disorders in cognitively impaired patients referred for geriatric assessment. *Journal of Addictive Diseases*, 12(1), 55–64.

Rehm, J., Mathers, C., Popova, S., Thavorncharoensap, M., Teerawattananon, Y. and Patra, J. (2009). Global burden of disease and injury and economic cost attributable to alcohol use and alcohol-use disorders. *Lancet*, 373, 2223–33.

Renvoize, E., Hanson, M. and Dale, M. (2011). Prevalence and causes of young onset dementia in an English health district. *International Journal of Geriatric Psychiatry*, 26, 106–8.

Ritchie, K. and Villebrun, D. (2008). Epidemiology of alcohol-related dementia. *Handbook of Clinical Neurology*, 89, 845–50.

Rosenbloom, M. J., Reilly, A. O., Sassoon, S. A., Sullivan, E. V. and Pfefferbaum, A. (2005). Persistent cognitive deficits in community-treated alcoholic men and women volunteering for research: limited contribution from psychiatric co-morbidity. *Journal on Studies of Alcohol*, 66(2), 254–65.

Salem, L. C., Andersen, B. B., Nielsen, T. R., Stokholm, J., Jørgensen, M. B., Rasmussen, M. H. and Waldemar, G. (2012). Overdiagnosis of dementia in young patients: a nationwide register-based study. *Dementia and Geriatric Cognitive Disorders*, 34, 292–9.

Saunders, P. A., Copeland, J. R. M., Dewey, M. E., Davidson, I. A., McWilliam, C., Sharma, V. and Sullivan, C. (1991). Heavy drinking as a risk factor for depression and dementia in elderly men: findings from the Liverpool Longitudinal Community Study. *British Journal of Psychiatry*, 159, 213–16.

Savage, L. (2014). Alcohol-related brain damage and neuropathology. In J. Svanberg, A. Withall, B. Draper and S. Bowden (eds), *Alcohol and the Adult Brain*. Hove: Psychology Press.

Scalzo, S., Bowden, S. and Hillbom, M. (2014). Wernicke-Korsakoff Syndrome. In J. Svanberg, A. Withall, B. Draper and S. Bowden (eds), *Alcohol and the Adult Brain*. Hove: Psychology Press.

Sechi, G. and Serra, A. (2007). Wernicke's encephalopathy: new clinical settings and recent advances in diagnosis and management. *Lancet Neurology*, 6, 442–55.

Smith, D. M. and Atkinson, R. M. (1993). Alcoholic dementia in an Alzheimer's Registry. Presented at the American Psychiatric Association Annual Meeting, Miami, Florida.

Smith, D. M. and Atkinson, R. M. (1995). Alcoholism and dementia. *The International Journal of the Addictions*, 30(13–14), 1843–69.

Smith, I. D. and Flanigan, C. (2000). Korsakoff's psychosis in Scotland: evidence for increased prevalence and regional variation. *Alcohol and Alcoholism*, 35(1), 8–10.

Stavro, K., Pelletier, J. and Potvin, S. (2012). Widespread and sustained cognitive deficits in alcoholism: a meta-analysis. *Addiction Biology*, 18, 203–13.

Sullivan E. V. and Pfefferbaum, A. (2009). Neuroimaging of the Wernicke-Korsakoff Syndrome. *Alcohol and Alcoholism*, 44, 155–65.

Takada, L. T., Caramelli, P., Radanovic, M, Anghinah, R., Hartmann, A. P., Guariglia, C. C., Bahia, V. S. and Nirtini, R. (2003). Prevalence of potentially reversible dementias in a dementia outpatient clinic of a tertiary university-affiliated hospital in Brazil. *Arquivos de neuro-psiquiatria*, 61(4), 925–9.

Teesson, M., Baillie, A., Lynskey, M., Manor, B. and Degenhardt, L. (2006). Substance use, dependence and treatment seeking in the United States and Australia: a cross-national comparison. *Drug and Alcohol Dependence*, 81(2).

Thomson, A. D., Guerrini, I. and Marshall, E. J. (2012). The evolution and treatment of Korsakoff's syndrome: out of sight, out of mind? *Neuropsychology Review*, 22(2), 81–92.

Thomson, A. D. and Marshall, E. J. (2006). The treatment of patients at risk of developing Wernicke's encephalopathy in the community. *Alcohol and Alcoholism*, 41(2), 159–67.

Thomson, A. D., Marshall, E. J. and Bell, D. (2013). Time to act on the inadequate management of Wernicke's encephalopathy in the UK. *Alcohol and Alcoholism*, 48(1), 4–8.

Torvik, A., Lindboe, C. F. and Rogde, S. (1982). Brain lesions in alcoholics: a neuropathological study with clinical correlations. *Journal of the Neurological Sciences*, 56, 233–48.

Wilson, K. (2015). The clinical rehabilitation of people with alcohol-related brain damage. In J. Svanberg, A. Withall, B. Draper and S. Bowden (eds), *Alcohol and the Adult Brain*. Hove: Psychology Press.

Withall, A., Draper, B., Seeher, K. and Brodaty, H. (2014). The prevalence and causes of younger onset dementia in Eastern Sydney, Australia. *International Psychogeriatrics*.

Withall, A. and Shafiee, S. (2015). Alcohol and cognitive impairment: Considerations with the older client. In J. Svanberg, A. Withall, B. Draper and S. Bowden (eds) *Alcohol and the Adult Brain*. Hove: Psychology Press.

United Nations Department of Economic and Social Affairs. (2001). World Population Ageing: 1950–2050. Retrieved 11 September 2013, from http://www.un.org/esa/population/publications/worldageing19502050/index.htm

Van Oort, R. and Kessels, R. P. C. (2009). Executive dysfunction in Korsakoff syndrome: time to revise the DSM criteria for alcohol-induced persisting amnestic disorder? *International Journal of Psychiatry in Clinical Practice*, 13(1), 78–81.

Victor, M., Adams, R. D. and Collins, G. H. (1989). *The Wernicke-Korsakoff Syndrome* (2nd edn). Philadelphia: F. A. Davis Co.

World Health Organization (WHO; 1992). *ICD-10 Classifications of Mental and Behavioural Disorders: Clinical Descriptions and Diagnostic Guidelines*. Geneva, Switzerland: WHO.

World Health Organization (2011). *Global Status Report on Alcohol and Health*. Geneva, Switzerland: WHO.

World Health Organization (2012). *Dementia: A Public Health Priority*. Geneva, Switzerland: WHO.

Zahr, N. M., Kaufman, K. L. and Harper, C. G. (2011). Clinical and pathological features of alcohol-related brain damage. *Nature Reviews: Neurology*, 7, 284–94.

4

CULTURAL CONSIDERATIONS IN ALCOHOL USE AND MISUSE

Carly Johnco and Brian Draper

Alcohol use has long been linked with cultural expression, whether it is its symbolic use during a religious ceremony such as a Christian liturgy, the ritual toasting of a newly married couple at the wedding reception, the wine routinely served at the opening night of an art exhibition or its social use as a marker of time and mood (Anderson and Baumberg, 2006). Culture is defined in the *Oxford Dictionary* as "the ideas, customs, and social behaviour of a particular people or society". In this chapter we will consider various aspects of cultural expression including ethnicity, socio-economic issues, employment, education, religion, living arrangements and issues faced by minority groups and indigenous people. We will consider how differences in alcohol use across different ethnic and cultural groups may influence health consequences of alcohol use, including alcohol-related brain damage.

Ethnicity

There is marked variability in levels of consumption between countries, with high levels of abstention in those countries in North Africa and South Asia with large Muslim populations (World Health Organization, 2011). High-risk drinking and alcohol-related harm is particularly prominent in the Russian Federation and Latin America. Even within Europe, the highest drinking region of the world, there is marked variability of alcohol consumption between countries ranging from Turkey, where in 2004 the per capita consumption was less than 5 litres per year, to Hungary where it was closer to 20 litres per year. These national consumption patterns are not static and in Europe since the 1970s a harmonization has been recorded with the traditionally high consumption in southern European countries diminishing and the lower consumption patterns of northern Europe increasing. There is also evidence of national variability in the way people drink: the type of alcohol, the drinking context (for example, with meals or in public) and the frequency (Anderson and Baumberg, 2006).

Genetic variations in the way individuals respond to alcohol can contribute to what might appear to be ethnic differences. For some populations, genetic vulnerability means low tolerance to alcohol and the inability to process it (International Center for Alcohol Policies, 2001). Some East Asians have heightened sensitivity to alcohol due to impairment of alcohol metabolism caused by a non-functional form of the enzyme alcohol dehydrogenase. Although this results in an acute reaction to even small amounts of alcohol, it might confer a protective effect for other alcohol-related harms by limiting alcohol consumption (International Center for Alcohol Policies, 2001). The sensitivity characterizes 25 to 40 per cent of the Japanese population, nearly 25 per cent of Han Chinese and between 15 and 30 per cent of Koreans (Maezawa et al., 1995; Shen et al., 1997). For other populations genetic vulnerability is an increased risk for alcohol abuse or dependence (International Center for Alcohol Policies, 2001).

Minority groups

It is important to consider the impact of minority group status, including indigenous populations and immigrants, on alcohol-use behaviors. There are a range of cultural influences present in these groups that are likely to impact on their alcohol-use behaviors, along with negative health and cognitive outcomes.

Indigenous people

Before European colonization, most areas of the world, with the exception of parts of the Pacific and North America, had indigenous versions of alcoholic drinks. These were quite varied in their composition, preparation and primary use, which included nutrition and medicinal purposes as well as alcohol's psychoactive properties (Dietler, 2006). The pre-colonial role of alcohol in indigenous societies was diverse, encompassing political, economic and religious dimensions. Modes of serving, consumption, expected drinking behavior and styles of inebriation were quite varied from culture to culture (Dietler, 2006).

European contact and colonization brought changes to the social, political and economic context of alcohol use in indigenous societies (Dietler, 2006; Westermeyer, 1996). For example, the social context of drinking in the Americas changed to include "frontier drinking", which was secular, individualistic, male-centered and often associated with bravado or confrontation as opposed to the more family-oriented drinking that tended to occur in groups and in religious rituals (Westermeyer, 1996). In West Africa, the importance of alcohol in the political economy is highlighted by the role of distilled spirits as a commodity and currency in establishing exchange relationships in the Atlantic slave trade (Dietler, 2006). Similarly, rum was used as currency in the early years of the convict settlement in Australia (Saggers and Gray, 1998).

There was no pre-European-contact use of alcohol by Indigenous Canadians and New Zealand Maori and limited use by Australian Aboriginal people; early post-contact reports from each country emphasized that the indigenous people had to be encouraged to drink alcohol (Saggers and Gray, 1998). However, once some of the indigenous people in these countries had acquired the taste for alcohol, patterns of consumption resembled that seen in the European colonists, with a mix of excessive use and abstinence (Saggers and Gray, 1998).

The decimation of indigenous populations by introduced diseases and violence over land possession resulted in many indigenous people becoming dispossessed fringe dwellers who consumed alcohol to excess. This prompted colonial jurisdictions to impose controls on indigenous alcohol use due to fears of outbreaks of violence and concerns about the health of indigenous people (Saggers and Gray, 1998). From the mid-19th century these controls included prohibition of the sale of alcohol to indigenous people in various parts of the USA, Canada, Australia and New Zealand and in some jurisdictions prohibition remained in force until the mid-20th century (Saggers and Gray, 1998; Westermeyer, 1996). Overall, prohibition was ineffective and had other negative consequences as it led to increased surveillance, exclusion from social spaces such as hotels and the development of riskier drinking patterns such as high-alcohol drinks without food (Wilson et al., 2010).

One of the myths about alcohol use in indigenous people is that they drink more alcohol and in a different pattern to their European counterparts, a view not supported by the evidence (May, 2005; Saggers and Gray, 1998; Westermeyer, 1996). Indeed, there is marked variation in alcohol use in indigenous groups within countries (Whitesell et al., 2012), with factors reinforcing use including low access to financial security, jobs and relationships (Spillane, Smith and Kahler, 2013). Another myth is that indigenous people have a biological vulnerability to alcohol hepatic metabolism and are thus prone to alcohol-use disorders (May, 2005; Saggers and Gray, 1998). For example, while there is evidence that some Native American populations have variants of the alcohol-metabolizing enzymes alcohol dehydrogenase (ADH) and aldehyde dehydrogenase (ALDH), the findings do not explain the high prevalence of harmful alcohol use (Ehlers, 2007). Yet there is evidence that alcohol-use disorders are more prevalent in indigenous people than in non-indigenous people in countries worldwide.

Psychosocial issues that have been identified as contributing to harmful alcohol consumption by contemporary indigenous peoples include land rights, with past dispossession of traditional lands and associated moves to reservations where different tribal groups were forced to cohabit; experiences of trauma, social exclusion, poor education, poverty and racism; and family disruption including the legally endorsed forced removal of children from parents (May, 2005; Saggers and Gray, 1998; Szlemko, Wood and Thurman, 2006; Westermeyer, 1996). For example, children of the Australian Aboriginal "stolen generation" have twice the risk of harmful alcohol and drug use compared with children of Aboriginals who were not separated from their parents (Zubrick et al., 2004). This combination of contemporary and historical experiences has resulted in alcohol being used by some indigenous people as a way of coping with often forced abandonment and loss of traditional lifestyles.

In Australia it is estimated that the prevalence of harmful alcohol use in Indigenous Australians is approximately double that reported in the general population

(Wilson *et al.*, 2010). Alcohol harm is responsible for 5.4 per cent of the total disease burden and 6.7 per cent of deaths in Indigenous Australians compared with only 2.3 per cent total disease burden and 0.8 per cent of deaths in the general population (Calabria *et al.*, 2010). New Zealand Maori have about a 50 per cent higher rate of alcohol abuse/dependence than non-Maori (Marie, Fergusson and Boden, 2012). Over 85 per cent of Venezuelan Native American males and 7.5 to 17.5 per cent of females have been reported to have "problem drinking" (Seale *et al.*, 2002; 2010). In the USA, alcohol-attributable deaths among American Indians and Alaska Natives is estimated to be double that of the general population (Centers for Disease Control and Prevention, 2008).

The extent to which the high prevalence of harmful alcohol use in indigenous populations translates into alcohol-related brain damage (ARBD) is unclear. Anecdotal reports speak of high rates of ARBD (e.g., Pollitt, 1997; Wilson, 2001); however, most reports of alcohol-related harm in indigenous people do not include a specific category of brain damage (e.g., Calabria *et al.*, 2010; Saggers and Gray, 1998) or only allude to it in a cursory fashion (e.g., Westermeyer, 1996; Wilson *et al.*, 2010). Older studies indicate possible concerns. A forensic neuropathology study reported that the incidence of Wernicke's Encephalopathy was approximately five times higher in Australian Aboriginal people than in the general population (Harper, 1983). There are few studies of dementia in indigenous people but two older methodologically flawed studies reported high rates of alcohol-related dementia. From a small sample of 192 community-dwelling Canadian Cree subjects, Hendrie and colleagues (1993) identified eight with dementia of whom two (25 per cent) had alcohol-related dementia. A study from north Queensland in Australia reported that alcohol-related dementia/Korsakoff's Syndrome was the main cause of dementia in a small sample of 133 Indigenous Australians aged 65 years and over (Zann, 1994). In the latter study most of the sample was living in residential care and their diagnoses were obtained from hospital records and/or a cognitive screening instrument unvalidated in the population.

More recent epidemiological studies of cognitive impairment in Indigenous Australians that utilized culturally appropriate methodologies have not found alcohol to be a major cause of dementia (Radford *et al.*, 2013; Smith *et al.*, 2010). One study in a rural Australian substance treatment in-patient population reported that 82 per cent of indigenous subjects and only 28 per cent of non-indigenous subjects were cognitively impaired on the Addenbrooke's Cognitive Examination – Revised (Allan, Kemp and Golden, 2012). The researchers noted that interpretation of these results was limited by the uncertainty of the validity of the screening tool in the indigenous population. It is worth noting, however, that some of the health factors that are associated with increased risk of the Wernicke-Korsakoff Syndrome, such as diabetes and poor nutrition, are prevalent in some indigenous populations and may indicate increased risk (Arpi *et al.*, 2006; Gubhaju *et al.*, 2013; Wijnia *et al.*, 2012). Cultural sensitivity of the care system also influenced the recognition and treatment of cognitive impairment – for example, due to a lack of culturally appropriate assessment measures, a lack of advocacy, difficulties in service provision in rural areas, the need for appropriate cohesion between traditional healing customs and western health care, and the need for language resources (Keightley *et al.*, 2009).

There are potential negative outcomes for cognition resulting from parental alcohol abuse. Foetal Alcohol Syndrome (FAS) is a condition that refers to the teratogenic effects of heavy maternal alcohol consumption upon the developing fetus such as growth retardation, characteristic facial features and central nervous system dysfunction which can include developmental delay, behavioral disorders and intellectual disability (O'Leary, 2004). High rates of FAS have been reported in some indigenous populations in Australia, the USA and Canada, being recognized as the main preventable non-genetic cause of intellectual impairment (O'Leary, 2004). There are concerns that findings from a few studies in select indigenous populations known to have high alcohol consumption have been extrapolated to be representative of indigenous populations as a whole thereby obscuring other factors such as poor education, poverty, unemployment and racism that might be responsible for cognitive outcomes (Hoy, 2012). Nevertheless, the potential intergenerational impact of FAS upon indigenous populations is of great concern.

Migration

Various patterns of harmful alcohol use have been described in immigrant populations, which do not simply reflect alcohol use in the country of birth, although little is known specifically about how this may relate to ARBD. Some examples illustrate this. Levels of alcohol consumption in various South Asian immigrant groups in Scotland are lower than in the general population (McKenzie and Haw 2006), while age-standardized alcohol-related mortality was comparatively low in immigrants from Pakistan, other parts of the UK and elsewhere in the world (Bhala, Fischbacher and Bhopal, 2010). In contrast, immigrants from the former Soviet Union residing in Israel have high rates of alcohol-related disorders (Weiss, 2008). A study comparing the alcohol use in Latinos born in the USA with that in recent Latino immigrants pre-immigration and post-immigration found that the post-immigration alcohol use of immigrants was lower than their pre-immigration use and that of US-born Latinos (De La Rosa *et al.*, 2012). In Germany, the drinking behavior of adolescent immigrants from Turkey and the former Soviet Union only partially conformed to expectations and the authors speculated on the role of acculturation in their findings (Donath *et al.*, 2011). An examination of alcohol-use disorders in Afghan migrants to Germany found that they were significantly associated with acculturation stress and mental distress whether or not alcohol was used prior to migration (Haasen, Sinaa and Reimer, 2008). The important role of acculturation in migrants was supported in a nationally representative sample of 952 Asian American adults extracted from the Wave 2 National Epidemiologic Survey of Alcohol and Related Conditions. After controlling for other factors, a positive relationship between ethnic drinking cultures and alcohol outcomes held for most drinking outcomes, with a moderating effect of integration into ethnic cultures as indicated by ethnic language use being found in US-born Asian Americans (Cook, Mulia and Karriker-Jaffe, 2012).

The studies considered here illustrate the complexity of understanding harmful alcohol use in immigrant populations and show little information specifically about ARBD.

Socio-economic status

There is a notable socio-economic gradient in relation to alcohol-related mortality and morbidity (Melchior *et al.*, 2011); however, this relationship is complex and multifaceted. Socio-economic status (SES) and disadvantage can refer to a range of issues, although most commonly it refers to combinations of low levels of education, unemployment and financial hardship. It is also relevant to consider the impact of both individual-level and area-level socio-economic disadvantage on both alcohol-use patterns and negative health outcomes. Hazardous use of alcohol increases the risk of a range of negative health outcomes, including ARBD. While the research on the impact of SES on ARBD is somewhat limited, understanding the impact of SES on hazardous alcohol-use patterns may provide some insight into high-risk groups in the community.

There are a number of different mechanisms proposed to underlie the effect of SES on substance use patterns, including psychological, social and environmental contributions. Investigations into the effect of SES on alcohol use and alcohol-related consequences are complex. There are often conflicting results due to the varying methodologies used. Studies vary in their definitions and classifications of SES, including varying combinations of education, income and employment as proxy indicators. Studies also vary in their measurement of what constitutes problematic drinking behaviors, ranging from frequency and quantity of consumption, to the experience of negative alcohol-related health outcomes.

There is evidence of area-level impact on alcohol use with residents of similar geographical areas showing similar patterns of consumption (Karriker-Jaffe, 2011), and higher rates of problematic alcohol use in areas of socio-economic disadvantage (Jones-Webb *et al.*, 1997; Stimpson *et al.*, 2007; Waitzman and Smith, 1998). While neighborhood disadvantage seems to play a role in increased use, perhaps through problematic social norms, high alcohol consumption is also seen in neighborhoods where there is high income inequality (Cutright and Fernquist, 2010), possibly indicating a role of upward social comparisons in increasing dissatisfaction and substance use. There is a clustering of negative alcohol-related outcomes in areas of socio-economic deprivation, including increased rates of ARBD (Chiang, 2002; MacRae and Cox, 2003) and higher rates of FAS (Abel, 1995). The impact of SES on alcohol use is evident in developed as well as less developed nations, including India and Sri Lanka (De Silva, Samarasinghe and Hanwella, 2011; Pillai *et al.*, 2013), where higher proportions of income is spent on alcohol in lower-income households compared with higher SES groups (De Silva, Samarasinghe and Hanwella, 2011). While area-level disadvantage does seem to have a role in alcohol use and outcomes, the effect is likely to be indirect, and often disappears when adjusting for individual-level mediating factors (Karriker-Jaffe, 2011).

Given the variability in measurement of individual-level SES and alcohol-use patterns it is unsurprising that the findings are complex. There are reasonably consistent findings between poorer SES and increased hazardous alcohol use and consequences. Some findings indicate that those with higher SES tend to have higher alcohol consumption, especially in relation to binge drinking patterns (Casswell, Pledger and Hooper, 2003; Chuang *et al.*, 2005; Huckle, You and Casswell, 2010; Keyes and Hasin, 2008; Melotti *et al.*, 2013; Sanchez *et al.*, 2013). The socioeconomic gradient is often more prominent when examining more extreme aspects of hazardous alcohol use, such as frequent hangovers, periods of alcohol-related unconsciousness, alcohol-specific hospitalizations and death (Paljarvi *et al.*, 2013).

Surrogate alcohol consumption (consumption of alcoholic substances not intended to be drunk, such as mouthwash or cleaning products with ethanol) is an especially dangerous form of alcohol abuse that is frequently seen in low SES populations (Tomkins *et al.*, 2007). Low SES appears to impact alcohol use in one of two directions, increasing the likelihood that a person would either abstain from alcohol use or have an alcohol-related problem (Bloomfield *et al.*, 2006; Casswell, Pledger and Hooper, 2003). It is likely that the complexity of this finding is partially due to the disparities between these two groups. Overall, findings do suggest increased rates of alcohol-related harm in those with poorer SES, including mortality, cirrhosis and hospitalizations (Bloomfield *et al.*, 2006; Harrison and Gardiner, 1999; Makela, Keskimaki and Koskinen, 2003), along with greater impact of alcohol use on cognitive abilities in low SES groups which may be due to lower cognitive reserve (Sabia *et al.*, 2011). It has been argued that those with lower SES may have increased negative outcomes related to their alcohol use due to factors that limit use of or access to protective health behaviors, such as health care, housing and nutrition, rather than necessarily due to heavier consumption (Huckle, You and Casswell, 2010; Makela and Paljarvi, 2008). Poverty is also a factor. In Sri Lanka, despite spending less on alcohol than those with higher incomes, the poor are likely to spend a higher proportion of their disposable income on alcohol (De Silva, Samarasinghe and Hanwella, 2011). The impact of other health behaviors is likely to exacerbate the negative impact of alcohol use among those experiencing socioeconomic disadvantage. Examples include poor nutrition, which increases the risk of ARBD, and smoking, which is independently associated with dementia (Almeida *et al.*, 2002; Arpi *et al.*, 2006; Murphy *et al.*, 2012). Findings in relation to the socioeconomic gradient on alcohol-use outcomes often suggest a different pattern for men and women (Batty *et al.*, 2012; Bloomfield *et al.*, 2006). Lower SES is often associated with higher risk of heavy use and abuse in men, but was associated with lower use and abuse patterns in women (Batty *et al.*, 2012; Bloomfield *et al.*, 2006; van Oers *et al.*, 1999). In the context of understanding the abstinence and abuse groups found in studies of low SES populations, it may be that women who are caring for children tend to be represented more in the abstinence groups, while men commonly fall into the hazardous-use groups. Unemployment was found to be the highest risk factor for hazardous drinking in men, while being on a disability pension increased the risk for women (Paljarvi *et al.*, 2013). The role of gender in drinking behaviors has historically been divided, with drinking being stigmatized as a sign of masculinity, particularly among young adult males. However, the increase of alcohol use in western women following the feminist movement may begin to negate some of the historical gender differences in years to come.

Employment

Unemployment is one aspect of SES that is frequently associated with increased and hazardous alcohol use (Droomers *et al.*, 1999; Henkel, 2011; Joutsenniemi *et al.*, 2007; Kriegbaum *et al.*, 2011). However, the nature of this relationship is likely to be bidirectional, with heavy alcohol use increasing the longitudinal risk of unemployment, and unemployment increasing the risk of subsequent alcohol use. There are some studies that suggest that unemployment increases the risk of excessive drinking, and that the risk increases with the number of job losses and duration of unemployment (Kriegbaum *et al.*, 2011). Unemployment is likely to have an impact on alcohol use through a number of psychosocial mechanisms, including drinking for entertainment or drinking to avoid the psychological distress associated with losing a job. Increased risk of subsequent problem drinking and alcohol-specific diagnoses following disengagement from the workforce is also seen in people on disability pensions, where increased alcohol-use problems are seen subsequent to their inability to maintain employment (Paljarvi *et al.*, 2013). Most studies find an association between unemployment and hazardous alcohol use, but do not specify a direction of this relationship (Huckle, You and Casswell, 2010; Paljarvi *et al.*, 2013), although there are some studies that fail to find this association (Backhans, Lundin and Hemmingsson, 2012). While there are psychosocial factors involved with unemployment that may increase the risk of problem drinking behaviors, it is also likely that the performance deficits or cognitive issues induced by chronic alcohol-use problems, including transient or more pervasive cognitive impairments, increase the chance of poor workplace functioning and dismissal.

Under-employment and low income are also relevant aspects of SES to consider in relation to alcohol-use behaviors. There appears to be a positive relationship between income and alcohol abuse in the general population, but a negative relationship between income and alcohol dependence (Keyes and Hasin, 2008). Findings suggest that more affluent people tend to drink more regularly, but tend to drink smaller quantities on a given occasion compared with lower income groups (Huckle, You and Casswell, 2010). Similar to findings with broad SES categorization, there appear to be increased risks of abstinence or heavy drinking (rather than light/moderate drinking) in those with sustained low income levels (Cerda, Johnson-Lawrence and Galea, 2011). It is likely that these are two distinct groups and that the increased high-risk drinking behaviors and health outcomes are more representative of those who neglect basic living expenses and needs in favor of alcohol use and abuse rather than those who are experiencing low income levels and allocate all available resources to living expenses, eliminating alcohol use.

There has long been evidence that some occupations are associated with higher levels of harmful alcohol consumption. A review from over 20 years ago found evidence of increased levels of alcohol-related harm, independent of demographic factors, in the construction and transportation industries (Mandell *et al.*, 1992). Subsequent research has generally confirmed that manual laborers with low qualifications have the highest rates of alcohol consumption and alcohol-related harm (Cheng *et al.*, 2012; Hemmingsson and Weitoft, 2001; Marchand, 2008). However, there is also evidence that upper managers have significantly higher rates of risky drinking (Marchand, 2008). Characteristics of the workplace environment are also important, as workplace harassment is associated with alcohol use and misuse (Marchand, 2008). Other occupational characteristics, such as working on a farm or in the hospitality industry, were also noted to be associated with binge drinking in North Dakota (Jarman *et al.*, 2007).

Education

Educational attainment is another common proxy of SES, and lower education is often associated with higher alcohol consumption (Droomers *et al.*, 1999; Paljarvi *et al.*, 2013; van Oers *et al.*, 1999), although binge drinking confounds this relationship (Paljarvi *et al.*, 2013). Similar to findings around the role of income, those with higher educational achievements tend to drink more regularly, but drink less hazardous quantities of alcohol on a single drinking occasion compared with those with lower education levels (Huckle, You and Casswell, 2010). Binge drinking is sometimes found to be higher in those with lower education (Bloomfield *et al.*, 2006) and at other times in those with higher education (van Oers *et al.*, 1999). Binge drinking patterns are important to consider in relation to the risk for ARBD, given the potential for the repeated neurotoxic effects to damage the brain more acutely than more chronic states of intoxication.

Religion

Religion is another prominent cultural factor that can affect alcohol consumption patterns but, as in most of the other cultural factors, there is little evidence that there is a specific impact on ARBD. Religions vary in their proscriptive practices regarding alcohol consumption, with some prohibiting consumption for a variety of reasons, others encouraging alcohol use as a part of religious practices, and others being less proscriptive in relation to alcohol. Identification with highly proscriptive religions has been associated with drinking practices, and there is an over-representation of ex-drinkers in some religious denominations (Michalak, Trocki and Bond, 2007).

There are several religions that directly prohibit the consumption of alcohol. Mormonism (members of the Church of Jesus Christ of Latter Day Saints) forbids the consumption of alcohol for health reasons (Hilton, 1986), as does Methodism (Schmidt, 1995) and Sikhism. Mormons and Methodists were historically allowed to consume alcohol; however, these denominations were strong supporters of the

US prohibition movement and subsequently forbade the consumption of alcohol (Schmidt, 1995). The Muslim religion forbids the consumption of alcohol, and forbids any involvement with alcohol, including serving, transporting, selling and producing it. Studies find particularly high rates of abstinence (over 70 per cent) in those identifying with these highly proscriptive religions, including those identifying as Mormons and Muslims, along with Pentecostals and Baptists (Michalak, Trocki and Bond, 2007). Islam prohibits the consumption of alcohol as it is against Islamic teachings to consume anything that makes you lose sensibility and/or judgment. Similarly, Buddhism discourages the use of alcohol given the potential to disrupt mindfulness and awareness, features central to the teaching of Buddhism. Although these religious denominations discourage or prohibit the use of alcohol, low levels of religiosity in individuals identifying with these religions are often associated with increased consumption of alcohol.

However, there are other religions that promote the consumption of alcohol. Some Christian religions, including Anglicans and Catholics, embrace alcohol into religious customs, with red wine being used during communion as a symbol for the blood of Christ. In fact, under-age children in Roman Catholic ceremonies will be encouraged to drink wine during Holy Communion. Monks have brewed spirits, wine and beer since the Middle Ages. Judaism prescribes wine with the Sabbath meal and drinking to excess is encouraged at some religious ceremonies, although general recommendations suggest moderation (Glassner, 1985). Moderate drinking patterns (less than five drinks on any occasion) are common in people identifying with Jews, Lutherans and Presbyterians (Michalak, Trocki and Bond, 2007). Although Christianity condemns excessive drinking and drunkenness, the drinking of wine is found throughout the Bible. Modern views suggest temperance rather than abstinence in Christian religions. However, in US population surveys, Catholics are at greater risk of heavy drinking, and frequent heavy drinking, relative to other denominations (Michalak, Trocki and Bond, 2007).

Other religious denominations are less proscriptive in their views of alcohol. Hinduism suggests the use of wine for medicinal reasons, although discourages drinking for non-medicinal reasons. Although Lutherans are typically perceived as conservative, this religion allows for wine in moderation and studies find very low rates of abstinence. Higher sense of religiosity in Lutherans was associated with a greater likelihood of alcohol consumption, and showed high rates of moderate drinking patterns rather than abstinence or heavy drinking (Michalak, Trocki and Bond, 2007).

Geography and living arrangements

There is limited information about geographical influences on ARBD and most of what is available comes from Scotland, where there is evidence of marked regional variations with rates higher in the west of Scotland, particularly Glasgow and Argyll and Clyde (McKenzie and Haw, 2006). In Korea, different patterns of harmful alcohol use were found in elderly men in urban and rural areas. In urban areas, alcohol-use disorders were associated with dementia and higher education, while in rural areas it was associated with lower education and lower rates of dementia (Kim *et al.*, 2002).

Elsewhere most data relates to alcohol consumption. In Sweden, there is higher consumption in the south compared with the north and it is speculated that this might be due to the south being closer to the European continent (Branstrom and Andreasson, 2008). In Australia, residents of the Northern Territory have higher rates of harmful alcohol consumption than residents of the other states and territories (Australian Institute of Health and Welfare, 2011), and alcohol consumption levels, alcohol-attributed morbidity and mortality are consistently found to be lower in major cities compared with regional and remote rural areas of Australia (National Preventative Health Taskforce, 2008). Higher rates of alcohol consumption and binge drinking were also reported in adolescents residing in rural Germany compared with urban centers (Donath *et al.*, 2011). The lack of alternative pastimes may be a factor in increased rural use.

High rates of ARBD have been reported in homeless people, with one study of 204 homeless hostel dwellers in inner Sydney reporting that 10 per cent were cognitively impaired, about a third due to alcohol (Buhrich, Hodder and Teesson, 2000), while a study from Glasgow reported that 21 per cent of homeless hostel dwellers had ARBD (Gilchrist and Morrison, 2005). This is generally regarded as tertiary homelessness as it is a form of supported accommodation most suitable for a cognitively impaired person and may overestimate the rates of ARBD in the broader homeless population. However, it is likely that people with ARBD do have an increased risk of homelessness due to their long-term disruption of family ties, unemployment and poverty.

Conclusions

In this chapter we have reviewed cultural factors that might contribute to ARBD. On the whole there is relatively little information that focuses on ARBD specifically, thus we have had to mainly rely on broader research on harmful alcohol use. Whether there are specific cultural factors that increase the likelihood that a person with harmful alcohol use will develop ARBD is yet to be determined.

References

Abel, E. L. (1995). An update on incidence of FAS: FAS is not an equal opportunity birth defect. *Neurotoxicology and Teratology*, 17(4), 437–43.

Allan, J., Kemp, M. and Golden, A. (2012). The prevalence of cognitive impairment in a rural in-patient substance misuse treatment programme. *Mental Health and Substance Use*, 5(4), 303–13.

Almeida, O. P., Hulse, G. K., Lawrence, D. and Flicker, L. (2002). Smoking as a risk factor for Alzheimer's disease: contrasting evidence from a systematic review of case-control and cohort studies. *Addiction*, 97(1), 15–28.

Anderson, P. and Baumberg, B. (2006). *Alcohol in Europe*. London: Institute of Alcohol Studies.

Arpi, S., Lustygier, V., Le Bon, O., Hanak, C., Streel, E., Pelc, I. and Verbanck, P. (2006). Wernicke-Korsakoff syndrome: demonstration of risk factors in alcohol-dependent patients. *Alcoologie et Addictologie*, 28(1, Special Issue), 16S–21S.

Australian Institute of Health and Welfare (2011). *2010 National Drug Strategy Household Survey Report. Drug Statistics Series No. 25*. Cat. no. PHE 145. Canberra: AIHW.

Backhans, M. C., Lundin, A. and Hemmingsson, T. (2012). Binge drinking: a predictor for or a consequence of unemployment? *Alcoholism: Clinical and Experimental Research*, 36(11), 1983–90.

Batty, D. G., Bhaskar, A., Emslie, C., Benzeval, M., Der, G., Lewars, H. and Hunt, K. (2012). Association of life course socioeconomic disadvantage with future problem drinking and heavy drinking: gender differentials in the west of Scotland. *International Journal of Public Health*, 57(1), 119–26.

Bhala, N., Fischbacher, C. and Bhopal, R. (2010). Mortality for alcohol-related harm by country of birth in Scotland, 2000–2004: potential lessons for prevention. *Alcohol and Alcoholism*, 45(6), 552–6.

Bloomfield, K., Grittner, U., Kramer, S. and Gmel, G. (2006). Social inequalities in alcohol consumption and alcohol-related problems in the study countries of the EU concerted action "Gender, Culture and Alcohol Problems: A Multi-national Study". *Alcohol and Alcoholism*, 41(Supplement 1), 26–36.

Branstrom, R. and Andreasson, S. (2008). Regional differences in alcohol consumption, alcohol addiction and drug use among Swedish adults. *Scandinavian Journal of Public Health*, 36(5), 493–503.

Buhrich, N., Hodder, T. and Teesson, M. (2000). Prevalence of cognitive impairment among homeless people in inner Sydney. *Psychiatric Services*, 51(4), 520–1.

Calabria, B., Doran, C. M., Vos, T., Shakeshaft, A. P. and Hall, W. (2010). Epidemiology of alcohol-related burden of disease among Indigenous Australians. *Australian and New Zealand Journal of Public Health*, 34, S47–S51.

Casswell, S., Pledger, M. and Hooper, R. (2003). Socioeconomic status and drinking patterns in young adults. *Addiction*, 98(5), 601–10.

Centers for Disease Control and Prevention. (2008). Alcohol-attributable deaths and years of potential life lost among American Indians and Alaska Natives: United States, 2001–2005. *Morbidity and Mortality Weekly Report*, 57, 938–41.

Cerda, M., Johnson-Lawrence, V. D. and Galea, S. (2011). Lifetime income patterns and alcohol consumption: investigating the association between long- and short-term income trajectories and drinking. *Social Science and Medicine*, 73(8), 1178–85.

Cheng, W. J., Cheng, Y., Huang, M.-C. and Chen, C.-J. (2012). Alcohol dependence, consumption of alcoholic energy drinks and associated work characteristics in the Taiwan working population. *Alcohol and Alcoholism*, 47(4), 372–9.

Chiang, C. C. P. (2002). Wernicke Korsakoff Syndrome in Argyll and Clyde: a literature review, needs assessment and recommendation for the prevention, treatment and provision of Wernicke Korsakoff Syndrome: Part II, Submission to the Faculty of Public Health Medicine.

Chuang, Y.-C., Ennett, S. T., Bauman, K. E. and Foshee, V. A. (2005). Neighborhood influences on adolescent cigarette and alcohol use: mediating effects through parent and peer behaviors. *Journal of Health and Social Behavior*, 46(2), 187–204.

Cook, W. K., Mulia, N. and Karriker-Jaffe, K. (2012). Ethnic drinking cultures and alcohol use among Asian American adults: findings from a national survey. *Alcohol and Alcoholism*, 47(3), 340–8.

Cutright, P. and Fernquist, R. M. (2010). Predictors of per capita alcohol consumption and gender-specific liver cirrhosis mortality rates: thirteen European countries, circa 1970–1984 and 1995–2007. *Omega: Journal of Death and Dying*, 62(3), 269–83.

De La Rosa, M., Sanchez, M., Dillon, F. R., Ruffin, B. A., Blackson, T. and Schwartz, S. (2012). Alcohol use among Latinos: a comparison of pre-immigration, post-immigration, and US born Latinos. *Journal of Immigrant and Minority Health*, 14(3), 371–8.

De Silva, V., Samarasinghe, D. and Hanwella, R. (2011). Association between concurrent alcohol and tobacco use and poverty. *Drug and Alcohol Review*, 30(1), 69–73.

Dietler, M. (2006) Alcohol: anthropological/archaeological perspectives. *Annual Review of Anthropology*, 35, 229–49.

Donath, C., Grassel, E., Baier, D., Pfeiffer, C., Karagulle, D., Bleich, S. and Hillemacher, T. (2011). Alcohol consumption and binge drinking in adolescents: comparison of different migration backgrounds and rural vs urban residence – a representative study. *BMC Public Health*, 11(84), 84.

Droomers, M., Schrijvers, C. T., Stronks, K., van de Mheen, D. and Mackenbach, J. P. (1999). Educational differences in excessive alcohol consumption: the role of psychosocial and material stressors. *Preventive Medicine: An International Journal Devoted to Practice and Theory*, 29(1), 1–10.

Ehlers, C. L. (2007) Variations in ADH and ALDH in Southwest California Indians. *Alcohol Research & Health: The Journal of the National Institute on Alcohol Abuse & Alcoholism*, 30(1), 14–17.

Gilchrist, G. and Morrison, D. S. (2005). Prevalence of alcohol related brain damage among homeless hostel dwellers in Glasgow. *European Journal of Public Health*, 15(6), 587–8.

Glassner, B. (1985). Jewish-Americans and alcohol: processes of avoidance and definition. In L. A. Bennett and G. M. Ames (eds), *The American Experience with Alcohol: Contrasting Cultural Perspectives* (pp. 93–108). New York: Plenum Press.

Gubhaju, L., McNamara, B. J., Banks, E., Joshy, G., Raphael, B., Williamson, A. and Eades, S. J. (2013). The overall health and risk factor profile of Australian Aboriginal and Torres Strait Islander participants from the 45 and up study. *BMC Public Health*, 13, 661.

Haasen, C., Sinaa, M. and Reimer, J. (2008). Alcohol use disorders among Afghan migrants in Germany. *Substance Abuse*, 29(3), 65–70.

Harper, C. (1983). Wernicke's encephalopathy in Western Australia: a common preventable disease. *Australian Alcohol/Drug Review*, 2(1), 71–3.

Harrison, L. and Gardiner, E. (1999). Do the rich really die young? Alcohol-related mortality and social class in Great Britain, 1988–94. *Addiction*, 94(12), 1871–80.

Hemmingsson, T. and Weitoft, G. R. (2001). Alcohol-related hospital utilization and mortality in different occupations in Sweden in 1991–1995. *Scandinavian Journal of Work, Environment and Health*, 27(6), 412–19.

Hendrie, H. C., Hall, K. S., Pillay, N., Rodgers, D., Prince, C., Norton, J., Brittain, H., Nath A., Blue A., Kaufert J., Shelton P., Postl B. and Osuntokun, B. (1993). Alzheimer's disease is rare in Cree. *International Psychogeriatrics*, 5, 5–14.

Henkel, D. (2011). Unemployment and substance use: a review of the literature (1990–2010). *Current Drug Abuse Reviews*, 4(1), 4–27.

Hilton, M. E. (1986). Abstention in the general population of the USA. *British Journal of Addiction*, 81(1), 95–112.

Hoy, H. (2012) "Never meant to be": porcupines and china dolls as a foetal-alcohol narrative. *Mosaic: A Journal for the Interdisciplinary Study of Literature*, 45(2), 95–112.

Huckle, T., You, R. Q. and Casswell, S. (2010). Socio-economic status predicts drinking patterns but not alcohol-related consequences independently. *Addiction*, 105(7), 1192–202.

International Center for Alcohol Policies (2001). *Alcohol and "Special Populations": Biological Vulnerability*. ICAP Report No. 10, November 2001, Washington DC.

Jarman, D. W., Naimi, T. S., Pickard, S. P., Daley, W. R. and De, A. K. (2007). Binge drinking and occupation, North Dakota, 2004–2005. *Preventing Chronic Disease*, 4(4).

Jones-Webb, R., Snowden, L., Herd, D., Short, B. and Hannan, P. (1997). Alcohol-related problems among black, Hispanic and white men: the contribution of neighborhood poverty. *Journal of Studies on Alcohol and Drugs*, 58(5), 539–45.

Joutsenniemi, K., Martelin, T., Kestila, L., Martikainen, P., Pirkola, S. and Koskinen, S. (2007). Living arrangements, heavy drinking and alcohol dependence. *Alcohol and Alcoholism*, 42(5), 480–91.

Karriker-Jaffe, K. J. (2011). Areas of disadvantage: a systematic review of effects of area-level socioeconomic status on substance use outcomes. *Drug and Alcohol Review*, 30(1), 84–95.

Keightley, M. L., Ratnayake, R., Minore, B., Katt, M., Cameron, A., White, R., Bellavance A., Longboat-White C. and Colantonio, A. (2009). Rehabilitation challenges for Aboriginal clients recovering from brain injury: a qualitative study engaging health care practitioners. *Brain Injury*, 23(3), 250–61.

Keyes, K. M. and Hasin, D. S. (2008). Socio-economic status and problem alcohol use: the positive relationship between income and the DSM-IV alcohol abuse diagnosis. *Addiction*, 103(7), 1120–30.

Kim, J. M., Shin, I. S., Stewart, R. and Yoon, J. S. (2002). Alcoholism in older Korean men: prevalence, aetiology, and comorbidity with cognitive impairment and dementia in urban and rural communities. *International Journal of Geriatric Psychiatry*, 17(9), 821–7.

Kriegbaum, M., Christensen, U., Osler, M. and Lund, R. (2011). Excessive drinking and history of unemployment and cohabitation in Danish men born in 1953. *European Journal of Public Health*, 21(4), 444–8.

McKenzie, K. and Haw, S. (2006) *Alcohol and Alcohol-Related Problems in Scotland: Summary and 2006 Update of Evidence*. Edinburgh/Glasgow: NHS Health Scotland.

MacRae, R. and Cox, S. (2003). *Meeting the Needs of People with Alcohol Related Brain Damage: a Literature Review on the Existing and Recommended Service Provision and Models of Care*. University of Stirling: Dementia Services Development Centre. Available at http://lx.iriss.org.uk/sites/default/files/resources/ARBD_MeetingNeeds.pdf. Accessed 24 February 2014.

Maezawa, Y., Yamauchi, M., Toda, G., Suzuki, H. and Sakurai, S. (1995). Alcohol-metabolizing enzyme polymorphisms and alcoholism in Japan. *Alcohol: Clinical and Experimental Research*, 19(4), 951–4.

Makela, P., Keskimaki, I. and Koskinen, S. (2003). What underlies the high alcohol related mortality of the disadvantaged: high morbidity or poor survival? *Journal of Epidemiology and Community Health*, 57(12), 981–6.

Makela, P. and Paljarvi, T. (2008). Do consequences of a given pattern of drinking vary by socioeconomic status? A mortality and hospitalisation follow-up for alcohol-related causes of the Finnish drinking habits surveys. *Journal of Epidemiology and Community Health*, 62(8), 728–33.

Mandell, W., Eaton, W. W., Anthony, J. C. and Garrison, R. (1992). Alcoholism and occupations: a review and analysis of 104 occupations. *Alcoholism: Clinical and Experimental Research*, 16(4), 734–46.

Marchand, A. (2008). Alcohol use and misuse: what are the contributions of occupation and work organization conditions? *BMC Public Health*, 8(1), 1–12.

Marie, D., Fergusson, D. M. and Boden, J. M. (2012). The links between ethnicity, cultural identity and alcohol use, abuse and dependence in a New Zealand birth cohort. *Alcohol and Alcoholism*, 47(5), 591–6.

May, P. A. (2005). History and challenges in substance abuse prevention among American Indian communities. In E. H. Hawkins and R. D. Walker (eds), *Best Practices in Behavioural Health Services for American Indians and Alaska Natives* (pp. 1–24). Portland Oregon: One Sky National Resource Center for American Indian and Alaska Native Substance Abuse Prevention and Treatment Services.

Melchior, M., Choquet, M., Le Strat, Y., Hassler, C. and Gorwood, P. (2011). Parental alcohol dependence, socioeconomic disadvantage and alcohol and cannabis dependence among young adults in the community. *European Psychiatry*, 26(1), 13–17.

Melotti, R., Lewis, G., Hickman, M., Heron, J., Araya, R. and Macleod, J. (2013). Early life socio-economic position and later alcohol use. birth cohort study. *Addiction*, 108(3), 516–25.

Michalak, L., Trocki, K. and Bond, J. (2007). Religion and alcohol in the US National Alcohol Survey: how important is religion for abstention and drinking? *Drug and Alcohol Dependence*, 87(2–3), 268–80.

Murphy, A., Roberts, B., Stickley, A. and McKee, M. (2012). Social factors associated with alcohol consumption in the former Soviet Union: a systematic review. *Alcohol and Alcoholism*, 47(6), 711–18.

National Preventative Health Taskforce. (2008). *Technical Report No. 3: Preventing Alcohol-Related Harm in Australia: A Window of Opportunity*. Canberra: Commonwealth of Australia.

O'Leary, C. M. (2004). Fetal alcohol syndrome: diagnosis, epidemiology, and developmental outcomes. *Journal of Paediatrics and Child Health*, 40(1–2), 2–7.

Oxford Dictionary Online. http://oxforddictionaries.com/definition/english/culture. Accessed 19 September 2013.

Paljarvi, T., Suominen, S., Car, J. and Koskenvuo, M. (2013). Socioeconomic disadvantage and indicators of risky alcohol-drinking patterns. *Alcohol and Alcoholism*, 48(2), 207–14.

Pillai, A., Nayak, M. B., Greenfield, T. K., Bond, J. C., Nadkarni, A. and Patel, V. (2013). Patterns of alcohol use, their correlates, and impact in male drinkers: a population-based survey from Goa, India. *Social Psychiatry and Psychiatric Epidemiology*, 48(2), 275–82.

Pollitt, P. (1997). The problem of dementia in Australian Aboriginal and Torres Strait Islander communities: an overview. *International Journal of Geriatric Psychiatry*, 12(2), 155–63.

Radford, K., Mack, H. A., Draper, B., Chalkley, S., Daylight, G., Cumming, B., Bennett, H. and Broe, G. A. (2013). Prevalence of dementia and cognitive impairment in urban and regional Aboriginal Australians. *Alzheimer's & Dementia*, DOI: 10.1016/j.jalz.2014.03.007

Sabia, S., Gueguen, A., Berr, C., Berkman, L., Ankri, J., Goldberg, M., Zins, M. and Singh-Manoux, A. (2011). High alcohol consumption in middle-aged adults is associated with poorer cognitive performance only in the low socio-economic group. Results from the GAZEL Cohort Study. *Addiction*, 106(1), 93–101.

Saggers, S. and Gray, D. (1998). *Dealing with Alcohol: Indigenous Usage in Australia, New Zealand and Canada*. Cambridge: Cambridge University Press.

Sanchez, Z. M., Locatelli, D. P., Noto, A. R. and Martins, S. S. (2013). Binge drinking among Brazilian students: a gradient of association with socioeconomic status in five geo-economic regions. *Drug and Alcohol Dependence*, 127(1–3), 87–93.

Schmidt, L. A. (1995). "A battle not man's but God's": Origins of the American temperance crusade in the struggle for religious authority. *Journal of Studies on Alcohol and Drugs*, 56(1), 110–21.

Seale, J. P., Seale, J. D., Alvarado, M., Vogel, R. L. and Terry, N. E. (2002). Prevalence of problem drinking in a Venezuelan Native American population. *Alcohol and Alcoholism*, 37(2), 198–204.

Seale, J. P., Shellenberger, S., Sanchez, N., Vogel, R. L., Villalobos, E., Girton, F. S., Seale, D. M. and Okosun, Ike S. (2010). Characteristics of problem drinking in an urban South American indigenous population. *Substance Use and Misuse*, 45(13), 2185–202.

Shen, Y. C., Fan, J. H., Edenberg, H. J., Li, T. K., Cui, Y. H., Wang, Y. F., Tian, C.-H., Zhou, C.-F., Zhou, R.-L., Wang, J, Zhao, Z.-L. and Xia, G. Y. (1997). Polymorphism of ADH and ALDH genes among four ethnic groups in China and effects upon the risk for alcoholism. *Alcoholism: Clinical and Experimental Research*, 21(7), 1272–7.

Smith, K., Flicker, L., Dwyer, A., Atkinson, D., Almeida, O. P., Lautenschlager, N. T. and LoGiudice, D. (2010). Factors associated with dementia in aboriginal Australians. *Australian and New Zealand Journal of Psychiatry*, 44(10), 888–93.

Spillane, N. S., Smith, G. T. and Kahler, C. W. (2013). Perceived access to reinforcers as a function of alcohol consumption among one First Nation group. *Alcoholism: Clinical and Experimental Research*, 37(Supplement 1), E314–E321.

Stimpson, J. P., Ju, H., Raji, M. A. and Eschbach, K. (2007). Neighborhood deprivation and health risk behaviors in NHANES III. *American Journal of Health Behavior*, 31(2), 215–22.

Szlemko, W. J., Wood, J. W. and Thurman, P. J. (2006). Native Americans and alcohol: past, present, and future. *Journal of General Psychology*, 133(4), 435–51.

Tomkins, S., Saburova, L., Kiryanov, N., Andreev, E., McKee, M., Shkolnikov, V. and Leon, D. (2007). Prevalence and socio-economic distribution of hazardous patterns of alcohol drinking: study of alcohol consumption in men aged 25–54 years in Izhevsk, Russia. *Addiction*, 102(4), 544–53.

van Oers, J., Bongers, I., Van de Goor, L. and Garretsen, H. (1999). Alcohol consumption, alcohol-related problems, problem drinking, and socioeconomic status. *Alcohol and Alcoholism*, 34(1), 78–88.

Waitzman, N. J. and Smith, K. R. (1998). Phantom of the area: poverty-area residence and mortality in the United States. *American Journal of Public Health*, 88(6), 973–6.

Weiss, S. (2008). Review: alcohol use and problems among immigrants from the former Soviet Union in Israel. *Substance Abuse*, 29(4), 5–17.

Westermeyer, J. (1996). Alcoholism among New World peoples: a critique of history, methods, and findings. *The American Journal on Addictions*, 5(2), 110–23.

Whitesell, N. R., Beals, J., Crow, C. B., Mitchell, C. M. and Novins, D. K. (2012). Epidemiology and etiology of substance use among American Indians and Alaska Natives: risk, protection, and implications for prevention. *American Journal of Drug and Alcohol Abuse*, 38(5), 376–82.

Wijnia, J. W., van de Wetering, B. J., Zwart, E., Nieuwenhuis, K. and Goossensen, M. (2012). Evolution of Wernicke-Korsakoff syndrome in self-neglecting alcoholics: preliminary results of relation with Wernicke-delirium and diabetes mellitus. *The American Journal on Addictions*, 21(2), 104–10.

Wilson, M., Stearne, A., Gray, D. and Saggers, S. (2010). The harmful use of alcohol amongst Indigenous Australians. *Australian Indigenous HealthInfoNet*. http://www.health-infonet.ecu.edu.au/health-risks/alcohol/reviews/our-review. Accessed 6 August 2013.

Wilson, S. (2001). Comorbidity and Indigenous Australians. In M. Teesson and L. Burns (eds), *National Comorbidity Project* (pp. 71–2). Canberra: Commonwealth Department of Health and Aged Care.

World Health Organization (2011) *Global Status Report on Alcohol and Health*. Geneva: WHO.

Zann, S. (1994) Identification of support, education and training needs of rural/remote health care service providers involved in dementia care. *Rural Health, Support, Education and Training (RHSET) Project Progress Report*. Northern Regional Health Authority, Queensland.

Zubrick, S., Lawrence, D., Silburn, S., Blair, E., Milroy, H., Wilkes, T., Eades, S., D'Antoine, H., Read, A. Ishiguchi, P. and Doyle, S. (2004). *The Western Australian Aboriginal Child Health Survey: The Health of Aboriginal Children and Young People*. Perth: Telethon Institute for Child Health Research.

5

COMORBIDITY AND COMPLEXITY IN CHRONIC ALCOHOL MISUSE

Apo Demirkol and Nicholas Lintzeris

The consumption of alcohol is associated with risks of adverse health and social consequences for drinkers and those around them (WHO, 2006). Aside from the immediate acute effects of alcohol use, almost each and every system in the human body can be adversely affected by excessive alcohol consumption (Demirkol, Haber and Conigrave, 2011).

There is evidence that those at greatest risk of becoming dependent on alcohol or other substances are more likely to have histories of mental ill health or adverse early life experiences (Dube *et al.*, 2002).

In the case of alcohol-related brain damage (ARBD), comorbidity is likely to be the norm rather than the exception, and multiple conditions may contribute to cognitive impairment. Wilson and colleagues (2012) found that a quarter of people with ARBD presenting to their service also had secondary microvascular stroke-related disorders and/or histories of head injury. Sumransub (2012) investigated a cohort of 101 people diagnosed with ARBD and found that 87 per cent of the cohort had evidence of significant comorbidity. In addition to ARBD, 50 per cent had diagnoses of other neurological conditions, including traumatic brain injury (TBI), epilepsy and stroke-related disorders; and 37 per cent had concurrent non-neurological conditions, including hepatic disorders, osteoporosis, psychological problems and poly-substance misuse.

Complex presentations require needs-led and flexible treatment strategies, for which there is little robust evidence, as most research studies investigating the effectiveness of particular interventions tend to exclude those people presenting with multiple morbidities.

This chapter will consider these issues, first, by outlining some of the consequences and comorbid conditions associated with acute and chronic alcohol misuse, including medical and psychiatric diagnoses and cognitive impairment and, second, by considering the evidence base for pharmacological and psychological management of complex presentations within populations using alcohol to excess.

Alcohol is a psychoactive substance with reinforcing properties that, in the context of social and environmental cues, leads to repeated consumption. The core neural pathway believed to be the basis of this reinforcement is the mesolimbic dopaminergic pathway, which includes the ventral tegmental area that projects mainly to the nucleus accumbens of the ventral striatum, as well as amygdala and hippocampus (Koob, Paolo Sanna and Bloom, 1998; Beaunieux, Eustache and Pitel, 2014). The endogenous opioid system is also believed to be involved in producing some of alcohol's rewarding effects (Koob, Paolo Sanna and Bloom, 1998).

Ongoing alcohol exposure can then lead to longer-term molecular changes in the brain known as neuroadaptation, which provides the basis for tolerance and the withdrawal syndrome (Littleton, 1998). Upon removal of alcohol, the adapted system overcompensates in the direction of excitation, resulting in a characteristic withdrawal syndrome that includes features of hyper-excitability, anxiety and even seizures (Bayard et al., 2004).

Health and social risks associated with acute intoxication

The psychoactive impact of alcohol leads to immediate effects on mood, motor function and thinking processes. Even a single occasion of excessive alcohol consumption can lead to a range of risk-taking behaviors, such as violence, unplanned and unprotected sex, accidents, falls, injuries sustained while driving vehicles or operating machinery, and acute alcohol poisoning, which may require intensive care admission. Intoxication can also be associated with a range of social and legal harms that may have far-reaching consequences for the individual and those around them. The consequences of these acute episodes of intoxication can result in chronic health problems such as disability in the case of injury, sexually transmitted diseases in the case of unprotected sexual activity and increased risk of blood-borne viruses such as hepatitis B, C and HIV, particularly where concurrent intravenous drug use is present.

The physical, psychological and social consequences of alcohol excess

Along with the injuries that may be caused by accidents or as a result of fights due to impaired judgment while intoxicated, almost each and every system in the human body is adversely affected by excessive alcohol consumption (Demirkol, Haber and Conigrave, 2011). This is partly due to alcohol's structure and small molecule size, which allows alcohol to travel through all cell membranes and tissue structures (Friel, Baer and Logan, 1995).

The physical health effects associated with chronic alcohol use vary considerably among individual drinkers. It appears that some people can consume large amounts of alcohol regularly over many years without any evidence of harm, while some people are unusually sensitive to end-organ damage, all of which indicates significant genetic variation (Haber *et al.*, 2009). The factors determining the severity and the extent of alcohol-related organ damage are thought to be alcohol metabolism, nutritional status, or immunological responses to the inflammation associated with alcohol-mediated tissue injury (Proude *et al.*, 2009). Table 5.1 summarizes the health and social problems associated with long-term excessive alcohol misuse.

Among all the organs, the liver is the most vulnerable. Repeated excessive alcohol consumption exposes the liver to hypoxia, harmful by-products of alcohol metabolism and reactive oxygen chemicals, and protein adducts. In addition, alcohol increases the levels of circulating lipopolysaccharides, which, together with the above toxins, cause liver damage (Cargiulo, 2007).

Alcohol can also exacerbate hepatitis C (HCV)-related liver disease (Jamal, Saadi and Morgan, 2006). More than half of all patients with HCV infection have a past history of heavy alcohol use. Current evidence suggests that alcohol consumption of more than five drinks per day in individuals with HCV increases the rate of liver

TABLE 5.1 Problems associated with excessive alcohol use

System	Problem
Nutritional	Protein deficiency, vitamin deficiency syndromes (esp. thiamine and folic acid), obesity
Metabolic	Ketoacidosis, hypoglycaemia or hyperglycaemia, electrolyte problems (i.e., low Mg or Na)
Neurologic	Alcohol withdrawal syndrome (including seizures and delirium tremens), Wernicke-Korsakoff Syndrome, cerebellar degeneration, dementia, peripheral neuropathy
Mental health	Insomnia, fatigue, anxiety disorders, depression, suicide and suicidal ideation, exacerbation of existing mental health problems
Behavioral	Disinhibition leading to health risk behaviors, such as unplanned or unprotected sex, or increased risk of assaults or injury. Use of other licit or illicit substances
Muscular	Myopathy
Gastrointestinal	Fatty liver, alcoholic hepatitis, cirrhosis, pancreatitis (chronic or clinically acute), gastroesophageal reflux disease, gastritis, chronic diarrhoea, malabsorption

(continued)

TABLE 5.1 Problems associated with excessive alcohol use (continued)

System	Problem
Endocrine	High uric acid/gout, low testosterone/impotence/testicular atrophy, gynaecomastia, irregular menstrual periods, impaired oestrogen metabolism, osteoporosis, sexual dysfunction
Blood	Macrocytosis, anaemia, leukopenia, destruction of platelets, coagulopathy (especially 2° to liver disease)
Cardiac	Hypertension, arrhythmias, dilated cardiomyopathy
Infectious diseases	Pneumonia, tuberculosis, sexually transmissible infections, hepatitis C
Social	Relationship problems, family breakdown, domestic violence, financial problems, workplace absenteeism or poor performance, child abuse/neglect, road safety

fibrosis, and the risk for cirrhosis, hepatocellular carcinoma and, possibly, death from liver disease (Zhang *et al.*, 2003).

It is suggested that the risk of developing certain malignancies, such as breast cancer and upper gastrointestinal cancers, increases from base risk levels with any alcohol consumption regardless of the amount. Other forms of malignancies such as hepatic, colon, or pancreatic cancers are more commonly observed among those who consume more than four standard drinks (Seitz *et al.*, 2001; Boffetta and Hashibe, 2006). Several mechanisms have been identified for alcohol-associated carcinogenesis, including acetaldehyde formation, induction of CYP2E1, leading to formation of reactive oxygen species and enhanced pro-carcinogen activation, and modulation of cellular regeneration (Baan *et al.*, 2007).

The negative effects of excessive alcohol use on the innate and adaptive immunity, both among episodic and chronic drinkers, have been well documented. These drinkers are often immunodeficient and as a result have an increased propensity to present with serious infectious diseases. Bacterial pneumonia, for example, is a leading cause of lower respiratory tract infection in this population (Brown *et al.*, 2006; Szabo and Mandrekar, 2009).

Alcohol has both positive and negative effects upon heart disease. While there is some evidence to show that light drinking on a daily basis may reduce the risks of coronary heart disease and all-cause mortality, excessive alcohol intake and binge drinking are detrimental to overall health (NMHRC, 2009; Demirkol, Haber and Conigrave, 2011). It is not recommended that non-drinkers start drinking in order to gain health benefits. Most of these cardiovascular benefits can be achieved by other means such as exercise or weight loss, which do not involve the potential risk of developing alcohol-related harms or an alcohol-use disorder.

Table 5.1 summarizes medical, social, neurological and mental health problems associated with excessive alcohol use. It is beyond to scope of this chapter to discuss the management of these conditions for which excellent treatment guidelines exist (Haber *et al.*, 2009). The sheer volume and diversity of conditions listed in the table indicates the importance of performing a comprehensive physical and mental health assessment of those patients with known alcohol-use problems, which includes cognitive screening, and of taking a substance-use history in patients presenting with the co-occurring disorders described in Table 5.1, as many individuals may not attribute any of these health problems to their drinking. The severity, complexity and chaotic nature of the way some patients present to health services can result in the underlying substance use, or other comorbidities, being overlooked in the attempt to address the presenting problem.

In developing a management plan for patients with alcohol-use problems and co-occurring conditions, it is important to remember that alcohol can exacerbate existing mental and physical disorders, can contribute to cognitive impairment, can adversely interact with other prescribed medications and may be associated with a wide variety of (intentional and unintentional) injury. All aspects of alcohol-related health and social harm need to be clearly explained to the patient. Brief interventions based on motivational techniques are effective in reducing alcohol consumption in those presenting with hazardous or harmful alcohol use, and can encourage dependent drinkers to enter alcohol treatment (Bien, Miller and Tonigan, 1993; Babor and Higgins-Biddle, 2001).

The relationship between mental health and alcohol use

Alcohol-use disorders frequently occur with other psychiatric conditions, and there may be complex relationships between symptoms of mental ill health and use of substances. The evidence suggests that the more adverse experiences, such as childhood sexual abuse, neglect or maltreatment, an individual is exposed to during childhood, the greater the risk that the individual will grow up to develop a range of physiological and psychological problems (Dube *et al.*, 2002). Experiencing four or more adverse experiences in childhood was found to increase the probability of developing alcoholism in adult life, as well as drug abuse, depression and suicide attempts, by over 500 per cent (Felitti *et al.*, 1998).

Epidemiological studies conducted in countries such as Australia, the UK and the USA consistently suggest that among people with alcohol dependence around one in five also meet the criteria for an anxiety disorder and almost one in four for an affective or mood disorder (Haber et al., 2009). Other common mental health diagnoses associated with alcohol dependence include other substance-use disorders, psychotic illness, personality disorders, post-traumatic stress disorder (PTSD) and complex PTSD (Degenhardt et al., 2000; Reynolds et al., 2005; Weaver et al., 2003). Suicidal behavior is also linked to intoxication, alcohol-use disorders and mental illness. Professionals working in both mental health and drug and alcohol settings find themselves dealing with challenging dilemmas about how to provide the best treatment to address co-occurring mental health and substance-use disorders. However, these findings highlight the importance of assessing for common mental health problems such as anxiety, depression and suicidal intent as a routine part of a standard drug and alcohol assessment.

One of the major challenges in assessment of coexisting mental health and drug and alcohol problems is in understanding the relationship between the substance and the mental health symptoms. For instance, the acute effects of alcohol intoxication or withdrawal from alcohol may cause symptoms of anxiety and depression. A period of abstinence lasting three or more weeks is often required in order to make a differential diagnosis. This period of abstinence is often sufficient to demonstrate which of the presenting mental health problems are comorbid and may require their own treatments according to appropriate guidelines (Schuckit and Hesselbrock, 1994; Schuckit et al., 1997). However, if a period of abstinence is not an achievable option, it is best to place a greater emphasis on the addressing the symptoms and functional impact of the mental health problems.

Population-based studies investigating the health service utilization among people with comorbid substance-use and mental health problems indicate that the probability of having a contact with a specialized mental health service is higher for people with a comorbid psychiatric disorder and alcohol-use disorder than the probability of the same group of patients seeking treatment through a drug and alcohol treatment centre (Wu, Kouzis and Leaf, 1999). This finding highlights the importance of a comprehensive assessment of substance use in mental health facilities and providing integrated care for these conditions. It is important to note that many people entering mental health treatment often have a range of other health and psychosocial issues that need to be addressed (e.g., relationship, housing, financial, employment), and that many people with comorbid disorders do not receive the specialized substance-abuse care they need.

Considerations around poly-substance use

Since the 1960s, the availability and popularity of psychoactive drugs have been expanded and, in some age groups or subcultures such as club goers, the use of psychoactive substances has been accepted as a part of many contemporary lifestyles.

Population studies indicate that alcohol is commonly used with other licit and illicit substances such as tobacco, prescribed medications (e.g., painkillers or sedatives), cannabis, amphetamine-like substances and cocaine. These studies indicate that other substance-use disorders are the most commonly seen comorbidity among people with alcohol-use disorders (Kessler *et al.*, 1996; Degenhardt *et al.*, 2000). This is an indication that the initial and ongoing assessment of a person with an alcohol-use disorder must include the assessment of the use of other substances.

Among the reasons why people might use other substances concomitantly are:

1) To enhance the effects of substances used together; for example, using benzodiazepines to boost and prolong the effect of alcohol intoxication.
2) To dampen the effect of one substance with another; for example, using benzodiazepines to "come off" amphetamine-type substances.
3) To replace one substance with the other due to availability or other problems; for example, increasing alcohol intake when no access to benzodiazepines.
4) To maintain tolerance when and if dependence to multiple substances has developed; for example, using both alcohol and heroin dependently.

A comprehensive assessment would facilitate the early detection of other drug use and potentially reduce the risks and complications associated with that particular substance. For poly-substance-dependent people seeking treatment, a stepped approach to detoxification with a focus on substances with more severe withdrawal and harm profile is often preferable, though not always practical (Haber *et al.*, 2009).

The management of a patient with alcohol-use disorder who uses other drugs is often challenging and more complex as the poly-substance use is associated with higher levels of physical and mental health comorbidities, poorer treatment outcomes and greater severity of dependence that would result in a more complicated withdrawal experience. The management principles of comorbid alcohol and other substance use disorders are no different than managing people with comorbid physical and mental health conditions. The main issue is the patient's involvement in the treatment plan. Although there may be some divergences between the patient's and treating clinicians' perceptions about which substance may be more problematic, for an effective treatment plan, patient's concerns should be prioritized.

Using motivational interviewing techniques will support an increase in the patient's awareness and knowledge regarding the impact of ongoing use of other drugs on the efficacy of both psychological and pharmacological interventions, as well as the individual's physical and mental health. This is paramount in establishing an effective working relationship with the patient.

The impact of cognitive impairment

Cognitive impairment associated with alcohol use varies in severity and duration, as is outlined in depth throughout this volume. Acute intoxication can impair a drinker's cognitive functioning, but the impairment is mostly reversible. Metabolic changes due to excessive alcohol intake such as electrolyte imbalances, or hepatic encephalopathy can cause acute confusion and significant cognitive impairment, which can be resolved with appropriate treatment. Persistent cognitive impairment associated with alcohol is a problem that a significant proportion of the heaviest drinkers may face due to brain damage in cases such as Wernicke-Korsakoff Syndrome or TBI sustained while intoxicated (Evert and Oscar-Berman, 1995; Oscar-Berman *et al.*, 1997; Scalzo, Bowden and Hillbom, 2015).

A majority of people with alcohol-use disorders have a degree of impairment in intellectual functioning, as well as changes in brain size and regional changes in brain-cell activity (Parsons, 1998). Impairment in both visuo-spatial abilities and higher cognitive functioning are most commonly seen in alcohol-related cognitive problems (Oscar-Berman and Marinković, 2007).

There is not a consensus on the duration or lifetime quantity of drinking that lead to cognitive problems. Some suggest that severity of cognitive performance is directly associated with the severity and duration of alcoholism (Parsons, 1998). Some other studies assert that social drinkers who consume more than 21 drinks a week, with no other apparent harm from alcohol, may also fit into this category (Beatty *et al.*, 2000).

Some of the alcohol-related cognitive impairments in problem-solving, short-term memory and visuo-spatial abilities are more severe during and soon after the detoxification, but improve significantly in time with abstinence. It is suggested that, over a period of several months to a year, abstinent ex-drinkers recover brain function and show significant improvements in their cognitive functioning (Sullivan, Rosenbloom and Pfefferbaum, 2000; Savage, 2015; Beaunieux, Eustache and Pitel, 2015).

Treatment of coexisting disorders

One of the challenges in planning treatment for clinicians working with patients with co-occurring mental health, drug and alcohol problems is that most of the current evidence on the efficacy of any given treatment comes from single-diagnosis studies. In the field of alcohol research, often people with mental health problems are excluded. The same applies to mental health: patients with co-occurring alcohol-related disorders are often excluded in intervention studies for the majority of the mental health diagnoses. However, the few studies investigating the efficacy of treating alcohol and mental health problems concurrently have shown some positive results. For example, a computer-based cognitive behavioral therapy (CBT) and motivational interviewing (MI) approach was found to be effective for comorbid depression and alcohol or cannabis misuse (Kay-Lambkin *et al.*, 2009). In addition, the cognitive behavioral integrated treatment approach (C-BIT) outlines an approach for integrating treatment for coexisting severe mental health and substance-use disorders (Graham *et al.*, 2004). International guidelines recommend treating substance-use disorders with co-occurring depression or anxiety in parallel, though there is recognition that the withdrawal syndrome should be diminished before accurate assessment of depression or anxiety can be completed (Haber *et al.*, 2009; NICE, 2011).

Engaging patients in treatment planning and goal setting is essential in this population. Long-term treatment is usually required in order to achieve successful outcomes, given the chronic relapsing nature of many mental health and alcohol-use disorders. A focus on raising patient's awareness of the interaction between alcohol use and symptoms of mental disorder often is an important point of engagement. As the rate of suicide is significantly higher among patients with comorbid mood and alcohol-use disorder (Sullivan, Fiellin and O'Connor, 2005), the risk should be regularly assessed and monitored.

Pharmacological approaches to treatment

The three medications that are used to treat alcohol-use disorders, namely disulfiram, naltrexone and acamprosate, have rarely been evaluated in the treatment of patients with coexisting mental health problems. However, some of the medications such as antidepressants and antipsychotics used to treat mental health conditions have been trialed in some studies among people with co-occurring substance-use and mental health problems.

Disulfiram is the oldest medication used clinically in the management of alcohol dependence. Any patient on a sufficient dose of disulfiram who drinks alcohol will experience substantial aversive reactions, including vomiting, flushing, headache and severe anxiety due to the interaction between the medication and acetaldehyde, a normal alcohol breakdown by product. The idea behind this treatment is that these reactions are strong enough to make most people completely stop drinking while taking disulfiram at its prescribed dose.

Early clinical reports from 1960s to early 1970s have suggested that disulfiram, at around a daily dose of 1–3g, may precipitate several psychiatric symptoms, including delirium, depression, anxiety symptoms, mania and psychosis. It is difficult to extrapolate from those findings to current-day practice for several reasons: current recommended dose varies between 200 and 500mg a day in different countries, which is significantly lower than doses that triggered the reported side effects (Larson *et al.*, 1992). Also, around that time the definitions of the psychiatric symptoms were not standardized, as we understand them now. Since then there have not been more than a few studies that explored the use of disulfiram in patients with comorbid psychiatric disorders.

There is no significant evidence suggesting clinically meaningful interactions between disulfiram and medications commonly prescribed to treat major psychiatric disorders (Larson *et al.*, 1992). Nevertheless, it is still appropriate to suggest caution when prescribing disulfiram for patients with psychiatric comorbidity, particularly those with a psychotic disorder.

Naltrexone is an opioid antagonist used in the treatment of alcohol dependence. Compared to a placebo, it is effective in reducing the levels of alcohol craving, the number of drinks consumed per occasion and the number of drinking days, although less effective in achieving total abstinence than disulfiram. Unlike disulfiram, naltrexone does not cause an aversive reaction if patients consume alcohol. It appears that naltrexone is more effective in individuals with the G-allele of the A118G polymorphism of the μ-opioid receptor gene (OPRM1) (Chamorro *et al.*, 2012).

There is a small evidence base to support using naltrexone and other opioid antagonists to treat patients with comorbid mental health disorders. Existing literature, which consists of small-scale clinical trials or case reports, suggests that naltrexone and other opioid antagonists are safe in treating people with comorbid mental diagnoses as they tend to improve treatment outcomes by reducing alcohol use and increasing retention (Volpicelli et al., 1992; O'Malley et al., 1996). However, further research evaluating its efficacy, tolerability and safety among different groups of patients with mental illness is necessary.

Acamprosate is a GABA-like drug that acts on the same glutamatergic NMDA receptor system affected by chronic alcohol use. By reducing alcohol cravings, it promotes abstinence from alcohol. It does not cause any adverse reactions if patients consume alcohol.

The majority of the research establishing its efficacy was conducted in patients without comorbid psychiatric disorders. Similar to naltrexone, existing small-scale studies and case reports imply that acamprosate does not cause any negative outcomes among people with comorbid mental health problems.

Antidepressants are inevitably considered as a treatment option in comorbid mood and alcohol disorders due to frequently overlapping symptoms and common neurobiological changes, as well as similar treatment frameworks which consist of pharmacological and psychosocial interventions (Pettinati, Oslin and Decker, 2000).

Among all antidepressants, the selective serotonin reuptake inhibitors (SSRIs) and the tricyclic antidepressants (TCAs) have been evaluated in patients with comorbid depression and alcohol use. Although they seem to be effective in treating depressive symptoms in this population, they did not produce any significant change in drinking behavior.

The TCAs have been found to be effective in treating depression among people with alcohol-use disorders (Kranzler, 1998); however, there is no consistent evidence that they are effective in decreasing alcohol consumption. With these mixed results and considering the potential for sedation, overdose and lowered seizure threshold, the use of TCAs in alcohol-abusing patients should only be undertaken with extreme caution.

The SSRIs, because they have fewer serious side effects than the older antidepressants, have become the first line of treatment for depressive disorders in mid- to high-income countries. Current literature suggests that SSRIs may be effective in reducing depressive symptoms in individuals with both depression and alcohol dependence; however, alone they have minimal impact upon alcohol consumption, and concurrent pharmacological and/or psychological treatment of alcohol-use disorder is recommended (Witte et al., 2012).

It is important to note that SSRIs' efficacy in decreasing alcohol use as well as depressive symptoms in patients with comorbid alcohol-use disorders and depression is rather modest. It is plausible that these medications may be effective only in certain subtypes of depressed individuals with alcohol-use disorder (Pettinati, Oslin and Decker, 2000). In treatment matching, a comprehensive assessment along with ongoing regular contact might help clinicians to observe if the chosen medication has been effective in treating depressive symptoms.

Medications for treating anxiety disorders include benzodiazepines, TCAs and SSRIs.

Benzodiazepines are first-line agents in managing acute alcohol withdrawal symptoms, as well as relieving acute symptoms of anxiety disorders; however, their long-term use among patients with comorbid alcohol-use disorders and anxiety disorders is controversial due to benzodiazepines' abuse/dependence liability, as well as their potential to worsen the motor and cognitive impairment associated with alcohol use and complicate the long-term management of seizures in this patient group. As a result, the use of benzodiazepines in this patient population is usually contraindicated outside of the management of alcohol withdrawal.

Both TCAs and SSRIs have been found effective in treating anxiety disorders, but the evidence on their utility among patients with comorbid anxiety and alcohol-use disorders is lacking. Due to their relatively minor side effects, the SSRIs often are the first line of treatment for anxiety disorders (Brady, Sonne and Roberts, 1995; Garbutt et al., 1999). Based on the fact that they have shown some promise in dually diagnosed patients with depression and alcohol-use disorders, further studies exploring their efficacy in this patient population are warranted.

Antipsychotic medications are the first line of treatment for patients with schizophrenia or psychotic disorders with a view to stabilize their acute psychotic symptoms due to the fact that acute psychosis limits patients' ability to participate in social, community and treatment activities. There is a paucity of evidence suggesting the superiority of any one type of antipsychotic in treating patients with comorbid psychotic illness and alcohol-use disorders.

It is reported that the newer antipsychotics are better at treating negative symptoms, with fewer side effects. As people with psychotic illness may use alcohol or other drugs to self-medicate the negative symptoms, newer antipsychotic medications may be effective in treating the psychotic symptoms, as well as alcohol use in this population. There is some evidence suggesting that while treating psychotic symptoms, risperidone and clozapine may be effective in reducing alcohol intake among dually diagnosed patients (Wobrock and Soyka, 2009).

Medication compliance is an important issue to consider in this patient population. It is also important to consider alcohol's interaction with the medication, such as its potential to increase its effects. Highly sedating medications or medications that reduce the seizure threshold in a patient with alcohol-use disorder may be problematic (Haber et al., 2009).

The "newer" medications such as baclofen and topiramate are widely and wildly used in some quarters. There is insufficient evidence regarding their safety and efficacy. Due to the concerns around potential harms and misuse, caution should be used, and specialist input should be sought prior to commencement.

Psychosocial and psychological treatments for coexisting problems

Psychosocial and psychological interventions have a strong evidence base in the treatment of both alcohol-use disorders and mental health disorders. Cognitive behavioral, behavioral, motivational, social network, behavioral couples therapy and environment-based therapies are recommended stand-alone interventions for harmful drinking and mild alcohol dependence, and in combination with pharmacological interventions for people with moderate to severe dependence (NICE, 2011; NHS Education for Scotland, 2011). There is promising preliminary evidence for the use of "third-wave" cognitive behavioral approaches, which use concepts from Buddhist philosophies to develop acceptance, and teach mindfulness meditation to enable detachment from the strong emotional and physiological responses that may occur in the early stages of abstinence from alcohol or other substances (Hayes *et al.*, 2004; Witkiewitz and Bowen, 2010).

Twelve-step programs have been the focus of controversy in the field of addiction medicine, particularly for the treatment of people with comorbid alcohol-use and mental health problems. It is obvious that these programs may be beneficial to many people; however, people with severe mental illness may feel alienated and, at times, may be disadvantaged if the group is against any intervention (e.g., medication for a coexisting psychiatric condition) other than the 12-step approach. In considering whether to refer a patient to a 12-step group, clinicians have to assess some factors such as the patient's motivation, barriers to attendance (including difficulties in relating to other people), previous experience with 12-step meetings and the expectations of the patients and their families. Special meetings for people with dual disorders may exist in some areas.

The efficacy of psychosocial and psychological treatments in treating a wide range of mental health disorders has also been well established. Among the specific psychological interventions that are known to be effective in treating common mental health problems are cognitive behavioral therapy, behavior therapy, interpersonal therapy, psychodynamic/psychoanalytic therapies and systemic and family therapies (Drake and Mueser, 2000; NHS Education for Scotland, 2011). These approaches have limitations in individuals with significant cognitive impairment, as may be the case among those with alcohol-use disorders, due to their reliance on executive functions, explicit memory and effortful cognitive processes (Bates, Buckman and Nguyen, 2013). However, there is evidence for the effectiveness of adapting CBT for common mental health problems in populations with brain injury, mild cognitive impairment and dementia (Khan-Bourne and Brown, 2003; Orgeta *et al.*, 2014; Soo and Tate, 2007).

Psychosocial and psychological techniques are also indicated where there are concurrent substance-use problems, such as contingency management, as well as specialist psychological interventions. There is a high prevalence of PTSD and complex PTSD in poly-substance-using populations (e.g., Najavits, 2001), and integrated or phase-based treatments are a promising way of structuring different stages of treatment in order to support stability and begin to address complex mental health problems (e.g., Najavits, 2006; Cloitre *et al.*, 2011). Integrated treatment programs for dual diagnosis recommend components including peer-oriented group work, residential interventions, intensive case management and family interventions, but further research is needed to assess their efficacy (Drake, Mueser and Brunette, 2007).

When considering co-occurring disorders, effective psychological treatments are important for patients for whom early abstinence may be associated with a worsening of psychiatric symptoms, such as patients with PTSD who may experience a recurrence of symptoms with the cessation of alcohol use. In such cases, a well-co-ordinated treatment plan, designed in collaboration with the patient, is essential to ensure that the patient is engaged with different stages of the treatment, and is supported to tolerate the increase in distress that abstinence can bring.

When used in collaboration with pharmacological treatments, psychological therapies such as motivational interviewing may enhance their efficacy by improving engagement and compliance with medication. Some behavioral interventions, such as supervised administration, administration by a significant other, or establishing written agreements on taking medications as prescribed, are shown to be effective in improving safety and overall treatment outcomes. In cases where pharmacotherapy may not be effective, suitable or may even be dangerous (such as the use of benzodiazepines among patients with comorbid alcohol-use and anxiety disorders), psycho-social and psychological interventions can improve treatment outcomes without introducing further complications.

It is suggested that, where possible, the same health professional should provide treatment for both alcohol-use and comorbid disorders. It is now well established that the abilities of the practitioner delivering psychological interventions are at least as important as the matching of the therapy to the mental health problems of the patient (Roth and Fonagy, 2005). This is perhaps most important for those patients with complex and comorbid presentations, who cross diagnostic categories. Evidence suggests that experienced therapists who are able to work flexibly, drawing on a range of therapeutic models, are more successful in engaging and treating these complex patients (NHS Education for Scotland, 2011). In patients presenting with comorbid alcohol and mental health problems, clarifying treatment priorities with the patient is important. It may be that in severely alcohol-dependent patients a focus on anxiety and depression may divert attention from reducing alcohol consumption early in treatment. Conversely, in patients with severe mental health problems such as acute psychosis or major depression, priority should be stabilizing the mental health problems rather than a sole focus on alcohol use.

Cognitive impairment can have a major impact upon the treatment of alcohol-use disorders. Rather than taking the fatalistic view that people with cognitive impairment may not be able to retain any treatment-related strategies presented, thereby would fail in their attempt to abstain, it is more productive to recognize that cognitive functioning may influence treatment outcome through a number of indirect pathways, affecting processes of change within and outside treatment (Allen, Goldstein and Seaton, 1997; Bates, Buckman and Nguyen, 2013). Treatment strategies should, therefore, be designed to target an individual's cognitive strengths, and recognize the limits of cognitive impairments (Bates, Buckman and Nguyen, 2013; Wilson, 2015). Focusing on improving factors such as nutrition, exercise and social isolation, as well as the treatment of comorbid mental or medical disorders, may be more effective than focusing solely on abstinence from alcohol (Allen, Goldstein and Seaton, 1997).

There has also been a promising expansion in research investigating interventions designed to harness the intact implicit memory and automatic cognitive processing systems in those with alcohol-related cognitive impairment, drawing on cognitive retraining, biofeedback, exercise, combined mental and physical training, and meditation techniques (Bates, Buckman and Nguyen, 2013). For those with the most severe impairments, environmental adaptations may be of most benefit, such as the provision of supported accommodation, or development of non-alcohol-using social networks (Buckman, Bates and Cisler, 2007; Wilson, 2015).

Changes to clinical systems and structures may be required in order to successfully treat patients with coexisting disorders. Drake, Mueser and Brunette (2007) suggest that when considering programs for severe mental illness and substance misuse, programs require: an ethos of recovery, with clinicians who convey optimism and hope regarding long-term recovery; reorganization to enable cross-disciplinary and multi-modal interventions that can be applied flexibly to those with co-occurring disorders; strong leadership to articulate a clear vision for service structures, and support staff to educate themselves about co-occurring disorders and their consequences; and, finally, quality improvement mechanisms in order to monitor progress and measure effectiveness.

Summary

Coexisting substance use, physical and mental health disorders are the norm rather than the exception, and a majority of people presenting to alcohol treatment services will also have cognitive impairments. Comprehensive assessments of need are essential for all those presenting to not only substance treatment services, but also mental health and general medical services. It is important that clinicians involved in treating people with alcohol-use disorders regularly assess cognitive functioning, and reconfigure the treatment plan by taking cognitive impairment into account. There have now been decades of research consistently showing the potential for the brain to recover, even after long-term heavy alcohol use (Bates, Buckman and Nguyen, 2013). The challenge now is to translate recent research advances into practice, to ensure the best possible outcomes for those with alcohol-use disorders and comorbid difficulties.

References

Allen, D. N., Goldstein, G. and Seaton, B. E. (1997). Cognitive rehabilitation of chronic alcohol abusers. *Neuropsychology Review*, 7(1), 21–39.

Baan, R., Straif, K., Grosse, Y., Secretan, B., Ghissassi, F. E., Bouvard, V., Altieri, A. and Cogliano, V. (2007). Carcinogenicity of alcoholic beverages. *The Lancet Oncology*, 8(4), 292–3.

Babor, T. F. and Higgins-Biddle, J. C. (2001). *Brief Intervention for Hazardous and Harmful Drinking: A Manual for Use in Primary Care*. Geneva: WHO.

Bates, M. E., Buckman, J. F. and Nguyen, T. T. (2013). A role for cognitive rehabilitation in increasing the effects of treatment for alcohol use disorders. *Neuropsychology Review*, 23, 27–47.

Bayard, M., McIntyre, J., Hill, K. R. and Woodside, J. Jr (2004). Alcohol withdrawal syndrome. *American Family Physician*, 69(6), 1443–50.

Beatty, W. W., Tivis, R., Stott, H. D., Nixon, S. J. and Parsons, O. A. (2000). Neuropsychological deficits in sober alcoholics: influences of chronicity and recent alcohol consumption. *Alcoholism: Clinical and Experimental Research*, 24(2), 149–54.

Beaunieux, H., Eustache, F. and Pitel, A.-L. (2015). The relation of alcohol-induced brain changes to cognitive function. In J. Svanberg, A. Withall, B. Draper and S. Bowden (eds), *Alcohol and the Adult Brain*. Hove: Psychology Press.

Bien, T. H., Miller, W. R. and Tonigan, J. S. (1993). Brief interventions for alcohol problems: a review. *Addiction*, 88, 315–36.

Boffetta, P. and M. Hashibe (2006). Alcohol and cancer. *The Lancet Oncology*, 7(2), 149–56.

Brady, K. T., Sonne, S. C. and Roberts, J. M. (1995). Sertraline treatment of comorbid post-traumatic stress disorder and alcohol dependence. *Journal of Clinical Psychiatry*, 56(11), 502–5.

Brown, L. A. S., Cook, R. T., Jerrells, T. R., Kolls, J. K., Nagy, L. E., Szabo, G., Wands, J. R. and Kovacs, E. J. (2006). Acute and chronic alcohol abuse modulate immunity. *Alcoholism: Clinical and Experimental Research*, 30(9), 1624–31.

Buckman, J. F., Bates, M. E. and Cisler, R. A. (2007). Social networks and their influence on drinking behaviours: differences related to cognitive impairment in clients receiving alcoholism treatment. *Journal of Studies on Alcohol and Drugs*, 68(5), 738–47.

Cargiulo, T. (2007). Understanding the health impact of alcohol dependence. *American Journal of Health-System Pharmacy*, 64(5, Supplement 3), S5–S11.

Chamorro, A. J., Marcos, M., Mirón-Canelo, J. A., Pastor, I., González-Sarmiento, R. and Laso, F. J. (2012). Association of μ-opioid receptor (OPRM1) gene polymorphism with response to naltrexone in alcohol dependence: a systematic review and meta-analysis. *Addiction Biology*, 17(3), 505–12.

Cloitre, M., Courtois, C. A., Charuvastra, A., Carapezza, R., Stolbach, B. C. and Green, B. L. (2011). Treatment of complex PTSD: results of the ISTSS expert clinician survey on best practices. *Journal of Traumatic Stress*, 24(6), 615–27.

Degenhardt, L., Hall, W., Teesson, M. and Lynskey, M. (2000). *Alcohol Use Disorders in Australia: Findings from the National Survey of Mental Health and Well-Being*. Sydney: National Drug and Alcohol Research Centre, UNSW.

Demirkol, A., Haber, P. and Conigrave, K. (2011). Problem drinking: detection and assessment in general practice. *Australian Family Physician*, 40(8), 570–4.

Drake, R. E. and Mueser, K. T. (2000). Psychosocial approaches to dual diagnosis. *Schizophrenia Bulletin*, 26(1), 105–18.

Drake, R. E., Mueser, K. T. and Brunette, M. F. (2007). Management of persons with co-occurring severe mental illness and substance use disorder: program implications. *World Psychiatry*, 6, 131–6.

Dube, S. R. Anda, R. F., Felitti, V. J., Edwards, V. J. and Croft, J. B. (2002). Adverse childhood experiences and personal alcohol abuse as an adult. *Addictive Behaviors*, 27(5), 713–25.

Evert, D. L. and Oscar-Berman, M. (1995). Alcohol-related cognitive impairments: an overview of how alcoholism may affect the workings of the brain. *Alcohol Health and Research World*, 19(2), 89–96.

Felitti, V. J., Anda, R. F., Nordenberg, D., Williamson, D. F., Spitz, A. M., Edwards, V., Koss, M. P. and Marks, J. S. (1998). Relationship of childhood abuse and household dysfunction to many of the leading causes of death in adults. *American Journal of Preventative Medicine*, 14(4), 245–58.

Friel, P. N., Baer, J. S. and Logan, B. K. (1995). Variability of ethanol absorption and breath concentrations during a large-scale alcohol administration study. *Alcoholism: Clinical and Experimental Research*, 19(4), 1055–60.

Garbutt, J. C., West, S. L., Carey, T. S., Lohr, K. N. and Crews, F. T. (1999). Pharmacological treatment of alcohol dependence. *JAMA (Journal of the American Medical Association)*, 281(14), 1318–25.

Graham, H. L., Copello, A., Birchwood, M. J., Mueser, K., Orford, J., McGovern, D., Atkinson, E., Maslin, J., Preece, M., Tobin, D. and Georgiou, G. (2004). *Cognitive-Behavioural Integrated Treatment (C-BIT): A Treatment Manual for Substance Misuse in People with Severe Mental Health Problems*. Chichester: John Wiley and Sons.

Haber, P., Lintzeris, N., Proude, E. and Lopatko, O. (2009). *Guidelines for the Treatment of Alcohol Problems*. Canberra: Australian Government Department of Health and Aged Care.

Hayes, S. C., Wilson, K. G., Gifford, E. V., Bissett, R., Piasecki, M., Batten, S. V. and Byrd, M. (2004). A preliminary trial of twelve-step facilitation and acceptance and commitment therapy with polysubstance-abusing methadone-maintained opiate addicts. *Behaviour Therapy*, 35(4), 667–88.

Jamal, M. M., Saadi, Z. and Morgan, T. R. (2006). Alcohol and hepatitis C. *Digestive Diseases*, 23(3–4), 285–96.

Kay-Lambkin, F. J., Baker, A. L., Lewin, T. J. and Carr, V. J. (2009). Computer-based psychological treatment for comorbid depression and problematic alcohol and/or cannabis use: a randomized controlled trial of clinical efficacy. *Addiction*, 104(3), 378–88.

Kessler, R. C., Nelson, C. B., McGonagle, K. A., Edlund, M. J., Frank, R. G. and Leaf, P. J. (1996). The epidemiology of co-occurring addictive and mental disorders: implications for prevention and service utilization. *American Journal of Orthopsychiatry*, 66(1), 17–31.

Khan-Bourne, N. and Brown, R. G. (2003). Cognitive behaviour therapy for the treatment of depression in individuals with brain injury. *Neuropsychological Rehabilitation*, 13(1–2), 89–107.

Koob, G. F., Paolo Sanna, P. and Bloom, F. E. (1998). Neuroscience of addiction. *Neuron*, 21, 467–76.

Kranzler, H. R. (1998). *Dual Diagnosis and Treatment: Substance Abuse and Comorbid Medical and Psychiatric Disorders*. New York: Marcel Dekker.

Larson, E. W., Olincy, A., Rummans, T. A. and Morse, R. M (1992). Disulfiram treatment of patients with both alcohol dependence and other psychiatric disorders: a review. *Alcoholism: Clinical and Experimental Research*, 16(1), 125–30.

Littleton, J. (1998). Neurochemical mechanisms underlying alcohol withdrawal. *Alcohol Health and Research World*, 22(1), 13–24.

Najavits, L. M. (2001). Helping "difficult" patients. *Psychotherapy Research*, 11(2), 131–52.

Najavits, L. M. (2006). Managing trauma reactions in intensive addiction treatment environments. *Journal of Chemical Dependency Treatment*, 8, 153–61.

NICE. (2011). *Alcohol-Use Disorders: Diagnosis, Assessment and Management of Harmful Drinking and Alcohol Dependence*. Guideline CG115. London: National Institute for Health and Clinical Excellence.

NHS Education for Scotland. (2011). *The "Matrix": Mental Health in Scotland. A Guide to Delivering Evidence-Based Psychological Therapies in Scotland*. Edinburgh: NES. http://www.nes. scot.nhs.uk/media/20137/Psychology%20Matrix%202013.pdf. Accessed 20 April 2014.

NMHRC (2009). *Australian Guidelines to Reduce Health Risks from Drinking Alcohol*. Canberra: National Health and Medical Research Council.

O'Malley, S. S., Jaffe, A. J., Rode, S. and Rounsaville, B. J. (1996). Experience of a "slip" among alcoholics treated with naltrexone or placebo. *The American Journal of Psychiatry*, 153(2), 281–3.

Orgeta, V., Qazi, A., Spector, A. E. and Orrell, M. (2014). Psychological treatments for depression and anxiety in dementia and mild cognitive impairment. *Cochrane Database of Systematic Reviews*, 22(1).

Oscar-Berman, M. and Marinković, K. (2007). Alcohol: effects on neurobehavioral functions and the brain. *Neuropsychology Review*, 17(3), 239–57.

Oscar-Berman, M., Shagrin, B., Evert, D. L. and Epstein, C. (1997). Impairments of brain and behavior. *Alcohol Health and Research World*, 21, 65–76.

Parsons, O. A. (1998). Neurocognitive deficits in alcoholics and social drinkers: a continuum? *Alcoholism: Clinical and Experimental Research*, 22(4), 954–61.

Pettinati, H., Oslin, D. and Decker, K. (2000). Role of serotonin and serotonin-selective pharmacotherapy in alcohol dependence. *CNS Spectrums*, 5(2), 33.

Proude, E., Lopatko, O., Lintzeris, N. and Haber, P. (2009). *The Treatment of Alcohol Problems: A Review of the Evidence*. Canberra: Australian Government Department of Health and Aged Care.

Reynolds, M., Mezey, G., Chapman, M., Wheeler, M., Drummond, C. and Baldacchino, A. (2005). Co-morbid post-traumatic stress disorder in a substance misusing clinical population. *Drug and Alcohol Dependence*, 77, 251–8.

Roth, A. and Fonagy, P. (2005). *What Works for Whom? A Critical Review of Psychotherapy Research* (2nd edn). London: Guilford Press.

Savage, L. (2015). Alcohol-related brain damage and neuropathology. In J. Svanberg, A. Withall, B. Draper and S. Bowden (eds), *Alcohol and the Adult Brain*. Hove: Psychology Press.

Scalzo, S., Bowden, S. and Hillbom, M. (2015). Wernicke-Korsakoff Syndrome. In J. Svanberg, A. Withall, B. Draper and S. Bowden (eds), *Alcohol and the Adult Brain*. Hove: Psychology Press.

Schuckit, M. A. and Hesselbrock, V. (1994). Alcohol dependence and anxiety disorders: what is the relationship? *The American Journal of Psychiatry*, December, 151, 12.

Schuckit, M. A., Tipp, J. E., Bergman, M., Reich, W., Hesselbrock, V. M. and Smith, T. L. (1997). Comparison of induced and independent major depressive disorders in 2,945 alcoholics. *The American Journal of Psychiatry*, 154(7), 948–57.

Seitz, H. K., Matsuzaki, H., Yokoyama, A., Homann, N., Väkeväinen, S. and Dong Wang, X. (2001). Alcohol and cancer. *Alcoholism: Clinical and Experimental Research*, 25(Supplement 1), 137S–143S.

Soo, C. and Tate, R. (2007). Psychological treatment for anxiety in people with traumatic brain injury (review). *Cochrane Database of Systematic Reviews*, 3.

Sullivan, E., Rosenbloom, M. J. and Pfefferbaum, A. (2000). Pattern of motor and cognitive deficits in detoxified alcoholic men. *Alcoholism: Clinical and Experimental Research*, 24(5), 611–21.

Sullivan, L. E., Fiellin, D. A. and O'Connor, P. G. (2005). The prevalence and impact of alcohol problems in major depression: a systematic review. *The American Journal of Medicine*, 118(4), 330–41.

Sumransub, P. (2012). Predicting functional dependence in alcohol related brain damage. Unpublished thesis, University of Glasgow.

Szabo, G. and Mandrekar, P. (2009). A recent perspective on alcohol, immunity, and host defense. *Alcoholism: Clinical and Experimental Research*, 33(2), 220–32.

Volpicelli, J. R., Alterman, A. I., Hayashida, M. and O'Brien, P. O. (1992). Naltrexone in the treatment of alcohol dependence. *Archives of General Psychiatry*, 49(11), 876.

Weaver, T., Madden, P., Charles, V., Stimson, G., Renton, A., Tyrer, P., Barnes, T., Bench, C., Middleton, H., Wright, N., Paterson, S., Shanahan, W., Seivewright, N. and Ford, C. (2003). Comorbidity of substance misuse and mental illness in community mental health and substance misuse services. *British Journal of Psychiatry*, 183, 304–13.

WHO (2006). *WHO Expert Committee on Problems Related to Alcohol Consumption. Second Report.* Geneva: WHO.

Wilson, K. (2015). The clinical rehabilitation of people with alcohol-related brain damage. In J. Svanberg, A. Withall, B. Draper and S. Bowden (eds), *Alcohol and the Adult Brain.* Hove: Psychology Press.

Wilson, K., Halsey, A., Macpherson, H., Billington, J., Hill, S., Johnstone, G., Raju, K. and Abbot, P., (2012). The psycho-social rehabilitation of patients with alcohol-related brain damage in the community. *Alcohol and Alcoholism,* 47(3), 304–11.

Witkiewitz, K. and Bowen, S. (2010). Depression, craving and substance use following a randomized trial of mindfulness-based relapse prevention. *Journal of Consulting and Clinical Psychology,* 78(3), 362–74.

Witte, J., Bentley, K., Evins, A. E., Clain, A. J., Baer, L., Pedrelli, P., Fava, M. and Mischoulon, D. (2012). A randomized, controlled, pilot study of acamprosate added to escitalopram in adults with major depressive disorder and alcohol use disorder. *Journal of Clinical Psychopharmacology,* 32(6), 787–96.

Wobrock, T. and Soyka, M. (2009). Pharmacotherapy of patients with schizophrenia and substance abuse. *Expert Opinion in Pharmacotherapy,* 10(3), 353–67.

Wu, L.-T., Kouzis, A. C. and Leaf, P. J. (1999). Influence of comorbid alcohol and psychiatric disorders on utilization of mental health services in the National Comorbidity Survey. *The American Journal of Psychiatry,* 156(8), 1230–6.

Zhang, T., Li, Y., Lai, J.-P., Douglas, S. D., Metzger, D. S., O'Brien, C. P. and Ho, W.-Z. (2003). Alcohol potentiates hepatitis C virus replicon expression. *Hepatology,* 38(1), 57–65.

6

ALCOHOL AND COGNITIVE IMPAIRMENT

Considerations with the older client

Adrienne Withall and Samaneh Shafiee

The global population is ageing. By the year 2030, the total number of older people worldwide is expected to exceed 1 billion, accounting for one in every eight persons (National Institute of Aging and US Department of State, 2007). Alcohol misuse in older adults presents unique challenges to clinicians and health professionals. It represents a growing but relatively neglected public health problem and it has been predicted that the number of older people requiring treatment for alcohol-use disorders (AUDs) will increase substantially in coming years (Han *et al.*, 2009). This is considered to be due partly to the size of the "Baby Boom" cohort (born after World War II, between 1946 and 1964) – particularly the higher rate of alcohol and other substance use among this group due to social acceptability and affordability, as well as the greater observed inclination of baby boomers to discuss personal and mental health concerns (Patterson and Jeste, 1999; Wang and Andrade, 2013). However, research into populations engaging in risky or problematic alcohol use has largely neglected those aged over 60 (Patterson and Jeste, 1999). There also remains a lack of awareness among primary health care, drug and alcohol, aged care and general practitioners about the extent and impacts of alcohol use and misuse in people aged over 60, possible impacts on cognition especially in midlife and a general reluctance to screen for alcohol-use disorders in this group.

In fact, older people are likely to have a greater sensitivity to cognitive impairment as a result of alcohol use, partly through the increased risk of cognitive impairment as a result of increasing age (Kumar *et al.*, 2005). Although alcohol-related brain damage (ARBD) is more common in midlife than later life (MacRae and Cox, 2003), alcohol use may complicate neurodegenerative and vascular dementias, and is the second most common cause of delirium and confusional states in older people (Kales *et al.*, 2003). Paradoxically, moderate alcohol intake may actually be neuroprotective (Collins *et al.*, 2009), highlighting the need for alcohol use guidelines specific to this age group.

Given the heightened effects of alcohol in late life due to poorer metabolism of alcohol, general frailty, physical health comorbidity, the potential for impaired vitamin absorption, prescribed medication interactions and the high risk of comorbid neu-ropsychiatric disorders, new strategies are needed in order to address safe drinking levels, as well as suitable assessment and treatment protocols.

Prevalence of alcohol-use disorders in older people

In developed countries, there is a growing body of epidemiological evidence indi-cating that alcohol (and other drug) abuse is a current public health concern in the older population (Wang and Andrade, 2013). It is further anticipated that this effect will spread to developing regions over the next few decades (Wang and Andrade, 2013). In general, the prevalence of alcohol-use disorders declines with increasing age and they are more common in men than women (Coulton, 2009), although many diagnostic methods do not have age-specific criteria (see later, this chapter). Estimates for the number of older people drinking at risky levels vary widely: mostly from 1 to 15 per cent (Blow and Barry, 2012) although higher rates have been reported in Europe. For example, data from Belgium indicated that 20.5 per cent of people aged 65 years and over drank in excess of the NIAAA guidelines (Hoeck and Van Hal, 2012). An Australian national community survey found that older adults in fact drink more frequently than younger age groups, albeit at lesser levels (Australian Institute of Health and Welfare, 2011). This same trend was shown in data from participants in the Netherlands Twin Register between 2009 and 2012. Daily alcohol use was mark-edly higher in the 55–64 year age band and highest in the 65 and over group; it was ten fold lower in prevalence in the 18–24 year age group (Geels et al., 2013). Men drank more than women across all age groups and hazardous drinking occurred in 12.7 per cent of men aged 65 years and over and 5.5 per cent of women, which was less than for younger age groups (Geels et al., 2013). Data from the 2001–2002 National Epidemiologic Survey of Alcohol and Related Conditions indicated that 16 per cent of participants aged 65 and over had a lifetime diagnosis of alcohol-use disorder and fewer than 2 per cent had this diagnosis during the past 12 months (Lin et al., 2011). Alcohol-use disorders were diagnosed with the *Diagnostic and Statistical Manual of Mental Disorders* (4th edn, DSM-IV; American Psychiatric Association, 1994).

Blazer and Wu (2009) examined pooled data from nearly 11,000 participants in the 2005 and 2006 US National Surveys on Drug Use and Health. Overall, 60 per cent of adults aged 50 or over had used alcohol in the past year, with elevated rates in the 50–64 year age band as compared to those aged 65 years and over. Further work indicated that the rate of past year alcohol-use disorders was twice as common in the 50–64 than the 65 and over age band (approximately 7 per cent vs 3.3 per cent; Blazer and Wu, 2011). This suggests that there is a cohort effect consistent with the observation of increased alcohol intake in the Baby Boomer generation (Patterson and Jeste, 1999).

Longitudinal data from the General Lifestyle Survey (Great Britain) cited in a paper by Knott and colleagues (2013) showed that between 1998 and 2010 daily alcohol consumption exceeding recommended limits has decreased in the 16–24 year age group (from 50 to 34 per cent for men and 41 to 31 per cent for women), while it has increased in those aged 65 and over (from 17 to 22 per cent for men and 4 to 11 per cent for women). This trend for a change in drinking habits in older adults is reinforced by the data modeled by Han and colleagues (2009) that indicated a conservative doubling in the number of adults aged 50 years and over diagnosed with substance use disorder by the year 2020.

In summary, there is variation between studies regarding the prevalence of harmful alcohol use and alcohol-use disorders in late life. This is often due to differences in methodology between studies (definition of an older person, community vs hospital or institution setting and diagnostic criteria) and a key challenge is the lack of any gold standard definition for alcohol-use disorders in older people (Coulton, 2009; Gilson, Bryant and Judd, 2014). However, it is evident that rates are increasing substantially, consistent with the increasing number of older people in the population and different drinking habits of the Baby Boomer generation. This increase in prevalence rates will put significant pressure upon health services and emphasizes the importance of developing diagnostic tools and treatment protocols that are suitable for this group.

Identification and assessment of alcohol-related issues in older people

The identification of alcohol-use disorders among the older population is generally quite poor. This is due to a wide range of issues including difficulties with defining hazardous drinking in the elderly, a lack of age-appropriate clinical guidelines, a reluctance of health professionals to screen for alcohol misuse and abuse in older people (due to insufficient knowledge about this group, as well as time constraints and competing demands), the misapprehension that alcohol-use disorders are not common in ageing, a reluctance by patients to report alcohol-use levels to their clinician, the potential for atypical presentations triggered by accidents, confusion or self-neglect and a lack of knowledge regarding the interplay between alcohol and cognitive impairment in late life (Dar, 2006; O'Connell *et al.*, 2003).

Identification of alcohol-use disorders in older people

There are challenges associated with defining an alcohol-use disorder in older people. Even the definition of "older" in the literature varies and this can depend on the clinical context. For example, drug and alcohol services can view older clients as those aged 40 to 50 and above; however, this cut-off usually increases to 65 years in an aged-care context. Furthermore, standard diagnostic criteria may not apply to this population. Given that older adults are often retired and may be socially isolated, it can be difficult for older people to meet DSM-IV diagnostic criteria (Patterson and Jeste, 1999). Tolerance can also be difficult to establish given biological changes with age that mean older people require less alcohol to achieve the same effects

(Patterson and Jeste, 1999). The newer DSM-5 (American Psychiatric Association, 2013) now utilizes a single diagnostic category, "alcohol-use disorder", which has 11 criteria that the person may meet to be diagnosed with an AUD (two symptoms minimum). While some of the same difficulties with older patients persist, the newer criteria provide a broader range that may be more inclusive of this group. This issue is intended to be addressed with the new revision of the International Classification of Diseases (ICD), which will include age-specific diagnostic criteria (B. Draper, personal communication, July 2014).

There is also a lack of clarity in clinical guidelines with respect to safe drinking levels for older adults, with considerable variation across countries. The majority of current guidelines are based on work in young adults and do not provide a recommended daily or weekly intake for older people. This is relevant since older people do not metabolize alcohol as efficiently and have the competing effects of frailty and concomitant medication use (prescribed and/or illicit) interacting with alcohol consumption (Ridley, Draper and Withall, 2013). The guidelines are also very country specific, with respect to the fact that different countries vary greatly in the grams of alcohol included in a standard drink and this needs to be considered. In particular, the highest per-capita alcohol consumption in the world is reported in Europe and accordingly alcohol-related deaths among older people in this region has markedly increased over the past decade (Hallgren, Hogberg and Andreasson, 2009). However, the majority of countries in the European Union do not have age-specific guidelines (Hoeck and Van Hal, 2012).

The current Australian guidelines do not have any specific recommendations for older adults (National Health and Medical Research Council, 2009). All adults aged 18 and over are advised to consume no more than two standard drinks on any single day (1 drink = 10g) in order to reduce the lifetime risk of harm from alcohol-related disease or injury. These guidelines, however, acknowledge that people aged 60 years and older are at an increased risk of harm from consuming alcohol and that, while less likely to binge drink, they are more likely to drink smaller quantities more regularly and are at risk of cumulative harm. The recent Invisible Addicts report released by the Working Group of the Royal College of Psychiatry in the UK (Crome et al., 2011) advocates that the upper "safe limit" for older people is 1.5 units per day or 11 units per week (1 drink = 8g). The NIAAA guidelines (National Institute on Alcohol Abuse and Alcoholism, 1998) are comparable, recommending that healthy adults over 65 years who are not taking any medications should not exceed one drink on a given day and seven drinks in total over the course of a week (1 drink = 14g). Interestingly, a recent analysis of nationally representative data from the Health Survey for England indicated that if the guidelines of the Working Group of the Royal College of Psychiatry were to be adopted then there would be a greater number of drinkers at risk of alcohol-related harm in the community in the 65+ age band than in the 16–24 year group (Knott et al., 2013). Furthermore, the number of older, at-risk drinkers would increase by 2.5 fold to exceed 3 million cases in England alone. This is a dramatic increase and caution needs be used in applying such criteria until we have a better grasp of the true impact of low-level daily drinking in late life.

Given that older people may also show more complex patterns of substance use (e.g., alcohol plus inappropriate use of prescribed medications) and need clear guidance on cognitive and physical comorbidities, the development of further age-specific guidelines, as well as research to prove their validity, is imperative. The impact of these lowered drinking levels, in particular how best to manage the number of people who would screen positive, also needs to be considered.

Tools to identify alcohol-use disorders in older people

Common screening tools to assess alcohol use and misuse in older clients currently screen for risky intake levels and alcoholism only. The Short Michigan Alcoholism Screening Instrument – Geriatric Version (SMAST-G) (Blow *et al.*, 1992) is a short form of the Michigan Alcoholism Screening Instrument that is specifically tailored to older adults. The Substance Abuse and Mental Health Services Administration (SAMHSA) Guidelines now recommend that a screening test like the SMAST-G be the first step in "SBIRT", a treatment protocol consisting of screening followed by brief intervention and referral to treatment as needed (Naegle, 2007). Scores on this scale can be a useful starting point to instigate a discussion with those who screen positive about the need to reduce their levels of alcohol consumption. The Alcohol-Use Disorders Identification Test (AUDIT) was developed by the World Health Organization as a brief screening tool mainly for use in primary care settings (Babor *et al.*, 2001). It consists of ten questions regarding both the quantity and frequency of alcohol use in adults, with the aim of identifying those drinking at hazardous or harmful levels. The screening cut-point for hazardous drinking and where brief intervention is indicated is a total score of eight or higher, although it is acknowledged that the elderly constitute an at-risk group and therefore a reduced score of six or seven might be more sensitive. The scale has also been further refined to briefer, three-item (AUDIT-C) and five-item versions (AUDIT-5) that have been shown to reliably identify heavy drinking and/or active alcohol abuse or dependence and to out-perform other scales (Bush *et al.*, 1998; O'Connell *et al.*, 2004). Though not developed specifically for an older population, the shortened versions of this scale have been shown to have good utility for both males and females in this age group (Bradley *et al.*, 2004; Bush *et al.*, 1998). The other common detection tool is the CAGE (Ewing, 1984), which screens for alcohol abuse or dependence. This tool is brief and is the most commonly administered; however, its main target is identifying alcoholism rather than current or shorter-term hazardous use (Crome *et al.*, 2011) and its performance in the elderly has been shown to be variable (O'Connell *et al.*, 2004).

A newer test developed by Fink and colleagues (2002a) is the Alcohol-Related Problems Survey (ARPS). The aim of this comprehensive 60-item tool is to provide a sliding threshold scale according to comorbid medical conditions and concomitant medications and it categorizes patients into non-hazardous, hazardous or harmful drinking. There is also a shortened version (Fink *et al.*, 2002a). Both versions of this scale have been shown to perform better than the AUDIT and the SMAST-G in older people and to have excellent sensitivity; however, both have poorer specificity (Moore *et al.*, 2002). Unlike the other scales, the ARPS is able to identify a cohort of people at risk of alcohol-related harm due to their comorbid medical illnesses or concomitant medications (Fink *et al.*, 2002b). While broad and comprehensive, a key disadvantage of the ARPS is its long length, which may serve as a deterrent to its use in clinical care.

Currently, the most commonly used tools for an older population are aimed at identifying cases of alcoholism. It would be beneficial if there were specific tools to identify a broad spectrum of AUDs in older adults and if these could distinguish between symptoms observed in "normal ageing" and those associated with alcohol misuse. To have optimum utility, this tool would be brief and able to be administered across a range of clinical settings. Another current gap in this literature is the older population presenting with cognitive impairment. There is currently no gold standard screening instrument to detect AUDs in this population and they constitute a particularly vulnerable group to the effects of alcohol, particularly as regards their clinical course (O'Connell *et al.*, 2004). Older people presenting to some memory clinics may be excluded if there are signs of AUDs, but may also struggle to engage with alcohol treatment services (where these are available for older groups) due to cognitive impairments (Wadd *et al.*, 2013). However, existing alcohol screening measures can be adapted for individuals presenting with cognitive impairment and recommendations suggest supplementing screening performance feedback with alcohol diaries and collateral information from family members and carers to provide accurate information on alcohol use (Wadd *et al.*, 2013). Our multidisciplinary, memory clinic in the Aged-Care Psychiatry service at Prince of Wales Hospital (NSW, Australia) accepts all referrals, regardless of age and aetiology, and we are currently working collaboratively with local drug and alcohol services (who are now cognitively screening all clients) to trial this clinic as a means of providing more in-depth assessment of ageing drug and alcohol patients who present with cognitive impairment. One gap that persists in the literature, however, is that more information is required regarding the differences in presentation of older people with cognitive impairment with comorbid alcohol misuse (or, more broadly, substance abuse) compared to those with common types of dementia.

Cognitive assessment of older adults with alcohol-use disorders

There is, likewise, currently no cognitive tool advocated for the older population to assess the impact of alcohol on cognitive performance although anecdotal evidence in our clinics suggests that the Montreal Cognitive Assessment (MoCA) has good acceptability and utility and is preferable to the Mini-Mental State Examination (MMSE). The MoCA was also highlighted as a quick, easy to administer and acceptable tool to use in substance misuse services to screen for cognitive impairment among older clients (Wadd *et al.*, 2013). This type of assessment is vital as cognitive capacity is a sensitive predictor of engagement in treatment (Bates and Pawlak, 2006); identifying cognitive deficits allows treatment to be modified to optimise outcomes for the patient (Wadd *et al.*, 2013).

The MoCA has been shown to be effective in distinguishing those with mild cognitive impairment (MCI) from control participants with intact cognition and from patients with conditions associated with impaired cognition in ageing, such as mild Alzheimer's disease (Lee *et al.*, 2008) and Parkinson's disease (Hoops *et al.*, 2009). It correlates well with the domains of a broad neuropsychological assessment, particularly memory, executive function and visuo-spatial function, and it can have particular utility in directing further in–depth assessment (Lam *et al.*, 2013). The strength of the performance of the MoCA on these domains makes it particularly suitable for differentiating between some of the difficulties observed in patients with many types of early dementia and those with alcohol-induced cognitive impairment.

There is also evidence of the utility of the MoCA as a cognitive screen in younger adults with substance abuse. The utility of this test has been compared to the full Neuropsychological Assessment Battery-Screening Module (NAB-SM), which assesses cognitive functioning across the five domains of attention, language, memory, visuo-spatial function and executive function (Stern and White, 2003) and has been used previously in drug and alcohol settings. The MoCA was shown to have criterion-related validity and good accuracy in correctly distinguishing cases of alcohol-related cognitive impairment (Copersino *et al.*, 2009). A weakness of the MoCA is that it does not examine psychomotor speed, visual learning or delayed recognition, although it is only a screening measure and as such cannot be expected to examine all cognitive domains. The study did also support the clinical utility of the test and showed that the patient acceptability was good. Within the group with ARBD, the MoCA memory sub-domain in particular has also been shown to be able to distinguish between those with Korsakoff's Syndrome and patients with alcohol-related cognitive impairment (non-Korsakoff's: Wester *et al.*, 2013).

The MoCA appears to be a useful brief screening tool to evaluate cognitive impairment in older people and in those with AUDs. This test should not be used as a substitute for further neuropsychological assessment but rather to complement this process and indicate patients where further evaluation is warranted.

Barriers to screening older people

A difficulty for clinicians as regards the diagnosis and assessment of AUDs is that the medical comorbidities that can be warning signs for alcohol misuse and abuse can also present as symptoms of medical illnesses associated with ageing. Examples of this include cognitive impairment, confusion and disorientation, gastrointestinal tract problems and falls. However, these conditions do provide an important opportunity for screening. The primary care setting in particular is a key environment for the screening of AUDs in older people since this age group is known to visit their physician regularly, on average at least six times each year (Schappert, 1999). Key opportunities for alcohol-use screening in primary care include at the initial con-sultation, if the patient has a fall, or when a new medication is commenced or existing medications are reviewed (Hunter and Lubman, 2010). Screening should also occur if the patient presents with symptoms of mental disturbance such as depression, sleep difficulties, anxiety or cognitive changes, if they present with conditions associated with the heart, liver, kidneys or gastrointestinal system, or in the case of nutritional problems (Hunter and Lubman, 2010). In these instances, the patient is likely to expect such questions and as such this may make the session less confronting for both the patient and practitioner.

Another barrier to screening and adequate detection rates of alcohol misuse in this group is the attitudes of health professionals working with older adults. There is a general consensus that older people reduce their alcohol intake as they age and therefore clinicians may perceive less impetus to ask this population about their consumption levels. There also appears to be a general reluctance to enter into such a conversation with an older client (Duru et al., 2010). Consistent with this are the relatively poor rates of detection of AUDs, being approximately a third of cases in hospital settings (Speckens, Heeren and Rooijmans, 1991; McInnes and Powell, 1994). There is also an expectation that cognitive function will decline, meaning this is not always seen as an impetus for further investigation or assessment.

More recently, Draper and colleagues (2014) screened a sample of over 200 elderly non-demented, non-delirious patients presenting to Australian aged-care hospital and community services. All participants were screened with the AUDIT-C and those who screened positive received further evaluation, which included the full AUDIT, CAGE and Addenbrooke's Cognitive Examination-Revised (ACE-R). The average age of participants was 81 years. Seventeen per cent screened positive for an AUD alone with a further 3.3 per cent screening positive for both alcohol and benzodiazepine misuse. Interestingly, the patients who screened positively reported significantly higher subjective quality of life but did not differ to screen negatives according to depression, functional or cognitive status. Importantly, a review of the medical records of patients who screened positive after three months revealed that nearly three-quarters had their alcohol consumption levels recorded in the file by medical staff (73 per cent), although in only 23 per cent of cases was the level documented as problematic and for only 14 per cent was there a management plan devised.

The views of older people themselves as regards testing for alcohol use can interact with those of the health professional. Older people can fear assessment due to the perceived shame at being labeled an "alcoholic". Some also view their alcohol intake as nobody's business but their own and therefore will not report their drinking levels to a clinician (Dar, 2006), even when they experience initial cognitive impairment. Many older adults consume alcohol for "medicinal purposes" (often low-level drinking; Aira, Hartikainen and Sulkava, 2008) because it is often promoted as protecting against dementia. The majority of older people are also often just unaware of safe drinking levels and guidelines, and particularly interactions with prescription and over-the-counter medications, and this information needs to be supplied by a health professional (Rakshi et al., 2011; Gilson, Bryant and Judd, 2014). Some older people also fear cognitive assessments lest they be diagnosed with a type of dementia, but if carried out on a routine basis (such as annually) then these tests can become standard practice and less confronting.

Alcohol misuse and cognitive function in later life

The impact of alcohol consumption on cognitive function in ageing is currently an area of great research interest, especially given that this is a modifiable risk factor for cognitive impairment and dementia. Older adults presenting with cognitive symptoms are often presumed to have a neurodegenerative disorder, such as Alzheimer's disease, and screening for their alcohol-use levels can easily be overlooked. The role of alcohol in late-life cognitive disorders is complex and the results have been mixed as to whether alcohol guards against cognitive decline in later life or whether it accelerates this process.

The effects of heavy alcohol use and alcohol-related cognitive disorders

Sustained, heavy use of alcohol has been associated with an increased risk of alcohol-related cognitive disorders including alcohol-related dementia (ARD), Wernicke's Encephalopathy, Korsakoff's Syndrome and ARBD (Oslin and Cary, 2003). In line with this, the DSM-5 criteria acknowledge alcohol abuse as a cause of major and minor neurocognitive disorder (terms analogous to dementia and MCI). The term "alcohol-related brain damage" has replaced "alcohol-related dementia" (DSM-IV alcohol-induced persisting dementia) in many clinical contexts (Jauhar and Smith, 2009), although the latter is still used mainly in an aged-care or geriatrics context. More specific criteria have also been proposed and validated for ARD, specifying that at least 35 standard drinks per week for males and 28 for women for a period of more than five years is sufficient to cause a dementia syndrome (Oslin and Cary, 2003; Ridley, Draper and Withall, 2013). To be diagnosed with ARD, these criteria also propose that the cognitive symptoms persist for at least 60 days after the person's last exposure to alcohol and that significant alcohol use must occur within three years of the onset of the cognitive deficits (Oslin and Cary, 2003).

Incidence and prevalence estimates of ARD vary in accordance with the lack of consistent guidelines and diagnostic criteria (Ridley, Draper and Withall, 2013; Ridley and Draper, 2014). A recent Australian epidemiological study of younger-onset dementia (onset of symptoms under 65 years) identified that ARD was the leading cause, accounting for nearly 20 per cent of cases (18.4 per cent; Withall et al., 2014). This was a significant increase from a rate of 10 per cent identified in a previous study in the UK, which occurred about a decade beforehand (Harvey, Skelton-Robinson and Rossor, 2003). A combination of DSM-IV criteria for alcohol-induced persisting dementia and Oslin and Cary's criteria for ARD were used. Most of the ARD cases were identified following hospital treatment for a medical illness and few received active follow-up and/or assessment for their cognitive difficulties following discharge (Withall et al., in press). This group, whose ages ranged from 38 to 75 years, were often isolated from family members and this created a further barrier to service provision.

The Australian Hospital Dementia Services Project provided additional support for this relatively high rate of cases (Draper et al., 2011). The study analysed data representing nearly 410,000 multi-day hospital admissions during 2006/7 for patients aged 50 years and over from 222 public hospitals across NSW. In total 300 patients with diagnosed ICD-10-AM ARD were admitted in this period, 268 with ARD (82 per cent male, mean age 65, range 50–86 years) and an additional 32 patients diagnosed with ARD plus another type of dementia (mean 71 years, range 53–84 years). From these figures, ARD represented approximately 20 per cent of the patients diagnosed with dementia in the 50–64 year age band and 1.4 per cent of the total number of patients identified with dementia. Digestive system illness was the leading cause of hospital admission for this group (16.3 per cent) and this was predominantly liver disease (11 per cent). Injuries accounted for a further 9.8 per cent of admissions and these were mostly fractures and head injuries. These patients often had coexisting medical conditions (mean = 5) and in fact 13 per cent of admissions had eight or more comorbidities. These results suggest that ARD is on the rise in the "young-old", a group who are too young for aged care and can be seen as too old for drug and alcohol services. The findings also bring attention to the issue of where these patients are best placed within the medical system in order to receive the assessment and clinical follow-up that is required for both their medical conditions but also their cognitive difficulties (Withall *et al.*, in press). In both of these studies, however, the identification of ARD was in an acute hospital setting and many more patients were given this diagnosis than could be confirmed during a case note review (Withall *et al.*, in press). It may be that many health professionals liberally combine a clinical history of heavy alcohol use and cognitive impairment into a diagnosis of ARD without patients receiving further testing; a lack of clinical follow-up was certainly one finding from the study by Withall and colleagues. This theory is supported by a Danish study investigating the validity of dementia diagnoses registered for younger-onset patients. They reported that the registered diagnosis was found to be correct in just over half the patients (59 per cent), with misdiagnosis occurring most frequently in those with depression or a history of alcohol abuse (Salem *et al.*, 2012). This suggests, therefore, that some caution is needed.

Further support for the harmful impact of heavy alcohol use has also come from recent longitudinal analyses from the Whitehall II cohort study examining the impact of midlife alcohol consumption (mean age 56, range 44–69 years at first assessment) on cognitive decline over the course of a ten-year period (Sabia *et al.*, 2014). Men who consumed greater than or equal to 36g/day of alcohol in midlife experienced a faster ten-year decline across both cognitive domains as well as a global cognitive function domain. Short-term verbal memory was assessed through immediate recall of a list of 20 one- or two-syllable words, presented orally at two-second intervals. Executive function was assessed with the Alice Heim 4-I (AH4-I) to test inductive reasoning (timed), phonemic fluency and semantic fluency. The evidence was not as robust for women, but indicated a decline in executive function at intake levels greater than 19g/day, which is consistent with the fact that women tolerate alcohol less well than men. As regards the effect of type of beverage, heavy consumption of spirits caused more decline than either beer or wine. An additional longitudinal study examining risk factors for younger-onset dementia with a follow-up period of 37 years also reported that number of episodes of hospital-treated alcohol intoxication was the single, most important contributor and was associated with diagnosed ARD, as well as vascular dementia and unspecified dementia (Nordström *et al.*, 2013).

Is light to moderate alcohol use neuroprotective in late life?

Conversely, a non-binge, light to moderate pattern of alcohol use has actually been suggested to have a neuroprotective role (Collins *et al.*, 2009). This has followed the observation from a number of studies that the association between alcohol consumption and cognition is represented by a J-shaped curve, with light to moderate consumption conferring more beneficial effects than either abstinence or heavy drinking (Kim *et al.*, 2012). Such findings have frequently been promoted to the public in the media and this has encouraged many older people to drink for "medicinal purposes" in order to improve their brain health. Moderate alcohol use is believed to bestow protective effects against coronary heart disease, as well as cognitive impairment and dementia. A review paper examining biological mechanisms that could underlie these findings reported that exposure to moderate levels of alcohol conveys protection against the damaging effects of ischemia, endotoxin, β-amyloid and gp120. Furthermore, mild anti-inflammatory mechanisms in the heart, vasculature and brain that serve to promote cellular survival pathways are triggered by moderate alcohol consumption (Collins *et al.*, 2009). These protective effects are believed to be optimal in the range of half to two drinks per day, with diminishing positive effects as consumption increases and a complete reversal to causing harm once six drinks per day is reached or exceeded (Corrao *et al.*, 2000). Wine seems to confer more beneficial effects that other beverages and the presence of the apolipoprotein E ε4 allele, which is a risk factor for Alzheimer's disease, promotes cognitive decline (Panza *et al.*, 2012).

Further support for the benefits of some alcohol intake in ageing was provided by a rigorous, systematic review and meta-analyses of 15 prospective studies examining the effect of alcohol as an independent predictor of dementia (Alzheimer's disease, vascular dementia and any dementia) and cognitive decline (Anstey, Mack and Cherbuin, 2009). Findings from included studies were mixed with respect to whether former drinkers had poorer outcomes and as such should be included in the same group as abstainers. Overall, light to moderate alcohol intake conferred a 25 to 28 per cent reduction in risk of Alzheimer's, vascular dementia and any dementia compared to abstinence. Heavy drinkers were not shown to have an increased risk of dementia, although it was acknowledged that this cohort might not be captured in such longitudinal studies due to ill health or premature mortality (Anstey, Mack and Cherbuin, 2009).

The role of genetics in moderating the harmful effects of alcohol on cognition in late life

Recently there has been a move towards studies that have considered the interaction between genetics and alcohol consumption on cognitive function. These studies have attempted to explain some of the variance in the research findings by exploring the impact of a person's genetic ability to process alcohol (i.e., alcohol dehydrogenase activity) as a mediating variable. For example, a variant of the alcohol dehydrogenase 1B (ADH1B) gene causes as much as an 80-fold reduction in the enzyme's ability to metabolize ethanol and those who possess the ability to metabolize alcohol more rapidly are at increased risk of AUDs, as well as alcohol-induced medical illnesses (Li, Zhao and Gelernter, 2011; Almeida *et al.*, 2014). The impact of alcohol consumption over the previous two to three months (g/day) on cognitive ability at age 70 was studied using the Lothian Birth Cohort 1936 (Ritchie *et al.*, 2014). After controlling for the participant's SES of origin (father's occupational level in 1936), their own attained SES (highest occupational level), years of education, smoking status and cognitive ability at age 11, there was a significant gene × alcohol consumption interaction on lifetime cognitive change. It was further revealed that greater alcohol consumption levels in subjects with high alcohol processing efficiency led to moderate increases in cognitive ability across the lifespan, while those with less metabolic activity displayed cognitive losses across the lifespan. This suggests that there are some people that are better able to handle their alcohol than others and may explain some of the variance observed in clinical patients presenting with cognitive impairment.

However, a further Mendelian randomization study that followed community-dwelling men aged 65–83 years for a six-year period found that alcohol consumption was not a predictor of cognitive impairment, as rated by performance on the MMSE (total score < 23; Almeida *et al.*, 2014). Overall, compared to the reference category of non-drinkers, those with moderate intake of alcohol (15–27 drinks per week; 1 drink = 10g of alcohol) had reduced odds of cognitive impairment six years later (OR = 0.60; 95 per cent CI = 0.40 − 0.89) and this effect remained significant after excluding abstainers from the reference group. However, the effects were no longer significant after controlling for age, education, marital status and cardiovascular disease. Heavy alcohol use (> 28 drinks per week) did not increase the risk of cognitive impairment and the G → A polymorphism was not found to reduce the risk of cognitive impairment as expected. Overall the study indicated that alcohol use, including heavy drinking and abuse, does not directly cause cognitive impairment in older men. Key methodological issues were that alcohol consumption was measured at baseline, with no consideration given to how usage levels may have changed over the six-year period as well as their impact. Also, cognitive impairment was measured as a dichotomous cut-point on the MMSE, which may have reduced the sensitivity of the analyses, as might the lack of measurement of executive functioning in the MMSE (see Svanberg, Morrison and Cullen, 2015).

In summary, alcohol has both neurotoxic and neuroprotective effects, although it is clear that there are still many issues to be resolved as to determining the protective or deleterious effects of alcohol upon cognitive function in ageing (Kim *et al.*, 2012). Of the studies that have been performed, most have been cross-sectional and there has been considerable variability according to outcome measures, types of alcoholic beverage considered, definition used for a standard drink (g alcohol), follow-up period, as well as varying consideration given to interactions with other lifestyle or genetic factors (Panza *et al.*, 2012). Another key factor has been the inclusion of former drinkers in the abstainers group, which is used in most studies as the reference category (Lobo *et al.*, 2010). Newer studies that have explored the impact of genetic factors on the cognitive impacts of drinking in later life have considerable potential and may help to explain some of the variance in findings. However, as with other studies, people refusing genetic testing and/or cognitive testing could be those most likely to be heavy drinkers and/or to have impairment and this may impact upon the results (Almeida *et al.*, 2014). One issue that remains unresolved is the number of cases of dementia in late life where heavy alcohol use is a contributing factor and, indeed, how often ARBD may complicate this clinical profile, although one review suggested that this figure may be as high as 24 per cent (Smith and Atkinson, 1995).

Why are older people vulnerable to alcohol-related harm?

Compared to younger people, older adults require less alcohol to achieve the same effects due to several age-related bodily changes. Ageing modifies the body's responses to alcohol, including the rate of absorption and excretion (Fink *et al.*, 2005). Additionally, there are bodily changes that increase the concentration of alcohol and these include a reduction in muscle mass, lean body mass and total body water, with an increase in adiposity (Dufour and Fuller, 1995). Reduced absorption of nutrients, in particular thiamine, may also place older people at greater risk of thiamine deficiency syndromes such as Wernicke's Encephalopathy (Bonner, 2014).

The physiological changes associated with normal ageing therefore result in older adults tolerating alcohol less well than younger adults and place older people at an increased risk of adverse physical effects even at relatively modest intake levels (Aira, Hartikainen and Sulkava, 2005). This renders older people more susceptible to alcohol-attributable injury and disease (such as falls or gastrointestinal complaints) from consumption levels that may previously have been safe for them. Other conditions associated with alcohol abuse and dependence in older adults include diabetes, heart disease and hypertension, cirrhosis of the liver, peripheral neuropathy, seizure disorders, delirium, nutritional deficiencies, incontinence and peptic ulcer disease (Fink *et al.*, 2005).

Interactions between medications and alcohol are common in older people. A population-based, random sample of 601 community-dwelling elderly people (aged 75 years or over) indicated that the majority (86.9 per cent) used both alcohol and regular medications. Furthermore, it was revealed that most of the risk for harm arose from interactions between alcohol and medications as opposed to the amount of consumed alcohol (Aira, Hartikainen and Sulkava, 2005). Recent cross-sectional data from the Irish Longitudinal Study on Ageing reported on results from a sample of 3,815 older adults aged 60 years and over, demonstrating that 72 per cent of participants were exposed to medications that interact with alcohol (Cousins *et al.*, 2014). These medications were predominantly cardiovascular and central nervous system (CNS) agents, including psychotropics, opioid analgesics, hypnotics and antidepressants. Within this subgroup, 60 per cent of those exposed to such medications reported concomitant alcohol use. Interestingly, the study also supported recent trends in the data of increasing alcohol use in older people, with 8 per cent of the sample (12.7 per cent of current drinkers) being identified as problem drinkers on the CAGE. This was partially attributed to the younger age of participants, which included the Baby Boomers. This high prevalence of potentially harmful interactions between alcohol and medication use suggests that greater education is needed for clinicians and that patients also need greater health literacy around this issue.

Management approaches for the older person

The acute period: withdrawal and the older client

Withdrawal from alcohol poses particular challenges for the older patient and it is more severe than for younger people, mostly due to the same physiological changes in ageing that increase sensitivity to alcohol (Coulton, 2009). Older people are also susceptible to withdrawal at lower levels of alcohol intake than younger people and they have a larger number of withdrawal symptoms that persist for a longer time period (Brower et al., 1994). They experience cognitive impairment, weakness, daytime sleepiness and high blood pressure (but not hallucinations) more frequently than younger people experiencing withdrawal (Brower et al., 1994). They may also experience cardiac instability and death, and these symptoms can begin as soon as six to 12 hours following their last intake of alcohol (Taheri et al., 2014). Older adults require close supervision during the withdrawal process, which will often need to be undertaken in a hospital setting, as they are susceptible to delirium or acute confusion, need monitoring of their vital signs and they present a falls risk, sometimes due to over-sedation (Kraemer, Mayo-Smith and Calkins, 1997; Rigler, 2000).

Delirium is one condition that should serve as a warning sign or flag for alcohol withdrawal, especially in older patients presenting to a hospital setting. In a study examining diagnosed delirium and associated confusional states in patients aged over 60 discharged from acute inpatient units (n = 267,947), alcohol intoxication or withdrawal delirium was the second most common cause and accounted for 18.7 per cent of cases (Kales et al., 2003). Delirium should not be confused with persisting cognitive impairment and a strong clinical history should be gained wherever possible from supportive people, such as carers, guardians or others who may know the usual level of functioning of the person.

Short-acting benzodiazepines should preferentially be used since this class of medication takes longer to be metabolized by older patients and has less likelihood of prolonged sedation and negative effects (Mayo-Smith et al., 2004). A recommended dosage is either 1–2mg of lorazepam (administered by oral, intravenous or intramuscular route) or 30–60mg of oxazepam (oral administration) given hourly (Kraemer, Conigliaro and Saitz, 1999). This should be supplemented by thiamine and electrolytes as needed (Rigler, 2000). The dosage of the short-acting benzodiazepine should also be titrated carefully as older patients will achieve efficacy at a lower dose than younger people. They will also need to be tapered off medication carefully in order to avoid withdrawal seizures or breakthrough symptoms (Mayo-Smith *et al.*, 2004). Nurses are in an ideal position to monitor these issues since they observe patients consistently over a longer period of the day and can be more sensitive to detecting both the onset of withdrawal and/or delirium, as well as the resolution of withdrawal symptoms (Kales *et al.*, 2003). A newer approach to managing alcohol withdrawal in older people is a symptom-triggered dosage regimen (Taheri *et al.*, 2014). One relatively small study in people aged 70 and older showed promising results; the average cumulative dose of lorazepam administered reduced significantly from 9mg to 3mg and the median duration of benzodiazepine administration also decreased from 96 to 48 hours. There was also a significant reduction in severe withdrawal symptoms (Taheri *et al.*, 2014).

Longer term approaches: why do older people misuse alcohol?

In order to understand how best to manage AUDs and cognitive impairment in older people it is first necessary to understand the factors that affect their success. There are two groups of clients within the category of older drinkers: the lifelong heavy drinker (the "survivor" of early onset drinking) and the late-onset drinker (the "reactor" to life's events; Christie *et al.*, 2013; Atkinson, Tolson and Turner, 1990). These groups vary in their characteristics and this can impact upon treatment modality and success. A study of an older cohort admitted to a Veterans Affairs geriatric alcoholism outpatient treatment program indicated that half of these participants had commenced their heavy drinking after the age of 40 (Atkinson, Tolson and Turner, 1990). Furthermore, late-onset alcohol abuse (at or after 60 years) was shown to be a milder, more confined issue than for early or midlife difficulties and with less likelihood of a family history. Late-onset heavy drinking was more often a reaction to losses in life, as opposed to psychological morbidity (Atkinson, Tolson and Turner, 1990). Additionally, late-onset drinkers tend to still have family support around them to help nurture the recovery process, unlike those with long-term alcohol abuse who tend to be estranged from family and more isolated (Brennan and Moos, 1996).

Older people who are drinking heavily or binge drinking often do so in order to cope with negative psychosocial factors, such as loss of identity and boredom due to retirement, social isolation, depressed mood, physical disability and pain, and divorce or separation (Lin *et al.*, 2011; Crome *et al.*, 2011). One study found that for older men, but not older women, there was a correlation between depression scores and drinking levels, suggesting that older men may use drinking as a coping strategy for mood symptoms (Choi and Dinitto, 2011). To improve detection rates, it was recommended that alcohol screening should coincide with depression screening in older men and vice versa. Older women who have had a partner with an AUD and/or are bereaved are more likely to drink heavily (Wilsnack and Wilsnack, 1995). However, in turn their heavy drinking might also contribute to social isolation and depressive symptoms, promoting a vicious cycle from which it is difficult to escape. Older people also drink to relieve stress or anxiety in a type of avoidant coping and those with a history of alcohol abuse prior to age 50 are at an increased risk of high-risk consumption in late life (Moos et al., 2010; Christie et al., 2013). For this group drinking is often a private affair, whereby they drink alone in their own home (McCabe, 2011; Christie et al., 2013).

A further, important enabler is the belief by many family members (and some clinicians) that alcohol misuse by older people is innocuous, manageable and is a pleasure that should not be taken away from the person (Benshoff, Harrawood and Koch, 2003). As such, the habit is promoted and deleterious effects are overlooked as just normal ageing. Public health campaigns have not assisted in this regard since AUDs and binge drinking tend to be promoted as only affecting young people, which reinforces the view that drinking is harmless in older people (Knott et al., 2013). In fact, given that the older drinker prefers to drink at home alone they go undetected since they are not inflicting their behavior upon members of the general public, as can be the case with alcohol-related violence among younger people. There has also been widespread promotion of the message that alcohol in moderation is good for brain health and this has encouraged many older people to take a daily drink.

There are also more positive factors that facilitate drinking in older adults. As mentioned earlier, some older people believe their alcohol consumption is promoting good brain health. Additionally, longitudinal research across ten-year and 20-year periods has shown that older people who have more financial resources and for whom drinking is an established social activity and promoted among their social network tend to consume alcohol at hazardous levels (Moos et al., 2010). About 10 per cent of older people with an AUD drink simply because they enjoy it (Christie et al., 2013).

Psychosocial variables, both positive and negative, can contribute to the exacerbation of a pre-existing difficulty with alcohol or the new development of an AUD in the elderly.

Benshoff, Harrawood and Koch (2003), however, warned against making causal associations between depression and psychosocial factors, citing circularity as a problem and posing the pertinent question "does increased drinking after retirement result from despair in the change of life status or an inability to manage unstructured free time?" (p. 44).

Treatment approaches for alcohol-use disorders in older clients

Drug and alcohol services are generally a "young man's game" and this is likely to be one reason why there are few older people within this specialist treatment system. Services are targeted towards young adults and this can lead to older people feeling ostracized, especially since there is considerable stigma about being identified as an "alcoholic", particularly for women (Blow, 2000); many regard their drinking, albeit heavy, as largely social. In fact, well under 10 per cent of drug and alcohol services have a program where the target population is ageing patients (Koenig, George and Schneider, 1994). Older clients also struggle to be referred to treatment services by health professionals, with one study indicating that only 15 per cent of older clients presenting with a diagnosis of alcohol dependence or abuse were referred on to rehabilitation services (Mulinga, 1999). This may be due to therapeutic nihilism, as mentioned above, with some clinicians believing the patient is too old for intervention or unable to complete a treatment program (McCabe, 2011). This is magnified for clients who present with comorbid cognitive impairment. As such, there is a tendency for these clients to fall through the gaps between services. This is compounded by the relatively little evidence regarding the most appropriate treatment approaches for older people with AUDs. However, the studies that have been performed indicate that older people respond relatively well to treatment and, in particular, have higher rates of maintaining abstinence than younger clients (Caputo et al., 2012; Whelan, 2003).

AUDs also cause difficulties for clinicians working in aged-care and geriatrics environments. Alcohol abuse can complicate the clinical picture and can expedite the progression of degenerative dementias (Teri, Hughes and Larson, 1990). In a study examining a range of factors that contribute to the progression of Alzheimer's disease, it was found that patients with lifetime or current alcohol abuse declined faster than any other group (including those with head injury or other neurodegenerative disease); an average of more than seven points per year on the MMSE, which was five points faster per year than adults without an AUD.

Brief interventions delivered by primary care physicians have been shown to be a particularly useful tool for reducing alcohol intake in older people. The Florida Brief Intervention and Treatment for Elders (BRITE) project involved nearly 3,500 participants aged 55 years and older who were screened for problematic substance use, as well as for depression and suicide risk in emergency and primary health care settings (Schonfeld et al., 2010). The program is based upon the "SBIRT" model (Babor et al., 2007) and those who received screening and brief intervention had decreased depression and alcohol usage, as well as improvements in inappropriate medication use. Project GOAL (Guiding Older Adult Lifestyles) utilized two ten- to 15-minute sessions of physician advice, education and counseling using a scripted workbook (Fleming et al., 1999). Overall, the intervention group had a 34 per cent reduction in alcohol use at 12-months follow-up and women responded particularly well. In particular, they had a significant reduction in their recent alcohol consumption, frequency of at-risk drinking and episodes of binge drinking. Another study has indicated that women respond well to feedback alone derived from screening measures (Blow, 2000) and given that many women drink at risky levels rather than those associated with abuse per se this may be a cost-effective and feasible intervention. Women, however, are more likely to have comorbid benzodiazepine and alcohol use or misuse than men and this may warrant additional attention (Blow, 2000). Finally, the Project SHARE Study utilized a broad intervention consisting of personalized reports, educational information, drinking diaries, brief physician advice and telephone counseling (Ettner et al., 2014). At 12 months, the intervention group not only reduced their at-risk drinking but had more alcohol-related discussions with their physician, and reduced health care utilization (both emergency admissions and assistance from a non-professional carer). Whether these brief interventions are effective for those with cognitive impairment remains to be seen.

Support for the older person with alcohol-related brain damage

These patients can present with complex comorbidities and as such it is recommended that services use a "mainstreaming" or integrated care approach (Rao and Shanks, 2011). Staff working with older adults would benefit from cross-training in aged care, mental health and substance abuse so that they can identify comorbid issues early and can also provide appropriate referrals to other services. Supervision and support is needed to provide this education to health professionals (Rao and Shanks, 2011). As indicated earlier in this chapter, it is not uncommon for AUDs to coexist not only with cognitive impairment but also with mood disorders and collaborative care is vital in this context (Rao and Shanks, 2011). Older patients who are drinking in excess and who are physically frail and/or cognitively impaired should also be referred to an aged-care psychiatry or geriatric service for further assessment (Rigler, 2000). Since many patients seen in an aged-care or geriatric service have a declining clinical course, the additional engagement of neuro-rehabilitative services can be a useful adjunct (Wilson *et al.*, 2012). Community health workers can also be engaged in order to facilitate these clients' access to supportive services such as home care, transport and assistance with meals (Rigler, 2000). Assertive outreach and a high level of inter-agency liaison is essential for working with this group to ensure that they do not fall into gaps between services (Wadd *et al.*, 2013).

Specialized, multidisciplinary care can also help some of the difficulties associated with these patients in the hospital setting, where they are particularly at risk of extended stays, high rates of discharge at own risk and discharge to residential care (MacPhail, McDonough and Ibrahim, 2013; Draper *et al.*, 2011). Reasons for this include their range of complex needs, challenging behaviors, difficulties with identifying appropriate medical and support services, and a lack of appropriate residential care facilities (MacPhail, McDonough and Ibrahim, 2013; Rota-Bartelink, 2006). In many respects the level of care required by these patients parallels that of people with dementia (particularly a high staff to client ratio), although they can differ in that they often have care needs that extend to promoting social skills and social support, as well as with ensuring adequate housing (Rota-Bartelink, 2006). The care pathway appropriate for patients with ARBD should not be any different in older clients; that is, withdrawal and medical stabilization, cognitive assessment, abstinence with support and repeat assessment, rehabilitation and, finally, establishment of long-term supports (Wilson and Halsey, 2010). If these patients are viewed as having a set of complex needs, rather than being defined by a diagnosis, then the stigma related to their condition being self-inflicted diminishes and expertise from a range of disciplines can be drawn upon to maximize their outcomes. Longitudinal assessment of these clients is vital and their cognitive function and activities of daily living should be regularly assessed in order to establish any improvement, stabilization, or deterioration (Ridley, Draper and Withall, 2013). Any care plan developed should also be regularly reviewed to allow adjustments for changes in cognitive and functional ability; in particular, over time and with sustained abstinence people with ARBD may be able to move to more independent living accommodation. Above all, as should be the right of any patient presenting to a health service, person-centered care is of key importance (Wilson *et al.*, 2012).

Summary

AUDs in later life are more common than previously thought and can lead to significant increases in physical and psychological morbidity. This is an important health policy message and health promotion campaigns should be directed towards this population. Health messages delivered to the public must be chosen judiciously, especially as regards cognitive effects of alcohol. It appears that some alcohol use in late life can be neuroprotective; however, there are limitations with the literature and this may not hold true for patients once they have been diagnosed with a cognitive disorder. More attention also needs to be given to promoting the negative effects of heavy alcohol use, especially given the lack of awareness among this group regarding guidelines for safe drinking levels.

It is recommended that screening for alcohol misuse occurs in primary health care settings as older people are more likely to be in regular contact with health professionals in these settings and interactions with medications need to be considered. However, it is also evident that health professionals from all sectors of community and hospital services need training in the prevalence of alcohol problems in this population, appropriate screening measures, impacts on cognition and other effects, and age-appropriate pathways to care. In particular, adequate treatment depends on identifying the reason(s) for the person's AUD and managing their coexisting life situations, such as bereavement and/or social isolation. Brief interventions have been shown to be effective for this group and older people can have better outcomes from treatment than younger cohorts. Future research is sorely needed across a number of areas, namely to determine appropriate safe drinking levels in late life, to evaluate the effects of alcohol abuse on older clients with cognitive impairment and dementia, to establish service models for older people with ARBD and to determine whether interventions are effective for older people with cognitive impairment who are misusing alcohol.

References

Aira, M., Hartikainen, S. and Sulkava, R. (2005). Community prevalence of alcohol use and concomitant use of medication: a source of possible risk in the elderly aged 75 and older? *International Journal of Geriatric Psychiatry*, 20(7), 680–5.

Aira, M., Hartikainen, S. and Sulkava, R. (2008). Drinking alcohol for medicinal purposes by people aged over 75: a community-based interview study. *Family Practice*, 25(6), 445–9.

Almeida, O. P., Hankey, G. J., Yeap, B. B., Golledge, J. and Flicker, L. (2014). Alcohol consumption and cognitive impairment in older men: a mendelian randomization study. *Neurology*, 82(12), 1038–44.

American Psychiatric Association. (1994). *Diagnostic and Statistical Manual of Mental Disorders* (4th edn). Washington DC: APA.

American Psychiatric Association. (2013). *Diagnostic and Statistical Manual of Mental Disorders* (5th edn). Arlington, VA: American Psychiatric.

Anstey, K. J., Mack, H. A. and Cherbuin, N. (2009). Alcohol consumption as a risk factor for dementia and cognitive decline: meta-analysis of prospective studies. *The American Journal of Geriatric Psychiatry*, 17(7), 542–55.

Atkinson, R. M., Tolson, R. L. and Turner, J. A. (1990). Late versus early onset problem drinking in older men. *Alcoholism: Clinical and Experimental Research*, 14(4), 574–9.

Australian Institute of Health and Welfare. (2011). *National Drug Strategy Household Survey Report*. Canberra: AIHW.

Babor, T. F., Biddle-Higgins, J. C., Saunders, J. B. and Monteiro, M. G. (2001). *AUDIT: The Alcohol Use Disorders Identification Test: Guidelines for Use in Primary Health Care* (2nd edn). Geneva, Switzerland: WHO.

Babor, T. F., McRee, B. G., Kassebaum, P. A., Grimaldi, P. L., Ahmed, K. and Bray, J. (2007). Screening, brief intervention, and referral to treatment (SBIRT) toward a public health approach to the management of substance abuse. *Substance Abuse*, 28(3), 7–30.

Bates, M. E. and Pawlak, A. P. (2006). Cognitive impairment influences drinking outcome by altering therapeutic mechanisms of change. *Psychology of Addictive Behaviours*, 20(3), 241–53.

Benshoff, J. J., Harrawood, L. K. and Koch, D. S. (2003). Substance abuse and the elderly: unique issues and concerns. *Journal of Rehabilitation*, 69(2), 43–8.

Blazer, D. G. and Wu, L.-T. (2009). The epidemiology of substance use and disorders among middle aged and elderly community adults: national survey on drug use and health. *The American Journal of Geriatric Psychiatry*, 17(3), 237–45.

Blazer, D. G. and Wu, L.-T. (2011). The epidemiology of alcohol use disorders and subthreshold dependence in a middle-aged and elderly community sample. *The American Journal of Geriatric Psychiatry*, 19(8), 685–94.

Blow, F. C. (2000). Treatment of older women with alcohol problems: meeting the challenge for a special population. *Alcoholism: Clinical and Experimental Research*, 24(8), 1257–66.

Blow, F. C. and Barry, K. L. (2012). Alcohol and substance misuse in older adults. *Current Psychiatry Reports*, 14(4), 310–19.

Blow, F., Brower, K., Schulenberg, J., Demo-Dananberg, L., Young, J. and Beresford, T. (1992). The Michigan alcoholism screening test-geriatric version (MAST-G): a new elderly specific screening instrument. *Alcoholism: Clinical and Experimental Research*, 16(2), 372.

Bonner, A. (2014). Alcohol, ageing and cognitive function: a nutritional perspective. In J. Svanberg, A. Withall, B. Draper and S. Bowden (eds), *Alcohol and the Adult Brain*. Hove: Psychology Press.

Bradley, K. A., Kivlahan, D. R., Zhou, X. H., Sporleder, J. L., Epler, A. J., McCormick, K. A., Merrill, J. O., McDonell, M. B. and Fihn, S. D. (2004). Using alcohol screening results and treatment history to assess the severity of at-risk drinking in veterans affairs primary care patients. *Alcoholism: Clinical and Experimental Research*, 28(3), 448–55.

Brennan, P. L. and Moos, R. H. (1996). Late-life drinking behavior: the influence of personal characteristics, life context, and treatment. *Alcohol Health and Research World*, 20, 197–204.

Brower, K. J., Mudd, S., Blow, F. C., Young, J. P. and Hill, E. M. (1994). Severity and treatment of alcohol withdrawal in elderly versus younger patients. *Alcoholism: Clinical and Experimental Research*, 18(1), 196–201.

Bush, K., Kivlahan, D. R., McDonell, M. B., Fihn, S. D. and Bradley, K. A. (1998). The AUDIT alcohol consumption questions (AUDIT-C): an effective brief screening test for problem drinking. *Archives of Internal Medicine*, 158(16), 1789–95.

Caputo, F., Vignoli, T., Leggio, L., Addolorato, G., Zoli, G. and Bernardi, M. (2012). Alcohol use disorders in the elderly: a brief overview from epidemiology to treatment options. *Experimental Gerontology*, 47(6), 411–16.

Choi, N. G. and Dinitto, D. M. (2011). Heavy/binge drinking and depressive symptoms in older adults: gender differences. *International Journal of Geriatric Psychiatry*, 26(8), 860–8.

Christie, M. M., Bamber, D., Powell, C., Arrindell, T. and Pant, A. (2013). Older adult problem drinkers: who presents for alcohol treatment? *Aging and Mental Health*, 17(1), 24–32.

Collins, M. A., Neafsey, E. J., Mukamal, K. J., Gray, M. O., Parks, D. A., Das, D. K. and Korthuis, R. J. (2009). Alcohol in moderation, cardioprotection, and neuroprotection: epidemiological considerations and mechanistic studies. *Alcoholism: Clinical and Experimental Research*, 33(2), 206–19.

Copersino, M. L., Fals-Stewart, W., Fitzmaurice, G., Schretlen, D. J., Sokoloff, J. and Weiss, R. D. (2009). Rapid cognitive screening of patients with substance abuse disorders. *Experimental and Clinical Psychopharmacology*, 17(5), 337–44.

Corrao, G., Rubbiati, L., Bagnardi, V., Zambon, A. and Poikolainen, K. (2000). Alcohol and coronary heart disease: a meta-analysis. *Addiction*, 95(10), 1505–23.

Coulton, S. (2009). Alcohol use disorders in older people. *Reviews in Clinical Gerontology*, 19(03), 217–25.

Cousins, G., Galvin, R., Flood, M., Kennedy, M.-C., Motterlini, N., Henman, M. C., Kenny, R.-A. and Fahey, T. (2014). Potential for alcohol and drug interactions in older adults: evidence from the Irish longitudinal study on ageing. *BMC Geriatrics*, 14, 57.

Crome, I., Dar, K., Jankiewicz, S., Rao, R. and Tarbuck, A. (2011). *Our Invisible Addicts: First Report of the Older Persons' Substance Misuse Working Group of the Royal College of Psychiatrists*. London: Royal College of Psychiatrists.

Dar, K. (2006). Alcohol use disorders in elderly people: fact or fiction? *Advances in Psychiatric Treatment*, 12(3), 173–81.

Draper, B., Karmel, R., Gibson, D., Peut, A. and Anderson, P. (2011). Alcohol-related cognitive impairment in New South Wales hospital patients aged 50 years and over. *Australian and New Zealand Journal of Psychiatry*, 45(11), 985–92.

Draper, B., Ridley, N., Johnco, C., Withall, A., Sim, W., Freeman, M., & Lintzeris, N. (2014). Screening for alcohol and substance use for older people in geriatric hospital and community health settings. *International Psychogeriatrics*. Available on CJO 2014.

Dufour, M. and Fuller, R. K. (1995). Alcohol in the elderly. *Annual Review of Medicine*, 46, 123–32.

Duru, O. K., Xu, H., Tseng, C.-H., Mirkin, M., Ang, A., Tallen, L., Moore, A. A. and Ettner, S. L. (2010). Correlates of alcohol-related discussions between older adults and their physicians. *Journal of the American Geriatrics Society*, 58(12), 2369–74.

Ettner, S. L., Xu, H., Duru, O. K., Ang, A., Tseng, C.-H., Tallen, L., Barnes, A., Mirkin, M., Ransohoff, K. and Moore, A. A. (2014). The effect of an educational intervention on alcohol consumption, at-risk drinking, and health care utilization in older adults: the Project SHARE study. *Journal of Studies on Alcohol and Drugs*, 75(3), 447–57.

Ewing, J. A. (1984). Detecting alcoholism. The CAGE questionnaire. *JAMA (Journal of the American Medical Association)*, 252(14), 1905–7.

Fink, A., Morton, S. C., Beck, J. C., Hays, R. D., Spritzer, K., Oishi, S. and Moore, A. A. (2002a). The alcohol-related problems survey: identifying hazardous and harmful drinking in older primary care patients. *Journal of the American Geriatrics Society*, 50(10), 1717–22.

Fink, A., Tsai, M. C., Hays, R. D., Moore, A. A., Morton, S. C., Spritzer, K. and Beck, J. C. (2002b). Comparing the alcohol-related problems survey (ARPS) to traditional alcohol screening measures in elderly outpatients. *Archives of Gerontology and Geriatrics*, 34(1), 55–78.

Fink, A., Elliott, M. N., Tsai, M. and Beck, J. C. (2005). An evaluation of an intervention to assist primary care physicians in screening and educating older patients who use alcohol. *Journal of the American Geriatrics Society*, 53(11), 1937–43.

Fleming, M. F., Manwell, L. B., Barry, K. L., Adams, W. and Stauffacher, E. A. (1999). Brief physician advice for alcohol problems in older adults: a randomized community-based trial. *Journal of Family Practice*, 48(5), 378–84.

Geels, L. M., Vink, J. M., van Beek, J. H., Bartels, M., Willemsen, G. and Boomsma, D. I. (2013). Increases in alcohol consumption in women and elderly groups: evidence from an epidemiological study. *BMC Public Health*, 13(1), 207.

Gilson, K.-M., Bryant, C. and Judd, F. (2014). Exploring risky drinking and knowledge of safe drinking guidelines in older adults. *Substance Use and Misuse*, 49(11), 1473–9.

Hallgren, M., Hogberg, P. and Andreasson, S. (2009). *Alcohol Consumption Among Elderly European Union Citizens: Health Effects, Consumption Trends and Related Issues*. Ostersund: Swedish National Institute of Public Health.

Han, B., Gfroerer, J. C., Colliver, J. D. and Penne, M. A. (2009). Substance use disorder among older adults in the United States in 2020. *Addiction*, 104(1), 88–96.

Harvey, R. J., Skelton-Robinson, M. and Rossor, M. N. (2003). The prevalence and causes of dementia in people under the age of 65 years. *Journal of Neurology, Neurosurgery, and Psychiatry*, 74(9), 1206–9.

Hoeck, S. and Van Hal, G. (2012). Unhealthy drinking in the Belgian elderly population: prevalence and associated characteristics. *European Journal of Public Health*, 23, 1069–75.

Hoops, S., Nazem, S., Siderowf, A. D., Duda, J. E., Xie, S. X., Stern, M. B. and Weintraub, D. (2009). Validity of the MoCA and MMSE in the detection of MCI and dementia in Parkinson disease. *Neurology*, 21, 1738–45.

Hunter, B. and Lubman, D. I. (2010). Substance misuse: management in the older population. *Australian Family Physician*, 39(10), 738–41.

Jauhar, S. and Smith, I. D. (2009). Alcohol-related brain damage: not a silent epidemic. *The British Journal of Psychiatry*, 194(3), 287–8.

Kales, H. C., Kamholz, B. A., Visnic, S. G. and Blow, F. C. (2003). Recorded delirium in a national sample of elderly inpatients: potential implications for recognition. *Journal of Geriatric Psychiatry and Neurology*, 16(1), 32–8.

Kim, J. W., Lee, D. Y., Lee, B. C., Jung, M. H., Kim, H., Choi, Y. S. and Choi, I.-G. (2012). Alcohol and cognition in the elderly: a review. *Psychiatry Investigation*, 9(1), 8–16.

Knott, C. S., Scholes, S. and Shelton, N. J. (2013). Could more than three million older people in England be at risk of alcohol-related harm? A cross-sectional analysis of proposed age-specific drinking limits. *Age and Ageing*, 42(5), 598–603.

Koenig, H. G., George, L. K. and Schneider, R. (1994). Mental health care for older adults in the year 2020: a dangerous and avoided topic. *Gerontologist*, 34(5), 674–9.

Kraemer, K. L., Conigliaro, J. and Saitz, R. (1999). Managing alcohol withdrawal in the elderly. *Drugs and Aging*, 14(6), 409–25.

Kraemer, K. L., Mayo-Smith, M. F. and Calkins, D. R. (1997). Impact of age on the severity, course, and complications of alcohol withdrawal. *Archives of Internal Medicine*, 157(19), 2234–41.

Kumar, R., Dear, K. B. G., Christensen, H., Ilschner, S., Jorm, A. F., Meslin, C., Rosenman, S. J. and Sachdev, P. S. (2005). Prevalence of mild cognitive impairment in 60- to 64-year-old community-dwelling individuals: the Personality and Total Health through Life 60+ study. *Dementia and Geriatric Cognitive Disorders*, 19(2–3), 67–74.

Lam, B., Middleton, L. E., Masellis, M., Stuss, D. T., Harry, R. D., Kiss, A. and Black, S. E. (2013). Criterion and convergent validity of the Montreal cognitive assessment with screening and standardized neuropsychological testing. *Journal of the American Geriatrics Society*, 61(12), 2181–5.

Lee, J. Y., Dong Woo, L., Cho, S. J., Na, D. L., Hong Jin, J., Kim, S. K., You Ra, L., Youn, J. H., Kwon, M., Lee, J. H. and Maeng, J. C. (2008). Brief screening for mild cognitive impairment in elderly outpatient clinic: validation of the korean version of the Montreal Cognitive Assessment. *Journal of Geriatric Psychiatry and Neurology*, 21(2), 104–10.

Li, D., Zhao, H. and Gelernter, J. (2011). Strong association of the alcohol dehydrogenase 1(ADH1B) with alcohol dependence and alcohol-induced medical diseases. *Biological Psychiatry*, 70(6), 504–12.

Lin, J. C., Karno, M. P., Grella, C. E., Warda, U., Liao, D. H., Hu, P. and Moore, A. A. (2011). Alcohol, tobacco, and nonmedical drug use disorders in US adults aged 65 years and older: data from the 2001–2002 National Epidemiologic Survey of Alcohol and Related Conditions. *The American Journal of Geriatric Psychiatry*, 19(3), 292–9.

Lobo, E., Dufouil, C., Marcos, G., Quetglas, B., Saz, P., Guallar, E., Lobo, A. (2010). Is there an association between low-to-moderate alcohol consumption and risk of cognitive decline? *American Journal of Epidemiology*, 172(6), 708–16.

MacPhail, A., McDonough, M. and Ibrahim, J. E. (2013). Delayed discharge in alcohol-related dementia: consequences and possibilities for improvement. *Australian Health Review*, 37(4), 482–7.

MacRae, R. and Cox, S. (2003). *Meeting the Needs of People with Alcohol Related Brain Damage: A Literature Review on the Existing and Recommended Service Provision and Models of Care.* Stirling: Dementia Services Development Centre.

Mayo-Smith, M. F., Beecher, L. H., Fischer, T. L., Gorelick, D. A., Guillaume, J. L., Hill, A., Jara, G., Kasser, C. and Melbourne, J. (2004). Management of alcohol withdrawal delirium: an evidence-based practice guideline. *Archives of Internal Medicine*, 164(13), 1405–12.

McCabe, L. F. (2011). Alcohol, ageing and dementia: a Scottish perspective. *Dementia*, 10(2), 149–63.

McInnes, E. and Powell, J. (1994). Drug and alcohol referrals: are elderly substance abuse diagnoses and referrals being missed? *British Medical Journal*, 308(6926), 444–6.

Moore, A. A., Beck, J. C., Babor, T. F., Hays, R. D. and Reuben, D. B. (2002). Beyond alcoholism: identifying older, at-risk drinkers in primary care. *Journal of Studies on Alcohol*, 63(3), 316–24.

Moos, R. H., Schutte, K. K., Brennan, P. L. and Moos, B. S. (2010). Late-life and life history predictors of older adults' high-risk alcohol consumption and drinking problems. *Drug and Alcohol Dependence*, 108(1–2), 13–20.

Mulinga, J. D. (1999). Elderly people with alcohol-related problems: where do they go? *International Journal of Geriatric Psychiatry*, 14(7), 564–6.

Naegle, M. A. (2007). *Alcohol Use Screening and Assessment for Older Adults*. Retrieved 20 June 2014, from http://consultgerirn.org/uploads/File/trythis/try_this_17.pdf

National Health and Medical Research Council. (2009). *Australian Guidelines to Reduce Health Risks from Drinking Alcohol*. Canberra: NHMRC.

National Institute of Aging and US Department of State. (2007). *Why Population Aging Matters: A Global Perspective. Publication No. 07-6134.* Washington DC.

National Institute on Alcohol Abuse and Alcoholism. (1998). *Alcohol and Aging. Alcohol Alert No. 40.* Retrieved 25 June 2014, from http://pubs.niaaa.nih.gov/publications/aa40.htm

Nordström, P., Nordström, A., Eriksson, M., Wahlund, L.-O. and Gustafson, Y. (2013). Risk factors in late adolescence for young-onset dementia in men: a nationwide cohort study. *JAMA Internal Medicine*, 173(17), 1612–18.

O'Connell, H., Chin, A.-V., Cunningham, C. and Lawlor, B. (2003). Alcohol use disorders in elderly people: redefining an age old problem in old age. *British Medical Journal*, 327(7416), 664–7.

O'Connell, H., Chin, A. V., Hamilton, F., Cunningham, C., Walsh, J., Coakley, D. and Lawlor, B. A. (2004). A systematic review of the utility of self-report alcohol screening instruments in the elderly. *International Journal of Geriatric Psychiatry*, 19(11), 1074–86.

Oslin, D. W. and Cary, M. S. (2003). Alcohol-related dementia: validation of diagnostic criteria. *The American Journal of Geriatric Psychiatry*, 11(4), 441–7.

Panza, F., Frisardi, V., Seripa, D., Logroscino, G., Santamato, A., Imbimbo, B. P., Scafato, E., Pilotto, A. and Solfrizzi, V. (2012). Alcohol consumption in mild cognitive impairment and dementia: harmful or neuroprotective? *International Journal of Geriatric Psychiatry*, 27(12), 1218–38.

Patterson, T. L. and Jeste, D. V. (1999). The potential impact of the baby-boom generation on substance abuse among elderly persons. *Psychiatric Services*, 50(9), 1184–8.

Rakshi, M., Wilson, I., Burrow, S. and Holland, M. (2011). How can older people's mental health services in the UK respond to the escalating prevalence of alcohol misuse among older adults? *Advances in Dual Diagnosis*, 4, 17–27.

Rao, R. and Shanks, A. (2011). Development and implementation of a dual diagnosis strategy for older people in south east London. *Advances in Dual Diagnosis*, 4, 28–35.

Ridley, N. J. and Draper, B. (2014). Alcohol-related dementia and brain damage: a focus on epidemiology. In J. Svanberg, A. Withall, B. Draper and S. Bowden (eds), *Alcohol and the Adult Brain*. Hove: Psychology Press.

Ridley, N. J., Draper, B. and Withall, A. (2013). Alcohol-related dementia: an update of the evidence. *Alzheimer's Research and Therapy*, 5(1).

Rigler, S. K. (2000). Alcoholism in the elderly. *American Family Physician*, 61(6), 1710–16, 1883.

Ritchie, S. J., Bates, T. C., Corley, J., McNeill, G., Davies, G., Liewald, D. C., Starr, J. M. and Deary, I. J. (2014). Alcohol consumption and lifetime change in cognitive ability: a gene × environment interaction study. *Age*, 36(3), 9638.

Rota-Bartelink, A. (2006). *Models of Care for Elderly People with Complex Care Needs Arising from Alcohol-related Dementia and Brain Injury*. Victoria, Australia: Wintringham.

Sabia, S., Elbaz, A., Britton, A., Bell, S., Dugravot, A., Shipley, M., Kivimaki, M. and Singh-Manoux, A. (2014). Alcohol consumption and cognitive decline in early old age. *Neurology*, 82(4), 332–9.

Salem, L. C., Andersen, B. B., Nielsen, T. R., Stokholm, J., Jørgensen, M. B., Rasmussen, M. H. and Waldemar, G. (2012). Overdiagnosis of dementia in young patients: a nationwide register-based study. *Dementia and Geriatric Cognitive Disorders*, 34(5–6), 292–9.

Schappert, S. M. (1999). Ambulatory care visits to physician offices, hospital outpatient departments, and emergency departments: United States, 1997. National Center for Health Statistics. *Vital Health Statistics*, 13(143).

Schonfeld, L., King-Kallimanis, B. L., Duchene, D. M., Etheridge, R. L., Herrera, J. R., Barry, K. L. and Lynn, N. (2010). Screening and brief intervention for substance misuse among older adults: the Florida BRITE project. *American Journal of Public Health*, 100(1), 108–14.

Smith, D. M. and Atkinson, R. M. (1995). Alcoholism and dementia. *International Journal of the Addictions*, 30(13–14), 1843–69.

Speckens, A. E., Heeren, T. J. and Rooijmans, H. G. (1991). Alcohol abuse among elderly patients in a general hospital as identified by the Munich Alcoholism Test. *Acta psychiatrica Scandinavica*, 83(6), 460–2.

Stern, R. A. and White, T. (2003). *Neuropsychological Assessment Battery: Administration, Scoring, and Interpretation Manual*. Lutz, FL: Psychological Assessment Resources.

Svanberg, J., Morrison, F. and Cullen, B. (2015). Neuropsychological assessment of alcohol-related cognitive impairment. In J. Svanberg, A. Withall, B. Draper and S. Bowden (eds), *Alcohol and the Adult Brain*. Hove: Psychology Press.

Taheri, A., Dahri, K., Chan, P., Shaw, M., Aulakh, A. and Tashakkor, A. (2014). Evaluation of a symptom-triggered protocol approach to the management of alcohol withdrawal syndrome in older adults. *Journal of the American Geriatrics Society*, 24 June.

Teri, L., Hughes, J. P. and Larson, E. B. (1990). Cognitive deterioration in Alzheimer's disease behavioral and health factors. *Journal of Gerontology*, 45(2), 58–63.

Wadd, S., Randall, J., Thake, A., Edwards, K., Galvani, S., McCabe, L. and Coleman, A. (2013). *Alcohol Misuse and Cognitive Impairment in Older People*. London: Alcohol Research UK.

Wang, Y.-P. and Andrade, L. H. (2013). Epidemiology of alcohol and drug use in the elderly. *Current Opinion in Psychiatry*, 26(4), 343–8.

Wester, A. J., Westhoff, J., Kessels, R. P. C. and Egger, J. I. M. (2013). The Montreal Cognitive Assessment (MoCA) as a measure of severity of amnesia in patients with alcohol-related cognitive impairments and Korsakoff syndrome. *Clinical Neuropsychiatry*, 10(3–4), 134–41.

Whelan, G. (2003). Alcohol: a much neglected risk factor in elderly mental disorders. *Current Opinion in Psychiatry*, 16(6), 609–14.

Wilsnack, S. C. and Wilsnack, R. W. (1995). Drinking and problem drinking in US women: patterns and recent trends. *Recent Developments in Alcoholism*, 12, 29–60.

Wilson, K. and Halsey, A. (2010) Commissioned services for people with alcohol-related brain damage. *Neuropsychiatry News: Newsletter of the Section of Neuropsychiatry*, Royal College of Psychiatrists. London: RCP.

Wilson, K., Halsey, A., Macpherson, H., Billington, J., Hill, S., Johnson, G., Raju, K. and Abbott, P. (2012). The psychosocial rehabilitation of patients with alcohol-related brain damage in the community. *Alcohol and Alcoholism*, 47(3), 304–11.

Withall, A., Draper, B., Seeher, K. and Brodaty, H. (2014). The prevalence and causes of younger onset dementia in Eastern Sydney, Australia. *International Psychogeriatrics*.

7

ALCOHOL-RELATED BRAIN DAMAGE AND NEUROPATHOLOGY

Lisa Savage

It has been well established that excessive and chronic alcohol consumption leads to permanent damage to the brain, resulting in functional motor and cognitive loss. However, there can be recovery of some brain structure and behavioral function with prolonged abstinence. Autopsy evaluation and in-vivo neuroimaging of the brains of people with diagnosed alcohol dependence have demonstrated that approximately 78 per cent of this population exhibit significant brain pathology (Goldstein and Shelley, 1980; Harper, 1998). However, the clinical presentation of brain damage in this group is heterogeneous, which is a result of the range of associated behavioral problems (such as poor eating habits, poly-drug abuse, physical accidents, repeated intoxication and withdrawal cycles) that accompany the lifestyle of those with alcohol dependence. The term "uncomplicated alcoholics" refers to patients that display *structural changes to the brain as a function of chronic alcohol consumption* (i.e., alcohol-related brain damage: ARBD), but have not been diagnosed with liver disease or nutritional deficiency states (Zahr, Kaufman and Harper, 2011). A history of heavy alcohol consumption is a cardinal feature in the criteria for ARBD. It has been suggested that more than 35 drinks/week for men or 28 drinks/week for women for a period of five years can produce a neurotoxic burden sufficient to lead to brain pathology (Oslin *et al.*, 1998). "Complicated alcoholics" refers to patients with a history of heavy drinking as well as other health problems, such as liver disease or nutritional deficiency, which in their own right can cause severe brain damage and dysfunction (Harper, 2009). However, even with this differentiation, the mechanisms that underlie ARBD are complex and include the direct neurotoxic effects of alcohol, thiamine deficiency, withdrawal syndromes, cerebrovascular disease, hepatic encephalopathy and head injury (Kopelman *et al.*, 2009).

Although the literature refers to the dichotomy of "uncomplicated" and "complicated" alcoholic populations, it is in fact difficult to differentially diagnose people with alcohol dependence along several dimensions. In addition, clinicians and researchers have referred to a *spectrum of ARBD* and the neuropsychological sequelae of that spectrum, which are graded through the range of those with "uncomplicated alcoholism" to include those with the added complication of thiamine deficiency or liver disease (e.g., Bowden, 1990; Joyce, 1994; Victor, Adams and Collins, 1989; Harper, 1998).

People with alcohol dependence are prone to nutritional deficiency because sustained heavy alcohol consumption often occurs at the expense of food consumption (Santolaria *et al.*, 2000). In a cohort of heavy drinkers, as much as 60 per cent of caloric intake came from alcohol (Manari, Preedy and Peters, 2003), and in this sample the intake of vitamins were below recommended levels. Thus, malnourishment often coexists with chronic alcoholism due to poor diet as well as decreased absorption and/or utilization of nutrients – in particular thiamine (B1). Thiamine status is altered in uncomplicated alcoholics (Alexander-Kaufman *et al.*, 2007; Pitel *et al.*, 2011). Those with alcohol dependence are at particular risk for the development of thiamine deficiency because of impaired thiamine absorption, storage and reduced phosphorylation (Zahr, Kaufman and Harper, 2011). As many as 80 per cent are deficient in thiamine to some extent (Galvin *et al.*, 2010) and if left untreated thiamine deficiency can lead to Wernicke's Encephalopathy (WE). Without restoration of thiamine, WE can further progress to Wernicke-Korsakoff Syndrome (WKS). WE, the acute phase of WKS, has been historically diagnosed by a classic triad of symptoms: oculomotor disturbances, motor-ataxia abnormalities and global confusion (Victor, Adams and Collins, 1971). The primary diagnostic feature of the permanent WKS is profound amnesia, both retrograde and anterograde (Victor, Adams and Collins, 1989), but there are also impairments of perceptual and abstract problem-solving skills (see Butters and Cermack, 1974; Oscar-Berman, 2012; Parsons and Nixon, 1993). Despite their clear diagnostic criteria, WE and WKS due to alcohol dependence are diagnosed more commonly at post-mortem autopsy than when the person is alive (Harper, 2007). Indeed, post-mortem prevalence rates of WKS are 1 to 2 per cent in the general population but 12 to 14 per cent in the population with alcohol dependence (Harper, Kril and Holloway, 1985; Harper, 1998). This is likely due to that fact that the classic triad of WE symptoms is only observed in a minority of patients.

This has led to a re-evaluation of WE-associated criteria due to alcoholism for both post-mortem evaluation (see Caine *et al.*, 1997) and patient clinical diagnosis (see Galvin *et al.*, 2010). An approach that has been endorsed by the European Federation of Neurological Societies requires the presence of only two of the following four signs: (1) history of dietary deficiencies, (2) oculomotor abnormalities, (3) cerebellar dysfunction and (4) altered mental state or memory impairment. A recent study by Pitel and colleagues (2011) categorized people with alcohol dependence according to the above criteria. It was found that 16 per cent had a diagnosis of WE (two or more signs), 57 per cent were at risk for WE (positive for one sign) and 27 per cent did not display any signs of WE. It is important to note that when these new criteria were used, the percentage of living patients with alcohol dependence who are diagnosed with WE/WKS matched post-mortem studies. The most prevalent signs were dietary deficiency (57 per cent) and ataxia (36 per cent). Further, these symptomatic subgroups did not differ in their lifetime consumption of alcohol or sobriety duration. Those with alcohol dependence that did not meet any of the criteria for WE risk did not differ from control participants on any neuropsychological measure. However, the groups who met one or two of the criteria showed significant graded deficits on memory measures (Wechsler memory scale), visuospatial tasks (Rey-Osterrieth complex figure task) and speed of processing (digital symbol subtest of the WAIS-R). In addition, those positive for two criteria displayed impaired executive functioning (trail-making task) and dysfunction in upper limb motor skills (fine finger movement test, grooved pegboard test). These findings provide evidence that mild to moderate thiamine deficiency likely plays a role in the heterogeneity observed in the neuropathology and resultant cognitive and motor dysfunctions observed in chronic alcoholism.

Similar to the continuum of behavioral neuropsychological deficits, a graded degree of neuropathology has also been observed in recent studies when uncomplicated alcoholic patients are compared to patients complicated with WKS. Prior to addressing the issue of whether a dichotomy or spectrum best describes ARBD, a review of neuropathology associated with chronic alcoholism is presented.

Neuropathology in alcohol-related disorders

The earliest reports of brain abnormalities in patients with excessive alcohol consumption were non-specific findings from computed tomography (CT) imaging and post-mortem data. For instance, CT studies in chronic alcoholism described reductions in total brain volume (Harper and Blumbergs, 1982) and clinical pathology reports revealed reduced brain weights in people with alcohol dependence compared to control participants. Pathology only occurred, however, in selective cortical and subcortical regions (Kril et al., 1997). As technology advanced, the most consistent findings were ventricular enlargement and sulcal widening associated with cortical white matter shrinkage, gray matter volume reductions and neural loss in the septal region and cerebellum (Cullen et al., 1997; Harper, 1998; Lishman, 1990; Parsons and Nixon, 1993; Pfefferbaum et al., 1992). Somewhat surprising was that while some imaging studies revealed hippocampal volume decreases in human chronic alcoholism (Sullivan and Marsh, 2003; Pitel et al., 2009), neuropathological examination found little to no neuronal loss in the hippocampus of those with alcohol dependence compared to control participants (Harding et al., 1997). One suggestion is that volume loss in the hippocampus may be caused by a reduction in white matter, not gray matter (Harding et al., 1997).

A cardinal feature of ARBD observed in both pathology examinations (Harper and Kril, 1990) and imaging studies (Pfefferbaum et al., 1996) is a reduction in white matter. Reduced corpus callosum volume and white matter degeneration in the cerebellum, particularly the vermis, have been reported (Sullivan et al., 2000a; Sullivan et al., 2000b). Alcohol-induced white matter loss across brain regions has contributed to both myelin loss and the degradation of axonal circuitry (Pfefferbaum and Sullivan, 2005). In uncomplicated alcoholics, thinning of the corpus callosum, documented by in-vivo magnetic resonance imaging (MRI), was associated with reductions in the frontal lobes (Pfefferbaum *et al.*, 1996) and concomitant compromise of ponto–cerebellar and cerebello–thalamocortical systems (Sullivan *et al.*, 2003). Such white matter loss is a key contributor to circuit-level dysfunction that will be discussed in a following section.

The most vulnerable cortical region to alcoholism appears to be the frontal cortex (Dirksen *et al.*, 2006; Oscar-Berman *et al.*, 2004; Pfefferbaum *et al.*, 1997; Ratti *et al.*, 2002). Examination of post-mortem tissue from the Australian brain bank has revealed decreased neuron density (15 to 23 per cent) in the frontal cortex of people with alcohol dependence (Harper and Matsumoto, 2005). Likewise in-vivo imaging methods have shown frontal cortex abnormalities, including decreased frontal lobe volume detected by MRI (Pfefferbaum *et al.*, 1997), abridged regional blood flow measurements (Gansler *et al.*, 2000) and decreased amplitude of event-related potentials during cognitive processing (Chen *et al.*, 2007).

Numerous studies have revealed significant neuropathological differences between WKS and non-WKS (uncomplicated) alcoholics. While non-WKS patients typically show some degree of structural abnormalities in several of the same regions as WKS patients, it is often less severe. For example, WKS patients have wider third ventricles, larger lateral ventricles and wider interhemispheric fissures than uncomplicated chronic alcoholics (Sullivan and Pfefferbaum, 2009). However, sulcal and Sylvian fissure widths are equivalent in those with WKS and non-WKS (Jacobson and Lishman, 1990). Adding further credence to the notion of a continuum of pathology, a graded pattern of volumetric deficits were observed, from mild in uncomplicated alcoholics to moderate and severe in WKS-diagnosed patients, in the frontal cortex, mammillary bodies, hippocampus, thalamus, cerebellum and pons (Sullivan and Pfefferbaum, 2009). However, even though chronic alcoholism is associated with mammillary body and cerebellar tissue volume loss, these markers do not distinguish between amnesic and non-amnesic cases (Shear *et al.*, 1996).

Studies by Harper and colleagues (1998, 2007) further suggest that thiamine deficiency is a key feature mediating ARBD. In WKS patients, regardless of aetiology of thiamine deficiency (different diseases or conditions that result in restricted eating or limit adequate vitamin absorption), a prominent neuropathological consequence is volume and neuronal loss in the anterior and midline thalamic nuclei, as well as the mammillary bodies (Mair *et al.*, 1991; Mayes *et al.*, 1988; Savage, Hall and Resende, 2012). This extent of pathology is not evident in patients without WKS. Recent studies suggest that the amnesic syndrome in WKS is due to damage in the diencephalic-hippocampal circuitry that relies upon the anterior thalamic nucleus and mammillary bodies (Sullivan and Marsh, 2003; Savage, Hall and Resende, 2012).

Harding and colleagues (2000) performed an extensive analysis of pathology of the diencephalon with a unique classification system for the brain of patients with chronic alcoholism. Patients were categorized into four groups: controls (no history of alcoholism: CON), alcohol dependence cases that did not have any mammillary body (MMB) pathology (defined in this study as uncomplicated alcoholics: ALC), alcohol dependence cases with MMB damage but not severe memory loss (WE) and alcohol dependence cases with MMB damage and severe memory loss (WKS). They found that MMB volume related to graded shrinkage across conditions (MMB size: CON>ALC>WE>WKS). Furthermore, MMB damage was correlated with duration of WE episode, which was determined by patient records. Volume and cell loss in the medial thalamus was also determined. In contrast to pathology of the MMB, the volume of the medial thalamus was not altered in uncomplicated alcoholics, slightly damaged in WE and severely reduced in WKS patients. Volume loss in the medial thalamus was correlated with atrophy of the cerebrum. Within the medial thalamus, the medial dorsal nucleus (MD) was the most consistently affected by WE (with and without amnesia). Pathology was extensive and included vascular hypertrophy and hyperplasia and neuronal loss. There was no MD neuronal loss in uncomplicated alcoholics relative to control subjects. Patients with WE displayed fewer neurons than alcoholics or controls, but the loss of neurons in MD was equal across WE brains regardless of whether diagnosis included amnesia. The extent of MD and anterior thalamus (AT) atrophy correlated with the duration of WE. There was no pathology in other thalamic nuclei, such as the lateral nucleus or the pulvinar nucleus of the thalamus. In the AT the loss of neurons, relative to controls, was only seen in WE patients who displayed amnesia (i.e., WKS patients). Neither uncomplicated alcoholics nor non-amnestic WE patients displayed significant loss of neurons in the AT. The loss of AT neurons correlated with the total volume of the AT. Although MD and MMB had been implicated as critical pathology in WE and WKS in prior studies (Victor, Adams and Collins, 1989), the stereological neuropathological analysis by Harding and colleagues (2000) provided quantitative evidence that the loss of AT neurons is critical for a diagnosis of WKS and may be the site of differential pathology critical of the amnestic state that can follow alcohol-related thiamine deficiency.

There exists a suggestion that alcohol toxicity and thiamine deficiency may have some overlap in cortical dysfunction, but there are clear distinctions in pathology with regard to specific diencephalic regions. In mice, seven months of chronic exposure to ethanol in drinking water produced about a 30 per cent loss of neurons in the mammillary bodies and the remaining neurons exhibited shrunken nuclei (Lescaudron et al., 1995). Furthermore, mice that drank high volumes of ethanol had a slight loss (about 9 to 15 per cent) of neurons in the AT and in the MD thalamus (Berecochea et al., 1987). The pyrithiamine-induced thiamine deficiency (PTD) model of WKS in rats results in dramatic loss of neurons (>50 per cent) in the medial mammillary bodies and a complete loss of neurons to the ventrolateral part of the anteroventral nucleus of the thalamus, but marginal loss to the ventral MD nucleus (Langlais and Savage, 1995; Savage, Hall and Resende, 2012; Vetreno, Hall and Savage, 2011; Vetreno et al., 2012). Thus, experimental models tell us that long-term heavy ethanol intake can reduce the integrity of the diencephalon slightly to moderately. However, whether thiamine deficiency starts to emerge in long-term ethanol exposure in these models is questionable. Subramanian, Subramanian and Said (2010) reported that chronic alcohol consumption in rats moderately reduces thiamine pyrophosphokinase, an enzyme involved in the regulation of thiamine metabolism. Extensive thiamine deficiency can produce persistent and significant loss of neurons in key diencephalic structures, such as the AT and medial mammillary bodies.

The opposite effect occurs in the hippocampus, where chronic ethanol treatment results in a 10 to 40 per cent reduction in neuronal populations (pyramidal cells, granule cells and interneurons) with a concomitant 20 to 60 per cent decrease in the density of dendritic processes (Bengoechea and Gonzalo, 1991; Franke *et al.*, 1997; Paula-Barbosa *et al.*, 1993; Riley and Walker, 1978; Walker *et al.*, 1980; Walker, King and Hunter, 1993). Neurogenesis is inhibited by chronic ethanol exposure by over 60 per cent (Herrea *et al.*, 2003). In contrast, cell loss in the hippocampus has not been documented after thiamine deficiency (Mair *et al.*, 1991) and hippocampal neurogenesis is only disrupted by about 20 per cent in the PTD model (Vetreno, Klintsova and Savage, 2011).

Although damage to the hippocampus is not always observed in WKS (Reed *et al.*, 2003; Squire, Amaral and Press, 1990; but see Sullivan and Marsh, 2003 and Pitel *et al.*, 2009), both the AT and mammillary bodies are directly connected to the hippocampus (Gabriel and Sparenborg, 1986; Gabriel, Sparenborg and Stolar, 1987; Van Groen and Wyss, 1995) and form the *hippocampal-diencephalic memory circuit* (see Aggleton and Brown, 2006; Savage, Chang and Gold, 2003). Thiamine deficiency creates significant cell loss in AT and mammillary bodies. This loss leads to impaired hippocampal functioning, particularly when the system is activated by behavioral demands (Savage, Hall and Resende, 2012).

A recent study directly compared brain damage in uncomplicated alcoholism to that in alcoholism complicated with WKS (Pitel *et al.*, 2012; Beaunieux, Eustache and Pitel, 2014). Several regions of interest were examined and a continuum of brain damage, rather than a dichotomy of distinct differences, was observed. First, although there was widespread gray matter loss in both patients with alcoholism and WKS patients compared to control participants, the cortical regions most significantly affected were the orbitofrontal cortex, parietal lobe, cingulate cortex, insula and medial temporal lobe. The cerebellum was also affected in both patient populations. Subcortical regions of the thalamus and hypothalamus (primarily the mammillary bodies) displayed significant reductions. Graded effects of volume deficits (total volume: CON>ALC>WKS) were found in the medial portion of the mammillary bodies and left insula. White matter volume loss was also observed in patients with alcoholism and WKS patients in the corpus callosum, fornix, cingulum and cerebellar peduncles. While there were graded effects of white matter loss in the corpus callosum, the reduction of thalamic fibers (left thalamic radiation) was only seen in WKS patients. Again, we see a pattern of results pointing towards thalamic pathology as key to the amnestic syndrome associated with WKS.

Circuit dysfunction

Papez circuit

Present data indicate that extensive damage to limbic structures combined with atrophy of prefrontal cortical regions is consistently associated with alcoholic-WKS, but significant limbic pathology is not observed in uncomplicated alcoholics (Moselhy, Georgious and Kahn, 2001; Oscar-Berman *et al.*, 2004; Pitel *et al.*, 2009). Volume/neuronal loss in the limbic thalamus is a critical neuropathological feature of WKS. Shrinkage is observed in the anterior and midline thalamic nuclei, as well as mammillary bodies (Caulo *et al.*, 2005; Harding, Halliday and Kril, 2000; Pitel *et al.*, 2012). Pitel and colleagues (2009) found significantly lower gray matter density in the thalamus and mammillary bodies of WKS patients, relative to controls. They also found reductions in gray matter density in the key limbic cortical regions of the hippocampus and parahippocampus, supporting the notion that medial temporal abnormalities can occur in WKS as previously reported by the same research group (Sullivan and Marsh, 2003). In addition to morphological abnormalities in these critical nuclei within the Papez circuit, Pitel and colleagues (2012) also reported disruption of white matter tracts that connect several limbic regions. The superior part of the fornix and inferior part of the cingulum bundle displayed decreased density. This loss of white matter likely impairs connectivity between the cingulate cortex, hippocampus and mammillary bodies.

Kim and colleagues (2009) conducted a resting-state functional connectivity study using fMRI to assess the strength between the AT and mammillary bodies in WE patients, patients with uncomplicated alcoholism and control participants. It was found that that WE patients had significantly reduced anterior thalamic-mammillary body connectivity relative to controls and the connective strength of alcoholics fell between the two groups. Furthermore, significant correlations were also seen between left-sided connectivity strength and several memory measures when the data of WE patients were combined with the data of controls, but was absent when patients with alcoholism were included.

The gray and white matter abnormalities within the limbic network, in particular the diencephalon (thalamus and mammillary bodies), appears to play a key role in presentation of the severe amnestic state associated with WKS (see Figure 7.1). Although slight damage to the diencephalon may occur in uncomplicated alcoholism, the pathology is not severe enough to result in functional loss within this circuit.

Fronto-cerebellar circuit

In contrast to the Papez/limbic circuit, the fronto-cerebellar circuit appears equally disrupted in both uncomplicated alcoholic and alcoholic-WKS patients. The frontal cortex displays extreme sensitivity to alcohol toxicity, and the superior cerebellar vermis is also a region of vulnerability. Examination of the brains of alcoholics with and without WKS revealed that cerebellar atrophy of the vermis occurs in 25 to 40 per cent of uncomplicated alcoholics and in about 35 to 50 per cent of WKS brains (Victor, Adams and Collins, 1989). Both in-vivo human neuroimaging and postmortem examination has revealed reductions in gray and white matter in the anterior superior vermis of the cerebellum in alcoholics with and without WKS, as well as a loss of vermis Purkinje cells (36 per cent) in WKS patients (Baker *et al.*, 1999; Sullivan *et al.*, 2000a). Pontine oedema occurring in both the superior and inferior vestibular nuclei is also seen in WKS patients (Sullivan and Pfefferbaum, 2001).

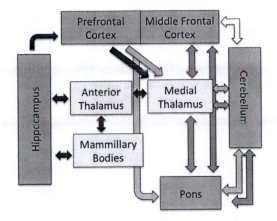

FIGURE 7.1 Brain regions damaged by thiamine deficiency (light gray) and by alcohol and thiamine deficiency (dark gray) Arrows mark circuits (black = limbic/Papez circuit; gray = frontocerebellar loops [see Chanraud *et al.*, 2013; light gray = executive loop; dark gray = motor loop; white = novel compensatory loop] that become altered in WKS patients (black and gray arrows) and in uncomplicated alcoholics (gray and white arrows).

Studies looking at concomitant loss across several selective brain regions have found changes to the main nodes and connections of the fronto-cerebellar circuitry linking the frontal cortex to the thalamus and cerebellum via the ventral pons (Sullivan, 2003; Sullivan *et al.*, 2003; Pitel *et al.*, 2009; see Figure 7.1). Fronto-cerebellar circuitry dysfunction has been implicated because volume shrinkage in the pons and thalamus are associated with volume loss in the cerebellum and cortex (Pfefferbaum and Sullivan, 2002; Pfefferbaum *et al.* 2005; Sullivan *et al.*, 2003). A study by Sullivan and colleagues (2003) found a significant correlation between volume of the thalamus and cortical gray matter. In addition, correlations were also found between both white and gray matter volumes in prefrontal cortex and the four regions of the vermis. The pattern of correlation observed in alcoholism patients (but not control patients) suggested that both the ponto-cerebellar and cerebello-thalamocortical circuits were distinctly disrupted by alcoholism. Disruption of these circuits is likely involved in the two primary classes of neurological impairment seen in patients with alcoholism and WKS patients: (1) gait and balance deficits and (2) and deficits in executive functioning (Oscar–Berman, 2012).

Other critical issues

Amount of alcohol consumed and age of drinking initiation

As we have read, malnourishment is a critical variable in ARBD; however, several key factors, such as amount of alcohol consumed across the lifespan, age at which alcohol dependent behaviors emerge, are also important in the expression of ARBD. Although Pitel and colleagues (2011) revealed that lifetime alcohol consumption did not influence the expression of diagnostic criteria of thiamine deficiency or impaired cognitive functioning, Ding and colleagues (2004) showed that the more alcohol consumed, the greater the expansion in the brain's ventricles. In moderate drinkers, it was found that total brain volume correlated with amount of alcohol consumed (Paul et al., 2008). Volume of both the cortical white matter and thalamus are negatively correlated with alcohol consumption (Kril et al., 1997). Specifically, lifetime alcohol consumption correlated with regional degradation of white matter in alcoholic men, but not women (Pfefferbaum et al., 2009). Lifetime alcohol consumption was also significantly associated with level of deficit for gait and balance (Sullivan, 2003; Sullivan et al., 2003). More intense adolescent binge drinking has been linked to smaller cerebellar volumes (Lisdal et al., 2013). Additionally, prefrontal cortex volume significantly correlates with alcohol consumption in a study that examined adolescent onset of alcoholism (De Bellis et al., 2005).

Vetreno, Qin and Crews (2013) reported that factors associated with neuroinflammation are increased in the orbital frontal cortex of uncomplicated alcoholics (post-mortem). Furthermore, there was a correlation between an increase in neuronal pro-inflammatory mediators involved in chronic inflammatory reactions associated with neurotoxicity (high-mobility-group box-1 [HMGB1] protein, acting as an activator of toll-like receptors [TLR] and receptors for advanced glycation end products [RAGE]) and an early, adolescent, age of drinking onset. Modeling early onset of alcohol exposure in rodents, these researchers also found that binge ethanol exposure, beginning at peri-adolescence and persisting throughout adolescence, led to an increase in the expression of TLR and HMGB1 in the prefrontal cortex that endured into adulthood. Up-regulation of the pro-inflammatory mediators was correlated with learning impairments. In sum, both the clinical and preclinical data point towards the conclusion that peri-adolescent/adolescent exposure to high levels of alcohol activates chronic inflammatory reactions in the brain, which likely contribute to later adult brain and behavioral pathologies associated with chronic alcoholism.

A recent study (Kroenke et al., 2014), in which rhesus monkeys self-administered (consumed) alcohol, revealed that volume change in the hippocampus was significantly negatively correlated with average daily ethanol intake following six months of drinking. In addition, following six and 12 months of access to alcohol, monkeys classified as heavy drinkers (more than 3g/kg consumed/day) displayed significant decreases in overall cerebral cortical gray matter. Specifically, after six months of consumption, there were correlations between loss of volume in the hippocampus, parietal, occipital, temporal and allocortex. The posterior cingulate and fasciolar gyri of the allocortex showed the most consistent decrease in volume over time. Greater volume shrinkage occurred in monkeys with younger onset of drinking that ultimately became heavier drinkers relative to monkeys with older drinking onset. None of these changes were observed in non-heavy drinkers.

This is an interesting preclinical finding, given that cases of alcohol-related dementia generally have a younger age of drinking onset (Ritchie and Villebrun, 2008).

Thus, the factors of age of drinking onset, level of consumption and gender all influence the relationship between amount of alcohol consumed and brain alterations.

Recovery of function

Harper (2009) has stated that the brain pathology of abusers of alcohol likely has two components: one involves permanent change, the other is transient. Partial recovery of white matter disturbances can occur with abstinence, and MRI studies indicate early reversibility of white matter shrinkage. Such reversal is accompanied by clinical improvement in cognitive and motor abilities (Sullivan and Pfefferbaum, 2009; Schulte *et al.*, 2010). The mechanism behind recovery from white matter damage is thought to involve the restoration of myelination and axonal integrity, but both are vulnerable to repeated disruption if drinking is resumed (Sullivan, Harris and Pfefferbaum, 2010).

Longitudinal MRI studies of abstinent alcoholics have found that with short-term (one-month) abstinence from alcohol, there is a recovery in overall brain tissue mass (Bartsch *et al.*, 2007; Gazdzinski, Durazo and Meyerhoff, 2005), with specific increases in cortical gray matter (Pfefferbaum *et al.*, 1995), including volume recovery within the frontal and temporal lobes (Cardenas *et al.*, 2005) and hippocampus (Gazdzinski *et al.*, 2008). Short-term recovery of hippocampal volume was associated with improved visuo-spatial memory (Gazdzinski *et al.*, 2008). In abstinent alcoholics, the corpus collosum did display regional recovery in microstructural integrity (genu and body improved, but the splenium did not) over a period of one year (Alhassoon *et al.*, 2012).

Long periods of sobriety have been associated with reduced volume of the third ventricle (Pfefferbaum *et al.*, 1995). However, with alcohol relapse, there is an expansion of the third ventricle and shrinkage of white matter (Pfefferbaum *et al.*, 1995). Maintenance of sobriety is associated with improvements in several behavioral domains: reduced volume of the lateral ventricle has been correlated with improvements in memory, whereas reduced volume of the fourth ventricle after abstinence is associated with improvement in balance (Rosenbloom *et al.*, 2007). Shrinkage in third ventricle volume across two to 12 months was significantly correlated with improvement in nonverbal short-term memory (Sullivan, Rosenbloom and Pfefferbaum, 2000). Significant correlations have been found between sobriety length and prefrontal gray matter volume and there was a trend for improvement on the Wisconsin card-sorting test (Sullivan *et al.*, 2003) with increased sobriety length. Some behavioral functions in abstinent alcoholics return faster (working memory vs postural stability; Rosenbloom, Pfefferbaum and Sullivan, 2004). Additionally, some behavioral processes recover more fully than others. Severe deficits in gait and postural stability persist even after prolonged abstinence and are more severe than those in the cognitive domain (Sullivan *et al.*, 2000b; Sullivan, Rosenbloom and Pfefferbaum, 2000).

Some functional recovery in uncomplicated alcoholics appears to involve unique compensatory mechanisms that invoke novel brain circuits. When performing a verbal working memory task, a group with alcohol dependence showed greater activation in the left prefrontal cortex and the right superior cerebellum, compared with controls. Within this group, patients with this unique pattern were able to perform the task successfully, suggesting a compensatory pathway in the brains of patients with alcoholism who display little to no cognitive impairment (Desmond et al., 2003).

As mentioned previously, a circuit that is dysfunctional in a large subset of those with alcoholism (both complicated and uncomplicated phenotypes) is the fronto-cerebellar loop involved in motor sequencing, planning and spatial working (see Sullivan, 2003). The role of fronto-cerebellar circuitry in such cognitive functions has been documented by in-vivo functional imaging (Habas et al., 2009; Buckner et al., 2011). There is evidence that the brains of well-functioning patients with alcoholism evoke alternative and compensatory loops within the fronto-cerebellar system. As outlined in Chanraud et al. (2013), there are distinct loops for (a) executive functioning, which engages the prefrontal cortex, thalamus, pons and cerebellular region VI, and (b) the motor planning loop that involves the primary motor cortex, thalamus, pons and cerebellar region VIII. These two loops appear to intersect in the thalamus. However, in alcohol-dependent patients with normal cognitive functioning an alternative system is activated that involves the dorsal mediofrontal frontal cortex, which bypasses the thalamus and pons, to make direct connections with both cerebellar regions.

Summary and conclusions

Over 50 per cent of cases of detoxified patients with alcoholism display some degree of cognitive impairment and 75 per cent of autopsied patients with chronic alcoholism have significant brain damage (Dufour, 1993; Parsons and Nixon, 1993; Smith and Atkinson, 1995; Zahr, Kaufman and Harper, 2011). There appears to be a continuum of brain and behavioral dysfunction in those with alcoholism without disease complications and those with nutrition complications (WE or WKS). Numerous imaging studies have revealed that cortical and subcortical shrinkage, as well as ventricular enlargement, is greater in those with complicated versus uncomplicated alcoholism (Sullivan and Pfefferbaum, 2009). The frontal cortex and cerebellum are damaged by both alcohol toxicity and thiamine deficiency; however, more extensive anterior thalamic and mammillary body is only observed in WKS patients. These clinical data have been previously observed in animal models of such disorders (see Vetreno, Hall and Savage, 2011).

A synergistic interaction of neuropathology across discrete nodes within the Papez/limbic circuit (such as the frontal cortex, hippocampus, thalamus and mammillary bodies) leads to circuit-level dysfunction and the dramatically impaired learning and memory performance commonly observed in WKS patients. In contrast, the fronto-cerebellar systems appear equally disrupted in uncomplicated alcoholics as well as those with WE/WKS. However, when the classification of WE is modified to use the criteria outlined by Caine et al., (1997), we see that behavioral dysfunction, assumed to be caused by brain pathology is graded based on the number of symptoms of thiamine deficiency. These data suggest that mild to moderate thiamine deficiency can account for a significant proportion of the behavioral dysfunction associated with chronic alcohol consumption. Another hypothesis is that alcohol-induced cognitive impairment arises from the degradation of several nodes or white matter tracts that modulate the interactions between cortical, subcortical and cerebellar regions (Sullivan and Pfefferbaum, 2005).

In cases of chronic alcoholism without a diagnosis of WE/WKS, some of the brain damage and cognitive impairment appears to be reversible if abstinence is achieved. There is a subset of abstinent patients who do not display cognitive impairment. Recent imaging data have revealed that these patients use a novel circuit that bypasses the thalamus, suggesting that the brains of functioning patients with alcoholism undergo compensatory reorganization that enables them to perform successfully on some tasks. A more complete understanding of the variety of brain and behavioral dysfunction is needed to improve the diagnostic criteria for alcohol-related neurological disorders and to develop therapeutic strategies that are effective for the recovery of cognitive functions after chronic alcohol addiction. The combination of preclinical translational work, new in-vivo imaging techniques and the use of well-screened human post-mortem brain tissue has led to new insights about extent of pathology and the ability of the brain to rebound with extended sobriety.

References

Aggleton, J. P. and Brown, M. W. (2006). Interleaving brain systems for episodic and recognition memory. *Trends in Cognitive Science*, 10, 455–63.

Alfonso-Loeches, S., Pascual, M., Gómez-Pinedo, U., Pascual-Lucas, M., Renau-Piqueras, J. and Guerri C. (2012). Toll-like receptor 4 participates in the myelin disruptions associated with chronic alcohol abuse. *Glia*, 60, 948–64.

Alhassoon, O. M., Sorg, S. F., Taylor, M. J., Stephan, R. A., Schweinsburg, B. C., Stricker, N. H., Gongvatana, A. and Grant, I. (2012). Callosal white matter microstructural recovery in abstinent alcoholics: a longitudinal diffusion tensor imaging study. *Alcoholism: Clinical and Experimental Research*, 36, 1922–31.

Alexander-Kaufman, K., Cordwell, S., Harper, C. and Matsumoto, I. (2007). A proteome analysis of the dorsolateral prefrontal cortex in human alcoholic patients. *Proteomics. Clinical Applications*, 1, 62–72.

Baker, K. G., Harding, A. J., Halliday, G. M., Kril, J. J. and Harper, C. G. (1999). Neuronal loss in functional zones of the cerebellum of chronic alcoholics with and without Wernicke's encephalopathy. *Neuroscience*, 91, 429–38.

Bartsch, A. J., Homola, G., Biller, A., Smith, S. M., Weijers, H. G., Wiesbeck, G. A., Jenkinson, M., De Stefano, N., Solymosi, L. and Bendszus, M. (2007). Manifestations of early brain recovery associated with abstinence from alcoholism. *Brain*, 130, 36–47.

Beaunieux, H., Eustache, F. and Pitel, A.-L. (2015). The relation of alcohol-induced brain changes to cognitive function. In J. Svanberg, A. Withall, B. Draper and S. Bowden (eds), *Alcohol and the Adult Brain*. Hove: Psychology Press.

Bengoechea, O. and Gonzalo, L. M. (1991). Effects of alcoholization on the rat hippocampus. *Neuroscience Letters*, 123, 112–14.

Beracochea, D., Lescaudron, L., Verna, A. and Jaffard, R. (1987). Neuroanatomical effects of chronic ethanol consumption on dorsomedial and anterior thalamic nuclei and on substantia innominata in mice. *Neuroscience Letters*, 73, 81–4.

Bowden, S. C. (1990). Separating cognitive impairment in neurologically asymptomatic alcoholism from Wernicke-Korsakoff syndrome: is the neuropsychological distinction justified? *Psychological Bulletin*, 107, 355–66.

Buckner, R. L., Krienen, F. M., Castellanos, A., Diaz, J. C. and Yeo, B. T. (2011). The organization of the human cerebellum estimated by intrinsic functional connectivity. *Journal of Neurophysiology*, 106, 2322–45.

Butters, N. and Cermak, L. S. (1974). The role of cognitive factors in the memory disorders of alcoholic patients with the Korsakoff syndrome. *Annals of the New York Academy of Sciences*, 233, 61–75.

Caine, D., Halliday, G. M., Kril, J. J. and Harper, C. G. (1997). Operational criteria for the classification of chronic alcoholics: identification of Wernicke's encephalopathy. *Journal of Neurology, Neurosurgery and Psychiatry*, 62, 51–60.

Cardenas, V. A., Studholme, C., Meyerhoff, D. J., Song, E. and Weiner, M. W. (2005). Chronic active heavy drinking and family history of problem drinking modulate regional brain tissue volumes. *Psychiatry Research*, 138, 115–30.

Caulo, M., Van Hecke, J., Toma, L., Ferretti, A., Tartaro, A., Colosimo, C., Romani, G. L. and Uncini, A. (2005). Functional MRI study of diencephalic amnesia in Wernicke-Korsakoff syndrome. *Brain*, 128, 1584–94.

Chanraud, S., Pitel, A. L., Müller-Oehring, E. M., Pfefferbaum, A. and Sullivan, E. V. (2013). Remapping the brain to compensate for impairment in recovering alcoholics. *Cerebral Cortex*, 23, 97–104.

Chen, A. C., Porjesz, B., Rangaswamy, M., Kamarajan, C., Tang, Y., Jones, K. A., Chorlian, D. B., Stimus, A. T. and Begleiter, H. (2007). Reduced frontal lobe activity in subjects with high impulsivity and alcoholism. *Alcohol: Clinical and Experimental Research*, 31, 156–65.

Cullen, K. M., Halliday, G. M., Caine, D. and Kril, J. J. (1997). The nucleus basalis (Ch4) in the alcoholic Wernicke-Korsakoff syndrome: reduced cell number in both amnesic and non-amnesic patients. *Journal of Neurology, Neurosurgery and Psychiatry*, 63, 315.

De Bellis, M. D., Narasimhan, A., Thatcher, D. L., Keshavan, M. S., Soloff, P. and Clark, D. B. (2005). Prefrontal cortex, thalamus, and cerebellar volumes in adolescents and young adults with adolescent-onset alcohol use disorders and comorbid mental disorders. *Alcohol: Clinical and Experimental Research*, 29, 1590–600.

Desmond, J. E., Chen, S. H., DeRosa, E., Pryor, M. R., Pfefferbaum, A. and Sullivan E. V. (2003). Increased frontocerebellar activation in alcoholics during verbal working memory: an fMRI study. *Neuroimage*, 19, 1510–20.

Ding, J., Eigenbrodt, M., Mosley, T., Hutchinson, R. G., Folsom, A. R., Harris, T. B. and Nieto, F. J. (2004). Alcohol intake and cerebral abnormalities on magnetic resonance imaging in a community-based population of middle aged adults. *Stroke*, 35, 16–21.

Dirksen, C. L., Howard, J. A., Cronin-Golomb, A. and Oscar-Berman, M. (2006). Patterns of prefrontal dysfunction in alcoholics with and without Korsakoff's syndrome, patients with Parkinson's disease, and patients with rupture and repair of the anterior communicating artery. *Neuropsychiatric Disease and Treatment*, 2, 327–39.

Dufour, M. C. (1993). The epidemiology of alcohol-induced brain damage. In W. A. Hunt and S. J. Nixon (eds), *Alcohol-Induced Brain Damage*. Rockville, MD: National Institute on Alcohol Abuse and Alcoholism, pp. 39–69.

Franke, H., Kittner, H., Berger, P., Wirkner, K. and Schramek, J. (1997). The reaction of astrocytes and neurons in the hippocampus of adult rats during chronic ethanol treatment and correlations to behavioral impairments. *Alcohol*, 14, 445–54.

Gabriel, M. and Sparenborg, S. (1986). Anterior thalamic discriminative neuronal responses enhanced during learning in rabbits with subicular and cingulate cortical lesions. *Brain Research*, 384, 195–8.

Gabriel, M., Sparenborg, S. P. and Stolar, N. (1987). Hippocampal control of cingulate cortical and anterior thalamic information processing during learning in rabbits. *Experimental Brain Research*, 67, 131–52.

Galvin, R., Bråthen, G., Ivashynka, A., Hillbom, M., Tanasescu, R. and Leone, M. A. (2010). EFNS guidelines for diagnosis, therapy and prevention of Wernicke encephalopathy. *European Journal of Neurology*, 17, 1408–18.

Gansler, D. A., Harris, G. J., Oscar-Berman, M., Streeter, C., Lewis, R. F., Ahmed, I. and Achong, D. (2000). Hypoperfusion of inferior frontal brain regions in abstinent alcoholics: a pilot SPECT study. *Journal of Studies on Alcohol and Drugs*, 61, 32–7.

Gazdzinski, S., Durazzo, T. C. and Meyerhoff, D. J. (2005). Temporal dynamics and determinants of whole brain tissue volume changes during recovery from alcohol dependence. *Drug and Alcohol Dependence*, 78, 263–73.

Gazdzinski, S., Durazzo, T. C., Yeh, P. H., Hardin, D., Banys, P. and Meyerhoff, D. J. (2008). Chronic cigarette smoking modulates injury and short-term recovery of the medial temporal lobe in alcoholics. *Psychiatry Research*, 162, 133–45.

Goldstein, G. and Shelly, C. (1980). Neuropsychological investigation of brain lesion localization in alcoholism. In H. Begleiter (ed.), *Biological Effect of Alcohol*. New York: Plenum Press, pp. 731–43.

Habas, C., Kamdar, N., Nguyen, D., Prater, K., Beckmann, C. F., Menon, V. and Greicius, M. D. (2009). Distinct cerebellar contributions to intrinsic connectivity networks. *Journal of Neuroscience*, 29, 8586–94.

Harding, A. J., Wong, A., Svoboda, M., Kril, J. J. and Halliday, G. M. (1997). Chronic alcohol consumption does not cause hippocampal neuron loss in humans. *Hippocampus*, 7, 78–87.

Harding, A., Halliday, G., Caine, D. and Kril, J. (2000). Degeneration of anterior thalamic nuclei differentiates alcoholics with amnesia. *Brain*, 123, 141–54.

Harper, C. G. (1998). The neuropathology of alcohol-specific brain damage, or does alcohol damage the brain? *Journal of Neuropathology and Experimental Neurology*, 57, 101–10.

Harper, C. G. (2007). The neurotoxicity of alcohol. *Human and Experimental Toxicology*, 26, 251–7.

Harper C. G. (2009). The neuropathology of alcohol-related brain damage. *Alcohol and Alcoholism*, 44, 136–40.

Harper, C. G. and Blumbergs, P. C. (1982). Brain weights in alcoholics. *Journal of Neurology, Neurosurgery and Psychiatry*, 45, 838–40.

Harper, C. G. and Kril, J. J. (1993). Neuropathological changes in alcoholics. *Research Monograph: Alcohol-Induced Brain Damage*, 22, 39–70.

Harper, C. G. and Matsumoto, I. (2005). Ethanol and brain damage. *Current Opinion in Pharmacology*, 5, 73–8.

Harper, C. G., Giles, M. and Finlay-Jones, R. (1986). Clinical signs in the Wernicke-Korsakoff complex: a retrospective analysis of 131 cases diagnosed at necropsy. *Journal of Neurology, Neurosurgery and Psychiatry*, 49, 341–5.

Harper, C. G., Kril, J. J. and Holloway, R. L. (1985). Brain shrinkage in chronic alcoholics: a pathological study. *British Medical Journal*, 290, 501–4.

Herrera, D. G., Yague, A. G., Johnsen-Soriano, S., Bosch-Morell, F., Collado-Morente, L., Muriach, M., Romero, F. J. and Garcia-Verdugo, J. M. (2003) Selective impairment of hippocampal neurogenesis by chronic alcoholism: protective effects of an antioxidant. *Proceedings of the National Academy of Sciences of the USA*, 100, 7919–24.

Jacobson, R. R. and Lishman, W. A. (1990). Cortical and diencephalic lesions in Korsakoff's syndrome: a clinical and scan study. *Psychological Medicine*, 20, 63–75.

Joyce, E. M. (1994). Aetiology of alcoholic brain damage: alcoholic neurotoxicity or thiamine malnutrition? *British Medical Bulletin*, 50, 99–114.

Kim, E., Ku, J., Namkoong, K., Lee, W., Lee, K. S., Park, J. Y., Lee, S. Y., Kim, J. J., Kim, S. I. and Jung, Y. C. (2009). Mammillothalamic functional connectivity and memory function in Wernicke's encephalopathy. *Brain*, 132, 369–76.

Kopelman, M. D., Thomson, A. D., Guerrini, I. and Marshall, E. J. (2009). The Korsakoff syndrome: clinical aspects, psychology and treatment. *Alcohol and Alcoholism*, 44, 148–54.

Kril, J. J. and Harper, C. G. (2012). Neuroanatomy and neuropathology associated with Korsakoff's syndrome. *Neuropsychology Review*, 22, 72–80.

Kril, J. J., Halliday, G. M., Svoboda, M. D. and Cartwright, H. (1997). The cerebral cortex is damaged in chronic alcoholics. *Neuroscience*, 79(4), 983–98.

Kroenke, C. D., Rohlfing, T., Park, B., Sullivan, E. V., Pfefferbaum, A. and Grant, K. A. (2014). Monkeys that voluntarily and chronically drink alcohol damage their brains: a longitudinal MRI study. *Neuropsychopharmarcology*, 39(4), 823–30.

Langlais, P. J. and Savage, L. M. (1995). Thiamine deficiency in rats produces cognitive and memory deficits on spatial tasks that correlate with tissue loss in diencephalon, cortex and white matter. *Behavioural and Brain Research*, 68, 75–89.

Lescaudron, L., Beracochea, D., Verna, A. and Jaffard, R. (1984). Chronic ethanol consumption induces neuronal loss in mammillary bodies of the mouse: a quantitative analysis. *Neuroscience Letters*, 50, 151–5.

Lisdahl, K. M., Thayer, R., Squeglia, L. M., McQueeny, T. M. and Tapert, S. F. (2013). Recent binge drinking predicts smaller cerebellar volumes in adolescents. *Psychiatry Research*, 211, 17–23.

Lishman, W. A. (1990). Alcohol and the brain. *British Journal of Psychiatry*, 156, 635–44.

Mair, R. G., Warrington, E. K. and Weiskrantz, L. (1979). Memory disorder in Korsakoff's psychosis: a neuropathological and neuropsychological investigation of two cases. *Brain*, 102, 749–83.

Mair, R. G., Otto, T. A., Knoth, R. L., Rabchenuk, S. A. and Langlais, P. J. (1991). Analysis of aversively conditioned learning and memory in rats recovered from pyrithiamine-induced thiamine deficiency. *Behavioural Neuroscience*, 105, 351–9.

Manari, A. P., Preedy, V. R. and Peters, T. J. (2003). Nutritional intake of hazardous drinkers and dependent alcoholics in the UK. *Addiction Biology*, 8, 201–310.

Mayes, A. R., Meudell, P. R., Mann, D. and Pickering, A. (1988). Location of lesions in Korsakoff's syndrome: neuropsychological and neuropathological data on two patients. *Cortex*, 24, 367–88.

Moselhy, H. F., Georgiou, G. and Kahn, A. (2001). Frontal lobe changes in alcoholism: a review of the literature. *Alcohol and Alcoholism*, 36, 357–68

Oscar-Berman, M. (2012). Function and dysfunction of prefrontal brain circuitry in alcoholic Korsakoff's syndrome. *Neuropsychology Review*, 22, 154–69.

Oscar-Berman, M., Kirkley, S. M., Gansler, D. A. and Couture, A. (2004). Comparisons of Korsakoff and non-Korsakoff alcoholics on neuropsychological tests of prefrontal brain functioning. *Alcohol: Clinical and Experimental Research*, 28, 667–75.

Oslin, D., Atkinson, R. M., Smith, D. M. and Hendrie, H. (1998). Alcohol related dementia: proposed clinical criteria. *International Journal of Geriatric Psychiatry*, 13, 203–12.

Parsons, O. A. and Nixon, S. J. (1993). Neurobehavioral sequelae of alcoholism. *Neurologic Clinics*, 11, 205–18.

Paul, C. A., Au, R., Fredman, L., Massaro, J. M., Seshadri, S., Decarli, C. and Wolf, P. A. (2008). Association of alcohol consumption with brain volume in the Framingham study. *Archives of Neurology*, 65, 1363–7.

Paula-Barbosa, M. M., Brandao, F., Madeira, M. D. and Cadete-Leite, A. (1993). Structural changes in the hippocampal formation after long-term alcohol consumption and withdrawal in the rat. *Addiction*, 88, 237–47.

Pfefferbaum, A. and Sullivan, E. V. (2005). Disruption of brain white matter microstructure by excessive intracellular and extracellular fluid in alcoholism: evidence from diffusion tensor imaging. *Neuropsychopharmacology*, 30, 423–32.

Pfefferbaum, A., Lim, K., Zipursky, R., Mathalon, D., Rosenbloom, M., Lane, B., Ha, C. N. and Sullivan, E. (1992). Brain grey and white matter volume loss accelerates with aging in chronic alcoholics: a quantitative MRI study. *Alcoholism: Clinical and Experimental Research*, 16, 1078–89.

Pfefferbaum, A., Sullivan, E. V., Mathalon, D. H., Shear, P. K., Rosenbloom, M. J. and Lim, K. O. (1995). Longitudinal changes in magnetic resonance imaging brain volumes in abstinent and relapsed alcoholics. *Alcoholism: Clinical and Experimental Research*, 19, 1177–91.

Pfefferbaum, A., Lim, K. O., Desmond, J. E. and Sullivan, E. V. (1996). Thinning of the corpus callosum in older alcoholic men: a magnetic resonance imaging study. *Alcoholism: Clinical and Experimental Research*, 20, 752–7.

Pfefferbaum, A., Sullivan, E. V., Mathalon, D. H. and Lim, K. O. (1997). Frontal lobe volume loss observed with magnetic resonance imaging in older chronic alcoholics. *Alcohol: Clinical and Experimental Research*, 21, 521–9.

Pfefferbaum, A., Rosenbloom, M., Rohlfing, T. and Sullivan, E. V. (2009). Degradation of association and projection white matter systems in alcoholism detected with quantitative fiber tracking. *Psychiatry*, 65, 680–90.

Pitel, A. L., Aupée, A. M., Chételat, G., Mézenge, F., Beaunieux, H., de la Sayette, V., Viader, F., Baron, J. C., Eustache, F. and Desgranges, B. (2009). Morphological and glucose metabolism abnormalities in alcoholic Korsakoff's syndrome: group comparisons and individual analyses. *PLoS One*, 4, e7748.

Pitel, A. L., Zahr, N. M., Jackson, K., Sassoon, S. A., Rosenbloom, M. J., Pfefferbaum, A. and Sullivan, E. V. (2011). Signs of preclinical Wernicke's encephalopathy and thiamine levels as predictors of neuropsychological deficits in alcoholism without Korsakoff's syndrome. *Neuropsychopharmacology*, 36, 580–8.

Pitel, A. L., Chételat, G., Le Berre, A. P., Desgranges, B., Eustache, F. and Beaunieux H. (2012). Macrostructural abnormalities in Korsakoff syndrome compared with uncomplicated alcoholism. *Neurology*, 78, 1330–3.

Ratti, M. T., Bo, P., Giardini, A. and Soragna, D. (2002). Chronic alcoholism and the frontal lobe: which executive functions are impaired? *Acta Neurologica Scandinavica*, 105, 276–81.

Reed, L. J., Lasserson, D., Marsden, P., Stanhope, N., Stevens, T., Bello, F., Kingsley, D., Colchester, A. and Kopelman, M. D. (2003). FDG-PET findings in the Wernicke-Korsakoff syndrome. *Cortex*, 39, 1027–45.

Riley, J. N. and Walker, D. W. (1978). Morphological alternations in hippocampus after long-term alcohol consumption in mice. *Science*, 201, 646–8.

Ritchie, K. and Villebrun, D. (2008). Epidemiology of alcohol-related dementia. *Handbook of Clinical Neurology*, 89, 845–50.

Rosenbloom, M. J., Pfefferbaum, A. and Sullivan, E. V. (2004). Recovery of short-term memory and psychomotor speed but not postural stability with long-term sobriety in alcoholic women. *Neuropsychology Review*, 18, 589–97.

Rosenbloom, M. J., Rohlfing, T., O'Reilly, A. W., Sassoon, S. A., Pfefferbaum, A. and Sullivan, E. V. (2007). Improvement in memory and static balance with abstinence in alcoholic men and women: selective relations with change in brain structure. *Psychiatry Research*, 155, 91–102.

Santolaria, F., Pérez-Manzano, J. L., Milena, A., González-Reimers, E., Gómez-Rodríguez, M. A., Martínez-Riera, A., Alemán-Valls, M. R. and de la Vega-Prieto, M. J. (2000). Nutritional assessment in alcoholic patients: its relationship with alcoholic intake, feeding habits, organic complications and social problems. *Drug and Alcohol Dependence*, 59, 295–304.

Savage, L. M., Chang, Q. and Gold, P. E. (2003). Diencephalic damage decreases hippocampal acetylcholine release during spontaneous alternation testing. *Learning and Memory*, 10, 242–6.

Savage, L. M., Hall, J. and Resende, L. S. (2012). Translational rodent models of Korsakoff syndrome reveal the critical neuroanatomical substrates of memory dysfunction and recovery. *Neuropsychology Review*, 22, 195–209.

Schulte, T., Müller-Oehring, E. M., Pfefferbaum, A. and Sullivan, E. V. (2010). Neurocircuitry of emotion and cognition in alcoholism: contributions from white matter fiber tractography. *Dialogues in Clinical Neuroscience*, 12, 554–60.

Shear, P. K., Sullivan, E. V., Lane, B. and Pfefferbaum, A. (1996). Mammillary body and cerebellar shrinkage in chronic alcoholics with and without amnesia. *Alcohol: Clinical and Experimental Research*, 20, 1489–95.

Smith, D. M. and Atkinson, R. M. (1995). Alcoholism and dementia. Intern J. *Addictions*, 30, 1843–69.

Squire, L. R., Amaral, D. G. and Press, G. A. (1990). Magnetic resonance imaging of the hippocampal formation and mammillary nuclei distinguish medial temporal lobe and diencephalic amnesia. *Journal of Neuroscience*, 10, 3016–17.

Subramanya, S. B., Subramanian, V. S. and Said, H. M. (2010). Chronic alcohol consumption and intestinal thiamin absorption: effects on physiological and molecular parameters of the uptake process. *American Journal of Physiology Gastrointestinal and Liver Physiology*, 299, G23–31.

Sullivan, E. V. (2003). Compromised pontocerebellar and cerebellothalamocortical systems: speculations on their contributions to cognitive and motor impairment in nonamnesic alcoholism. *Alcohol: Clinical and Experimental Research*, 27, 1409–19.

Sullivan, E. V. and Marsh, L. (2003). Hippocampal volume deficits in alcoholic Korsakoff's syndrome. *Neurology*, 61, 1716–19.

Sullivan, E. V. and Pfefferbaum, A. (2001). Magnetic resonance relaxometry reveals central pontine abnormalities in clinically asymptomatic alcoholic men. *Alcohol: Clinical and Experimental Research*, 25, 1206–12.

Sullivan, E. V. and Pfefferbaum, A. (2005). Neurocircuitry in alcoholism: a substrate of disruption and repair. *Psychopharmacology (Berl)*, 180, 583–94.

Sullivan E. V. and Pfefferbaum, A. (2009) Neuroimaging of the Wernicke Korsakoff syndrome. *Alcohol and Alcoholism*, 45, 155–65.

Sullivan, E. V., Harris, R. A. and Pfefferbaum, A. (2010). Alcohol's effects on brain and behaviour. *Alcohol Research and Health*, 33, 127–43.

Sullivan, E. V., Rosenbloom, M. J. and Pfefferbaum, A. (2000). Pattern of motor and cognitive deficits in detoxified alcoholic men. *Alcohol: Clinical and Experimental Research*, 24, 611–21.

Sullivan, E. V., Deshmukh, A., Desmond, J. E., Lim, K. O. and Pfefferbaum, A. (2000a). Cerebellar volume decline in normal aging, alcoholism, and Korsakoff's syndrome: relation to ataxia. *Neuropsychology*, 14, 341–52.

Sullivan, E. V., Rosenbloom, M. J., Lim, K. O. and Pfefferbaum, A. (2000b). Longitudinal changes in cognition, gait, and balance in abstinent and relapsed alcoholic men: relationships to changes in brain structure. *Neuropsychology*, 14, 178–88.

Sullivan, E. V., Harding, A. J., Pentney, R., Dlugos, C., Martin, P. R., Parks, M. H., Desmond, J. E., Chen, S. H. A., Pryor, M. R., De Rosa, E. and Pfefferbaum, A. (2003). Disruption of frontocerebellar circuitry and function in alcoholism. *Alcohol: Clinical and Experimental Research*, 27, 301–9.

Torvik, A. (1982). Brain lesions in alcoholics: a neuropathological study with clinical correlations. *Journal of the Neurological Sciences*, 56, 233–48.

Van Groen, T. and Wyss, J. M. (1995). Projections from the anterodorsal and anteroventral nucleus of the thalamus to the limbic cortex in the rat. *Journal of Comparative Neurology*, 358, 584–604.

Vetreno, R. P., Hall, J. and Savage, L. M. (2011). Alcohol-induced amnesia and dementia: what animal models have told us about the relationships between etiological factors, neuropathology, neurochemical dysfunctions and cognitive impairments. *Neurobiology of Learning and Memory*, 96, 596–608.

Vetreno, R. P., Klintsova, A. and Savage, L. M. (2011). Stage-dependent alterations of progenitor cell proliferation and neurogenesis in an animal model of Wernicke-Korsakoff syndrome. *Brain Research*, 1391, 132–46.

Vetreno R. P., Qin, L. and Crews, F. T. (2013). Increased receptor for advanced glycation end product expression in the human alcoholic prefrontal cortex is linked to adolescent drinking. *Neurobiology of Disease*, 59, 52–62.

Vetreno, R. P., Ramos, R. L., Anzalone, S. and Savage, L. M. (2012). Brain and behavioral pathology in an animal model of Wernicke's encephalopathy and Wernicke-Korsakoff syndrome. *Brain Research*, 1436, 178–92.

Victor, M., Adams, R. D. and Collins, G. H. (1971). *The Wernicke-Korsakoff Syndrome*. Philadelphia: F. A. Davis.

Victor, M., Adams, R. C. and Collins, G. H. (1989). *The Wernicke-Korsakoff Syndrome and Related Neurological Disorders due to Alcoholism and Malnutrition* (2nd edn). Philadelphia: F. A. Davis.

Walker, D. W., King, M. A. and Hunter, B. E. (1993). Alterations in the structure of the hippocampus after long-term ethanol consumption. In W. A. Hunt and S. J. Nixon (eds), *Alcohol-Induced Brain Damage*. Rockville, MD: National Institute on Alcohol Abuse and Alcoholism, pp. 231–48.

Walker, D. W., Barnes, D. E., Zornetzer, S. F., Hunter, B. E. and Kubanis, P. (1980). Neuronal loss in hippocampus induced by prolonged ethanol consumption in rats. *Science*, 209, 711–13.

Zahr, N. M. Kaufman, K. L. and Harper, C. G. (2011). Clinical and pathological features of alcohol-related brain damage. *Nature Reviews Neurology*, 7, 284–94.

8

THE RELATION OF ALCOHOL-INDUCED BRAIN CHANGES TO COGNITIVE FUNCTION

Hélène Beaunieux, Francis Eustache and Anne-Lise Pitel

Alcohol dependence is a major public health problem in the developed world. For example, the lifetime prevalence rate of alcohol abuse in the USA is 17.8 per cent and of dependence 12.5 per cent, with higher levels in men than women (Compton *et al.*, 2007; Grant *et al.*, 2004; Hasin *et al.*, 2007). In France, 5 million people (i.e., 8 per cent of the population) experience medical, psychological, or social difficulties attributable in part to alcohol consumption, and 2 million people (i.e., 3 per cent of the population) are alcohol dependent, again with men drinking more than women (Expertise Collective de l'Inserm, 2003). Among other medical consequences, chronic alcoholism can lead to persistent brain damage and attendant functional compromise involving motor, gait and balance and cognitive brain systems. Alcohol-related structural brain abnormalities will be detailed in the first section. In the second section, we will describe how chronic and excessive alcohol consumption affects the memory circuit of Papez, the executive fronto-cerebellar circuit, the decision-making and motivation brain networks.

Alcohol-related brain damage

Neuropathological studies

In their classic work, Victor, Adams and Collins (1971) described the neuropathology underlying Wernicke-Korsakoff Syndrome as including neuronal loss, microhaemorrhages and gliosis in the paraventricular and periaqueductal gray matter, along with macroscopic cortical atrophy in 27 per cent of their group with alcoholism.

Neuropathological studies also examined brain weights in people with alcoholism using automated quantitative analytical methods for volume measurements and cell counts. Those investigations indicated that reduction in brain weight observed in this group is largely due to reduction of white matter volume rather than gray matter volume (de la Monte, 1988; Harper and Kril, 1985). Cerebellar white matter

A) Gray matter

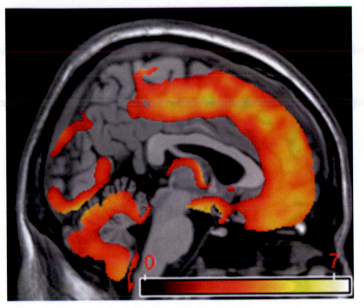

B) White matter

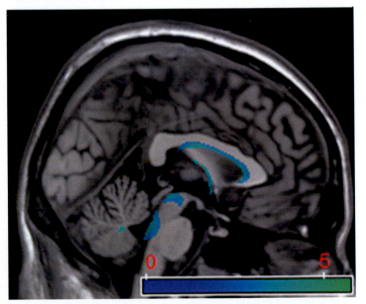

FIGURE 8.1 Gray and white matter shrinkage in uncomplicated alcoholic patients compared to healthy controls
A p value cut-off of p < 0.05 corrected for false discovery rate (FDR) was used. Cluster size > 200 voxels.
Pitel *et al.* (2012), 1330–3.

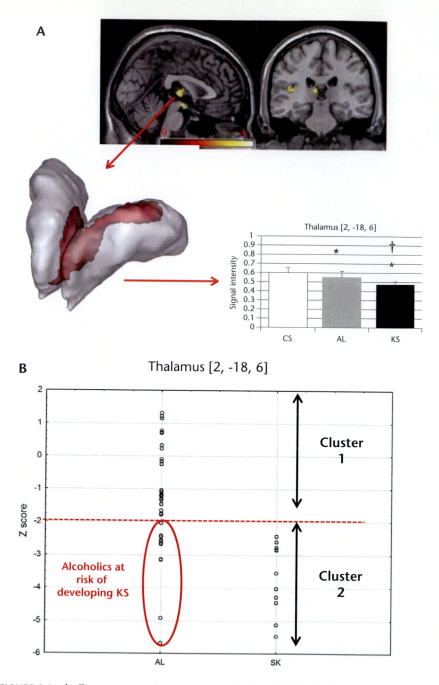

FIGURE 8.2   A. Gray matter regions more severely damaged in KS than in AL in Papez's circuit B. Distribution of thalamic volumes in AL and KS patients

KS: alcoholics with Korsakoff's Syndrome; AL: non-Korsakoff alcoholics; CS: control subjects

*: significant difference compared to controls

†: significant difference compared to alcoholics

For Z scores, the expected value of the controls is 0 (standard deviation = 1); low values of volume reflect volume deficits. The cluster analysis revealed that AL with Z scores inferior to 2 standard deviations from the control subjects are classified within the same cluster as KS patients

Pitel *et al.* (2012), 1330–3.

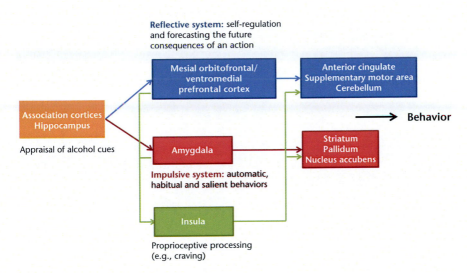

FIGURE 8.5 A brain network of alcohol addiction illustrating functional role for three key neural systems

Impulsive system (in red), reflective system (in blue) and the insula (in green). Based on Noël *et al.* (2013).

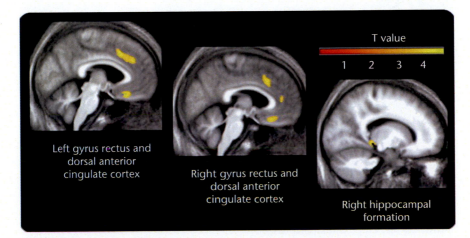

FIGURE 8.6 Positive correlations between the decision–making measure and brain voxels with reduced gray matter volume in the alcoholic group

Reproduced from Le Berre *et al.* (2014).

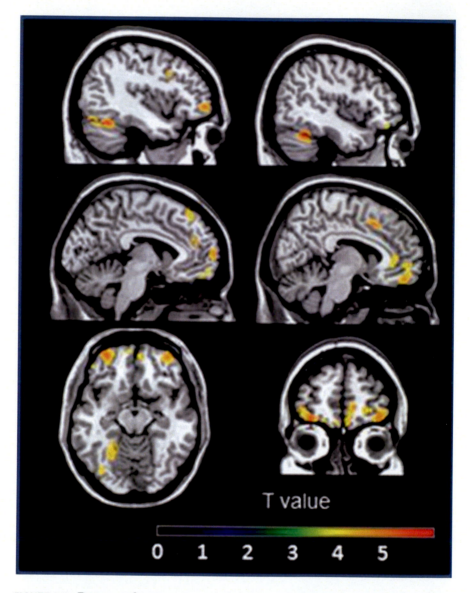

FIGURE 8.7 **Pattern of grey matter shrinkage** in alcoholic patients with low-level motivation to change drinking behavior

Red shaded areas mark regions with significant difference compared with high-level motivation alcoholic patients. Results are displayed at an uncorrected significance threshold of p < 0.001. Reproduced from *Le Berre et al.* (2013).

volume (especially in the vermis) is also reduced (Phillips, Harper and Kril, 1987) and the corpus callosum is significantly thinned in individuals with alcoholism (Harper and Kril, 1988; Tarnowska–Dziduszko, Bertrand and Szpak, 1995). At a microscopic level, Harper, Kril and Daly (1987) reported a reduction of 22 per cent in the number of neurons specifically localized in the superior frontal cortex in patients with chronic alcoholism compared with that in controls matched for age and sex. Brain weight loss in these patients has been shown to correlate with the rate and amount of alcohol consumed over a lifetime (Harding *et al.*, 1996), but occurred independently of the presence of Wernicke's Encephalopathy, indicating that alcohol consumption is more important than nutritional deficiency in causing a reduction in brain weight (de la Monte and Kril, 2014). The mechanisms underlying such brain weight loss remains unknown; this phenomenon probably involves cell body death and changes in both myelination and axonal integrity (Harper and Matsumoto, 2005).

In-vivo imaging studies

The CT investigations conducted in alcoholism have confirmed postmortem studies by showing the existence of widespread brain abnormalities including ventricular enlargement and sulcal widening (Bergman *et al.*, 1980; Carlen *et al.*, 1978; Jernigan *et al.*, 1982; Ron *et al.*, 1982). The percentage of people with alcoholism showing evidence of brain atrophy varies from 60 per cent (Bergman *et al.*, 1980) to 100 per cent (Carlen *et al.*, 1978). MRI studies have specified that those with alcoholism have regional cortical volume deficits (Jernigan *et al.*, 1991; Pfefferbaum *et al.*, 1992). Among these individuals, cerebral shrinkage is more pronounced in older patients than in younger ones, suggesting that the ageing brain is more vulnerable to alcohol-related brain damage (Pfefferbaum *et al.*, 1997; Pfefferbaum *et al.*, 1993). Chronic alcohol consumption damages both gray and white matter (Harper, 1998; Kril *et al.*, 1997). Alcohol-related brain structural damage, although widespread (Pfefferbaum *et al.*, 1992; Sullivan *et al.*, 1998), targets more specifically certain brain systems while others remain relatively intact (for review, see Chanraud *et al.* 2011).

Abnormal functioning of certain brain networks is associated with various neuropsychological deficits. MRI studies have revealed significant alterations of gray matter volume in focal brain areas such as the frontal cortex, the thalamus, the insular cortex, the hippocampus and the cerebellum, as well as damage of white matter volume in periventricular areas, corpus callosum, pons and cerebellar peduncles (Figure 8.1; Cardenas *et al.*, 2007; Chanraud *et al.*, 2007; Mechtcheriakov *et al.*, 2007; Pfefferbaum *et al.*, 1997; Pitel *et al.*, 2012).

Frontal lobes

Many studies have shown that the frontal lobes are more vulnerable to chronic and excessive alcohol consumption than other cerebral regions (Moselhy, Georgiou and Kahn, 2001; Oscar-Berman *et al.*, 2004; Pfefferbaum *et al.*, 1997). In accordance with

A) Gray matter   B) White matter

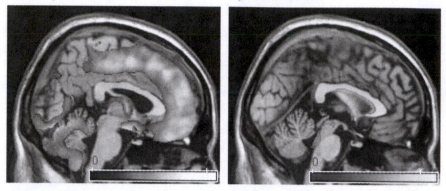

FIGURE 8.1 Gray and white matter shrinkage in uncomplicated alcoholic patients compared to healthy controls. See Figure 8.1 in plate section for a color version of this illustration.
A p value cut-off of p < 0.05 corrected for false discovery rate (FDR) was used. Cluster size > 200 voxels.
Pitel *et al.* (2012), 1330–3.

neuropathological studies that revealed decreased neuron density in the superior frontal cortex (Harper and Matsumoto, 2005), structural MRI studies showed shrinkage of the frontal lobes (Chanraud *et al.*, 2007; Pfefferbaum *et al.*, 1997; Pitel *et al.*, 2012). Some authors suggest that functional abnormalities such as blood flow (Nicolás *et al.*, 1993) or metabolism (Volkow *et al.*, 1994) in the frontal lobe may decrease before significant shrinkage becomes detectable (Nicolás *et al.*, 1993; Wang *et al.*, 1993).

Cerebellum

The cerebellum is a brain structure that is located at the back of the brain, underlying the occipital and temporal lobes of the cerebral cortex. The cerebellum coordinates voluntary motor function, balance and eye movements. It is also essential to the brain networks underlying executive functions (Schmahmann, 2010; Sullivan, 2003). Atrophy of the cerebellum is commonly associated with alcoholism (see Zahr *et al.*, 2010, for review): post-mortem studies revealed cerebellar atrophy in about 27 per cent of people with alcoholism (Lindboe and Løberg, 1988; Torvik, Lindboe and Rogde, 1982). Cerebellar atrophy has been confirmed by CT scan (Diener *et al.*, 1986; Melgaard and Ahlgren, 1986) and MRI studies (Shear *et al.*, 1996; Sullivan, 2003), showing volume deficits in both gray and white matter (Pentney *et al.*, 2002; Sullivan, Rosenbloom and Pfefferbaum, 2000) of the vermis in patients with chronic alcohol dependence.

Thalamus

The thalamus is a midline symmetrical structure located between the cerebral cortex and the midbrain and is part of the limbic system. MRI studies showed shrinkage of the thalamus in those with uncomplicated alcoholism compared with controls (Chanraud *et al.*, 2007; Sullivan *et al.*, 2003) and direct comparisons of brain damage in Korsakoff Syndrome (KS) and uncomplicated alcoholism revealed more severe thalamic damage in patients with uncomplicated alcoholism compared with KS patients (Figure 8.2; Pitel *et al.*, 2012; Sullivan and Pfefferbaum, 2009). Pitel *et al.* (2012) reported that in some people with alcoholism the shrinkage of the medial thalamic nuclei was as severe as in KS patients, which suggested that this subgroup may be at risk for developing KS (Figure 8.2).

Mammillary bodies

The mammillary bodies are a pair of small round bodies that are part of the limbic system. They are located at the ends of the anterior arches of the fornix. They serve as a relay for impulses coming from the amygdala and hippocampus, via the mammillo-thalamic tract, to the thalamus. As with the thalami, MRI studies have revealed smaller volumes of the mammillary bodies in groups with uncomplicated alcoholism compared with healthy controls (Sullivan *et al.*, 1999) and direct comparisons between those with uncomplicated alcoholism and alcoholism with KS revealed a graded pattern of shrinkage (Pitel *et al.*, 2012; Sullivan and Pfefferbaum, 2009).

Hippocampus

The hippocampus is a structure located in the medial temporal lobe and belongs to the limbic system. Structural neuroimaging studies that have demonstrated hippocampal volume shrinkage in alcoholism (Agartz *et al.*, 1999; Beresford *et al.*, 2006; Kurth *et al.*, 2004). Chanraud *et al.* (2009) also reported regional microstructural alteration of gray matter in parahippocampal areas in patients with uncomplicated alcoholism. Structural brain deficits in the hippocampus show a graded effect from those with uncomplicated alcoholism to patients with KS (Sullivan and Pfefferbaum, 2009), who have hippocampal shrinkage as severe as in patients with Alzheimer's disease (Sullivan and Marsh, 2003).

Amygdala

The amygdala is a small structure, deep within the temporal lobe. This highly connected region underpins the processing of motivational or affective significance of stimuli (Amaral *et al.*, 2003). The amygdala is also considered as a part of the limbic system. A significant reduction of gray matter volume in the amygdala of those with uncomplicated alcoholism has been reported (Cardenas *et al.*, 2011; Fein, McGillivray and Finn, 2006).

Insula

The insula is a distinct lobe entirely hidden and located in the depth of the Sylvian fissure. The insular cortex has widespread connections with other parts of the

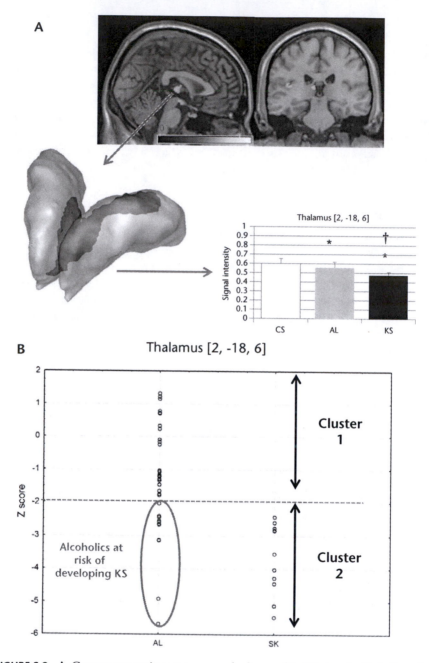

FIGURE 8.2 A. Gray matter regions more severely damaged in KS than in AL in Papez's circuit B. Distribution of thalamic volumes in AL and KS patients. See Figure 8.2 in the plate section for a color version of this illustration.

KS: alcoholics with Korsakoff's Syndrome; AL: non-Korsakoff alcoholics; CS: control subjects

*: significant difference compared to controls

†: significant difference compared to alcoholics

For Z scores, the expected value of the controls is 0 (standard deviation = 1); low values of volume reflect volume deficits. The cluster analysis revealed that AL with Z scores inferior to 2 standard deviations from the control subjects are classified within the same cluster as KS patients

Pitel *et al.* (2012), 1330–3.

brain: frontal, parietal and temporal lobes, the anterior cingulate gyrus and subcortical structures such as the amygdala, brainstem, thalamus and basal ganglia. The insula plays a crucial role in promoting the motivation to seek alcohol (Naqvi and Bechara, 2009). Insula shrinkage in alcoholism has been frequently described in MRI studies (Cardenas *et al.*, 2007; Chanraud *et al.*, 2007; Mechtcheriakov *et al.*, 2007).

Brainstem

The brainstem is the inferior part of the brain, adjoining and structurally continuous with the spinal cord and the cerebellum. The brainstem is considered critical for the development and maintenance of drug dependence (Koob, 2009). Included in the brainstem, the medulla oblongata, the pons and midbrain have been described to be altered in MRI studies conducted in those with alcoholism (Chanraud *et al.*, 2007; Sullivan, 2003).

White matter fibers

White matter is highly organized in fiber bundles that connect different areas of gray matter (nodes) within functional brain networks. Neuropathological studies have reported compromised white matter integrity in people with alcoholism. Thus chronic alcoholism may disrupt the fiber bundles linking the nodes of the functional brain networks (de la Monte, 1988; Harper and Kril, 1985; Jensen and Pakkenberg, 1993) and result in their dysfunction.

Shrinkage of the corpus callosum has consistently been found in structural MRI studies of people with alcoholism, with the genu being predominantly affected (Hommer *et al.*, 1996; Pfefferbaum *et al.*, 1996). White matter volume deficits in alcoholism may be explained by fewer white matter fibers in this group than controls (Chanraud *et al.*, 2009). Diffusion tensor imaging (DTI), a brain imaging technique notably designed to study white matter microstructure, provides quantitative information about the integrity of the fiber tracks. DTI studies have identified microstructural abnormalities in the corpus callosum of people with alcoholism (Pfefferbaum and Sullivan, 2005; Pitel *et al.*, 2010) especially with advancing age (Pfefferbaum, Adalsteinsson and Sullivan, 2006). Pfefferbaum *et al.* (2009) reported that alcoholism affects the microstructure of frontal and superior sites (frontal forceps, internal and external capsules, fornix and superior cingulate and longitudinal fasciculi) whereas more posterior and inferior bundles are relatively spared. The microstructure of mesencephalic white matter bundles composing the cortico–cerebellar network (Chanraud *et al.*, 2009), as well as the fronto–occipital fasciculus bundles (Bagga *et al.*, 2014), is also damaged in alcoholism.

Affected brain networks and associated neuropsychological deficits

The association of localized gray matter regional shrinkage with alterations in specific white matter bundles suggests that alcohol-related brain damage targets certain anatomical and functional brain networks. Dysfunction of the brain circuitry may account, at least in part, for the neuropsychological deficits observed in individuals with alcoholism. In the next sections, we will discuss how chronic and excessive alcohol consumption affects the fronto-cerebellar circuit associated with executive functions, the circuit of Papez associated with memory and the brain network implicated in addiction, associated with decision-making and motivation.

Fronto-cerebellar circuit and executive functions

"Executive functions" is an umbrella term for the management (regulation, control) of cognitive processes including judgment, reasoning, flexibility, inhibition and planning (Shallice and Burgess, 1998). Deficits of executive functions are frequently observed in alcoholism (Moselhy, Georgiou and Kahn, 2001; Oscar-Berman and Marinković, 2007). Inhibition, flexibility, categorization, deduction of rules, organization and planning have mostly been found to be impaired in this group (Fama, Pfefferbaum and Sullivan, 2004; Ihara, 2000; Pitel *et al.*, 2007). Executive deficits were first related to prefrontal lobe damage (Moselhy, Georgiou and Kahn, 2001; Nicolás *et al.*, 1993, 1997). More recent investigations highlighted that alterations of the fronto-cerebellar circuit (Figure 8.3) may be better predictors of executive dysfunction than damage of the prefrontal lobes (Sullivan, 2003; Zahr *et al.*, 2010). The fronto-cerebellar circuit includes top–down fiber bundles through the pons and bottom–up fiber bundles through the thalamus (mesencephalic bundles).

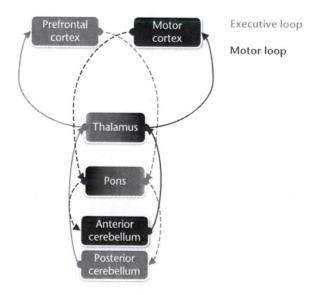

FIGURE 8.3   The **fronto–cerebellar circuit** encompasses a motor loop (in black) and a cognitive one (in gray).

The fronto-cerebellar circuit includes top–down fiber bundles through the pons and bottom–up fiber bundles through the thalamus.

This functional brain network encompasses two loops: a motor one involving the anterior cerebellum (e.g., cerebellar lobules IV, V, VI) and the motor cerebral cortices, as well as an executive one involving the posterior cerebellum (e.g., cerebellar lobule VII, lobule VIII, Crus I, and Crus II) and the prefrontal cortical sites (e.g., BA9 and 46).

Executive deficits in alcoholism have been related to the gray matter shrinkage of the frontal lobes, pons, thalamus and cerebellum (Chanraud et al., 2007; Sullivan, 2003). Moreover, using a tractography approach in people with alcoholism, Chanraud et al. (2009) showed that the number of white matter fibers reconstructed between the midbrain and the pons correlated with executive deficits. Thus, alcohol-related damage in the fronto-cerebellar circuit may at least partially contribute to the executive deficits frequently reported in alcoholism, either by disruption of nodes themselves or by disconnection within the circuitry.

In addition to the fronto-cerebellar circuit, macrostructural and microstructural abnormalities of the corpus callosum seem to be predictive of executive dysfunction (Pfefferbaum et al., 2000; Pfefferbaum, Adalsteinsson and Sullivan, 2006; Schulte, Pfefferbaum and Sullivan, 2004; Schulte et al., 2005).

Papez's circuit and episodic memory

Episodic memory functioning relies on a brain circuitry that encompasses two loops (Figure 8.4): a central one, which includes notably the hippocampus–anterior–thalamus axis called Papez's circuit (in gray) and a secondary one, more diffuse and extended which involves the internal temporal and frontal cortices (in white; Aggleton and Brown, 1999). In Papez's circuit, the anterior thalamus receives direct input from the hippocampus via the fornix and indirect input from the hippocampus through the mammillary bodies via the mamillothalamic tract.

Mild to moderate episodic memory deficits have been described in people with alcoholism (Chanraud et al., 2009a; Noël et al., 2012; Pitel et al., 2007). Pitel et al. (2007) suggested that alcohol-related structural abnormalities within the medial temporal lobe may underlie episodic memory alteration in these patients. Indeed, different components of episodic memory were shown to be impaired in patients with alcoholism (learning, encoding, retrieval and autonoetic consciousness), but those episodic memory impairments were not related to executive dysfunction, suggesting that episodic memory alteration observed in alcoholism could not be regarded as the consequences of frontal-based executive dysfunction, but rather as genuine hippocampal episodic memory deficits. Reduced hippocampal volume was reported in people with alcoholism with preserved episodic memory abilities, but no relationship was found between hippocampal volume and episodic memory performance (Sullivan et al., 1995). These findings suggest that hippocampal shrinkage itself cannot explain alcohol-related episodic memory deficits.

Even though shrinkage of gray matter nodes and white matter bundles of Papez's circuit have been reported in alcoholism (see previously in this chapter), little is known about the relations between episodic memory abilities and the

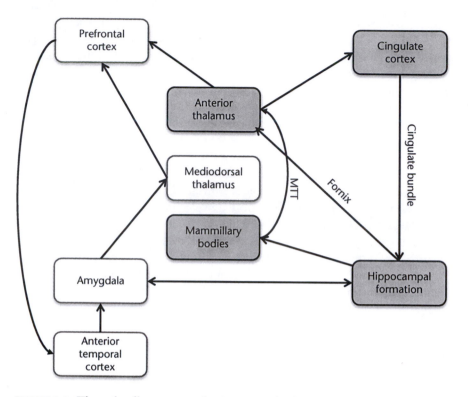

FIGURE 8.4 The **episodic memory brain networks** (based on Aggleton and Brown, 1999)

The Papez's circuit (gray) involves the hippocampus, anterior thalamus, mammillary bodies and cingulate cortex, which are connected by the formix, mamillothalamic tract (MTT) and cingulate bundle. The secondary circuit involves the amygdala, mediodorsal thalamus and temporal and frontal cortices, and plays a modulatory role.

integrity of Papez's circuit in uncomplicated alcoholism. Studies conducted in groups with uncomplicated alcoholism have suggested that episodic memory deficits are associated with compromised white matter in the temporal lobe (Gazdzinski et al., 2005) and microstructural gray matter abnormalities in hippocampal formation (Chanraud et al., 2009). More recently, Trivedi et al. (2013) reported a link between episodic memory deficits and the white matter integrity of the cingulum bundle and uncinate fasciculus, which connect gray matter nodes within Papez's circuit.

Most of our knowledge regarding the effect of chronic alcohol consumption on Papez's circuit comes from studies of KS. KS, which results from the combination of heavy alcohol consumption and thiamine deficiency, is one of the most severe neurological complications of alcoholism. KS has previously been characterized by a disproportionate impairment of episodic memory compared with other aspects of cognitive function (Kopelman, 1995; 2002). Neuropathological studies showed macrostructural abnormalities of thalamic nuclei and mammillary bodies in KS (Mair, Warrington and Weiskrantz, 1979; Mayes *et al.*, 1988; Sheedy *et al.*, 1999; Victor, Adams and Collins, 1971). In-vivo neuroimaging investigations confirmed reduced volume in thalami and mammillary bodies in KS (Jauhar and Montaldi, 2001; Reed *et al.*, 2003; Shimamura *et al.*, 1988; Squire, Amaral and Press, 1990; Sullivan *et al.*, 1999) and revealed widespread cerebral damage with the nodes and connections of the fronto-cerebellar circuit, with the limbic circuit being especially affected (Pitel *et al.*, 2009).

Neuroradiological comparison of people with alcoholism with and without KS showed graded volume deficits from mild to moderate volume deficits in uncomplicated alcoholism to more severe volume deficits in KS (Sullivan and Pfefferbaum, 2009). Using a voxelwise approach, Pitel *et al.* (2012) found that even though volume deficits were found in Papez's circuit in both alcoholism with and without KS, key structures of this circuit (thalamus, mammillary bodies and thalamic radiation) were more severely damaged in KS than in uncomplicated alcoholism (Figure 8.2). These findings suggest that the severity of the episodic memory disorder observed in KS may be related to the degradation of structures of or to the integrity of Papez's circuit.

The impulsive/reflective system and decision-making abilities

People dependent on alcohol usually favor the instant gratification of alcohol use and ignore its long-term negative consequences, suggesting impaired decision-making abilities (Goudriaan *et al.*, 2005; Le Berre *et al.*, 2012; Noël *et al.*, 2007). According to the somatic marker theory, decision-making abilities involve an extended brain network, which is mediated by two types of neural circuitry: the impulsive and reflective systems (Figure 8.5). During the development of alcohol addiction, the impulsive system, with the amygdala being the main substrate, triggers somatic states from stimuli (emotion, alcohol) present in the immediate environment (in red in Figure 8.5). The behaviors of those dependent on alcohol become progressively controlled by alcohol-associated information that has acquired the property to automatically generate alcohol-related actions and craving. Chronic alcohol consumption results in the strengthening of implicit "wanting", motivation-relevant associative memories and generate automatic approach tendencies (Stacy and Wiers, 2010). The reflective system controls the impulsive system and allows more the flexible pursuit of long-term goals (in blue in Figure 8.5). The reflective system is based on two neural networks: a "cold" and a "hot" executive functioning system. The "cold" executive functions, which refer to executive functions as described in the section "Fronto-cerebellar circuit and executive functions" on p. 132, are mediated by fronto-cerebellar and frontoparietal networks (Kerr and Zelazo, 2004; Zahr *et al.*, 2010). The "hot" executive functions rely on a brain circuitry that encompasses paralimbic orbitomedial and ventromedial fronto-limbic structures involved in triggering somatic states from cognition (Bechara *et al.*, 2005). Thus, adequate decision-making results in 1) an integration of "cold" and "hot"

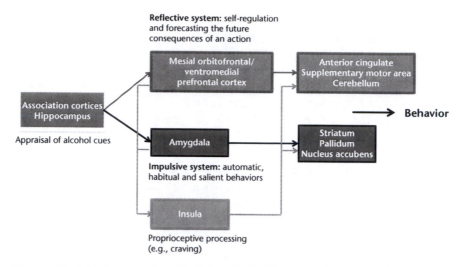

FIGURE 8.5 A brain network of alcohol addiction illustrating functional role for three key neural systems

Impulsive system (in dark gray), reflective system (in mid-gray) and the insula (in light gray). See Figure 8.5 in plate section for a color version of this illustration. Based on Noël *et al.* (2013).

executive functions and 2) the ability to consider short- and long-term gains or losses (Damasio, 1996; Figure 8.5; Noël, Brevers and Bechara, 2013; Verdejo-García and Bechara, 2009).

Several regions belonging to the somatic marker brain network are known to be damaged in chronic alcoholism, especially the frontal cortices, amygdala, hippocampus, striatum and cerebellum. Le Berre *et al.* (2014) reported that decision-making deficits in alcoholism are associated with reduced gray matter volume in the ventromedial prefrontal cortex (gyrus rectus and pregenual anterior cingulate cortex), the dorsal portion of the anterior cingulate cortex and the hippocampal formation (Figure 8.6). These results suggest that decision-making deficits in this group may result from impairment of both impulsive and reflective brain networks. These deficits may lead people with alcoholism to suffer from "myopia" for the future, contributing to their tendency to choose instant gratification (i.e., the immediate advantages of their alcohol consumption). This "myopia" may dim the person's awareness of the problems arising from substance abuse and may keep them in denial about their illness (Verdejo-García and Pérez-García, 2008).

A brain network of addiction and motivation

The brain network of addiction and motivation proposed by Noël *et al* (2013) includes the reward system, the impulsive/reflective system and incorporates the modulatory role of the insula on decision-making circuits (Figure 8.5). This model

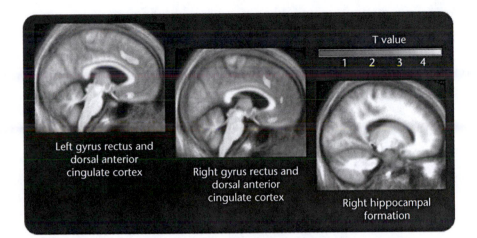

T value

1   2   3   4

Left gyrus rectus and dorsal anterior cingulate cortex

Right gyrus rectus and dorsal anterior cingulate cortex

Right hippocampal formation

FIGURE 8.6   Positive correlations between the decision-making measure and brain voxels with reduced gray matter volume in the alcoholic group
Reproduced from Le Berre *et al.* (2014). See Figure 8.6 in the plate section for a color version of this illustration.

proposed a functional role for three key brain circuits in addiction: (1) the "impulsive system", which excites the reward system involved in the execution of motivational states to seek alcohol (in red in Figure 8.5); (2) the "reflective system", which forecasts the future consequences of a behaviour, such as seeking alcohol (in blue in Figure 8.5); (3) the insula (in green in Figure 8.5) that integrates interoceptive states into conscious feelings (such as craving), which in turn influence decision-making. High motivation to stop alcohol consumption is a crucial triggering factor to patients' engagement in clinical treatment. However, motivation to stop addictive behavior may be jeopardized by their episodic memory (Blume *et al.*, 2005, Le Berre *et al.*, 2012) and decision-making deficits (Le Berre *et al.*, 2012). In accordance with the addiction and motivation brain network proposed by Noël *et al.* (2013), Le Berre *et al.* (2013) showed that people with alcoholism with low-level motivation to stop their drinking behavior had decreased gray matter volumes in the frontal cortex, including the lateral orbitofrontal cortex (OFC), the ventromedial, dorsomedial and dorsolateral prefrontal cortices and the anterior cingulate cortex, when compared with a control group (Figure 8.7).

These results suggest that shrinkage of gray mater nodes of impulsive and reflective systems may result in a low motivation to stop drinking. These brain volume deficits may result in impairments of decision-making and executive functions. Yet, those abilities may be needed to resolve ambivalence towards alcohol addiction and to apply "processes of change", which are essential for activating the desire to stop problematic behavior. Thus, resistance to change drinking habits may not only reflect psychological processes, but also neuropsychological impairments associated with shrinkage of gray mater nodes of impulsive and reflective systems.

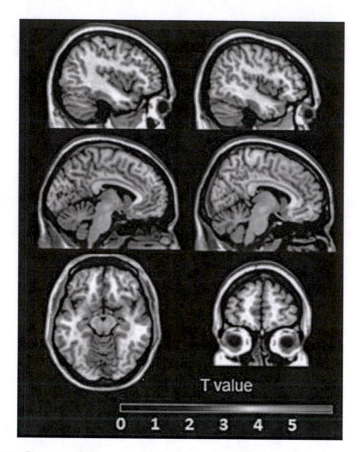

FIGURE 8.7 Pattern of grey matter shrinkage in alcoholic patients with low-level motivation to change drinking behavior
Shaded areas mark regions with significant difference compared with high-level motivation
alcoholic patients. Results are displayed at an uncorrected significance threshold of p < 0.001.
Reproduced from *Le Berre et al.* (2013). See Figure 8.7 in plate section for a color version of this
illustration.

Conclusion

Chronic and excessive alcohol consumption can cause widespread structural and functional brain damage. However, this damage is not diffuse and predominantly affects specific cerebral networks, resulting in a particular pattern of spared and impaired cognitive abilities. Disruption of fronto-cerebellar, Papez's, decision-making and reward/motivation circuits are associated with deficits of executive functions and working memory, episodic memory and decision-making, as well as reduced motivation to change, respectively. These neuropsychological disabilities can hamper treatment of alcohol dependence and can also indirectly interfere with successful treatment outcomes (Bates *et al.*, 2013). Cognitive impairments may impede positive treatment outcome by interrupting treatment processes, which in turn mediate the influence of impairment on these outcomes. Deficits may also serve to moderate the influence of treatment processes by reducing or enhancing their influence on treatment outcomes. Neuropsychological impairments must therefore be detected at treatment entry and taken into account to provide the most appropriate treatment. Structural brain examination of people with alcohol dependence may be less relevant to clinical decision-making, except to exclude other etiologies that could explain the observed cognitive deficits in this group.

References

Agartz, I., Momenan, R., Rawlings, R. R., Kerich, M. J. and Hommer, D. W. (1999). Hippocampal volume in patients with alcohol dependence. *Archives of General Psychiatry*, 56(4), 356–63.

Aggleton, J. P. and Brown, M. W. (1999). Episodic memory, amnesia, and the hippocampal-anterior thalamic axis. *The Behavioral and Brain Sciences*, 22(3), 425–44.

Amaral, D. G., Bauman, M. D., Capitanio, J. P., Lavenex, P., Mason, W. A., Mauldin-Jourdain, M. L. and Mendoza, S. P. (2003). The amygdala: is it an essential component of the neural network for social cognition? *Neuropsychologia*, 41(4), 517–22.

Bagga, D., Sharma, A., Kumari, A., Kaur, P., Bhattacharya, D., Garg, M. L., Khushu, S. and Singh, N. (2014). Decreased white matter integrity in fronto-occipital fasciculus bundles: relation to visual information processing in alcohol-dependent subjects. *Alcohol*, 48(1), 43–53.

Bates, M. E., Buckman, J. F. and Nguyen, T. T. (2013). A role for cognitive rehabilitation in increasing the effectiveness of treatment for alcohol use disorders. *Neuropsychology Review*, 23, 27–47.

Bechara, A., Damasio, H., Tranel, D. and Damasio, A. R. (2005). The Iowa Gambling Task and the somatic marker hypothesis: Some questions and answers. *Trends in Cognitive Sciences*, 9(4), 159–162.

Beresford, T. P., Arciniegas, D. B., Alfers, J., Clapp, L., Martin, B., Du, Y., Dengfeng, L., Dinggana, S. and Davatzikos, C. (2006). Hippocampus volume loss due to chronic heavy drinking. *Alcoholism: Clinical and Experimental Research*, 30(11), 1866–70.

Bergman, H., Borg, S., Hindmarsh, T., Ideström, C. M. and Mützell, S. (1980). Computed-tomography of the brain and neuropsychological assessement of alcoholic patients. *Advances in Experimental Medicine and Biology*, 126, 771–86.

Blume, A. W., Schmaling, K. B. and Marlatt, A. M. (2005). Memory, executive cognitive function, and readiness to change drinking behavior. *Addictive Behaviours*, 30(2), 301–14.

Cardenas, V. A., Studholme, C., Gazdzinski, S., Durazzo, T. C. and Meyerhoff, D. J. (2007). Deformation-based morphometry of brain changes in alcohol dependence and abstinence. *NeuroImage*, 34(3), 879–87.

Cardenas, V. A., Durazzo, T. C., Gazdzinski, S., Mon, A., Studholme, C. and Meyerhoff, D. J. (2011). Brain morphology at entry into treatment for alcohol dependence is related to relapse propensity. *Biological Psychiatry*, 70(6), 561–7.

Carlen, P. L., Wortzman, G., Holgate, R. C., Wilkinson, D. A. and Rankin, J. C. (1978). Reversible cerebral atrophy in recently abstinent chronic alcoholics measured by computed tomography scans. *Sciences*, 200(4345), 1076–8.

Chanraud, S., Pitel, A. L. and Sullivan, E. V. (2011). Structural imaging in substance abuse. In Martha E. Shenton and Bruce I. Turetsky (eds), *Understanding Neuropsychiatric Disorders Insights from Neuroimaging*. Cambridge: Cambridge Medicine.

Chanraud, S., Martelli, C., Delain, F., Kostogianni, N., Douaud, G., Aubin, H.-J., Reynaud, M. and Martinot, J.-L. (2007). Brain morphometry and cognitive performance in detoxified alcohol-dependents with preserved psychosocial functioning. *Neuropsychopharmacology: Official Publication of the American College of Neuropsychopharmacology*, 32(2), 429–38.

Chanraud, S., Leroy, C., Martelli, C., Kostogianni, N., Delain, F., Aubin, H.-J., Reynaud, M. and Martinot, J.-L. (2009a). Episodic memory in detoxified alcoholics: contribution of grey matter microstructure alteration. *PloS One*, 4(8), e6786.

Chanraud, S., Reynaud, M., Wessa, M., Penttila, J., Kostogianni, N., Cachia, A., Artiges, E., Delain, F., Perrin, M., Aubin, H.-J., Cointepas, Y., Martelli, C. and Martinot, J.-L. (2009b). Diffusion tensor tractography in mesencephalic bundles: relation to mental flexibility in detoxified alcohol-dependent subjects. *Neuropsychopharmacology*, 34, 1223–32.

Compton, W. M., Thomas, Y., Stinson, F. S. and Grant, B. F. (2007). Prevalence, correlates, disability, and comorbidity of DSM-IV drug abuse and dependence in the United States: results from the national epidemiologic survey on alcohol and related conditions. *Archives of General Psychiatry*, 64, 566–76.

Damasio, A. R. (1996). The somatic marker hypothesis and the possible functions of the prefrontal cortex. *Philosophical Transactions of the Royal Society of London. Series B, Biological Sciences*, 351(1346), 1413–20.

de la Monte, S. M. (1988). Disproportionate atrophy of cerebral white matter in chronic alcoholics. *Archives of Neurology*, 45(9), 990–2.

de la Monte, S. M. and Kril, J. J. (2014). Human alcohol-related neuropathology. *Acta Neuropathologica*, 127(1), 71–90.

Diener, H. C., Müller, A., Thron, A., Poremba, M., Dichgans, J. and Rapp, H. (1986). Correlation of clinical signs with CT findings in patients with cerebellar disease. *Journal of Neurology*, 233(1), 5–12.

Expertise Collective de l'Inserm. (2003). *Dommages Sociaux, Abus et Dépendance*. Paris: Inserm.

Fama, R., Pfefferbaum, A. and Sullivan, E. V. (2004). Perceptual learning in detoxified alcoholic men: contributions from explicit memory, executive function, and age. *Alcoholism: Clinical and Experimental Research*, 28(11), 1657–65.

Fein, G., McGillivray, S. and Finn, P. (2006). Normal performance on a simulated gambling task in treatment-naive alcohol-dependent individuals. *Alcoholism: Clinical and Experimental Research*, 30(6), 959–66.

Gazdzinski, S., Durazzo, T. C., Studholme, C., Song, E., Banys, P. and Meyerhoff, D. J. (2005). Quantitative brain MRI in alcohol dependence: preliminary evidence for effects of concurrent chronic cigarette smoking on regional brain volumes. *Alcoholism: Clinical and Experimental Research*, 29(8), 1484–95.

Goudriaan, A. E., Oosterlaan, J., de Beurs, E. and van den Brink, W. (2005). Decision making in pathological gambling: a comparison between pathological gamblers, alcohol dependents, persons with Tourette syndrome, and normal controls. *Brain Research. Cognitive Brain Research*, 23(1), 137–51.

Grant, B. F., Stinson, F. S., Dawson, D. A. and Chou, S. P. (2004). Prevalence and co-occurrence of substance use disorders and independent mood and anxiety disorders. *Archives of General Psychiatry*, 61, 807–16.

Harding, A. J., Halliday, G. M., Ng, J. L., Harper, C. G. and Kril, J. J. (1996). Loss of vasopressin-immunoreactive neurons in alcoholics is dose-related and time-dependent. *Neuroscience*, 72(3), 699–708.

Harper, C. G. (1998). The neuropathology of alcohol-specific brain damage, or does alcohol damage the brain? *Journal of Neuropathology and Experimental Neurology*, 57(2), 101–10.

Harper, C. G. and Kril, J. J. (1985). Brain atrophy in chronic alcoholic patients: a quantitative pathological study. *Journal of Neurology, Neurosurgery and Psychiatry*, 48, 211–17.

Harper, C. G. and Kril, J. J. (1988). Corpus callosal thickness in alcoholics. *British Journal of Addiction*, 83(5), 577–80.

Harper, C. and Matsumoto, I. (2005). Ethaë and brain damage. *Current Opinion in Pharmacology*, 5(1), 73–8.

Harper, C., Kril, J. and Daly, J. (1987). Are we drinking our neurones away? *British Medical Journal (Clinical Research Edn)*, 294(6571), 534–6.

Hasin, D., Stinson, F. S., Ogburn, E. and Grant, B. F. (2007). Prevalence, correlates, disability, and comorbidity of DSM-IV alcohol abuse and dependence in the United States: results from the National Epidemiologic Survey on Alcohol and Related Conditions. *Archives of General Psychiatry*, 64(7), 830–42.

Hommer, D., Momenan, R., Rawlings, R., Ragan, P., Williams, W., Rio, D. and Eckardt, M. (1996). Decreased corpus callosum size among alcoholic women. *Archives of Neurology*, 53, 359–63.

Ihara, H. (2000). Group and case study of the dysexecutive syndrome in alcoholism without amnesia. *Journal of Neurology, Neurosurgery and Psychiatry*, 68(6), 731–7.

Jauhar, P. and Montaldi, D. (2000). Wernicke-Korsakoff syndrome and the use of brain imaging. *Alcohol and Alcoholism*, 35(1), 21–3.

Jensen, G. B. and Pakkenberg, B. (1993). Do alcoholics drink their neurons away? *Lancet*, 342(8881), 1201–4.

Jernigan, T. L., Zatz, L. M., Ahumada, A. J., Pfefferbaum, A., Tinklenberg, J. R. and Moses, J. A. (1982). CT measures of cerebrospinal fluid volume in alcoholics and normal volunteers. *Psychiatry Research*, 7(1), 9–17.

Jernigan, T. L., Butters, N., DiTraglia, G., Schafer, K., Smith, T., Irwin, M., Grant, I., Schuckit, M. and Cermak, L. S. (1991). Reduced cerebral grey matter observed in alcoholics using magnetic resonance imaging. *Alcoholism: Clinical and Experimental Research*, 15(3), 418–27.

Kerr, A. and Zelazo, P. D. (2004). Development of "hot" executive function: the children's gambling task. *Brain and Cognition*, 55(1), 148–57.

Koob, G. F. (2009). Neurobiological substrates for the dark side of compulsivity in addiction. *Neuropharmacology*, 56 (Supplement 1), 18–31.

Kopelman, M. D. (1995). The Korsakoff syndrome. *The British Journal of Psychiatry: The Journal of Mental Science*, 166(2), 154–73.

Kopelman, M. D. (2002). Disorders of memory. *Brain: A Journal of Neurology*, 125(Part 10), 2152–90.

Kril, J. J., Halliday, G. M., Svoboda, M. D. and Cartwright, H. (1997). The cerebral cortex is damaged in chronic alcoholics. *Neuroscience*, 79(4), 983–98.

Kurth, C., Wegerer, C.A.V., Reulbach, U., Lewczuk, P., Kornhuber, J., Steinho, B. J. and Bleich, S. (2004). Analysis of hippocampal atrophy in alcoholic patients by a Kohonen feature map. *Neuroreport*, 15(2), 67–71.

Le Berre, A. P., Vabret, F., Cauvin, C., Pinon, K., Allain, P., Pitel, A.-L., Eustache, F. and Beaunieux, H. (2012). Cognitive barriers to readiness to change in alcohol-dependent patients. *Alcoholism: Clinical and Experimental Research*, 36(9), 1542–9.

Le Berre, A. P., Rauchs, G., La Joie, R., Segobin, S., Mézenge, F., Boudehent, C., Vabret, F., Viader, F., Eustache, F., Pitel, A.-L. and Beaunieux, H. (2013). Readiness to change and brain damage in patients with chronic alcoholism. *Psychiatry Research*, 213(3), 202–9.

Le Berre, A. P., Rauchs, G., La Joie, R., Mézenge, F., Boudehent, C., Vabret, F., Segobin, S., Viader, F., Allain, P., Eustache, F., Pitel, A.-L. and Beaunieux, H. (2014). Impaired decision-making and brain shrinkage in alcoholism. *European Psychiatry: The Journal of the Association of European Psychiatrists*, 29(3), 125–33.

Lindboe, C. F. and Løberg, E. M. (1988). The frequency of brain lesions in alcoholics. Comparison between the 5-year periods 1975–1979 and 1983–1987. *Journal of the Neurological Sciences*, 88(1–3), 107–13.

Mair, W. G. P., Warrington, E. K. and Weiskrantz, L. (1979). Memory disorder in Korsakoff's psychosis a neuropathological and neuropsychological investigation of two cases. *Brain*, 102(4), 749–83.

Mayes, A. R., Meudell, P. R., Mann, D. and Pickering, A. (1988). Location of lesions in Korsakoff's syndrome: neuropsychological and neuropathological data on two patients. *Cortex: A Journal Devoted to the Study of the Nervous System and Behavior*, 24(3), 367–88.

Mechtcheriakov, S., Brenneis, C., Egger, K., Koppelstaetter, F., Schocke, M. and Marksteiner, J. (2007). A widespread distinct pattern of cerebral atrophy in patients with alcohol addiction revealed by voxel-based morphometry. *Journal of Neurology, Neurosurgery, and Psychiatry*, 78(6), 610–14.

Melgaard, B. and Ahlgren, P. (1986). Ataxia and cerebellar atrophy in chronic alcoholics. *Journal of Neurology*, 233(1), 13–15.

Moselhy, H. F., Georgiou, G. and Kahn, A. (2001). Frontal lobe changes in alcoholism: a review of the literature. *Alcohol and Alcoholism*, 36(5), 357–68.

Naqvi, N. H. and Bechara, A. (2009). The hidden island of addiction: the insula. *Trends in Neurosciences*, 32(1), 56–67.

Nicolás, J. M., Catafau, A. M., Estruch, R., Lomeña, F. J., Salamero, M., Herranz, R., Monforte, R., Cardenal, C. and Urbano-Marquez, A. (1993). Regional cerebral blood flow-SPECT in chronic alcoholism: relation to neuropsychological testing. *Journal of Nuclear Medicine: Official Publication, Society of Nuclear Medicine*, 34(9), 1452–9.

Nicolás, J. M., Estruch, R., Salamero, M., Orteu, N., Fernandez-Solà, J., Sacanella, E. and Urbano-Márquez, A. (1997). Brain impairment in well-nourished chronic alcoholics is related to ethanol intake. *Annals of Neurology*, 41(5), 590–8.

Noël, X., Brevers, D. and Bechara, A. (2013). A neurocognitive approach to understanding the neurobiology of addiction. *Current Opinion in Neurobiology*, 23(4), 632–8.

Noël, X., Bechara, A., Dan, B., Hanak, C. and Verbanck, P. (2007). Response inhibition deficit is involved in poor decision making under risk in nonamnesic individuals with alcoholism. *Neuropsychology*, 21(6), 778–86.

Noël, X., Van der Linden, M., Brevers, D., Campanella, S., Hanak, C., Kornreich, C. and Verbanck, P. (2012). The contribution of executive functions deficits to impaired episodic memory in individuals with alcoholism. *Psychiatry Research*, 198(1), 116–22.

Oscar-Berman, M. and Marinković, K. (2007). Alcohol: effects on neurobehavioral functions and the brain. *Neuropsychology Review*, 17(3), 239–57.

Oscar-Berman, M., Kirkley, S. M., Gansler, D. A. and Couture, A. (2004). Comparisons of Korsakoff and non-Korsakoff alcoholics on neuropsychological tests of prefrontal brain functioning. *Alcoholism: Clinical and Experimental Research*, 28(4), 667–75.

Pentney, R. J., Mullan, B. A., Felong, A. M. and Dlugos, C. A. (2002). The total numbers of cerebellar granule neurons in young and aged Fischer 344 and Wistar-Kyoto rats do not change as a result of lengthy ethanol treatment. *Cerebellum*, 1(1), 79–89.

Pfefferbaum, A. and Sullivan, E.V. (2005). Disruption of brain white matter microstructure by excessive intracellular and extracellular fluid in alcoholism: evidence from diffusion tensor imaging. *Neuropsychopharmacology*, 30(2), 423–32.

Pfefferbaum, A., Adalsteinsson, E. and Sullivan, E.V. (2006). Supratentorial profile of white matter microstructural integrity in recovering alcoholic men and women. *Biological Psychiatry*, 59(4), 364–72.

Pfefferbaum, A., Lim, K. O., Zipursky, R. B., Mathalon, D. H., Rosenbloom, M. J., Lane, B., Ha, C. N. and Sullivan, E.V. (1992). Brain gray and white matter volume loss accelerates with aging in chronic alcoholics: a quantitative MRI study. *Alcoholism, Clinical and Experimental Research*, 16(6), 1078–89.

Pfefferbaum, A., Sullivan, E. V., Rosenbloom, M. J., Shear, P. K., Mathalon, D. H. and Lim, K. O. (1993). Increase in brain cerebrospinal fluid volume is greater in older than in younger alcoholic patients: a replication study and CT/MRI comparison. *Psychiatry Research*, 50(4), 257–74.

Pfefferbaum, A., Lim, K. O., Desmond, J. E. and Sullivan, E. V. (1996). Thinning of the corpus callosum in older alcoholic men: a magnetic resonance imaging study. *Alcoholism: Clinical and Experimental Research*, 20(4), 752–7.

Pfefferbaum, A., Sullivan, E. V., Mathalon, D. H. and Lim, K. O. (1997). Frontal lobe volume loss observed with magnetic resonance imaging in older chronic alcoholics. *Alcoholism: Clinical and Experimental Research*, 21(3), 521–9.

Pfefferbaum, A., Sullivan, E. V., Hedehus, M., Adalsteinsson, E., Lim, K. O. and Moseley, M. (2000). In vivo detection and functional correlates of white matter microstructural disruption in chronic alcoholism. *Alcoholism: Clinical and Experimental Research*, 24(8), 1214–21.

Pfefferbaum, A., Rosenbloom, M., Rohlfing, T. and Sullivan, E. V. (2009). Degradation of association and projection white matter systems in alcoholism detected with quantitative fiber tracking. *Biological Psychiatry*, 65(8), 680–90.

Phillips, S., Harper, C. and Kril, J. (1987). A quantitative histological study of the cerebellar vermis in alcoholic patients. *Brain: A Journal of Neurology*, 110, 301–14.

Pitel, A. L., Beaunieux, H., Witkowski, T., Vabret, F., Guillery-Girard, B., Quinette, P., Desgranges, B. and Eustache, F. (2007). Genuine episodic memory deficits and executive dysfunctions in alcoholic subjects early in abstinence. *Alcoholism: Clinical and Experimental Research*, 31(7), 1169–78.

Pitel, A. L., Aupée, A.-M., Chételat, G., Mézenge, F., Beaunieux, H., de la Sayette, V., Viader, F., Baron, J.-C., Eustache, F. and Desgranges, B. (2009). Morphological and glucose metabolism abnormalities in alcoholic Korsakoff's syndrome: group comparisons and individual analyses. *PloS One*, 4(11), e7748.

Pitel, A. L., Chanraud, S., Sullivan, E.V and Pfefferbaum, A. (2010). Callosal microstructural abnormalities in Alzheimer's disease and alcoholism: same phenotype, different mechanisms. *Psychiatry Research*, 184(1), 49–56.

Pitel, A.-L., Chételat, G., Le Berre, A. P., Desgranges, B., Eustache, F. and Beaunieux, H. (2012). Macrostructural abnormalities in Korsakoff syndrome compared with uncomplicated alcoholism. *Neurology*, 78(17), 1330–3.

Reed, L. J., Lasserson, D., Marsden, P., Stanhope, N., Stevens, T., Bello, F., Kingsley, D., Colchester, A. and Kopelman, M. D. (2003). FDG-PET findings in the Wernicke-Korsakoff syndrome. *Cortex*, 39(4–5), 1027–45.

Ron, M. A., Acker, W., Shaw, G. K. and Lishman, W. A. (1982). Computerized tomography of the brain in chronic alcoholism. *Brain*, 105(3), 497–514.

Schmahmann, J. D. (2010). The role of the cerebellum in cognition and emotion: personal reflections since 1982 on the dysmetria of thought hypothesis, and its historical evolution from theory to therapy. *Neuropsychological Review*, 20, 236–60.

Schulte, T., Pfefferbaum, A. and Sullivan, E.V. (2004). Parallel interhemispheric processing in aging and alcoholism: relation to corpus callosum size. *Neuropsychologia*, 42(2), 257–71.

Schulte, T., Sullivan, E. V., Müller-Oehring, E. M., Adalsteinsson, E. and Pfefferbaum, A. (2005). Corpus callosal microstructural integrity influences interhemispheric processing: a diffusion tensor imaging study. *Cerebral Cortex*, 15(9), 1384–92.

Shallice, T. and Burgess, P. (1998). Domain of supervisory processes and the temporal organization. In A. Roberts, T. Robbins and L. Weiskrantz (eds), *The Frontal Cortex*. Oxford: Oxford University Press, pp. 22–35.

Shear, P. K., Sullivan, E. V., Lane, B. and Pfefferbaum, A. (1996). Mammillary body and cerebellar shrinkage in chronic alcoholics with and without amnesia. *Alcoholism: Clinical and Experimental Research*, 20(8), 1489–95.

Sheedy, D., Lara, A., Garrick, T. and Harper, C. (1999). Size of mamillary bodies in health and disease: useful measurements in neuroradiological diagnosis of Wernicke's encephalopathy. *Alcoholism: Clinical and Experimental Research*, 23(10), 1624–8.

Shimamura, P., Jernigan, L., Squire, R. and Findings, C. T. (1988). Korsakoff's syndrome: radiological(CT) findings and neuropsychological correlates. *The Journal of Neuroscience: The Official Journal of the Society for Neuroscience*, 8(11), 4400–10.

Squire, L. R., Amaral, D. G. and Press, G. A. (1990). Magnetic resonance imaging of the hippocampal formation and mammillary nuclei distinguish medial temporal lobe and diencephalic amnesia. *The Journal of Neuroscience: The Official Journal of the Society for Neuroscience*, 10(9), 3106–17.

Stacy, A. W. and Wiers, R. W. (2010). Implicit cognition and addiction: a tool for explaining paradoxical behavior. *Annual Review of Clinical Psychology*, 6, 551–75.

Sullivan, E. V. (2003). Compromised pontocerebellar and cerebellothalamocortical systems: speculations on their contributions to cognitive and motor impairment in nonamnesic alcoholism. *Alcoholism: Clinical and Experimental Research*, 27(9), 1409–19.

Sullivan, E. V. and Marsh, L. (2003). Hippocampal volume deficits in alcoholic Korsakoff's syndrome. *Neurology*, 61(12), 1716–19.

Sullivan, E. V and Pfefferbaum, A. (2009). Neuroimaging of the Wernicke-Korsakoff syndrome. *Alcohol and Alcoholism*, 44(2), 155–65.

Sullivan, E. V., Rosenbloom, M. J. and Pfefferbaum, A. (2000). Pattern of motor and cognitive deficits in detoxified alcoholic men. *Alcoholism: Clinical and Experimental Research*, 24(5), 611–21.

Sullivan, E. V., Marsh, L., Mathalon, D. H., Lim, K. O. and Pfefferbaum, A. (1995). Anterior hippocampal volume deficits in nonamnesic, aging chronic alcoholics. *Alcoholism: Clinical and Experimental Research*, 19(1), 110–22.

Sullivan, E. V., Mathalon, D. H., Lim, K. O., Marsh, L. and Pfefferbaum, A. (1998). Patterns of regional cortical dysmorphology distinguishing schizophrenia and chronic alcoholism. *Biological Psychiatry*, 43(2), 118–31.

Sullivan, E. V., Lane, B., Deshmukh, A, Rosenbloom, M. J., Desmond, J. E., Lim, K. O. and Pfefferbaum, A. (1999). In vivo mammillary body volume deficits in amnesic and nonamnesic alcoholics. *Alcoholism: Clinical and Experimental Research*, 23(10), 1629–36.

Sullivan, E. V., Rosenbloom, M. J., Serventi, K. L., Deshmukh, A. and Pfefferbaum, A. (2003). Effects of alcohol dependence comorbidity and antipsychotic medication on volumes of the thalamus and pons in schizophrenia. *The American Journal of Psychiatry*, 160(6), 1110–16.

Tarnowska-Dziduszko, E., Bertrand, E. and Szpak, G. M. (1995). Morphological changes in the corpus callosum in chronic alcoholism. *Folia Neuropathologica*, 33(1), 25–9.

Torvik, A., Lindboe, C. F. and Rogde, S. (1982). Brain lesions in alcoholics: a neuropathological study with clinical correlations. *Journal of the Neurological Sciences*, 56(2–3), 233–48.

Trivedi, R., Bagga, D., Bhattacharya, D., Kaur, P., Kumar, P., Khushu, S., Tripathi, R. P. and Singh, N. (2013). White matter damage is associated with memory decline in chronic alcoholics: a quantitative diffusion tensor tractography study. *Behavioural Brain Research*, 250, 192–8.

Verdejo-García, A. and Bechara, A. (2009). A somatic marker theory of addiction. *Neuropharmacology*, 56 (Supplement 1), 48–62.

Verdejo-García, A. and Pérez-García, M. (2008). Substance abusers' self-awareness of the neurobehavioral consequences of addiction. *Psychiatry Research*, 158(2), 172–80.

Victor, M., Adams, R. and Collins, G. (1971). The Wernicke-Korsakoff syndrome: a clinical and pathological study of 245 patients, 82 with post-mortem examinations. *Contemporary Neurology Series*, 7, 1–206.

Volkow, N. D., Hitzemann, R., Fowler, J. S., Overall, J. E., Burr, G. and Wolf, A. P. (1994). Alcoholics. *The American Journal of Geriatric Psychiatry*, 151(2), 178–83.

Wang, G.-J., Volkow, N. D., Roque, C. T., Cestaro, V. L., Hitzemann, R. J., Cantos, E. L., Levy, A. V. and Dhawan, A. P. (1993). Functional importance of ventricule enlargement and cortical atrophy in healthy subjects and alcoholics as assessed with PET, MRI imaging, and neuropsychologic testing. *Radiology*, 186, 55–8.

Zahr, N. M., Pitel, A.-L., Chanraud, S. and Sullivan, E. V. (2010). Contributions of studies on alcohol use disorders to understanding cerebellar function. *Neuropsychology Review*, 20(3), 280–9.

9

ALCOHOL, AGEING AND COGNITIVE FUNCTION

A nutritional perspective

Adrian Bonner

The role of nutrition in the development of alcohol-related cognitive dysfunction, within a life cycle approach, is reviewed in this chapter. From prenatal exposure to alcohol, underage drinking, binge drinking in adolescents and adults and drinking problems in older people, the interaction of alcohol and poor nutrition can have an adverse effect on cognitive performance. These brain-related effects occurring across the life span can have a significant impact on the process of ageing and the development of dementia. The progression of chronic alcohol misuse includes:

- Changes in dietary selection and eating behavior
- Impaired metabolism, including:
  - decreased efficiency of the liver
  - impaired absorption of nutrients via the gut
  - increased vulnerability to diabetes
- Damage to tissues and organs due to oxidative stress
- Cognitive impairment
- Use of alcohol to self-medicate for anxiety, depression and other mental health problems
- Disruption of sleep and other circadian rhythms

Alcohol and nutrition

From a socio-economic perspective, health inequalities are increased in people abusing alcohol who are often consuming as much as 50 per cent of their daily calories from alcohol (Lieber, 2003). The consequences of chronic alcohol abuse and dependence result in a wide range of pathological indications found in muscle, bone and major organ systems, including the brain, cardiovascular system, digestive system and the liver (Albano, 2006). In populations using alcohol to excess, a wide range of health problems have been attributed to poor diet and heavy alcohol consumption. Morbidity and mortality result from heavy alcohol use, and disproportionately affect people of lower socio-economic status (Makela, 1999). Households with higher incomes are more likely to have better-quality diets, consuming more fruit and vegetables (Darmon and Drewnowski 2008; Johansson *et al.*, 1999). Lower socio-economic status and income have been linked to poorer overall health, negative health behaviors, such as smoking and alcohol misuse, and to shorter life expectancy. Individuals living in less deprived areas of the UK can expect to live ten years longer than those in more deprived areas, and to spend more life-years free of chronic illness and disabilities (van Oers *et al.*, 1999). Lifestyle factors such as diet and alcohol consumption may partly explain such health differentials. Socio-economic differences in nutrition are evident in that families who are less affluent, less educated or employed in less prestigious jobs have diets that are least concordant with official recommendations, both in general and specifically in relation to fruit and vegetable consumption in Europe and in the UK (Billson, Pryer and Nichols, 1999; Lindstrom *et al.*, 2001). It is well established that the consumption of alcohol is implicated in both the cause and progression of chronic liver disease. Increased consumption of alcohol over the lifetime, the amount consumed on any one occasion and the frequency of drinking all contribute to health risks more or less in a linear pattern for both men and women. This conclusion, from a major European review conducted within the *Addictions and Lifestyles in Contemporary Europe: Reframing Addictions Project* (ALICE-RAP Consortium, 2012), provides strong support for the idea that there is no drinking level without risk. The frequency of high-risk drinking is related directly to both risk and the severity of alcohol dependence, as shown in large-scale, general population-based studies.

Individuals who binge or are chronic drinkers have different health outcomes when compared to social drinkers. Therefore, knowing a person's drinking pattern is important in understanding the extent of the individual's dependence on alcohol and on the severity of liver damage, as well as other related metabolic disturbances that are modulated by drinking behavior. Genetic factors also contribute to some of the differences in alcohol metabolism in the population.

The metabolism of alcohol changes the level of oxidation in the liver, leading to alterations in lipid (fat), carbohydrate, protein, lactate and uric acid metabolism. Comorbid conditions such as type 2 diabetes, infection with hepatitis B or C and/or human immunodeficiency virus (HIV), hemochromatosis, or obesity are often present in alcohol-dependent individuals. The quantity and frequency of alcohol consumption has a major impact on metabolic processes underlying these comorbid conditions (Zakhari and Li, 2007).

The major pathways of alcohol metabolism and genetic factors have been investigated in cellular and molecular biology studies, indicating the role of factors such as nutritional and other environmental factors which result in some individuals having an increased vulnerability to organ damage. The risks of heavy drinking and adverse health conditions such as alcoholic liver disease (ALD), dementia and alcohol dependence are well known. However, not everyone who drinks chronically develops ALD or dementia, and the major risk factors for disease development and the mechanisms by which this occurs remain unclear (Li, 2008).

Nutrition and alcohol across the life cycle

Long-term, longitudinal research such as the National Longitudinal Study of Adolescent Health highlight the benefit of a life-course approach to promoting health through adolescence and young adulthood. Parental education, income and family structure, parental health conditions (asthma, diabetes, obesity, migraines) and early health challenges (physical abuse, presence of a disability and parental alcoholism and smoking) are significant predictors of health and well-being in later life. These family-of-origin mediators of a young person's health and health behaviors are reflected in obesity, depression, smoking, drinking and inactivity. These health status indicators, especially obesity, become more adverse with age and should be addressed in young adulthood with a view to promoting healthy lifestyles in later adulthood (Bauldry et al., 2012).

Fetal Alcohol Syndrome (FAS)

From a life-course perspective, fetal alcohol spectrum disorders (FASD) are the leading non-genetic cause of neurodevelopmental disability in children. In addition to the teratogenic effect of alcohol, environmental factors such as socio-economic status and nutrition significantly influence the risk of FASD. Iron deficiency without anemia (Rufer et al., 2012), choline (Bernhard et al., 2013) and folate (Hewitt et al., 2011) are potent and synergistic modifiers of FASD risk. Alcohol consumption during pregnancy can disrupt brain development of the fetus, leading to a variety of neurocognitive deficits associated with the activation of oxidative-inflammatory cascade in different brain regions. These events are found in postnatal ethanol exposure (Tiwari and Chopra, 2012). The death of newly formed neurons within the brain of adults with chronic alcohol misuse is related to oxidative stress (see later section, Oxidative stress), postulated to be a mechanism mediating cognitive deficits observed in alcoholism (Herrera et al., 2003). The dyad of a mother with alcohol dependence and her fetus is a very complex entity in which several elements play a role at different stages in the development of fetal brain damage. The cumulative effects of environmental factors and interaction with maternal and fetal genetic background have severe and life-long consequences (Guerrini, Thomson and Gurling, 2007).

Disordered eating behavior reflected in satiety problems and self-regulation is common in prenatal alcohol exposure (PAE), resulting in altered acquisition and distribution of body mass with increasing age. Children with PAE may be at risk of nutritional deficiencies, which are influenced by inappropriate food preferences, disordered eating patterns, medication use and the stressful dynamics surrounding food preparation and mealtime (Werts et al., 2013). There is substantial evidence suggesting that alcohol affects brain function and behavior differently during adolescence than during adulthood; adolescents are more vulnerable to the long-term effects of alcohol abuse. The adolescent brain may be especially sensitive to a harmful combination of alcohol abuse and nutritional deficiencies that have a significant impact on structural and functional brain development, which takes place during the teenage years (Guerri and Pascual, 2010; Sher, 2008).

Alcohol consumption impairs information processing and cognitive performance on a range of tasks (Koelega, 1995; Maylor *et al.*, 1992). It is possible that certain patterns of consumption may accelerate the alcohol-induced decline of brain function and promote mental health and cognitive issues occurring in both young and older adults. For example, depression and suicidal behavior in adolescents are frequently comorbid with alcohol and drug abuse. These mental health issues have been linked to adverse health behaviors, including maladaptive eating behavior and dietary selection. Alcohol abuse may lead to the deficiency of micronutrients including selenium, an essential trace element (Sher, 2008). During the period of brain and behavioral maturation many of the changes that take place during the second decade of life are novel and do not simply represent changes in neuronal plasticity in neuroadaptation, which occurs during development.

Currently there is concern over the increasing consumption of alcohol by older people (Geels *et al.*, 2013; Rao, 2013; Withall and Shafiee, 2015). Due to a range of socio-economic changes and improvements in health care, people are living longer in most countries. This demographic change is reflected in increases in diseases such as cancer, diabetes, dementia and Alzheimer's disease (AD). Nutritional status underpins sleep disruption resulting from desynchronization of biological rhythms, a problem common to both problematic alcohol users and the elderly. These age-related changes will be adversely affected by changes in the digestive system resulting in poor absorption of macro- and micronutrients (vitamins). Pathological changes in the ageing circulatory system include atherosclerosis and thrombosis, which may lead to cognitive impairment through cerebral infarcts. Oxidative stress is now seen as a major contributor to the process of atherogenesis (Kalmijn *et al.*, 1997).

Cognitive impairment

A well-documented severe form of brain damage in alcohol misusers is Wernicke's Encephalopathy (WE). This acute brain syndrome is a life-threatening, neurological disorder that occurs when there is thiamine (vitamin B1) deficiency resulting in neurocognitive impairment. WE is associated with severe short-term cognitive impairment, mental confusion, eye movement abnormalities and poor muscular co-ordination. Inadequate treatment of this acute syndrome may lead to the chronic deficit state of Korsakoff's Syndrome (KS), characterized by impairment of anterograde and retrograde memory, and confabulation (Cook, Hallwood and Thomson, 1998). WE and KS can be thought of as acute and chronic stages of the same disorder, with common underlying neuropathology, now commonly described as Wernicke-Korsakoff Syndrome (WKS; see Scalzo, Bowden and Hillbom, 2015). The clinical presentation of WE is highly variable. Lough (2012) illustrated this in a review considering clinical signs, brain imaging and thiamine blood levels, considering case reports from 2001 to 2011. From this review, 81 per cent of cases (43/53) were non-alcohol related. KS or chronic cognitive neurological changes occurred in 28 per cent (15/53), suggesting that existing diagnostic tools need to be improved (Lough, 2012). A longitudinal study by Schafer showed that, in addition to the chronic neurotoxic effect of alcohol, a number of different medical and psychiatric factors, as well as the cellular effects of alcohol, contribute to the cognitive scores of patients at various points in the clinical course (Schafer et al., 1991). A high incidence (15 per cent) of diabetes is found in WKS patients, perhaps providing support to the idea that, in addition to the direct toxic effect of alcohol on the brain, metabolic disruptions in carbohydrate and other nutritional processes contribute to the development of WKS (Wijnia et al., 2012).

The range of organic brain syndromes, with a variety of cognitive and motor deficits, found in people with alcohol dependence, may be considered as variants of the WKS, indicating the need to address the nutritional status of all patients who abuse alcohol. This approach has been used in the diagnosis of preclinical signs of WE by measurements of thiamine in blood. Some with alcohol dependence have severe neuropsychological deficits, whereas others, with a similar drinking history, exhibit preserved performance. Whole blood thiamine levels have been found to be selectively related to memory performance in alcohol-dependent groups providing the opportunity to identify "uncomplicated" alcoholics who are at risk for neuropsychological complications (Pitel et al., 2011). Further research into the role of both diet and alcohol via valid, reliable and easily administered tools for measurement of both diet and alcohol is needed (Wrieden et al., 2004). The supplementation of thiamine in the diet of people at risk of problematic alcohol use is discussed later in this chapter.

Metabolic perspectives on brain function

Chronic alcohol abuse can have adverse effects in the selection of diet and eating behavior resulting in suboptimal intake of nutrients required for the complex metabolic mechanisms underpinning physiological and behavioral functioning. Pathological effects resulting from this disruption of the homeostatic control of physiological processes and behavior include impaired absorption of nutrients, via the gastro intestinal tract, and liver damage. An important consequence or cause of nutritionally related problems associated with alcohol consumption is diabetes.

Diabetes

Excessive consumption of alcohol is a risk factor for both diabetes and poor adherence in alcohol treatment programs. Since the mid-1990s several large prospective studies have demonstrated a significant reduction in risk of type 2 diabetes in moderate drinkers; typically a 40 per cent risk reduction after controlling for other major risk factors. A J- or U-shaped association between level of alcohol consumption and incidence of diabetes has been found in some cohorts drawn from the general population (Conigrave and Rimm, 2003). A lower risk of diabetes has been found in people who frequently drink in moderation. This has not been found in groups of health professionals, groups containing few heavy drinkers. The effect of alcohol is moderated by bodyweight, but there is little information on the type of beverage. Longitudinal studies, but not cross-sectional studies, suggest that moderate long-term changes in alcohol consumption are positively related with the levels and changes in high-density lipoprotein cholesterol in healthy adult men and women (Koppes et al., 2005). Insulin resistance and pancreatic β-cell dysfunction are pre-requisites for the development of diabetes. However, alcohol consumption in diabetes is controversial. The causes of dysregulation of various processes in metabolic diseases, such as diabetes, include a defect in the insulin-mediated glucose function of adipocytes and an impaired insulin action in the liver (Kim and Kim, 2012). Increased levels of leptin in chronic alcohol abuse has been proposed as one of the main mechanisms that result in insulin resistance in people with alcoholism. Peptides and neurotrophic factors regulate appetite. This and other processes, such as alcohol consumption that precede the onset of diabetes, highlight the interplay between alcohol dependency and diabetes (Ju et al. 2011).

Most cases of diabetes mellitus result from decreased insulin secretion (type 1, insulin-dependent) or altered insulin action (type 2, insulin-independent). The most common pancreatic disease that causes diabetes mellitus is chronic pancreatitis that results from alcohol abuse (Greenhouse and Lardinois, 1996). Glucose intolerance and diabetes mellitus are both prevalent not only in alcoholic liver cirrhosis, but also in chronic alcoholism without cirrhosis. Excessive oxidation is thought to play a significant role in the pathogenesis of ethanol-induced glucose intolerance. Gluconeogenesis from glycogen, fatty acids, amino acids and lactate are also impaired during ethanol metabolism. Thus, ethanol-induced hypoglycaemia is closely related to depressed hepatic gluconeogenesis produced by ethanol, whereas ethanol-induced hyperglycemia or diabetes is due to hepatic and tissue insulin resistance and impairment of pancreatic endocrine system (Ishii and Ito, 1996). Data from a ten-year follow-up of a defined general population (n = 159,200) of native, urban Swedes indicated a six- to 13-fold and four- to six-fold excess rates of subjects with brain infarction among people with diabetes and alcoholism, respectively (Lindegard and Hillbom, 1987).

Some psychiatric disorders, such as depression, have a significant and negative effect on diabetes outcomes. It is well established that individuals with diabetes, alcohol and drug abuse/dependence have a significantly higher mortality (Jackson et al., 2007; Prisciandaro et al., 2011).

The conclusion from these studies is that there is a delicate balance between the harmful and beneficial effects of alcohol on the incidence of diabetes. Despite evidence that moderate drinking can protect against type 2 diabetes under some circumstances, research into the global burden of disease indicates that both clinical and public health measures are needed to address the problem of diabetes associated with excessive alcohol consumption. Reducing alcohol consumption in populations is predicted to have a significant beneficial influence on a range of health measures including diabetes.

Neurotransmission and brain function

Chronic alcohol abuse can have adverse effects in the selection of diet and eating behavior resulting in suboptimal intake of nutrients required for the complex metabolic mechanisms underpinning physiological and behavioral functioning. Pathological effects resulting from this disruption of the homeostatic control of physiological processes and behavior include impaired absorption of nutrients, via the gastrointestinal tract, and liver damage.

Tryptophan, serotonin and brain function

A discussion of the metabolism of serotonin (5-HT) is pertinent in this chapter as it is an important neurotransmitter in the brain, and its synthesis is significantly affected by dietary sources of tryptophan (Trp), an essential amino acid. Many of the effects of ethanol on behavior involve perturbations of 5-HT and related systems either by direct impact of ethanol causing the degeneration of 5-HT axons and axon terminals (Halliday, Baker and Harper, 1995) or via other aspects of the metabolism of tryptophan, the precursor of 5-HT. Acutely, ethanol depletes brain serotonin in normal subjects, which may contribute to alcohol-induced aggression (Pihl *et al.*, 1995) in susceptible individuals and also the incidence of depression and suicide in alcohol misusers (Meyer, Chrousos and Gold, 2001). Melatonin and related metabolites, pivotal in the regulation of the sleep–wake cycle is synthesized from 5-HT in the dark phase.

Trp availability to the brain is increased before the appearance of the alcohol-withdrawal syndrome (AWS), raising the possibility that the associated behavioral disturbances seen in AWS are related to this metabolic change (Oretti *et al.*, 1996; Badawy *et al.*, 1998; Oretti *et al.*, 2000). Trp metabolism is also implicated in the predisposition to becoming alcohol dependent (Badawy, 1996; 1999). Eating disorders and sleep problems, which are often associated with concurrent mental health problems, are frequently found in problematic alcohol users. Feeding disturbances, depression and suicide, impulsivity and violence, anxiety and harm avoidance, obsessive-compulsive features, seasonal variation of symptoms, as well as disturbances in neuroendocrine and vascular tissues, occur in patients with alcohol problems and eating disorders. These clinical features indicate the involvement of serotonin (5-HT) and its dysregulation, as well as other neurochemical systems linked to 5-HT. The control of food intake has been linked with behavioral impulsivity and mood. Concurrent or sequential periods of binge eating and drinking, behavioral impulsivity and depression in patients with eating disorders are determined by the modulation of the central nervous system by serotonin (Jimerson and Lesem, 1990).

The role of serotonin in eating behavior and the sleep–wake cycle, as noted above, indicates the extent to which 5-HT is involved in a wide range of neuropsychiatric and related conditions – including depression, insomnia, hypertension, behavioral disinhibition (Badawy, 1996; Le Marquand, Phil and Benkelfat, 1999; Mulder and Joyce, 2002), pathological and suicidal aggression, aggression (Pihl *et al.*, 1995), delirium (Cleare and Bond, 1995; Freese *et al.*, 1990) and the control of mood and cognitive performance (Altman and Normile, 1988; Maes *et al.*, 1999). Brain 5-HT is dependent on the availability of Trp, which is derived from the diet, and competes with other large neutral amino acids (LNAAs) for transport into the brain via the blood–brain barrier (Fernstrom, Munro and Wurtman, 1977). Mental performance is significantly affected by changes in the Trp/LNAA ratio (Bellisle *et al.*, 1998; Markus, Olivier and de Haan, 2002; Rosenthal *et al.*, 1989). This ratio is modulated by the relative proportions of carbohydrate and protein in the diet across the day, and is decreased following consumption of ethanol over a two- to three-hour time period (Badawy *et al.*, 1995). In addition to being a precursor for serotonin and melatonin, dietary tryptophan also can be metabolized into kynurenine and other related compounds, a number of which have significant influences on the brain. The kynurenine pathway is the major route for tryptophan metabolism and has been implicated in brain dysfunction in AD, Huntington's disease and acquired immuno-deficiency syndrome (AIDS)-dementia complex (Stone and Darlington, 2002).

The enzyme tryptophan dioxygenase (TDO) is formed in the liver and its synthesis is controlled by cortisol (the stress-related hormone), oestrogen and circulating Trp. Following the induction of the enzyme TDO, circulating Trp will be diverted into the kynurenine pathway with a subsequent reduction in the availability of Trp for synthesis into 5-HT in the brain. This reduction of brain 5-HT synthesis is exacerbated by the competition between Kynurenine and Trp for the same transporters through the blood–brain barrier (Young, 1981). The consequences of reduced brain 5-HT have been outlined above. Furthermore, cortisol activation of this metabolic pathway may be an important biological determinant of the ethanol withdrawal syndrome (Badawy *et al.*, 1998). High concentrations of the kynurenines are excreted in the urine of patients with rheumatoid arthritis, tuberculosis, leukemia, Hodgkin's disease and bladder tumours.

The kynurenine metabolite Quinolinic acid (QA) has been implicated in neurologic diseases and neurodegeneration, including Huntington's disease, temporal lobe epilepsy, glutaric aciduria, hepatic encephalopathy and coma (Freese *et al.*, 1990). QA destroys neuronal cell bodies; cortical cells with N-methyl-D-aspartate (NMDA) receptors are particularly sensitive to QA. NMDA receptors mediate the actions of many of the excitatory amino acids such as glutamate. This is central to memory function and learning via long-term potentiation. QA is a selective excitant (agonist) of the NMDA receptor while Kynurenic acid (KA) is an antagonist (Freese *et al.*, 1990), providing neuroprotection. Neurotoxicity induced by QA primarily occurs in the hippocampus, striatum and neocortex, brain areas that are particularly affected by the disorders mentioned above. Excitotoxicity results in overstimulation of NMDA receptors in the hippocampus affecting long-term potentiation and the cellular basis of learning. The link with ethanol consumption stems from observation of increased sensitivity of NMDA receptors in alcohol withdrawal (Nagy and

Laszlo, 2002; Oretti *et al.*, 1996a) and excitotoxic damage due to neural compensation for sustained alcohol levels and nutritional deficits underlying alcohol-related brain damage. The specific nutritional deficit here is thiamine (Lovinger, 1993). Other studies have demonstrated the role of reduced hippocampal glutamate decarboxylase in cell death occurring during ethanol dependence (Davidson, Wilce and Shanley, 1993). The development of brain damage in binge drinkers is more likely due to increased vulnerability of the brain to these neurotoxic mechanisms (Hunt, 1993).

Oxidative stress

Neurocognitive deficits, neuronal injury and neurodegeneration are well documented in people with alcoholism (Haorah *et al.*, 2008). There is considerable evidence that alcohol-related neurodegenerative disorders result from a range of metabolic disturbances, in particular free radicals and the resulting imbalance between them and the endogenous antioxidant defences, considered to be pivotal in these pathological responses (Herrera *et al.*, 2003). As protection becomes less efficient, reductive oxygen species (ROS) may damage critical biological molecules in the brain, such as proteins, cell membrane lipids (Joseph *et al.*, 1999) and nucleic acids (Tokumaru, Iguchi and Kojo, 1996). Of all organs of the body, the brain is particularly vulnerable to oxidative abuse because of its high content of polyunsaturated fatty acids (PUFAs) in the membranes and low levels of enzymatic and non-enzymatic antioxidant defences. In order to prevent free radical-induced cellular damage, the body has developed a defence mechanism, the antioxidative system. Exogenous and endogenous antioxidants in the CNS are at low concentrations compared to those in other tissues, which, in relation to the high level of PUFAs, makes the CNS exceptionally susceptible to free radical damage. The antioxidant enzymes superoxide dismutase, catalase, glutathion peroxidase and glutathione reductase are present in the CNS; these are in the cortex, cerebellum, hypothalamus, striatum and spinal cord, regions controlling physical and cognitive functioning (Martin and Bonner, 2000).

A life cycle approach to nutrition in alcohol-related ageing

Nutritional supplements are used extensively in all age groups, supported by a burgeoning market in health food products. These products include multivitamin preparations for various age groups and PUFA supplements (Kalmijn *et al.*, 1997) such as Souvenaid, which is a formulation of omega-3, uridine, choline and vitamins (Cummings, 2012; Scheltens *et al.*, 2012). Phytochemicals, including polyphenols and anthocyanins, have been marketed as health food products on the basis of their anti-ageing properties (Horvath *et al.*, 2012; Lantier *et al.*, 2014; Singh *et al.*, 1980; Spencer, 2010). The cellular and molecular interactions underpinning the antioxidant effects of flavonoids and other phytochemicals present in antioxidant-rich foods, such as spinach, may be beneficial in retarding functional age-related CNS and cognitive behavioral deficits and, perhaps, may have some benefit in neurodegenerative disease (Joseph *et al.*, 1998). A large group of people, mainly in the USA, take melatonin daily believing that it is the "fountain of youth". This interest has been generated by reports that life could be prolonged by replacement melatonin therapy by protecting the individual from the ravages of old age by minimizing the onset of Parkinson's disease and Alzheimer's disease (Koushali, Hajiamini and Ebadi, 2012).

The possibility that nutritional manipulation may protect against cognitive decline and dementia is an inviting prospect. However, data supporting a beneficial effect of a particular dietary pattern is limited. Various studies have demonstrated a health benefit from dietary plans that are high in fiber, whole grains, natural sugar and fish while maintaining lower intake in meat, dairy and poultry. However, the identification of the most salient factors of these diets has been unsuccessful. Several aspects of diet have been studied in detail and provided support for potential mechanisms for improving cognition. Although some clinical trials have been undertaken to demonstrate the beneficial effects of dietary manipulation, research to investigate the mechanisms of these interventions is in its infancy.

Alcohol-abuse history in older diabetic subjects presents an increased risk for cognitive impairment (Hudetz and Warltier, 2007). The well-established use of thiamine (vitamin B1) supplementation employed and shown to have a therapeutic benefit in alcohol-dependent sub-populations indicates the importance of nutritional interventions in mitigating against severe cognitive decline. Thomson found that, in a group of alcohol-dependent patients, thiamine absorption was significantly inhibited, and improvements in absorption did not return to normal levels in malnourished patients until after treatment with a nutritious diet (Thomson, 2000). This discovery and later research into the effectiveness of dosing regimes and the optimization of nutritional support, led to the publication of guidelines for the management of WE patients in accident and emergency departments (Thomson *et al.*, 2002). The principle recommendation of these guidelines is that patients suspected of having a poor diet should be treated as soon as possible with intravenous or intramuscular injections of B vitamins. The underlying physiological basis of this nutritional intervention is to increase levels of vitamin B1, which is essential in the basic energy-generating process within brain cells, and offsetting the production of free radicals causing cytotoxicity due to oxidative stress, leading to the death of neurones. Blood levels of thiamine in those at risk of alcohol-related neuropsychological damage have been demonstrated to indicate preclinical WE (Pitel *et al.*, 2011).

Thiamine is a water-soluble vitamin occurring in free or phosphorylated forms in most plant and animal tissues. Lipid-soluble precursors of thiamine have a higher bioavailability than the basic thiamine molecule. Benfotiamine (s-benzoylthiamine) has been found to prevent the progression of diabetes, but does not alter brain levels of thiamine. More effective lipid-soluble compounds, such as allithiamine and synthetic sulbutiamine and fursultiamine, do increase levels of brain thiamine (Volvert *et al.*, 2008).

Since 1991, in response to the high population incidence of WKS in Australia, there is mandatory enrichment of baking flour in Australia (but not in New Zealand), resulting in a significant reduction of WKS (Truswell, 2000; Harper *et al.*, 1998).

Consumption of vitamin supplements appears to bring thiamine levels closer to those seen in control participants. Supplementation of dietary intake of thiamine in people who are alcohol dependent remains an important measure for the prevention of WKS in this population (Rees and Gowing, 2013).

Amino acids, vitamins and minerals

From the information discussed in the earlier parts of this chapter, it is clear that an important aspect of alcohol-related brain function is the neurotoxic effect of oxidation processes causing tissue damage and the pathological consequences of disrupted metabolism. Long-term alcohol use seems to be associated with glycemic control in type 2 diabetes, probably due to changes in insulin sensitivity (Pietraszek, Gregersen and Hermansen, 2010). The increasing incidence of diabetes in young individuals is particularly concerning. There is growing evidence that excess generation of highly reactive free radicals, largely due to hyperglycemia, causes oxidative stress, which further exacerbates the development and progression of diabetes and its complications (Thandavarayan et al., 2011).

Earlier in this chapter attention was drawn to the opposing action of the Trp metabolites: QA, a neurotoxic compound and the neuroprotective KA. In the development of neuroprotective agents, pharmacological compounds designed as KA pro-drugs and KA analogues are being produced. These compounds are presently being investigated in a number of clinical trials focusing on neurodegenerative disorders. Clinical trials for stroke, AD, Parkinson's disease and related disorders, cerebral ischaemia, HIV, schizophrenia, epilepsy and depression are being pursued. Commercially produced compounds include KA derivatives, designed as NMDA antagonists (e.g., L705022, L701324), and pro-drugs of KA (e.g., SC49468, 4,6-dichlorokynurenine) have been developed. Modulators of QA and KA concentrations (e.g., 540C91) lower the concentrations of TDO and NCR631 and inhibit 3-hydroxyanthranilic acid, reducing loss of hippocampal cells (Stone and Darlington, 2002). Despite this extensive work on pharmacologically designed neuroprotectants, to date, therapeutic trials have yet to be undertaken on participants with alcohol-related brain damage.

Results from preliminary experiments in abstinent people with alcohol dependence by the author and colleagues provided evidence that following nutritionally balanced interventions containing tryptophan and vitamins, concentrations of the neurotoxic metabolite 3-HK and the neuroprotectant KA were significantly elevated. This is an important finding in view of the increased cytotoxic damage associated with alcohol withdrawal, and linked with alcohol withdrawal-induced seizures.

Melatonin, synthesized from Trp, plays an important role in the ageing process to offset oxidative damage, a likely cause of age-associated brain dysfunction. As age advances, the nocturnal production of melatonin decreases (Esteban et al., 2004; Garau et al., 2006). Light at night disrupts the endogenous circadian rhythm and specifically suppresses nocturnal production of the pineal hormone melatonin and its secretion into the blood. Light intensity and hours of daylight have a greater impact than nutritional factors, such as intake of vegetables, caffeine and some vitamins and minerals, in maintaining the sleep–wake cycle. The International Agency for Research on Cancer (IARC) Working Group concluded that "shift-work that involves circadian disruption is probably carcinogenic to humans" (Mehlmann *et al.*, 2007). This information should be seriously considered in the residential support of people with alcohol-related problems and those working in older persons' care settings.

The metabolism of amino acids and related compounds, as discussed above, is dependent on an adequate supply of vitamins and minerals. For example, zinc ions play a major role in a wide range of normal brain functions, including the cellular basis of learning (via LTP and synaptic plasticity), cognitive functions, gene regulation and transcription and antioxidant response (Mocchegiani *et al.*, 2007; Vasto *et al.*, 2006). Zinc plays a key role in the regulation of NMDA receptors and counterbalances the actions of excitotoxins such as QA and alcohol, by modulating glutamate-induced NMDA receptors excitability. On the other hand, zinc deficiency may synergistically act with neurotoxins to cause neuronal death by enhancing excito-toxicity damage brought by an excess of glutamate.

The endocannabinoid system, involved in brain metabolism, offers therapeutic potential by targeting this system and certain plant-derived cannabinoids, such as cannabidiol and Δ9-tetrahydrocannabivarin, which has a number of psychotropic effects and possesses potent anti-inflammatory and/or antioxidant properties (Horvath *et al.*, 2012).

Conclusion

This chapter provides an insight into the basic nutritional-dependent mechanisms involved in cognitive decline in chronic alcohol misuse. Degenerative changes in the alcoholic brain possibly provide an insight into premature ageing. The extensive research into nutritional factors linked with alcohol dependency, withdrawal and comorbidity with diabetes reinforces the importance of nutritional screening, monitoring and nutritional interventions in vulnerable people.

Approaches to reducing alcohol-related harm and the promotion of successful ageing are high priority objectives in contemporary health policy in the UK and many other countries. Clearly healthy lifestyle choices, including social networks, meaningful activities and optimal nutrition, are important in addressing these objectives. In addition to biomedical interventions in supporting people with alcohol problems, psychosocial aspects, such as patient education, behavioral medicine and psychiatric issues should be considered. These include treatments for depression, anxiety disorders, eating disorders and dependence on nicotine (Petrak *et al.*, 2005).

For those people who are excluded from society, due to a range of biological, psychological and social issues, screening, assessing and monitoring may suggest the need for interventions to offset pathological and behavioral problems linked to alcohol abuse (Bonner, 2006). In the case of chronic alcohol users, detoxification and relapse prevention are interventions that are commonly used to reduce alcohol-related harm.

In the process of ageing, the degeneration of tissues and organs and the desynchroni-zation of biological rhythms are accompanied by lifestyle changes such as retirement from employment, bereavement of a spouse and reduced mobility, issues which should be considered in supporting people to maintain their quality of life.

Structural and functional damage, due to long-term alcohol consumption, results in neuropsychological impairment, mood disorders and personality changes. Associations have been suggested between happiness, homicide and omega-3 (Hibbeln, 2007). In both alcohol-related harm and the process of ageing psychoso-cial stress, anxiety and cognitive dysfunction impact on physical and mental health and can contribute to suicidal tendencies in these groups (Bonner and Luscombe, 2009; Morin *et al.*, 2013). Psychological therapies can lead to improved performance. However, these methods are likely to be limited in their effectiveness if cellular mechanisms of brain function are compromised by neurotoxic factors, which mainly emanate from nutritional imbalances. Self-medication of physiologically active compounds such as melatonin and omega-3 is becoming more commonplace, as the ageing population has become more health aware.

A principal aim of evidence-based strategies should be to promote neuroadapta-tion and minimize neurodegeneration. Lifestyle and life cycle approaches with ref-erence to exercise, sleep–wake activities, nutrition and a harm-reduction approach to alcohol should be encouraged (ALICE-RAP Consortium, 2012). From a public health perspective, alcohol-related harm is related to the availability and con-sumption of alcohol in the community. The World Health Organization's global strategy to reduce the harmful use of alcohol provides robust evidence for alcohol control policies to reduce the frequency and intensity of alcohol consumption in at-risk populations, via restrictions on alcohol marketing and other proposed policy actions (Babor *et al.*, 2012).

References

Albano, E. (2006). Alcohol, oxidative stress and free radical damage. *Proceedings of the Nutrition Society*, 65(3), 278–90.

ALICE-RAP Consortium. (2012). Alcohol: the neglected addiction *ALICE RAP: Addictions and Lifestyles in Contemporary Europe: Reframing Addictions Project*. EU.

Altman, H. J. and Normile, H. J. (1988). What is the nature of the role of the serotonergic nervous system in learning and memory: prospects for development of an effective treat-ment strategy for senile dementia. *Neurobiology of Aging*, 9(5–6), 627–38.

Asbun, J. and Villarreal, F. J. (2006). The pathogenesis of myocardial fibrosis in the setting of diabetic cardiomyopathy. *Journal of the American College of Cardiology*, 47(4), 693–700.

Babor, T., Rehm, J., Jernigan, D., Vaeth, P., Monteiro, M. and Lehman, H. (2012). Alcohol, diabetes, and public health in the Americas. *Revista Panamerica de Salud Publica*, 32(2), 151–5.

Badawy, A. A. (1996). Tryptophan metabolism and disposition in relation to alcohol and alcoholism. *Advances in Experimental Medicine and Biology*, 398, 75–82.

Badawy, A. A. (1999). Tryptophan metabolism in alcoholism. *Advances in Experimental Medicine and Biology*, 467, 265–74.

Badawy, A. A., Morgan, C. J., Lovett, J. W., Bradley, D. M. and Thomas, R. (1995). Decrease in circulating tryptophan availability to the brain after acute ethanol consumption by normal volunteers: implications for alcohol–induced aggressive behaviour and depression. *Pharmacopsychiatry*, 28 (Supplement 2), 93–7.

Badawy, A. A., Rommelspacher, H., Morgan, C. J., Bradley, D. M., Bonner, A., Ehlert, A., Blum, S. and Spies, C. D. (1998). Tryptophan metabolism in alcoholism: tryptophan but not excitatory amino acid availability to the brain is increased before the appearance of the alcohol-withdrawal syndrome in men. *Alcohol and Alcoholism*, 33(6), 616–25.

Bauldry, S., Shanahan, M. J., Boardman, J. D., Miech, R. A. and Macmillan, R. (2012). A life course model of self-rated health through adolescence and young adulthood. *Social Science and Medicine*, 75(7), 1311–20.

Bellisle, F., Blundell, J. E., Dye, L., Fantino, M., Fern, E., Fletcher, R. J., Lambed, J., Roberfroid, M., Specter, S., Westenhöfer, J. and Westerterp-Plantenga, M. S. (1998). Functional food science and behaviour and psychological functions. *British Journal of Nutrition*, 80 (Supplement 1), S173–S193.

Bernhard, W., Full, A., Arand, J., Maas, C., Poets, C. F. and Franz, A. R. (2013). Choline supply of preterm infants: assessment of dietary intake and pathophysiological considerations. *European Journal of Nutrition*, 52(3), 1269–78.

Billson, H., Pryer, J. A. and Nichols, R. (1999). Variation in fruit and vegetable consumption among adults in Britain: an analysis from the dietary and nutritional survey of British adults. *European Journal of Clinical Nutrition*, 53(12), 946–52.

Bonner, A. B. (2006). *Social Exclusion and The Way Out: An Individual and Community Perspective on Social Dysfunction*. Chichester: John Wiley.

Bonner, A. B. and C. Luscombe (2009). Suicide and homelessness. *Journal of Public Mental Health*, 8(3), 7–19.

Cleare, A. J. and Bond, A. J. (1995). Relationship of plasma tryptophan and blood serotonin to aggression, mood and anxiety in males. *Journal of Serotonin Research*, 2, 77–84.

Conigrave, K. M. and Rimm, E. B. (2003). Alcohol for the prevention of type 2 diabetes mellitus? *Treatments in Endocrinology*, 2(3), 145–52.

Cook, C. C., Hallwood, P. M. and Thomson, A. D. (1998). B vitamin deficiency and neuropsychiatric syndromes in alcohol misuse. *Alcohol and Alcoholism*, 33(4), 317–36.

Cummings, J. L. (2012). Food for thought: Souvenaid in mild Alzheimer's disease. *Journal of Alzheimer's Disease*, 31(1), 237–8.

Darmon, N. and Drewnowski, A. (2008). Does social class predict diet quality? (review). *American Journal of Clinical Nutrition*, 87(5), 1107–17.

Davidson, M. D., Wilce, P. and Shanley, B. C. (1993). Increased sensitivity of the hippocampus in ethanol-dependent rats to toxic effect of N-methyl-D-aspartic acid in vivo. *Brain Research*, 606(1), 5–9.

Esteban, S., Nicolaus, C., Garmundi, A., Rial, R. V., Rodriguez, A. B., Ortega, E. and Ibars, C. B. (2004). Effect of orally administered L-tryptophan on serotonin, melatonin, and the innate immune response in the rat. *Molecular and Cellular Biochemistry*, 267(1–2), 39–46.

Fernstrom, J. D., Munro, H. N. and Wurtman, R. J. (1977). Brain tryptophan in rats on a high fat diet. *Nature*, 265(5591), 277.

Freese, A., Swartz, K. J., During, M. J. and Martin, J. B. (1990). Kynurenine metabolites of tryptophan: implications for neurologic diseases. *Neurology*, 40(4), 691–5.

Garau, C., Aparicio, S., Rial, R. V., Nicolau, M. C. and Esteban, S. (2006). Age related changes in the activity–rest circadian rhythms and c-fos expression of ring doves with aging: effects of tryptophan intake. *Experimental Gerontology*, 41(4), 430–8.

Geels, L. M., Vink, J. M., van Beek, J. H. D. A., Bartels, M., Willemsen, G. and Boomsma, D. I. (2013). Increases in alcohol consumption in women and elderly groups: evidence from an epidemiological study. *BMC Public Health*, 13(207), 1–13.

Greenhouse, L. and Lardinois, C. K. (1996). Alcohol-associated diabetes mellitus: a review of the impact of alcohol consumption on carbohydrate metabolism. *Archives of Family Medicine*, 5(4), 229–33.

Guerri, C. and Pascual, M. (2010). Mechanisms involved in the neurotoxic, cognitive, and neurobehavioral effects of alcohol consumption during adolescence. *Alcohol*, 44(1), 15–26.

Guerrini, I., Thomson, A. D. and Gurling, H. D. (2007). The importance of alcohol misuse, malnutrition and genetic susceptibility on brain growth and plasticity (review). *Neuroscience and Biobehavioural Reviews*, 31(2), 212–20.

Halliday, G., Baker, K. and Harper, C. (1995). Serotonin and alcohol-related brain damage. *Metabolic Brain Disease*, 10(1), 25–30.

Haorah, J., Ramirez, S. H., Floreani, N., Gorantla, S., Morsey, B. and Persidsky, Y. (2008). Mechanism of alcohol-induced oxidative stress and neuronal injury. *Free Radical Biology and Medicine*, 45(11), 1542–50.

Harper, C. G., Sheedy, D. L., Lara, A. I., Garrick, T. M., Hilton, J. M. and Raisanen, J. (1998). Prevalence of Wernicke-Korsakoff syndrome in Australia: has thiamine fortification made a difference? *Medical Journal of Australia*, 168(11), 542–5.

Herrera, D. G., Yague, A. G., Johnsen-Soriano, S., Bosch-Morell, F., Collado-Morente, L., Muriach, M., Romero, F. J. and Garcia-Verdugo, J. M. (2003). Selective impairment of hippocampal neurogenesis by chronic alcoholism: protective effects of an antioxidant. *Proceedings of the National Acadamy of Sciences USA*, 100(13), 7919–24.

Hewitt, A. J., Knuff, A. L., Jefkins, M. J., Collier, C. P., Reynolds, J. N. and Brien, J. F. (2011). Chronic ethanol exposure and folic acid supplementation: fetal growth and folate status in the maternal and fetal guinea pig. *Reproductive Toxicology*, 31(4), 500–6.

Hibbeln, J. R. (2007). From homicide to happiness: a commentary on omega-3 fatty acids in human society. Cleave Award Lecture. *Nutrition and Health*, 19(1–2), 9–19.

Horvath, B., Mukhopadhyay, P., Hasko, G. and Pacher, P. (2012). The endocannabinoid system and plant-derived cannabinoids in diabetes and diabetic complications. *American Journal of Pathology*, 180(2), 432–42.

Hudetz, J. A. and Warltier, D. C. (2007). Cognitive function in older diabetic subjects with a history of alcohol abuse. *Psychological Reports*, 101(3, Part 2), 1125–32.

Hunt, W. A. (1993). Are binge drinkers more at risk of developing brain damage? *Alcohol*, 10(6), 559–61.

Ishii, H. and Ito, D. (1996). Pathogenesis of glucose intolerance in alcoholics. *Nihon Rinsho*, 54(10), 2733–8.

Jackson, C. T., Covell, N. H., Drake, R. E. and Essock, S. M. (2007). Relationship between diabetes and mortality among persons with co-occurring psychotic and substance use disorders. *Psychiatric Services*, 58(2), 270–2.

Jimerson, D. C. and Lesem, M. D. (1990). Eating disorders and depression: is there a serotonin connection? *Biological Psychiatry*, 28(5), 443–53.

Johansson, L., Thelle, D. S., Solvoll, K., Bjorneboe, G. E. and Drevon, C. A. (1999). Healthy dietary habits in relation to social determinants and lifestyle factors. *British Journal of Nutrition*, 81(3), 211–20.

Joseph, J. A., Shukitt-Hale, B., Denisova, N. A., Prior, R. L., Cao, G., Martin, A., Taglialatela, G. and Bickford, P. C. (1998). Long-term dietary strawberry, spinach, or vitamin E supplementation retards the onset of age-related neuronal signal-transduction and cognitive behavioral deficits. *Journal of Neuroscience*, 18(19), 8047–55.

Joseph, C. D., Praveenkumar, V., Kuttan, G. and Kuttan, R. (1999). Myeloprotective effect of a non-toxic indigenous preparation Rasayana in cancer patients receiving chemotherapy and radiation therapy: a pilot study. *Journal of Experimental and Clinical Cancer Research*, 18(3), 325–9.

Ju, A., Cheon, Y. H., Lee, K. S., Lee, S. S., Lee, W. Y., Won, W. Y., Park, S. I., Kim, W. H. and Kim, D. J. (2011). The change of plasma ghrelin and leptin levels by the development of type 2 diabetes mellitus in patients with alcohol dependence. *Alcoholism: Clinical and Experimental Research*, 35(5), 905–11.

Kalmijn, S., Feskens, E. J., Launer, L. J. and Kromhout, D. (1997). Polyunsaturated fatty acids, antioxidants, and cognitive function in very old men. *American Journal of Epidemiology*, 145(1), 33–41.

Kim, S. J. and Kim, D. J. (2012). Alcoholism and diabetes mellitus. *Diabetes and Metabolism Journal*, 36(2), 108–15.

Koelega, H. S. (1995). Alcohol and vigilance performance: a review. *Psychopharmacology (Berl)*, 118(3), 233–49.

Koppes, L. L., Twisk, J. W., Van Mechelen, W., Snel, J. and Kemper, H. C. (2005). Cross-sectional and longitudinal relationships between alcohol consumption and lipids, blood pressure and body weight indices. *Journal of Studies on Alcohol and Drugs*, 66(6), 713–21.

Koushali, A. N., Hajiamini, Z. and Ebadi, A. (2012). Comparison of nursing students' and clinical nurses' attitude toward the nursing profession. *Iranian Journal of Nursing and Midwifery Research*, 17(5), 375–80.

Lantier, L., Drouet, F., Guesdon, W., Mancassola, R., Metton, C., Lo-Man, R., Werts, C., Laurent, F. and Lacroix-Lamande, S. (2014). Poly(I:C)-induced protection of neonatal mice against intestinal cryptosporidium parvum infection requires an additional TLR5 signal provided by the gut flora. *Journal of Infectious Diseases*, 209(3), 457–67.

Le Marquand, D., Phil, R. O. and Benkelfat, C. (1994). Serotonin and alcohol intake, abuse, and dependence: clinical evidence. *Biological Psychiatry*, 36, 326–37.

Li, T. K. (2008). Quantifying the risk for alcohol-use and alcohol-attributable health disorders: present findings and future research needs. *Journal of Gastroenterology and Hepatology*, 23 (Supplement 1), S2–8.

Lieber, C. S. (2003). Relationships between nutrition, alcohol use, and liver disease. *Alcohol Research and Health*, 27(3), 220–31.

Lindegard, B. and Hillbom, M. (1987). Associations between brain infarction, diabetes and alcoholism: observations from the Gothenburg population cohort study. *Acta Neurologica Scandinavica*, 75(3), 195–200.

Lindstrom, M., Hanson, B. S., Wirfalt, E. and Ostergren, P. O. (2001). Socioeconomic differences in the consumption of vegetables, fruit and fruit juices: the influence of psychosocial factors. *European Journal of Public Health*, 11(1), 51–9.

Lough, M. E. (2012). Wernicke's encephalopathy: expanding the diagnostic toolbox. *Neuropsychology Review*, 22(2), 181–94.

Lovinger, D. M. (1993). Excitotoxicity and alcohol-related brain damage. *Alcoholism: Clinical and Experimental Research*, 17(1), 19–27.

Maes, M., Lin, A. H., Verkerk, R., Delmeire, L., Van Gastel, A., Van der Planken, M. and Scharpe, S. (1999). Serotonergic and noradrenergic markers of post-traumatic stress disorder with and without major depression. *Neuropsychopharmacology*, 20(2), 188–97.

Makela, P. (1999). Alcohol-related mortality as a function of socio-economic status (research support, non-US government). *Addiction*, 94(6), 867–86.

Markus, C. R., Olivier, B. and de Haan, E. H. (2002). Whey protein rich in alpha-lactalbumin increases the ratio of plasma tryptophan to the sum of the other large neutral amino acids and improves cognitive performance in stress-vulnerable subjects. *American Journal of Clinical Nutrition*, 75(6), 1051–6.

Martin, C. R. and Bonner, A. B. (2000). A pilot investigation of the effect of tryptophan manipulation on the affective state of male chronic alcoholics. *Alcohol and Alcoholism*, 35(1), 49–51.

Maylor, E. A., Rabbitt, P. M., James, G. H. and Kerr, S. A. (1992). Effects of alcohol, practice, and task complexity on reaction time distributions. *Quarterly Journal of Experimental Psychology, Section A: Human Experimental Psychology*, 44(1), 119–39.

Mehlmann, M., Bonner, A. B., Williams, J. V., Dankbar, D. M., Moore, C. L., Kuchta, R. D., Podsiad, A. B., Tamerius, J. D., Dawson, E. D. and Rowlen, K. L. (2007). Comparison of the MChip to viral culture, reverse transcription-PCR, and the QuickVue influenza A+B test for rapid diagnosis of influenza. *Journal of Clinical Microbiology*, 45(4), 1234–7.

Meyer, S. E., Chrousos, G. P. and Gold, P. W. (2001). Major depression and the stress system: a life span perspective. *Developmental Psychopathology*, 13(3), 565–80.

Mocchegiani, E., Giacconi, R., Cipriano, C., Costarelli, L., Muti, E., Tesei, S., Giuli, C., Papa, R., Marcellini, F., Mariani, E., Rink, L., Herbein, G., Varin, A., Fulop, T., Monti, D., Jajte, J., Dedoussis, G., Gonos, E. S., Trougakos, I. P. and Malavolta, M. (2007). Zinc, metallothioneins, and longevity – effect of zinc supplementation: zincage study. *Annals of the New York Academy of Sciences*, 1119, 129–46.

Morin, J., Wiktorsson, S., Marlow, T., Olesen, P. J., Skoog, I. and Waern, M. (2013). Alcohol use disorder in elderly suicide attempters: a comparison study. *American Journal of Geriatric Psychiatry*, 21(2), 196–203.

Mulder, R. T. and Joyce, P. R. (2002). Relationship of temperament and behaviour measures to the prolactin response to fenfluramine in depressed men. *Psychiatry Research*, 109(3), 221–8.

Nagy, J. and Laszlo, L. (2002). Increased sensitivity to NMDA is involved in alcohol-withdrawal induced cytotoxicity observed in primary cultures of cortical neurones chronically pre-treated with ethanol. *Neurochemistry International*, 40(7), 585–91.

Oretti, R., Bano, S., Morgan, C. J., Badawy, A. A. B., Bonner, A., Buckland, P. and McGuffin, P. (1996). Prevention by cycloheximide of the audiogenic seizures and tryptophan metabolic disturbances of ethanol withdrawal in rats. *Alcohol and Alcoholism*, 31(3), 243–7.

Oretti, R. G., Bano, S., Azani, M. O., Badawy, A. A., Morgan, C. J., McGuffin, P. and Buckland, P. R. (2000). Rat liver tryptophan pyrrolase activity and gene expression during alcohol withdrawal. *Alcohol and Alcoholism*, 35(5), 427–34.

Petrak, F., Herpertz, S., Albus, C., Hirsch, A., Kulzer, B. and Kruse, J. (2005). Psychosocial factors and diabetes mellitus: evidence-based treatment guidelines. *Current Diabetes Reviews*, 1(3), 255–70.

Pietraszek, A., Gregersen, S. and Hermansen, K. (2010). Alcohol and type 2 diabetes: a review. *Nutrition, Metabolism and Cardiovascular Diseases*, 20(5), 366–75.

Pihl, R. O., Young, S. N., Harden, P., Plotnick, S., Chamberlain, B. and Ervin, F. R. (1995). Acute effect of altered tryptophan levels and alcohol on aggression in normal human males. *Psychopharmacology (Berl)*, 119(4), 353–60.

Pitel, A. L., Zahr, N. M., Jackson, K., Sassoon, S. A., Rosenbloom, M. J., Pfefferbaum, A. and Sullivan, E. V. (2011). Signs of preclinical Wernicke's encephalopathy and thiamine levels as predictors of neuropsychological deficits in alcoholism without Korsakoff's syndrome. *Neuropsychopharmacology*, 36(3), 580–8.

Priscindaro, J. J., Gebregziabher, M., Grubaugh, A. L., Gilbert, G. E., Echols, C. and Egede, L. E. (2011). Impact of psychiatric comorbidity on mortality in veterans with type 2 diabetes. *Diabetes Technology and Therapeutics*, 13(1), 73–8.

Rao, T. (2013). Trends in alcohol related admissions for older people with mental health problems: 2002 to 2012. Alcohol Concern.

Rees, E. and Gowing, L. R. (2013). Supplementary thiamine is still important in alcohol dependence. *Alcohol and Alcoholism*, 48(1), 88–92.

Rosenthal, N. E., Genhart, M. J., Caballero, B., Jacobsen, F. M., Skwerer, R. G., Coursey, R. D., Rogers, S. and Spring, B. J. (1989). Psychobiological effects of carbohydrate- and protein-rich meals in patients with seasonal affective disorder and normal controls. *Biological Psychiatry*, 25(8), 1029–40.

Rufer, E. S., Tran, T. D., Attridge, M. M., Andrzejewski, M. E., Flentke, G. R. and Smith, S. M. (2012). Adequacy of maternal iron status protects against behavioral, neuroanatomical, and growth deficits in fetal alcohol spectrum disorders. *PLoS One*, 7(10), e47499.

Scalzo, S., Bowden, S. and Hillbom, M. (2015). Wernicke-Korsakoff Syndrome. In J. Svanberg, A. Withall, B. Draper and S. Bowden (eds), *Alcohol and the Adult Brain*. Hove: Psychology Press.

Schafer, K., Butters, N., Smith, T., Irwin, M., Brown, S., Hanger, P., Grant, I. and Schuckit, M. (1991). Cognitive performance of alcoholics: a longitudinal evaluation of the role of drinking history, depression, liver function, nutrition, and family history. *Alcohol: Clinical and Experimental Research*, 15(4), 653–60.

Scheltens, P., Twisk, J. W., Blesa, R., Scarpini, E., von Arnim, C. A., Bongers, A., Harrison, J., Swinkels, S. H. N., Stam, C. J., de Waal, H., Wurtman, R. J., Wieggers, R. L., Vellas, B. and Kamphuis, P. J. (2012). Efficacy of Souvenaid in mild Alzheimer's disease: results from a randomized, controlled trial. *Journal of Alzheimers Disease*, 31(1), 225–36.

Sher, L. (2008). Depression and suicidal behavior in alcohol abusing adolescents: possible role of selenium deficiency. *Minerva Pediatrics*, 60(2), 201–9.

Singh, N., Nath, R., Kulshrestha, V. K. and Kohli, R. P. (1980). An experimental evaluation of dependence liability of methaqualone diphenhydramine (combination) and methaqualone in rats. *Psychopharmacology (Berl)*, 67(2), 203–7.

Spencer, J. P. (2010). Beyond antioxidants: the cellular and molecular interactions of flavonoids and how these underpin their actions on the brain. *Proceedings of the Nutrition Society*, 69(2), 244–60.

Stone, T. W. and Darlington, L. G. (2002). Endogenous kynurenines as targets for drug discovery and development. *Nature Reviews. Drug Discovery*, 1(8), 609–20.

Thandavarayan, R. A., Giridharan, V. V., Watanabe, K. and Konishi, T. (2011). Diabetic cardiomyopathy and oxidative stress: role of antioxidants. *Cardiovascular and Hematological Agents in Medical Chemistry*, 9(4), 225–30.

Thomson, A. D. (2000). Mechanisms of vitamin deficiency in chronic alcohol misusers and the development of the Wernicke-Korsakoff syndrome. *Alcohol and Alcoholism Supplement*, 35 (Supplement 1), 2–7.

Thomson, A. D., Cook, C. C. H., Touquet, R. and Henry, J. A. (2002). The Royal College of Physicians report on alcohol: guidelines for managing Wernicke's encephalopathy in the accident and emergency department. *Alcohol and Alcoholism*, 37(6), 513–21.

Tiwari, V. and Chopra, K. (2012). Attenuation of oxidative stress, neuroinflammation, and apoptosis by curcumin prevents cognitive deficits in rats postnatally exposed to ethanol. *Psychopharmacology (Berl)*, 224(4), 519–35.

Tokumaru, S., Iguchi, H. and Kojo, S. (1996). Change of the lipid hydroperoxide level in mouse organs on ageing. *Mechanisms of Ageing and Development*, 86(1), 67–74.

Truswell, A. S. (2000). Australian experience with the Wernicke-Korsakoff syndrome. *Addiction*, 95(6), 829–32.

van Oers, J. A., Bongers, I. M., van de Goor, L. A. and Garretsen, H. F. (1999). Alcohol consumption, alcohol-related problems, problem drinking, and socioeconomic status. *Alcohol and Alcoholism*, 34(1), 78–88.

Vasto, S., Mocchegiani, E., Candore, G., Listi, F., Colonna-Romano, G., Lio, D., Malavolta, M., Giacconi, R., Cipriano, C. and Caruso, C. (2006). Inflammation, genes and zinc in ageing and age-related diseases. *Biogerontology*, 7(5–6), 315–27.

Volvert, M. L., Seyen, S., Piette, M., Evrard, B., Gangolf, M., Plumier, J. C. and Bettendorff, L. (2008). Benfotiamine, a synthetic S-acyl thiamine derivative, has different mechanisms of action and a different pharmacological profile than lipid-soluble thiamine disulfide derivatives. *BMC Pharmacology*, 8, 10.

Werts, R. L., Van Calcar, S. C., Wargowski, D. S. and Smith, S. M. (2013). Inappropriate feeding behaviors and dietary intakes in children with fetal alcohol spectrum disorder or probable prenatal alcohol exposure. *Alcoholism: Clinical and Experimental Research*, 38(3), 871–8.

Wijnia, J. W., van de Wetering, B. J., Zwart, E., Nieuwenhuis, K. G. and Goossensen, M. A. (2012). Evolution of Wernicke-Korsakoff syndrome in self-neglecting alcoholics: preliminary results of relation with Wernicke-delirium and diabetes mellitus. *American Journal of Addiction*, 21(2), 104–10.

Withall, A. and Shafiee, S. (2015). Alcohol use disorders in older adults. In J. Svanberg, A. Withall, B. Draper and S. Bowden (eds), *Alcohol and the Adult Brain*. Hove: Psychology Press.

Wrieden, W. L., Connaghan, J., Morrison, C. and Tunstall-Pedoe, H. (2004). Secular and socio-economic trends in compliance with dietary targets in the north Glasgow MONICA population surveys 1986–1995: did social gradients widen? *Public Health and Nutrition*, 7(7), 835–42.

Young, S. N. (1981). Mechanism of decline in rat brain 5-hydroxytryptamine after induction of liver tryptophan pyrrolase by hydrocortisone: roles of tryptophan catabolism and kynurenine synthesis. *British Journal of Pharmacology*, 74(3), 695–700.

Zakhari, S. and Li, T. K. (2007). Determinants of alcohol use and abuse: impact of quantity and frequency patterns on liver disease. *Hepatology*, 46(6), 2032–9.

10

NEUROPSYCHOLOGICAL ASSESSMENT OF ALCOHOL-RELATED COGNITIVE IMPAIRMENT

Jenny Svanberg, Fraser Morrison and Breda Cullen

Excessive alcohol use causes changes to the structure and functioning of the brain, some permanent and some reversible with abstinence (Harper, 2009). Particularly sensitive to change are the frontal lobes, limbic system and cerebellum (Oscar-Berman and Marinkovic, 2007; Sullivan, 2003). This leads to well-documented neuropsychological changes in those drinking alcohol to excess, in particular the memory impairment (Bates, Bowden and Barry, 2002; Pitel *et al.*, 2011; Kopelman, 2009; Sullivan, 2003) and executive dysfunction commonly associated with Korsakoff's Syndrome (KS), the chronic stage of Wernicke-Korsakoff Syndrome (WKS). However, a wide range of cognitive presentations may be seen at different stages of development of alcohol-related brain damage (ARBD), outlined in greater detail elsewhere in this volume (Scalzo, Bowden and Hillbom, 2015; Wilson, 2015).

Alcohol-use disorders occur when an individual consumes alcohol to the extent that he or she is at risk of negative physical, mental or social consequences (hazardous drinking), experiencing such consequences (harmful drinking), or experiencing such consequences to the extent that there are withdrawal symptoms when alcohol use is stopped, the individual feels unable to control their alcohol use and alcohol is prioritized over other parts of the person's life (NICE, 2011). Although 50 to 80 per cent of individuals with alcohol-use disorders are thought to experience mild to moderate neurocognitive impairment (Bates, Bowden and Barry, 2002; Bates *et al.*, 2004) and 10 per cent severe impairment (Sullivan, 2003), cognitive assessment is not routinely carried out within addiction treatment settings. This has major implications for treatment outcome, given the emphasis of many treatment programs on motivation to change, and the possibility that impaired brain functioning as a result of alcohol use may prevent some from engaging with standard treatment programs. Cognitive impairment in those seeking treatment for substance-use disorders leads to a range of poor treatment outcomes (Copersino *et al.*, 2009) including an increased risk of alcohol relapse (Morrison, 2011). It may be underestimated or misinterpreted by treatment providers as low motivation, denial of problem and inattention (Bates *et al.*, 2004; Knight and Longmore, 1994), risking further deterioration in health and well-being in those cognitively unable to alter drinking behavior (e.g., Mental Welfare Commission for Scotland, 2006). The cognitive impairment in the early stages of ARBD is only slight and may lead to subtle executive functioning difficulties that make it more difficult for the person to make changes in their alcohol use and gain insight into their own deterioration (Le Berre *et al.*, 2013). As such, early cognitive impairments relating to alcohol use may not be recognized by mainstream health or alcohol treatment services, and individuals may not seek help themselves. Instead, deterioration may lead to the person coming the attention of services through problems in the living situation, or reports from social care providers, police, or concerned family members. In addition, the health risks posed by a long history of alcohol excess mean that there is a higher likelihood of hepatic or vascular damage and greater risk of traumatic brain injury (Oscar-Berman and Marinković, 2007), leading to the possibility of multiple routes to impaired cognition. With increasing age, there may be increased likelihood of concurrent degenerative dementia, particularly if there has been a history of alcohol excess in the midlife period. Use of other prescribed and illicit substances may also impact on cognition.

Taking all of these factors into consideration, it is clear that a comprehensive psychological assessment for those presenting for treatment of alcohol-use disorders should include assessment of cognitive functioning (NICE, 2011). Early identification of cognitive impairment among those entering alcohol treatment programs would allow more informed rehabilitation (Allen, Goldstein and Seaton, 1997; Bates, Bowden and Barry, 2002) and better treatment matching, with a corresponding benefit to outcomes. In addition, earlier recognition of impairment would give a greater possibility of recovery of function for some, and the potential to prevent further damage (Harper, 2009). Effective assessment of the presence of cognitive impairment can be achieved using screening measures, described further in the next section. Recognizing cognitive impairment early is crucial when considering the consequences of missing early signs of Wernicke's Encephalopathy (WE), such as development of the chronic KS (75 per cent) and/or death (20 per cent; Thomson and Marshall, 2006).

In order to improve earlier recognition of WKS in the acute phase, Caine and colleagues (1997) defined operational criteria to diagnose WE and classify neurological complications of alcohol dependence, requiring any two of the following: dietary deficiency, oculomotor abnormalities, cerebellar dysfunction and altered mental state or mild memory impairment. Using these criteria improved diagnostic accuracy from 31 per cent using the classic triad of signs associated with WE (eye signs, gait disturbance and altered mental state) to 100 per cent (Caine *et al.*, 1997). These criteria have since been incorporated into guidelines for identifying early thiamine deficiency and those at risk of WE (Thomson *et al.*, 2008). They have also shown predictive capacity in the identification of subgroups of people with alcohol dependence either showing signs of cognitive impairment, or at risk of such impairment due to subclinical WE (Pitel *et al.*, 2011). This latter study has been described in detail elsewhere in this volume (Savage, 2015; Beaunieux, Eustache and Pitel, 2015; Scalzo, Bowden and Hillbom, 2015), and illustrates the use of Caine and her colleagues' criteria in combination with protocols for diagnosis and treatment of WE (Thomson *et al.*, 2002; Thomson and Marshall, 2006) to detect and treat those at risk of impairment before this becomes irreversible, thus offering significant opportunity to prevent harm.

Assessment of alcohol-related brain damage

Due to the complexity and heterogeneity of ARBD, as described above and elsewhere in this volume (see in particular Scalzo, Bowden and Hillbom, 2015; Wilson, 2015), assessment of ARBD should be a multidisciplinary and staged process, with specific components depending on the referral route and specific presentation of the individual.

Cognitive screening

In an acute setting, an early measure of cognitive functioning is important to obtain, even when it may be difficult to assess the length of any period of abstinence. A cognitive screen will give a snapshot of "functional" cognitive status so that staff can be aware if an individual is particularly incapacitated; whether this is due to intoxication, withdrawal or residual impairment, it is useful information for informed management of the individual's needs. However, as a snapshot of an individual's presentation at a particular time, it is important to record as far as possible how much time has passed since any recent substance use, to estimate quantity of use and record available markers of physiological dysfunction such as hepatic function tests.

Cognitive screening will give a baseline for monitoring change, whether improvement or deterioration. Following medical stabilization and detoxification, there may be a need to support an extended period of abstinence in order to offer a more comprehensive assessment, clarify diagnosis and develop a care plan. This can be difficult if accommodation is not available, and if the individual struggles to remain abstinent outside a supported environment. During the first 12 weeks, assessment may be ongoing as there may be significant improvements in cognition as a result of abstinence and nutritional treatment (see also Wilson, 2015).

A cognitive screen carried out in an acute setting should always be interpreted cautiously, and a low cognitive score should not automatically lead to diagnosis of ARBD or other neurological disorders, but should only be a small part of a comprehensive assessment. In addition, over-reliance on cognitive screening may be a contributory factor in missing diagnosis of ARBD in its early stages (ARBIAS, 2011). To avoid this, and in cases where more detailed information is needed about the person's profile of cognitive strengths and impairments, a more detailed neuropsychological assessment should be carried out. This will pick up early evidence of impairment before other overt clinical signs are apparent, and specify the nature of this impairment, providing opportunities to prevent deterioration and design appropriate treatment plans.

How soon can cognition be assessed following abstinence?

There is a lack of consensus over when it is most appropriate to test cognition following abstinence from alcohol and other substances. Testing cognition too soon after detoxification runs the risk of finding impairment related to residual intoxication or withdrawal, rather than underlying brain changes. However, suggestions range from one week post detoxification from any substance (Miller, 1985; Copersino *et al.*, 2009), through three to six weeks to allow cognitive recovery to plateau following alcohol detoxification (Ryan and Butters, 1986), to not less than six weeks post detox in order to ensure reliability of test results (Walvoort, Wester and Egger, 2013). Criteria for diagnosing alcohol-related dementia (Oslin *et al.*, 1998) require a period of 60 days' abstinence, and suggest the Mini-Mental State Examination (MMSE) as a screening tool, although this will not pick up subtle or executive deficits. More sensitive screening tools include the Addenbrooke's Cognitive Examination (ACE; Mioshi *et al.*, 2006) or the Montreal Cognitive Assessment (MoCA; Nasreddine *et al.*, 2005), both of which have been used within populations with substance-related cognitive impairment (Gilchrist and Morrison, 2005; Copersino *et al.*, 2009).

Neuropsychological assessment of alcohol-related cognitive impairment

A comprehensive neuropsychological assessment is recommended to support diagnosis of ARBD (ARBIAS, 2011), and may be particularly useful in cases where cognitive impairment may be subtle, or where there appears to be a mismatch between performance on screening tools and functioning in the community. Specialist neuropsychological assessment may be able to answer questions about the nature and extent of impairment, the likely consequences of impairment and the interactions between cognitive deficits and psychological problems such as mood or anxiety, and the potential impact of confounding factors such as prescribed or illicit substances, or current physiological dysfunction on cognition. Neuropsychological assessment can also support individual rehabilitation planning, and may be requested to support assessment of decision-making capacity (Evans, 2010).

The initial assessment should give consideration to biological, psychological and social factors that may impact on the person's cognitive functioning. This is essential as populations presenting to drug and alcohol services are likely to have high prevalence of psychological and physical comorbidities that will impact on cognitive performance. Neuropsychological assessment with alcohol and drug using populations may take the following format:

1. Review of referral information

   The referral may contain a wealth of information or very little, and it may be useful to clarify the particular question(s) for which the referrer is seeking answers. It can also be useful to review the patient's medical records, with consent, particularly in cases where there has been a lengthy history. Information on the trajectory of any cognitive changes will be contained within records, and brain imaging may have been carried out in the past. The neuropsychological assessment is an opportunity to formulate information from medical, psychological and social domains and consider how these may impact on cognition, mood behavior and everyday functioning.

Initial review of information prior to the clinical interview is also an opportunity to consider particular areas of emphasis and risk – for example, if the person is elderly, they may be more sensitive to illicit and prescription drug and alcohol use (Withall and Shafiee, 2015). The impact of alcohol and other substances may be less predictable and more potent due to age-related changes, and their impact less well understood.

2. Obtaining consent

There may be limitations to obtaining consent from an individual with cognitive impairment, as addressed in national legislative guidelines. Informed consent should underpin all contact with clients, including information on the purpose of assessment, possible risks and benefits and the limits of confidentiality (British Psychological Society, 2008; see also Perkins and Hopkins, 2015).

In cases where decision-making capacity may be in question, or may be the reason for assessment, a pragmatic approach of "assent" rather than "consent" to assessment is often taken, where a person's lack of objection to assessment is seen as sufficient to proceed, provided that information has been offered on the purpose of assessment, that the person's best interests and preferences are taken into account and that consent has been sought from any person or organization with the legal authority to speak on behalf of the client (British Psychological Society, 2008; Johnson-Greene et al., 1997).

3. The clinical interview

A vital role of the clinical interview session is to help the person feel at ease and engage with the purpose of cognitive testing. A comprehensive neuropsychological assessment can be lengthy and tiring, and may have been requested in order to assess difficulties of which the person is not wholly aware. The initial interview is a chance to develop a therapeutic relationship in the same way as in any therapeutic encounter, and to support the person to understand the purpose of the assessment, which may include discussion of the pros and cons of the assessment and its consequences. Forming a good rapport at initial assessment may also reduce the person's anxiety at the assessment situation and prevent this from impacting on performance.

It is important to interview a relative or carer who knows the person well, due to the possibility of impaired memory and insight, particularly in alcohol-related cognitive impairment. KS is also associated with confabulation, so a carer's account can provide useful corroboration. A carer's account of executive abilities, behavior and personality change is often more informative than the patient's (Hodges, 2007). It is helpful to interview patient and carer individually, so that the carer can express concerns that may otherwise be hidden in order to protect the patient, and the patient has the opportunity to discuss issues that may be personal or confidential. The interview should provide enough qualitative information to form a provisional formulation of difficulties, and will allow major deficits to be assessed (Hodges, 2007). It will also allow for targeting the main areas of cognitive functioning that should be assessed in detail using standardized measurements. The initial interview may seek information on the following, although will be tailored to the referral question, the person's individual presentation and needs, and any practical limitations such as time or location pressures.

Cognitive difficulties

- The person's thoughts on their difficulties and the reasons for them. Was the person aware of the referral and the reasons for it?
- When did the difficulties first appear, or how did the person first become aware of them? How has this impacted on life, work, activities, relationships etc.?
- Were the changes gradual or sudden, and if problems have been progressive then at what rate? Information on initial changes and progression can be key in supporting diagnosis. If changes were sudden, were they associated with any other health concern (such as TIA, stroke or following a head injury)?
- If cognitive difficulties appear to be alcohol or substance related, are they acute or chronic?
- What has changed, and when did this change become noticeable? If the person is not aware of difficulties, have others pointed things out to them and what is the person's interpretation of this? It is useful to seek out examples of when the difficulties arise in the person's daily life, and if particular problems are most apparent in different settings, such as home, work, driving, managing finances, self-care, home–care, social situations (Hodges, 2007).
- How have these difficulties impacted on the person's family or social network?
- Are there any difficulties that may impact on the psychometric assessment – for example, concentration, comprehension or motivational difficulties (Evans, 2010)? How might a neuropsychological assessment need to be adapted to enhance performance – for example, through shortened sessions, using regular breaks, testing at the time of day when the person feels most alert?

Medical and psychiatric history

- Family history of psychiatric or medical problems, including alcohol and drug use. It can be useful to draw a comprehensive family tree, which also provides information about possible support networks for future rehabilitation.
- Past medical history, particularly seeking information about head injuries involving loss of consciousness or post-traumatic amnesia of over an hour, neurosurgery, skull fracture, seizures and CNS infections (Hodges, 2007).

- Past psychiatric history, including history of mood or anxiety disorders, hallucinations or delusions. It can be useful to ask about previous contact with psychological or psychiatric services.
- Any current emotional difficulties? There are high levels of psychiatric comorbidities in alcohol- and substance-using populations, including personality disorders, complex trauma, depression, anxiety disorders, attention deficit hyperactivity disorder (ADHD; Weaver *et al.*, 2003). Self-report scales can be used to help elicit symptoms, and should include measures to evaluate symptom validity.
- Any current physical difficulties or comorbid health problems? Physical problems such as pain or motor difficulties may affect test performance, and comorbid health problems may also impact on cognition. In alcohol- and drug-using populations, there are high levels of comorbid medical conditions – for example, vascular disease, malnutrition, liver cirrhosis, head injury.

Psychosocial history

- Much of this information can be obtained through drawing the person's family tree, as, if sensitively done, this can elicit information on parental and sibling relationships and early life experiences.
- Were there indications of abuse or neglect such as parental substance misuse, domestic violence? Adverse childhood experiences increase the risk of earlier exposure to and use of alcohol and other substances (Dube *et al.*, 2006), with a corresponding impact on brain development if used to excess. This may have implications for interpretation of psychometric test scores, as well as for responsive rehabilitation planning.
- Educational and occupational history. If this was limited, what was the person's experience at school? Were there signs of dyslexia, diagnosed or undiagnosed? Questioning around premorbid ability in conjunction with standardized testing allows the assessment of whether poor performance on cognitive testing represents deterioration, or whether a lack of support to attain educational goals compromised early learning.

Alcohol and drug use

- When did alcohol/drug use begin and become regular?
- What are the drugs/alcohol of choice? In particular, ask about super-strength beers and lagers and use of cannabis.
- What is the pattern of use, and are there indicators of alcohol dependence, tolerance and withdrawal?
- When was the last use, and will intoxication or withdrawal compromise assessment?
- What impact does the person think the alcohol/drug use is having, if any?
- A number of self-report scales are available to support assessment of alcohol and drug use and dependency (see NICE, 2011).

- What other prescribed medications are being taken, and will these have an impact on cognition? It is worth asking in particular about benzodiazepines and over-the-counter medications.

4. Standardized testing

There is no consensus over a particular test battery to use for neuropsychological assessment with alcohol and substance-using populations, and interpretation of results may seek to disentangle a number of potential causes of impairment, including intoxication or withdrawal effects, comorbid neurological, physiological or psychological disorders and variable effort. This means that interpretation of results must be undertaken cautiously, and with attention to the referral question. Rather than specifying particular neuropsychological tests to use, it is arguably more useful to use the referral question and hypotheses formed during initial assessment and interview to guide test selection. Tests selected to assess the presence of a cognitive impairment may be different to those designed to guide rehabilitation, so much depends on the purpose of assessment, any time constraints and, often, what might be available in a service's test cupboard. Whichever tests are chosen, the assessment should seek to cover the following cognitive domains, in order to specify areas of strength as well as deficit, and assess overall intellectual functioning:

- Orientation and basic attention,
- Working memory and processing speed,
- Memory (learning, recall and recognition; autobiographical memory),
- Language (expressive and receptive),
- Numeracy,
- Perception and visuo-spatial function,
- Executive functioning (multitasking, abstract thinking, flexibility, planning, problem solving, impulsivity etc.),
- Mood state and effort.

It will also be important to include tests of cognitive symptom validity using measures that minimize the false-positive rate (e.g., Sollman and Berry, 2011). See also Scalzo, Bowden and Hillbom (2015) for recommendations of the core cognitive abilities that should be covered.

Supporting differential diagnosis

As described elsewhere in this volume (Scalzo, Bowden and Hillbom, 2015), when considering a diagnosis of chronic WKS, or KS, a lack of discrepancy between overall intellectual functioning and memory should not necessarily be an exclusion factor. If there is evidence in the history of neurological signs of WE or acute WKS – for example, using Caine's criteria, or cognitive impairment of any kind (Bowden, 1990; Reuler, Girard and Cooney, 1985) – WKS should be considered.

There may also be a number of factors to consider when attempting to differentiate alcohol-related cognitive impairment from other aetiologies in a neuropsychological assessment. There are inconsistencies in the literature in this area as a result of differences in nosology, and varying criteria for inclusion and exclusion. However, a number of studies have compared those diagnosed with alcohol-related dementia as defined by Oslin and colleagues (1998) with those diagnosed with Alzheimer's disease or vascular dementia. According to Oslin's criteria, the presence of language impairment, focal neurological signs (excluding peripheral neuropathy or ataxia), or evidence of infarction or ischaemia would suggest aetiologies other than alcohol-related dementia, and language impairment, particularly of confrontation naming, has been found to differentiate those with Alzheimer's disease from those with alcohol-related dementia (Saxton et al., 2000). Schmidt and colleagues (2005) found that the executive control deficits in both alcohol-related and vascular dementia were similar, but those with alcohol-related dementia performed better on delayed memory tasks than those with Alzheimer's disease, and worse than those with vascular dementia (Schmidt et al., 2005). It can be more difficult to differentiate alcohol-related from vascular cognitive impairment in the early stages of both diseases, and cerebrovascular disease has been suggested as a component of the dementia syndrome in older people with alcoholism (Fisman, Ramsey and Weiser, 1996).

When considering the comorbidities associated with a history of alcohol excess, whether the increased risk of vascular damage, or that of traumatic brain injury, as well as the range of cognitive presentations that can be associated with ARBD, it is clear that it can be difficult to differentiate alcohol-related damage from other causes. Arguably, the most useful role for assessment will be to define the domains of impairment, profile strengths and weaknesses, and relate these to functional abilities, in order to inform treatment and design individual rehabilitation packages. Recent research suggests the need for more sophisticated uses of neuropsychological assessment of people with alcohol-use disorders in order to evaluate how specific domains of impairment may influence specific behavioral, cognitive and social treatment outcomes for people at different stages of severity (Bates, Buckman and Nguyen, 2013).

Diagnostic disclosure and feedback following assessment

Following assessment the results should be fed back to the individual, and any carers they may wish to involve. This should be done in such a way as to answer any questions they may have had regarding their cognition, and to provide information on areas of impairment, and areas of strength that may be used to compensate. It may be clinically very valuable to the individual and their family to learn about areas of impairment and how these may be contributing to difficulties in daily living. In addition, understanding the potential for cognitive recovery in abstinence, and the potential positive consequences of this in terms of relationships, emotional regulation or employment, may support motivation to reduce or curtail alcohol use, or engage in alcohol treatment (Bates, Buckman and Nguyen, 2013).

Although there is little literature on the impact of a diagnosis of ARBD on the person and their family, diagnostic disclosure should be done sensitively, with access to psychosocial support to enable adjustment, with information about potential prognosis and rehabilitation. It is worth considering the diagnostic terms used and how these might be perceived, due to the potential for perceived stigmatization. However, a diagnosis of ARBD or WKS may also be seen as progress for some, as it may provide an explanation for difficulties experienced, and may also guide access to resources and support.

Assessing decision-making capacity

When cognitive impairment is apparent in the context of alcohol or substance misuse, questions may arise over whether this impairment affects the person's ability to make decisions regarding their treatment, finances or welfare. Legislation supporting the determination of mental capacity or incapacity varies across different jurisdictions, and ethical and legal issues are discussed in greater detail in Perkins and Hopkins (2015). However, the considerations for assessment of decision-making capacity are the same across jurisdictions, recognizing that capacity is decision and time specific. Decision-making capacity is not simply present or absent, but can be recognized as a continuum influenced by insight and understanding (Hazelton, Sterns and Chisholm, 2003; Sullivan, 2004). As such, there is no one test for capacity, but the assessment needs to be tailored to the specific question and consider the degree to which capacity is present (Sullivan, 2004).

The process of assessment

When approaching assessment of capacity, the same issues apply as in the previous section, particularly as regards delaying assessment until the acute phase of intoxication and withdrawal is over. This phase may be prolonged if people have comorbid physical or neurological problems, and it is vital to ensure that assessment results are reliable. As with any neuropsychological assessment, a period of information-gathering prior to formal psychometric testing will inform the assessment. The following questions may be helpful in framing an assessment:

- Gather information about the decision to be made: what are the options and the consequences of each option?
- Gather information about the person's context and history: are there any friends or family members that may have a vested interest? Is anything known about the person's prior wishes and behavior as regards this decision?
- Gather information about the person's current functional abilities, including reports from other staff, carers and family members. An occupational therapy assessment can be important in providing evidence for self-care abilities.

Once the information-gathering phase is complete and it is appropriate to proceed to more formal assessment, a number of other considerations may be important.

Moye and colleagues (2006) suggest a number of ways of maximizing decision-making capacity as regards consent to treatment in older people with dementia, but the strategies are applicable to other populations with cognitive impairment and other decisions. A number of strategies to maximize decision-making capacity are outlined below:

- Assess at varying times of the day on a number of occasions in order to obtain a reliable and consistent picture of the person's cognitive abilities.
- Ensure any environmental distractions are minimized.
- Consider the impact of physical distractions such as pain, fatigue or timing of medication and attempt to structure assessment times to minimize these.
- Ensure that any required communication aids are accessible.
- Ensure that the person has information regarding the reason for the assessment and why the assessment is necessary, and provide relevant information in a form the person can understand. Visual cues can be useful, whether these are written, pictorial or diagrammatic.
- Provide a summary of key information relating to the decision, including consequences of different choices.
- Break information into manageable chunks and discuss one piece of information at a time, regularly inquiring about the person's understanding of the information. Repeat and rephrase information if necessary to ensure understanding, and provide corrective feedback as necessary.
- Allow extra time for the assessment, to slow down the discussion and allow for increased response latency.

A two-stage model of assessment of decision-making capacity has been proposed by Sullivan (2004), recommending an initial stage requiring assessment of fundamental cognitive abilities, followed by a second stage of assessment of the knowledge specific to the decision being made. This model proposes that formal neuropsychological assessment is carried out as the first stage, particularly in cases where cognitive functioning may be borderline, rather than where impairment is clear. A comprehensive assessment may also provide a profile of strengths and weaknesses that can be used to support the person to exercise any residual capacity and overcome barriers to decision-making. Other models have expanded on these two stages – for example, Marson (2001) presents a model of financial decision-making capacity which combines three elements: specific financial abilities or tasks relevant to areas of financial activity; general domains of financial activity relevant to independent functioning; and overall financial capacity.

The initial stage of assessment should cover the cognitive domains specified in the previous section. In an assessment of decision-making capacity, the importance of assessing executive function has been particularly highlighted due to the roles of organization, planning, self-regulation and goal-directed behavior in decision-making. In addition, attention, language and memory have been highlighted as important abilities underlying decision-making (Freedman, Stuss and Gordon, 1991).

A comprehensive assessment covering all cognitive domains allows for the identification of areas of strength that may be used to bypass any deficits and maximize capacity.

The second stage assessing decision-specific knowledge should use the information gathered in the initial stages of the assessment. Vignettes or scenarios tailored to the decision to be made can be used as a way of providing some structure and support for the person to consider possible scenarios. Vignettes have been found to be useful tools to use in capacity assessments in patients with diagnoses of dementia (Fazel, Hope and Jacoby, 1999), although it is unclear whether vignette-based assessments improve agreement between professional ratings of capacity (Sullivan, 2004). At this stage of the assessment it may also be important to include discussion about the specific concerns that may underlie a person's choices. For example, in assessing capacity to consent to treatment there may be concerns about pain or religious or cultural beliefs influencing decisions. With decisions around welfare, concerns about "burdening others", or giving up independence may be at the forefront. Financial worries may also influence decision-making, particularly in situations where a decision to move from independent living to a supported environment may impact on personal finances. It is important to consider suggestibility or undue influence, particularly with those who may have presented as vulnerable in their community in the time preceding involvement with services.

A number of purpose-built competency tests and recommended question sets are also available, but these do not offer information on the cognitive difficulties that may underlie diminished capacity, and therefore cannot offer insight into strategies to maximize the person's strengths and, potentially, their decision-making (Sullivan, 2004). In a review of available tools for assessment of capacity to consent to treatment or participation in clinical research, Dunn and colleagues (2006) recommended the MacArthur Competence Assessment Tools for Clinical Research and Treatment (Appelbaum and Grisso, 2001; Grisso, Appelbaum and Hill-Fotouhi, 1997), and highlighted a number of tools for use in different clinical settings. However, they also acknowledged that these tools should be used as aids to capacity assessment, rather than as stand-alone assessments (Dunn et al., 2006).

Specific considerations in the context of ARBD

There are a number of specific considerations when assessing decision-making capacity in adults presenting with alcohol-related cognitive impairment. Impaired decision-making through alcohol or drug intoxication or dependence alone, in the absence of other deficits, is not sufficient to deem a person legally incompetent (Spike, 1997). However, it can be very difficult to determine when someone using alcohol in a chronic and dependent fashion becomes someone unable to make informed decisions about their behavior and welfare due to a diagnosable mental disorder. In clinical practice, there may be dilemmas over whether someone is making a "choice to drink" and whether this choice is informed, or whether it is influenced by underlying cognitive impairment that may prevent the person from problem-solving, changing old behavioral patterns or thinking flexibly without external intervention, illustrating the fundamental ethical tension between autonomy and protection at the heart of personal competency legislation.

Given the cognitive impairments associated with chronic alcohol excess, this highlights the importance of assessing executive functions when considering decision-making capacity, as they are likely to be affected before other signs of impairment are apparent, and may disproportionately affect functioning and the ability to engage with treatment programs (Bates, Bowden and Barry, 2002). The preservation of language ability may also mask subtle impairments, and make the person appear more able than they actually are (Hazelton, Sterns and Chisholm, 2003), as will the presence of confabulation to mask the memory impairment. Confabulations in WKS are thought to relate in particular to temporal confusion in episodic memory, and can be highly plausible without external validation (Borsutsky et al., 2008), demonstrating the need to obtain an accurate history and reports from significant others wherever possible. In cases where it is difficult to obtain a reliable assessment of cognitive functioning as a result of continued alcohol use, but a person is repeatedly coming to the attention of health, social care or criminal justice services, consideration should be given to the need to assess decision-making capacity and consider legislation in order to protect a person's welfare, health and safety (Mental Welfare Commission for Scotland, 2006).

Hazelton and colleagues (2003) recommend a number of particular considerations in assessing decision-making capacity in those with alcohol-related cognitive impairment, outlined in Table 10.1.

There can be severe consequences of missing alcohol-related cognitive impairment in the context of decision-making capacity. The Mental Welfare Commission for Scotland presented a case, in 2006, of a man who presented to health and social care services due to his chronic alcohol abuse and the health consequences of this, over a period of many years (Mental Welfare Commission for Scotland, 2006).

TABLE 10.1 Suggestions regarding the evaluation of personal care competency of patients with alcohol abuse

- Wherever possible, assessment should be delayed until the acute effects of intoxication and delirium are over.
- Evidence of impaired judgment prior to hospitalization should be considered in addition to presentation at the time of assessment.
- Attempts should be made to differentiate between alcohol-related cognitive deficits and denial secondary to addiction.
- A comprehensive cognitive examination, including tests of executive function, should be performed.
- Patient preference should be respected to the greatest degree possible and least-restrictive measures should be employed.
- Where there is evidence of gradual improvement, competency should be reassessed during hospitalizations or even after placement in a nursing home.

Reprinted from Hazelton, Sterns and Chisholm. © (2003) with permission from Elsevier.

They concluded that a lack of intervention earlier in the course of "Mr H's" deterioration resulted in a more extreme list of legislative powers having to be sought, and recognized that early intervention was not provided as a result of: "the values, prejudices and misconceptions present in the wider society about individual responsibility and autonomy in relation to serious prolonged abuse of alcohol" (p. 17).

The issue of stigma against those presenting with alcohol- and substance-related problems is widespread within society, and has been recognized within health care settings (Thomson *et al.*, 2012). In many countries, alcohol is seen as an important part of societal tradition and culture, and there is recognition that professionals cannot be immune to societal attitudes towards the use and abuse of alcohol. This can influence beliefs about whether recovery from alcoholism is possible, whether people "deserve" care and treatment or whether they have "brought the problem on themselves", and whether professionals feel able to comment on another person's "right to drink", which can mean that individuals do not receive treatment or intervention until problems are already severe, and the possibility of recovery is diminished (Scottish Executive, 2004). There is a need to campaign against this stigma among health care professionals (Thomson *et al.*, 2012) and within wider society in order to ensure equality of care for some of the most vulnerable in our society.

References

Allen, D. N., Goldstein, G. and Seaton, B. E. (1997). Cognitive rehabilitation of chronic alcohol abusers. *Neuropsychology Review*, 7(1), 21–39.

Appelbaum, P. S. and Grisso, T. (2001). *MacCAT-CR: MacArthur Competence Assessment Tool for Clinical Research*. Sarasota, FL: Professional Resource Press.

ARBIAS. (2011). *Looking Forward: Information and Specialised Advice on Alcohol Related Brain Impairment* (4th edn). Available at http://www.arbias.org.au/content/documents/ Lookingforward_ABI2nd.pdf. Accessed 30 June 2014.

Bates, M. E., Bowden, S. C. and Barry, D. (2002). Neurocognitive impairment associated with alcohol use disorders: implications for treatment. *Experimental and Clinical Psychopharmacology*, 10(3), 193–212.

Bates, M. E., Buckman, J. F. and Nguyen, T. T. (2013). A role for cognitive rehabilitation in increasing the effectiveness of treatment for alcohol use disorders. *Neuropsychology Review*, 23, 27–47.

Bates, M. E., Barry, D., Labouvie, E. W., Buckman, J. F., Fals-Stewart, W. F. and Voelbel, G. (2004). Risk factors and neuropsychological recovery in alcohol use disordered clients exposed to different treatments. *Journal of Consulting and Clinical Psychology*, 72(6), 1073–80.

Beaunieux, H., Eustache, F. and Pitel, A.-L. (2015). The relation of alcohol-induced brain changes to cognitive function. In J. Svanberg, A. Withall, B. Draper and S. Bowden (eds), *Alcohol and the Adult Brain*. Hove: Psychology Press.

Borsutzky, S., Fujiwara, E., Brand, M. and Markowitsch, H. J. (2008). Confabulations in alcoholic Korsakoff patients. *Neuropsychologia*, 46(13), 3133–43.

Bowden, S. C. (1990). Separating cognitive impairment in neurologically asymptomatic alcoholism from Wernicke-Korsakoff syndrome: is the neuropsychological distinction justified? *Psychological Bulletin*, 107, 355–66.

British Psychological Society. (2008). *Generic Professional Practice Guidelines* (2nd edn.). Leicester: British Psychological Society.

Caine, D., Halliday, G. M., Kril, J. J. and Harper, C. G. (1997). Operational criteria for the classification of chronic alcoholics: identification of Wernicke's encephalopathy. *Journal of Neurology, Neurosurgery and Psychiatry*, 62(1), 51–60.

Copersino, M. L., Fals-Stewart, W., Fitzmaurice, G., Schretlen, D. J., Sokoloff, J. and Weiss, R. D. (2009). Rapid cognitive screening of patients with substance use disorders. *Experimental and Clinical Psychopharmacology*, 17(5), 337–44.

Dube, S. R., Miller, J. W., Brown, D. W., Giles, W. H., Felitti, V. J., Dong, M. and Anda, R. F. (2006). Adverse childhood experiences and the association with ever using alcohol and initiating alcohol use during adolescence. *Journal of Adolescent Health*, 38(4), 444e1–444e10.

Dunn, L. B., Nowrangi, M. A., Palmer, B. W., Jeste, D. V. and Saks, E. R. (2006). Assessing decisional capacity for clinical research or treatment: a review of instruments. *American Journal of Psychiatry*, 163, 1323–34.

Evans J. J. (2010). Basic concepts and principles of neuropsychological assessment. In J. Gurd, U. Kischka and J. Marshall (eds), *The Handbook of Clinical Neuropsychology* (2nd edn). Oxford: Oxford University Press.

Fazel, S., Hope, T. and Jacoby, R. (1999). Assessment of competence to complete advance directives: validation of a patient centred approach. *British Medical Journal*, 318, 493–7.

Fisman, M., Ramsey, D. and Weiser, M. (1996). Dementia in the elderly male alcoholic: a retrospective clinicopathological study. *International Journal of Geriatric Psychiatry*, 11(3), 209–18.

Freedman, M., Stuss, D. and Gordon, M. (1991). Assessment of competency: the role of neurobehavioural deficits. *Annals of Internal Medicine*, 115, 203–8.

Gilchrist, G. and Morrison, D. S. (2005). Prevalence of alcohol related brain damage among homeless hostel dwellers in Glasgow. *European Journal of Public Health*, 15(6), 587–8.

Grisso, T., Appelbaum, P. S. and Hill-Fotouhi, C. (1997). The MacCAT-T: a clinical tool to assess patients' capacities to make treatment decisions. *Psychiatric Services*, 48, 1415–19.

Harper, C. (2009). The neuropathology of alcohol related brain damage. *Alcohol and Alcoholism*, 44(2), 136–40.

Hazelton, L. D., Sterns, G. L. and Chisholm, T. (2003). Decision-making capacity and alcohol abuse: clinical and ethical considerations in personal care choices. *General Hospital Psychiatry*, 25(2), 130–5.

Hodges, J. (2007). *Cognitive Assessment for Clinicians*. Cambridge: Oxford University Press.

Johnson-Greene, D., Hardy-Morais, C., Adams, K. M., Hardy, C. and Bergloff. (1997). Informed consent and neuropsychological assessment: ethical considerations and proposed guidelines. *The Clinical Neuropsychologist*, 11(4), 454–60.

Knight, R. G. and Longmore, B. E. (1994). *Clinical Neuropsychology of Alcoholism*. East Sussex: Lawrence Erlbaum Associates.

Kopelman, M. D., Thomson, A. D., Guerrini, I. and Marshall, E. J. (2009). The Korsakoff syndrome: clinical aspects, psychology and treatment. *Alcohol and Alcoholism*, 44(2), 148–54.

Le Berre, A. P., Rauchs, G., La Joie, R., Segobin, S., Mézenge, F., Boudehent, C., Vabret, F., Viader, F., Eustache, F., Pitel, A. L. and Beaunieux, H. (2013). Readiness to change and brain damage in patients with chronic alcoholism. *Psychiatry Research*, 213(3), 202–9.

Marson, D. C. (2001). Loss of financial competency in dementia: conceptual and empirical approaches. *Aging, Neuropsychology, and Cognition: A Journal on Normal and Dysfunctional Development*, 8(3), 164–81.

Mental Welfare Commission for Scotland. (2006). *Inquiry into the Care and Treatment of Mr H*. Edinburgh: MWCScot. Available at http://www.mwcscot.org.uk. Accessed 30 June 2014.

Miller, L. (1985). Neuropsychological assessment of substance abusers: review and recommendations. *Journal of Substance Abuse Treatment*, 2(1), 5–17.

Mioshi, E., Dawson, K., Mitchell, J., Arnold, R. and Hodges, J. R. (2006). The Addenbrooke's Cognitive Examination Revised (ACE-R): a brief cognitive test battery for dementia screening. *International Journal of Geriatric Psychiatry*, 21(11), 1078–85.

Morrison, F. (2011). Neuropsychological impairment and relapse following inpatient detoxification in severe alcohol dependence. *International Journal of Mental Health and Addiction*, 9, 151–61.

Moye, J., Karel, M. J., Gurrera, R. J. and Azar, A. R. (2006). Neuropsychological predictors of decision-making capacity over 9 months in mild-to-moderate dementia. *Journal of General Internal Medicine*, 21(1), 78–83.

Nasreddine, Z. S., Phillips, N. A., Bedirian, V., Charbonneau, S., Whitehead, V., Collin, I., Cummings, J. L. and Chertkow, H. (2005). The Montreal Cognitive Assessment, MoCA: a brief screening tool for mild cognitive impairment. *Journal of the American Geriatric Society*, 53(4), 695–9.

NICE. (2011). *Alcohol-Use Disorders: Diagnosis, Assessment and Management of Harmful Drinking and Alcohol Dependence*. Guideline CG115. London: NICE.

Oscar-Berman, M. and Marinković, K. (2007). Alcohol: effects on neurobehavioural functions and the brain. *Neuropsychological Review*, 17, 239–57.

Oslin D., Atkinson R., Smith D. and Hendrie H. (1998). Alcohol related dementia: proposed clinical criteria. *International Journal of Geriatric Psychiatry*, 13, 203–12.

Perkins, C. and Hopkins, J. (2015). Ethical issues associated with alcohol-related cognitive impairment. In J. Svanberg, A. Withall, B. Draper and S. Bowden (eds), *Alcohol and the Adult Brain*. Hove: Psychology Press.

Pitel, A.-L., Zahr, N., Jackson, K., Sassoon, S., Rosenbloom, M., Pfefferbaum, A. and Sullivan, E. (2011). Signs of preclinical Wernicke's encephalopathy and thiamine levels as predictors of neuropsychological deficits in alcoholism without Korsakoff's syndrome. *Neuropsychopharmacology*, 36, 580–8.

Reuler, J. B., Girard, D. E. and Cooney, T. G. (1985). Wernicke's encephalopathy. *New England Journal of Medicine*, 312, 1035–9.

Ryan, C. and Butters, N. (1986). The neuropsychology of alcoholism. In D. Wedding, A. M. Horton Jr and J. S. Webster (eds), *The Neuropsychology Handbook*. New York: Springer.

Saxton, J., Munro, C. A., Butters, M. A., Schramke, C. and Mcneil, M. A. (2000). Alcohol, dementia and Alzheimer's disease: comparison of neuropsychological profiles. *Journal of Geriatric Psychiatry and Neurology*, 13(3), 141–9.

Savage, L. (2015). Alcohol-related brain damage and neuropathology. In J. Svanberg, A. Withall, B. Draper and S. Bowden (eds), *Alcohol and the Adult Brain*. Hove: Psychology Press.

Scalzo, S., Bowden, S. and Hillbom, M. (2015). Wernicke-Korsakoff Syndrome. In J. Svanberg, A. Withall, B. Draper and S. Bowden (eds), *Alcohol and the Adult Brain*. Hove: Psychology Press.

Schmidt, K. S., Gallo, J. L., Ferri C., Giovannetti T., Sestito N., Libon D. J. and Schmidt P. S. (2005). The neuropsychological profile of alcohol-related dementia suggests cortical and subcortical pathology. *Dementia and Geriatric Cognitive Disorders*, 20(5), 286–91.

Scottish Executive. (2004). *A Fuller Life: Report of the Expert Group on Alcohol Related Brain Damage*. Stirling: Dementia Services Development Centre. Available at http://lx.iriss. org.uk/sites/default/files/resources/ARBD_afullerlife.pdf. Accessed 30 June 2014.

Sollman, M. J. and Berry, D. T. R. (2011). Detection of inadequate effort on neuropsychological testing: a meta-analytic update and extension. *Archives of Clinical Neuropsychology*, 26, 774–89.

Spike, J. (1997). A paradox about capacity, alcoholism, and noncompliance. *Journal of Clinical Ethics*, 8(3), 303–6.

Sullivan, E. (2003). Compromised pontocerebellar and cerebellothalamocortical systems: speculations on their contributions to cognitive and motor impairment in nonamnesic alcoholism. *Alcoholism: Clinical and Experimental Research*, 27, 1409–19.

Sullivan, K. (2004). Neuropsychological assessment of mental capacity. *Neuropsychology Review*, 14(3), 131–42.

Thomson, A. D. and Marshall, E. J. (2006). The treatment of patients at risk of developing Wernicke's encephalopathy in the community. *Alcohol and Alcoholism*, 41(2), 159–67.

Thomson, A. D., Cook, C. C., Touquet, R. and Henry, J. A. (2002). The Royal College of Physicians report on alcohol: guidelines for managing Wernicke's encephalopathy in the accident and emergency department. *Alcohol and Alcoholism*, 37(6), 513–21.

Thomson A. D., Cook C. C., Guerrini I., Sheedy, D., Harper, C. and Marshall, J. (2008). Wernicke's encephalopathy: "Plus ça change, plus c'est la même chose". *Alcohol and Alcoholism*, 43(2), 180–6.

Thomson, A. D., Guerrini, I., Bell, D., Drummond, C., Duka, T., Field, M., Kopelman, K., Lingford-Hughes, A., Smith, I., Wilson, K. and Marshall, E. J. (2012). Alcohol-related brain damage: report from a Medical Council on Alcohol Symposium, June 2010. *Alcohol and Alcoholism*, 47(2), 84–91.

Walvoort, S. J., Wester A. J. and Egger J. L. (2013). The neuropsychology of cognitive functions in alcohol abstinence. *Tijdshdrift voor Psychiatrie*, 55(2), 101–11.

Weaver, T., Madden, P., Charles, V., Stimson, G., Renton, A., Tyrer, P., Barnes, T., Bench, C., Middleton, H., Wright, N., Paterson, S., Shanahan, W., Seivewright, N. and Ford, C. (2003). Comorbidity of substance misuse and mental illness in community mental health and substance misuse services. *British Journal of Psychiatry*, 183, 304–13.

Wilson, K. (2015). The clinical rehabilitation of people with alcohol-related brain damage. In J. Svanberg, A. Withall, B. Draper and S. Bowden (eds), *Alcohol and the Adult Brain*. Hove: Psychology Press.

Withall, A. and Shafiee, S. (2015). Alcohol and cognitive impairment: considerations with the older client. In J. Svanberg, A. Withall, B. Draper and S. Bowden (eds), *Alcohol and the Adult Brain*. Hove: Psychology Press.

11

ETHICAL ISSUES ASSOCIATED WITH ALCOHOL-RELATED COGNITIVE IMPAIRMENT

Chris Perkins and John Hopkins

Alcohol can affect cognitive function in a variety of ways, as described in this book. These include acute intoxication, withdrawal delirium, severe memory deficit, as in Korsakoff's Syndrome (KS), now known as "major neurocognitive disorder amnesic-confabulatory type" (American Psychiatric Association, 2013) and frontal lobe damage affecting judgment, motivation and volition. Although these are described as discrete conditions, in reality it is often difficult to distinguish between them so that the discussion below may apply to them all. It is estimated one in ten cases of dementia are caused by alcohol (Wilson, 2011), but the difference between alcohol-related brain damage (ARBD) and other forms of dementia is the potential for recovery with abstinence and for further damage with continued drinking.

In this chapter, we address the ethical issues associated with ARBD. Both the ethics of cognitive impairment and those of substance dependence are relevant when working with people with this condition.

The classical medical ethics framework calls for balancing the principles of:

- Autonomy: the state of being self-governing
- Beneficence: doing good
- Non-maleficence: not doing harm
- Justice: fairness, especially in the distribution of resources

Discourse, that is talking the matter over, helps us to resolve dilemmas where these principles clash, such as when there is a tension between protecting a vulnerable person's well-being (beneficence) and their right as an individual to make decisions, even if these are personally harmful (autonomy). There are no standard or "correct" answers. In each case different weight will be ascribed to each principle to come up with the best solution depending on individual circumstances – for example, if a person is likely to die as a result of alcohol use we might be more likely to override autonomy than if he/she is suffering only minor physical problems and managing his/her own self-care.

Autonomy

Autonomy is the state of having self-directing freedom and moral independence. Most legal jurisdictions assume that people are autonomous and thus have the capacity (also called competence) to make decisions unless proven otherwise. Individual autonomy is not always part of a person's cultural or ethnic beliefs. The clinician should attempt to understand the person's belief system and his or her own, in order to not impose a view that is not held by the patient. Similarly, older people might be more open and desiring of family input into decisions, rather than making an individual decision (Rabins and Black, 2010).

Capacity

To be autonomous a person needs to have decisional capacity – that is, the ability to make and communicate decisions. The person needs to be adequately informed of and aware of their situation, to have a choice and know that they have a choice. They must be able to understand the information provided, appreciate the significance of the situation, reason with the information (weigh up consequences, consider alternatives), communicate their choice or decision and be consistent. Capacity is not an all-or-nothing concept; there is a range of possibilities between the two poles of total incapacity and full capacity. This would include the ability to make decisions about some things and not others, fluctuating capacity or partial capacity where the person needs support to make or communicate decisions, but can have a say in what happens. If a cause for impaired capacity can be found and ameliorated, then capacity may be re-established. Every effort should be made to enhance autonomy by improving mental and physical health and hence capacity (Rabins and Black, 2010).

The effect of alcohol on capacity

In order to make a free choice a person must exercise self-determination without undue internal or external coercion. Whether this is possible when dependent on a substance is arguable, raising the question of the degree to which people addicted to substances lack the ability to exercise free will (Geppert and Bogenschulz, 2009). "Chronic addiction may diminish and even perhaps eliminate the individual's ability for rational and voluntary choice so critical for informed consent and the motivation and ability to change integral to addiction treatment" (Geppert and Bogenschulz, 2009, p. 288). Fadda and Rossetti (1998) suggest that the states of chronic alcohol consumption and dependence lead to functional and anatomic brain changes, even before the onset of recognizable alcoholic brain damage. Heavy substance use could lead to volitional and cognitive impairments that reduce the ability to provide informed consent for treatment or research and may contribute to the persistence of alcohol dependence. Lambert, Scheiner and Campbell (2010, p.169), argue that "the impaired, drug-abusing individual deserves to be considered within the category of individuals without capacity to make fully informed decisions". Other coercive pressures on people with ARBD include legal, family and social pressures, powerlessness, social stigmatization, desperation, poverty, anxiety and depression (Geppert and Bogenschulz, 2009).

Capacity assessment

For informed consent the person needs to be given adequate person-centered information including diagnosis, proposed treatment and risks and benefits. The sorts of decisions that people with ARBD need to make include: accommodation (e.g., whether to live in an environment that limits access to alcohol), financial (e.g., whether someone else should control their money) and health (such as who decides on medical or rehabilitative treatments). The capacity assessment needs to be directed towards the issue at hand.

A typical assessment (Appelbaum, 2007) includes determining whether the person has the ability to:

• Communicate a choice
• Comprehend information
• Reason about options, risks and benefits
• Appreciate the effect of choices on their life course and values.

Damage to the frontal lobes is common with alcohol dependence and this may be difficult to detect on routine questioning or standard cognitive testing. Symptoms of frontal lobe dysfunction, such as amotivation, poor judgment and personality change, can be difficult to distinguish from the effects of alcohol use if the person is still drinking. A particular challenge is to decide what is denial, common in substance dependence, and what is *lack of insight* associated with frontal lobe damage.

Frontal lobe testing may indicate difficulties with planning, organization, problem-solving, disinhibition and perseveration, with visuo-spatial impairments also particularly common (Wilson, 2011). The Addenbrooke's Cognitive Examination-Revised version, (ACE-R; Mioshi *et al.*, 2006) or Montreal Cognitive Assessment, (MoCA; Nasreddine *et al.*, 2005) are more likely to show frontal abnormalities than the Mini-Mental Status Examination (MMSE; Folstein, Folstein and McHugh, 1975) and as such they are now replacing the MMSE as the preferred bedside cognitive assessment instrument. Bossers and colleagues (2012) recommend verbal fluency and trail-making B tests for measuring potentially damaged executive function (Bossers *et al.*, 2012). In-depth neuropsychological assessment may be required to determine the degree of cognitive damage and its effect on capacity.

While cognitive assessment can support a capacity assessment, the true test will be the person's understanding of the issue confronting them, such as whether they are safe to return home, understanding of their medical condition or the risks of continuing alcohol intake. For fuller accounts of capacity assessment, see, for example,

Molloy, Darzins and Strang (1999), Appelbaum, (2007) or elsewhere in this volume (Svanberg, Morrison and Cullen, 2015).

It is not always obvious whether the person's incapacity is a temporary or permanent feature. Bodani, Reed and Kopelman (2009) note that the global confusion associated with Wernicke's Encephalopathy (WE) begins to dissipate after two to three weeks of abstinence and can clear completely after one to two months. Hannay and colleagues (2004) suggest that a significant improvement in neuropsychological deficits occurs after the first two weeks of stopping drinking and continues for weeks or months (Hannay *et al.*, 2004). However, the rate of improvement levels off after three to six weeks. Younger people may recover to normal in three months, though older people remain relatively impaired for longer. Initial capacity assessment should thus be delayed for at least three to four weeks after the person stops drinking. This may require a long hospital stay and the agreement of the patient to remain alcohol-free during this period, both of which can be difficult to achieve. With abstinence, decisional capacity can continue to improve over months or years. In such cases, making the sorts of permanent legal arrangements that suit people with a progressive degenerative condition is not necessarily appropriate. Thus, capacity should be regularly reassessed, especially if someone has been compulsorily required to accept treatment or placement.

Vignette 1

A 66-year-old woman, with a long history of anxiety, benzodiazepine dependence and excessive alcohol consumption, entered aged residential care at the instigation of her daughter (who held Enduring Power of Attorney [EPOA]) with a diagnosis of alcoholic dementia (ACE-R score = 43/100; cut-off for dementia: 82/100; Mioshi et al., 2006). She then stopped drinking. Two years later, following a delirium, she was transferred to a secure dementia unit using the authority of the EPOA. Within six months, she complained that she didn't belong with the other residents as she was less impaired than they were and requested a transfer to a non-secure facility in the same complex. Her frustrations then expressed themselves via antisocial behavior including stealing. A repeat ACE-R was 89/100!

The law

Three types of legislation potentially apply to the person with ARBD. These are laws applying specifically to substance abuse, mental health laws and guardianship provisions. Clinicians may use any of these depending on the circumstances.

Drug and alcohol legislation

Some countries have specific drug and alcohol legislation. These laws may either allow for protective custody of acutely intoxicated individuals (Geppert and Bogenschulz, 2009), or for compulsory treatment for the person to detoxify and regain capacity and thus restore autonomy. The person may then choose to undergo treatment rather than being subjected to long periods of compulsory rehabilitation. The New Zealand Law Commission, reviewing the local drug and alcohol legislation, state their opinion thus: "Once capacity has been restored, and there has been an opportunity to engender motivation, we think that people must be free to determine for themselves whether to undertake ongoing treatment on a voluntary basis" (The Law Commission, 2010, p. 5).

Mental health legislation

Mental health laws generally preclude committal solely on the basis of substance-use disorders, but may apply in the presence of other psychiatric symptoms such as depression, psychosis or cognitive deficit (along with the necessary risk to self or others). If it is unclear whether there is permanent ARBD it may be justified to admit, detoxify and assess someone under a mental health act.

Guardianship legislation

Most countries or states have guardianship laws that make provision for managing the personal and financial affairs of someone who lacks capacity. Guardianship laws are rarely used until someone has developed persistent or permanent cognitive impairment. A Scottish report states, "As long as an individual retains some capacity to change their drinking behaviour, it is not acceptable for the state, or anyone else, to intervene compulsorily to prevent even a reasonably predictable downward spiral" (Cox, Anderson and McCabe, 2004, p. 11). The degree of intervention allowed is generally the least restrictive option out of respect for autonomy. There will, however, be times when community treatment is impossible because of the risk of harm to self or others. Once a person is found to lack capacity, a guardian is appointed to make decisions for that person. Surrogate decision-making can either be via *substituted judgment*, where the patient's previous wishes are known, or via *best interests*, when the previous wishes are unknown. The wishes and decisions of the incapacitated person still need to be acknowledged and protected, and the person lacking capacity encouraged to be involved in decision-making as much as possible (Lambert, Scheiner and Campbell, 2010).

Sometimes surrogate decision-makers seem to be making decisions in their own interests. If, after exploring the issues, the clinician remains concerned about this, then the case may need to be referred to the courts (Rabins and Black, 2010). As in any case of compulsory treatment it is helpful and less worrying ethically if the family agrees with the treating clinicians. This is not always so as the case in Vignette 2 illustrates.

Even when capacity appears recovered, it is often the case that the person who is now "autonomous" resumes drinking in a manner that is likely to again impair their capacity. Once a person has regained capacity, must the clinician implement his or her wishes? Is there a case to enforce abstinence, by whatever means, on

> **Vignette 2**
>
> *A 70-year-old woman was admitted with a ten-year history of alcohol use of up to a gallon of gin per day with multiple end-organ damage (cerebellar ataxia, liver damage and peripheral neuropathy). MMSE = 21/30. She was placed temporarily under a court order in a secure dementia unit. Her cognition and function improved, though her capacity remained impaired. Her husband was also thought to be a drinker. The couple challenged the interim placement order and any extension of this. She did not require secure dementia level care, other than for enforcing abstinence, and her husband was clearly opposed to this.*

people who are known to have a history of repeated, self-injurious relapses? What is a compelling reason to override the wishes of a possibly only temporarily competent decision-maker? (Lambert, Scheiner and Campbell, 2010).

The difficult question, challenging clinicians and law-makers worldwide, is to determine under what circumstances it is justified to use compulsion to treat people whose alcohol use is causing physical, cognitive and/or social damage if they do not or cannot stop drinking? It remains very difficult to estimate an individual's potential for improvement or to predict the outcome of compulsory treatment.

Confidentiality

The control of information about oneself, what one wishes to keep private or make public is an aspect of autonomy. Because of the societal stigma associated with substance abuse clinicians need to be especially vigilant about confidentiality. However, as in any other type of mental illness there are times when the individual's right to confidentiality must be overridden because of risks to the person or to others, such as suicide or homicide threats, abuse of incompetent elders or children. Clinicians must remind the client of these limits to confidentiality when starting treatment (Geppert and Bogenschulz, 2009). If their patient poses a risk to others, these other people must be informed, though ideally the clinician will tell the patient first before breaking confidentiality.

If driving ability is impaired and the person will not stop voluntarily (or forgets to), then it may be necessary to discuss the risk with the family and/or notify the relevant authority. This often totally disrupts clinical rapport; people who do not usually recall much, often remember with persisting rage the person who "removed" their licence to drive. If the person is still drinking alcohol the issue becomes more complicated. Should they be allowed to "dry out" (if possible) and then be tested for driving skills? Should the licensing authority be notified of the ongoing problem? When a person drives to an appointment intoxicated, the clinician may need to arrange for alternate transport home or a chance to sober up before leaving. Is the clinician liable if there is a serious accident? Even if not held legally or professionally responsible, the clinician is bound to feel a certain level of guilt or, at least, regret if an innocent party is harmed by their patient's driving. At what stage of the assessment process should the person be warned against driving? To be safe, this could occur during the first interview if there is a possibility of cognitive impairment, but this may be unnecessary and too heavy-handed as many people rely on driving to maintain their independence.

Should a landlord be told about a forgetful or intoxicated person smoking in bed? Can a family ask the liquor shop not to sell to someone, or the bank to limit access to funds to buy alcohol? What about the use of devices tracking the person's movements (often regarded as an intrusion on privacy) if they are inclined to get lost or end up in a hotel bar? In each of these cases, breaking confidentiality must be balanced against the seriousness of the risk the person presents by their actions. The prudent clinician will seek the opinions of his or her colleagues and consider local privacy laws when considering the options.

If a clinician believes the family should be involved but the patient declines this, then an assessment of capacity will guide further action. Obviously one should not override the wishes of a person with capacity, but it may be in the best interests of the person to do this if they lack capacity. In some cultures, respect for an elder may always mean that their requests must be adhered to (Rabins and Black, 2010). Consultation with other professionals or members of that culture can help resolve such difficult dilemmas and in most areas sharing information with other health providers is acceptable. Clinical information should be recorded in a factual and non-judgmental manner (Geppert and Bogenschulz, 2009), especially as this may be available to the patient on request.

Truth-telling

To support someone's autonomy, even if it is limited, one must be honest about any actions that might affect them. Health professionals are obliged to discuss the risks of treatment and non-treatment with their patients (Ryan *et al.*, 2010). If someone is intoxicated, explanations may be better left until they sober up and if cognitively impaired, explanation must be couched in language the person can comprehend. Some families disable the car or hide ("lose") the keys to prevent a person driving. They may water down a person's wine or top up the whiskey decanter with coloured water. Is this deception justified if it reduces the number of times a person falls, slows the rate of cognitive decline or prevents them driving dangerously? By the time families have resorted to this, they have little interest in the niceties of truth-telling. Should the clinician ever suggest this course of action to others? Once again, the balance of harm done by deception must be weighed up against the good achieved, and reviewed if the situation changes.

Beneficence

This is about active goodness, kindness or charity. "Morality requires not only that we treat persons autonomously and refrain from harming them, but that we contribute to their welfare" (Lambert, Scheiner and Campbell, 2010, p. 169). Doing good has to be balanced against the risks of doing harm, including loss of autonomy – for example, by depriving a person of freedom – and against the principle of justice, such as funding other health initiatives.

It is under the principle of beneficence that we consider enforced treatment to protect the life and health of people with ARBD, especially in order for them to recover autonomy (Geppert and Bogenschulz, 2009). However, unless we can provide good care for such people, we should not be infringing on other principles. The "concept of reciprocity" means that if someone's freedom is removed, we have "an ethical responsibility to ensure that any imposed care is appropriate" (Cox, Anderson and McCabe, 2004).

Unfortunately, that good care is not always available; as the above vignettes demonstrate, people may be detained in unsuitable facilities against their will. People with ARBD are not a group that is generally attractive to care-providers. Often they are judged as having brought their condition on themselves and this seems to make them less worthy than other people to receive care. They may be difficult to manage and belligerent, lacking insight if they have frontal lobe damage, yet appearing superficially intact and in control of their behavior. If they have drunk for a long time and/or continue to drink, they can be seen as hopeless cases. They have alienated friends and families and may have multiple physical complications. There are few facilities available for specifically dealing with this group. However, the provision of good care would greatly help. KS is often perceived as untreatable, but, in fact, only 25 per cent show no recovery, 25 per cent experiencing slight, 25 per cent significant and 25 per cent complete recovery of memory with abstinence (Smith and Hillman, 1999). For a chronic condition, these are good outcomes and something towards which we should strive. Despite the generally negative attitudes to homeless people with ARBD, a "cost-effective and dignified care solution" for these people has been demonstrated – for example, by the Wicking Project carried out by Wintringham Specialist Aged Care (Rota-Bartelink, 2012, p. 4). In this trial of psychosocial approaches, staff identified recreational interests and worked to engage participants in these rather than alcohol-seeking activities. The total amount of alcohol consumed was reduced by 62 per cent, behavioral issues diminished and mental health and quality of life improved.

Fidelity (or faithfulness) by the treating team to the patient is a virtue relating to the patient's ultimate good. Dealing with people with ARBD can be difficult and frustrating. When there are years of treatment with multiple relapses, the clinician may lose hope and consider discharging the patient. However, the natural history of substance misuse is not always an inevitable slide in to worsening dependence; in an American study of problem drinkers, in 45 per cent of cases alcohol was no longer causing difficulties at the 20–year follow–up (Wilson, 2011). Whether persistent clinicians could improve these percentages is not clear. However, the Wicking Project (Rota-Bartelink, 2012, above) suggests that the quality of life of even the most recalcitrant recidivist can be improved significantly.

> **Vignette 3**
>
> *A 66-year-old male was admitted with WE, which progressed to Korsakoff's psychosis. For one month on the medical ward he did not know who or where he was (ACE-R = 47/100). A guardianship order was obtained for placement in a secure dementia unit. Two months later, his cognition and capacity had recovered to the extent that he no longer required secure care and so was transferred to residential care closer to the family home. However, he soon began returning home every day, drinking while there and returning to the facility intoxicated and sleepy or disruptive. This resulted in a second period of secure care and, after four months, he returned home, this time more successfully. Ten months later he was living a quiet, home-centered life, drinking approximately two glasses of wine per day and, despite this, had had no further hospital contacts or admissions and no further episodes of acute confusion.*

Beneficence might be about educating in-patient and emergency doctors to reduce the damage done by alcohol by providing detoxification to avoid dangerous withdrawal symptoms and suitable vitamin replacement to prevent brain damage. On the public health front, Wernicke-Korsakoff prevalence can be reduced by supplemental thiamine in staple food like bread, as has been done for years in some countries (USA, UK and Australia) with great success. Harper (2009) suggests that this preventative measure should be considered in all countries where alcohol-related disorders are common.

Non-maleficence

This is about doing no harm by our actions or, at the very least, minimizing harm done to individuals entrusted to the clinician's care (Lambert, Scheiner and Campbell, 2010). Some harms might be: the removal of freedoms to go wherever one wishes, enforced treatment (e.g., with disulfiram) and loss of the option to partake of a substance that most people in the western world enjoy. There are times when harm *will* be done, but it must be minimized and balanced against the potential good. "Minimum intervention and net benefit proportionality requires that the limits imposed on a person's right to refuse treatment go no further than is necessary. The benefits of those limits must outweigh the harm that impinging on rights will cause" (The Law Commission, 2010).

Where there is no dedicated service for people with alcohol-related cognitive impairment, the patient risks being "bounced" between services, passed between addiction and mental health services, medical wards, liaison psychiatry and older people's services. This lack of a joined-up service can delay appropriate treatment so that by the time the person does get help, their chances of recovery have diminished.

Stigmatization can and often does produce harm. Stigma in ARBD comes from its connection with alcohol, mental health problems and dementia; it is expressed at individual, institutional and societal levels (Cox, Anderson and McCabe, 2004). The negative attitudes of staff can be harmful if they put people off coming for treatment, and treatment given with bad grace deters patients from returning for help in future. Societal stigma deters people from acknowledging their condition and seeking help. "Victim-blaming" of people with ARBD gives governments and health providers the opportunity to opt out. Because most people use alcohol without too much problem this absolves the majority, including the liquor industry, from responsibility for those who are harmed.

However, the risk for alcohol dependence arises from a combination of genetic, personality and social factors, with estimates that 50 to 60 per cent of the liability to alcohol dependence results from genetic factors (Welch, 2011). Are alcohol-damaged people the predictable consequence of the widespread availability of alcohol? Does this mean that we should absolve these people of responsibility, thus perhaps reducing stigma? If so how do we understand and relate to individuals who, despite their genetic loading, manage to become and remain abstinent?

To reduce the possibility of harm, clinicians need to work within their level of competence, keep up to date, have suitable skills and use interventions that have little or no risk. This includes not reinforcing the self-blame or guilt that families of people with ARBD may feel (Whittinghill, 2002) and treating the person with the addiction with respect. To reduce clinical neglect and nihilism we need better education in diagnosis and treatment and dissemination of evidence-based treatments. It is important that clinicians consider their own personal philosophy on the uses and abuses of alcohol as this may negatively affect the decisions they make about their patient's health and well-being.

A final question is whether people with ARBD should ever be provided with alcohol to make their situation more manageable. Is this ever justified when the gold standard is total abstinence?

Vignette 4

Staff at a care home noticed that pictures were going missing from their walls. Eventually they worked out that a resident was taking and selling them to pay for alcohol. Naturally, the management was annoyed, but agreed to keep the man on and started giving him a couple of beers in the evenings. This reduced his need to buy alcohol (and saved the remaining pictures).

The Wicking Project carried out by Wintringham Specialist Aged Care in Australia (treating homeless men with ARBD) provides alcohol and cigarettes in a controlled program. They report positive benefits and "respite from the daily hardship arising from not knowing when and how the next drink or cigarette was to be acquired" (Rota-Bartelink, 2012, p. 3). It appears that the potential harm of providing a limited amount of alcohol may be outweighed by the benefit of being able to keep people in treatment.

Justice

Justice is about fairness and the equitable sharing of resources: the equal and fair access to services that individuals have a right to. There are, of course, constant arguments about how to share limited health resources. Should they go to those most in need? Where do you get the best value for money? Who is most deserving? In the Oregon priority-setting exercise, the ranking of conditions to be funded depended on the assessment of severity of impact of the condition and the effectiveness of treatment (Sabin and Daniels, 1999). It is difficult to justify discrimination against treatment for substance-use disorders because they represent valid, treatable disorders that often (as noted) have a genetic basis. Outcomes are as good, or better, than many other chronic diseases (Geppert and Bogenschulz, 2009). Some argue that moral obligations are greater to those most in need, in this situation poor, old, brain-damaged people (Lambert, Scheiner and Campbell, 2010). On these criteria ARBD should have high priority for funding of treatment.

However, there are very few specific residential and community services for people with ARBD. The peak age of those presenting with ARBD is between 50 and 60 years of age (Cox, Anderson and McCabe, 2004). They are often placed in residential care with older people and this can be unsuitable and especially challenging if they are intoxicated. Many drug and alcohol services fail to acknowledge those whose substance abuse has reduced their insight and volition and who cannot voluntarily attend the programs on offer.

Substance abuse affects people across all socio-economic, gender and ethnic groups, but services (when they are provided) are not equally suited to all groups (Lambert, Scheiner and Campbell, 2010). People in the criminal justice system, rural populations, women and certain ethnic groups may not have access to appropriate care (Geppert and Bogenschulz, 2009).

There is often an assumption that substance-abuse problems belong to the younger generation and/or that older problem drinkers are hopeless to treat. Problem drinking in older people is often invisible. Physicians underestimate the frequency of alcohol problems and are less likely to screen and treat older people for alcohol abuse (Sharp and Vacha-Haase, 2011; Caputo et al., 2012). There are few services specifically for ageing people and some residential services refuse admission to those over a certain age. While residential treatment outcomes for older people were similar to those of middle-aged people, lower rates of engagement by older people in traditional out-patient substance-abuse services may indicate the need for more age-appropriate treatment options (Oslin et al., 2005). Caputo and colleagues (2012) noted comparable outcomes to treatment with younger people (e.g., 20 per cent abstinent at four years) and urge that attention be paid to the physical frailty of older people and the interaction of commonly prescribed medication with alcohol. Further research into treatment of older people is needed, including those in long-term care (Sharp and Vacha-Haase, 2011).

Vignette 5

Lawrence (72) lives with his wife Jean. She describes him as a "bully" and spoke of having experienced years of physical abuse prior to him becoming less mobile. He continues to be extremely demanding. She only leaves him alone for brief periods, but on numerous occasions he has phoned the police to report her missing. Jean provides good physical care and meals for her husband and keeps an immaculate home. Jean has difficulty standing up to her husband and buys him approximately three litres of spirits weekly. She fears that her husband will refuse respite care. Staff are concerned about her mental and physical health and believe she is at the end of her tether. She has no close family or friends. The specialist addiction service has set up a review to look at the needs and possible options for the couple.

The lack of service provision throws the burden of care unfairly onto others, who are perhaps ill-equipped to manage. The stress for individuals caring for people with alcohol dependence is enormous and they too deserve support.

Finally, there is the enormous expense of alcohol-related problems to society in justice, relationships and employment, as well as health. In Australia, in 1987, one in five admissions to public hospital was due to alcohol-related problems (Baum, 2001). In the absence of consistent pathways to follow, people may remain as in-patients much longer than they might need to (Wilson, 2011). However, people who are discharged prematurely, without access to appropriate treatment, become "revolving-door" clients.

Vignette 6

A 52-year-old male with 150 alcohol-related presentations to emergency departments was compulsorily placed (under guardianship legislation) in aged residential care with a diagnosis of alcoholic dementia (ACE-R = 80/100). When this placement failed, he was transferred to a second facility and provided with 1:1 staffing, but would still walk to the local bottle shop (with the 1:1 "buddy" trailing behind) and return intoxicated and aggressive. He became paranoid and hallucinated. He was later controversially admitted to a mental health unit under the Mental Health Act for "drying out", assessment and treatment of psychosis and confirmation of cognitive impairment. When dry, his capacity returned (ACE-R = 92/100) and the psychosis disappeared. He was subsequently released to independent living. He was lost to follow-up and died within a year.

Despite an enormous cost to the health service, the outcome in this case was poor. Should people have the "right" to drink themselves to death? Is this the best way they can live their lives? Perhaps specifically targeted treatment for this man and others like him would be a more effective way of using scarce health resources (Wilson *et al.*, 2012). It has been demonstrated that adequate treatment of substance-induced disorders saves seven dollars for every dollar spent (Lambert, Scheiner and Campbell, 2010).

Conclusion

The traditional principles of medical ethics provide a guide to approaching decisions around treatment of ARBD, but balancing the principles without being able to predict the outcomes of intervention is difficult. Discussion with clinical and legal colleagues, as well as the person with ARBD and their family, will aid decision-making. The most challenging decisions are about whether to compulsorily treat a person with impaired capacity who continues to drink, especially when treatment facilities are not ideal. People can improve with abstinence and capacity can be regained. Although relapse is common, outcomes are, nevertheless, better than many clinicians assume.

Negative judgment of people perceived to have brought their problem on themselves can deter them from seeking help. Stigma in the wider community and among health care-providers means that treatment may be inadequate, unco-ordinated and poorly funded. Provision of suitable programs of care would not only improve the quality of life of people with ARBD and their care-givers, but also free up general hospital beds and more effectively use limited health care resources.

Acknowledgments

Thanks to Elizabeth Niven and Ashley Koning for their contributions to this chapter.

References

American Psychiatric Association. (2013). *Diagnostic and Statistical Manual of Mental Disorders* (5th edn). Arlington, VA: APA.

Appelbaum, P. (2007). Assessment of patients' capacity to consent to treatment. *New England Journal of Medicine*, 357, 1834–40.

Baum, F. (2001). *The New Public Health: An Australian Perspective* (p. 375). Melbourne: Oxford University Press.

Bodani, M., Reed, L. and Kopelman, M. (2009). Addictive and toxic disorders. In A. David, S. Fleminger, M. Kopelman, S. Lovestone and J. Meller (eds), *Lishman's Organic Psychiatry* (4th edn) (pp. 689–743). Chichester: Wiley Blackwell.

Bossers, W., van der Woude, L., Boersma, F., Scherder, E. and van Heuvelen, M. (2012). Recommended measures for the assessment of cognitive and physical performance in older patients with dementia: a systematic review. *Dementia and Geriatric Cognitive Disorders Extra*, 2(1), 589–609.

Caputo, F., Vignoli, T., Leggio, L., Addolorato, G., Zoli, G. and Bernardi, M. (2012). Alcohol use disorders in the elderly: a brief overview from epidemiology to treatment options. *Experimental Gerontology*, 47, 411–16.

Cox, S., Anderson, I. and McCabe, L. (2004). *A Fuller Life: Report of the Expert Group on Alcohol Related Brain Damage*. Stirling: Dementia Services Development Centre, University of Stirling.

Fadda, F. and Rossetti, Z. (1998). Chronic alcohol consumption: from neuroadaptation to neurodegeneration. *Progress in Neurobiology*, 56, 385–431.

Folstein, M., Folstein, S. and McHugh, P. (1975) "Mini-mental state": a practical method for grading the cognitive state of patients for the clinician. *Journal of Psychiatric Research*, 12, 189–98.

Geppert, C. and Bogenschulz, M. (2009). Ethics in substance use disorder treatment. *Psychiatric Clinics of North America*, 32, 283–97.

Hannay, H., Howieson, D., Loring, D., Fischer, J. and Lezak, M. (2004) Neuropathology for the neuropsychologist. In M. Lezak, D. Howieson and D. Loring (eds), *Neuropsychological Assessment* (4th edn) (pp. 157–285). Oxford: Oxford University Press.

Harper, C. (2009). The neuropathology of alcohol-related brain damage. *Alcohol and Alcoholism*, 4(2), 136–40.

Lambert, B., Scheiner, N. and Campbell, D. (2010) Ethical issues and addiction. *Journal of Addictive Diseases*, 29, 164–74.

The Law Commission: Te Aka Matua o te Ture (2010). *Compulsory Treatment for Substance Dependence: A Review of the Alcoholism and Drug Addiction Act 1966*, REPORT 118. Wellington: The Law Commission.

Mioshi, E., Dawson, K., Mitchell, J., Arnold, R. and Hodges, J. (2006) The Addenbrooke's Cognitive Examination Revised (ACE-R): a brief cognitive test battery for dementia screening. *International Journal of Geriatric Psychiatry*, 21(11), 1078–85.

Nasreddine, Z., Phillips, N., Bedirian, V., Charbonneau, S., Whitehead, V., Collin, I., Cummings, J. and Chertkow, H. (2005). The Montreal Cognitive Assessment, MoCA: a brief screening tool for mild cognitive impairment. *Journal of the American Geriatrics Society*, 53, 695–9.

Molloy, D., Darzins, P. and Strang, D. (1999). *Capacity to Decide*. Troy, Canada: Newgrange Press.

Oslin, D., Slaymaker, V., Blow, F., Owen, P. and Colleran, C. (2005). Treatment outcomes for alcohol dependence among middle-aged and older adults. *Addictive Behaviours*, 30, 1431–6.

Rabins, P. and Black, B. (2010) Ethical issues in geriatric psychiatry. *International Review of Psychiatry*, 22(3), 267–73.

Rota-Bartelink, A. (2012). *The Wicking Project: Older People with Acquired Brain Injury and Associated Complex Behaviours: A Psychosocial Model of Care Final Report, Executive Summary*. Melbourne: Wintringham Specialist Aged Care. http://www.wintringham.org.au/news/wickingresearchpublished.aspx. Accessed 21 August 2013.

Ryan, C., Nielssen, O., Paton, M. and Large, M. (2010) Clinical decisions in psychiatry should not be based on risk assessment. *Australasian Psychiatry*, 18(5), 398–403.

Sabin J. and Daniels N. (1999). Ethical issues in mental health resource allocation. In S. Bloch, P. Chodoff and S. Green (eds), *Psychiatric Ethics* (3rd edn) (pp. 383–99). Oxford: Oxford University Press.

Sharp, L. and Vacha-Haase, T. (2011). Physician attitudes regarding alcohol use screening in older adult patients. *Journal of Applied Gerontology*, 30, 226–40.

Smith I. and Hillman A. (1999) Management of alcohol Korsakoff syndrome. *Advances in Psychiatric Treatment*, 5, 271–8.

Svanberg, J., Morrison, F. and Cullen, B. (2015) Neuropsychological assessment of alcohol-related cognitive impairment. In J. Svanberg, A. Withall, B. Draper and S. Bowden (eds), *Alcohol and the Adult Brain*. Hove: Psychology Press.

Welch K. A. (2011) Neurological complications of alcohol and misuse of drugs, Review. *Practical Neurology*, 11, 206–19.

Whittinghill, D. (2002) Ethical considerations for the use of family therapy in substance abuse treatment. *The Family Journal*, 10(1), 75–8.

Wilson, K. (2011) Alcohol related brain damage: a 21st-century management conundrum. *The British Journal of Psychiatry*, 199(3), 176–7.

Wilson K., Halsey A., Macpherson H., Billington, J., Hill S., Johnson G., Raju, K. and Abbott, P. (2012) The psycho-social rehabilitation of patients with alcohol related brain damage in the community. *Alcohol and Alcoholism*, 47(3), 304–11.

12

THE CLINICAL REHABILITATION OF PEOPLE WITH ALCOHOL-RELATED BRAIN DAMAGE

Ken Wilson

Stigma (Boughy, 2007) and ignorance (MacRae and Cox, 2003) tend to foster the myth that people with brain damage as a consequence of prolonged exposure to alcohol and malnutrition are "hopeless" cases. This pessimism is reflected in the lack of service provision and care, resulting in patients being "bounced from pillar to post" (Boughy, 2007), denied access to appropriate care (e.g., Mental Welfare Commission, 2006) and being dumped in inappropriate institutions, resulting in increased disability, ongoing alcohol misuse, readmission and premature death (Price *et al.*, 1988). The main thrust of this chapter is to dispel some of these misinformed assumptions by examining the natural course of alcohol-related brain damage (ARBD), exploring the evidence supporting active intervention and examining the implications of the evidence in the context of service provision.

"Alcohol-related brain damage" is now an accepted clinical term across the UK and Europe, founded through practical experience and incorporating the term "alcohol-related dementia". The latter term can lead to associations with neurode-generative disorders, implying a progressive and deteriorating condition. However, the great majority of people with ARBD will improve in the context of abstinence, appropriate nutrition and care (MacRae and Cox, 2003). "Alcohol-related brain damage" is a generic term that includes a wide range of syndromes primarily caused through prolonged misuse of alcohol and thiamine deficiency. Necessarily, the term encompasses the Wernicke/Korsakoff spectrum, cerebellar dysfunction, related amnesiac presentations and the most common presentation of dysexecutive syndrome.

Due to the underdiagnosis of Wernicke's Encephalopathy (WE) and high frequency of comorbid problems, most cases of ARBD are not diagnosed or, if they are, rarely receive appropriate intervention. As a result, cases may deteriorate in the community, presenting to services at a later stage of the syndrome. Many hospital wards, accident and emergency units, alcohol treatment services and primary care services will readily recognize the individual presenting with a history of recurrent

withdrawals, hospital admissions, personal neglect, social, financial and family breakdown, malnutrition and chronic alcohol-related physical problems. It is this population that is of high risk and is the most easily identified. However, the subtle
presentation of frontal lobe dysfunction is more difficult to recognize and assess.
Such patients may still be in employment and be functioning fairly well. However,
time will tell through loss of social awareness and higher-order thinking, including
increasing problems in planning and complex decision-making. The person will
eventually experience difficulty in synthesizing information, become increasingly
impulsive and may develop progressively irrational behavior. Eventually memory
problems become more difficult to mask from others and may be seen alongside
increasing incompetence at work, frequently confounded by ongoing drinking
and lack of insight. In the absence of appropriate assessment of cognition and
capacity these vulnerable people are often missed and will deteriorate as drinking
and self-neglect continues. Common sense dictates that people attending alcohol
services for detoxification and treatment may be of particularly high risk of
presenting with these more subtle presentations. This chapter will review the literature relating to the management of people presenting into acute care and also
explore the issues relating to people presenting through community alcohol treatment services.

With regard to both groups of patients, the main question to consider is this: are
abstinence and long-term nutritional support and supplementation sufficient to
lead to optimal levels of cognitive, social and behavioral improvement, or do patients
require and benefit from specific or specialized interventions? In the absence of
robust research, this question is impossible to answer with any certainty. It is evident
that abstinence and nutritional stabilization are seminal to the recovery process. A
comprehensive (but not systematic) review of the literature provides some descriptive
reports that help to inform the debate. Examples of long-term follow-up studies
include two fairly old studies from Australia: Price and colleagues (1988) followed up
37 patients for one year following discharge into non-specialized community care.
Ten of these patients (27 per cent) were successfully placed, a further 20 (54.1 per
cent) were described as dysfunctional and the remaining seven were dead. Two years
earlier, Lennane (1986), within a specialized service, followed up 104 patients for
between eight months and two years. Fifty-three of these patients were classified as
successful placements, 11 (10.6 per cent) had been readmitted into hospital and the
remainder were lost to follow-up or presumed dead. Based on a comparison of
the outcomes of these studies, Price and colleagues make the case for specialized
service provision (Price *et al.*, 1988). The potential benefit of specifically commissioned specialist services is represented by Wilson and colleagues' (Wilson *et al.*,
2012) study, which demonstrated relatively good cognitive, behavioral and social
outcomes. Outcome studies of drug- or alcohol-abusing patients with cognitive
dysfunction in long-term specialist residential settings have demonstrated better outcomes (Fals-Stewart and Schafer, 1992; DeLeon, 1984; DeLeon and Jainhill, 1981)
than when placed in generic institutions. These findings are supported by Blansjaar,
Takens and Zwinderman (1992) and Ganzelves, Geus and Wester (1994) in which

ARBD patients referred to specialized nursing homes showed better cognitive preservation, improvement in social functioning and enhanced speed of information processing than when in non-specialist homes. In a study of alcohol management, Rychtarik and colleagues (2000) described a better outcome in people with cognitive impairment when treated for alcohol dependency in institutional settings, compared to out-patient clinics (Rychtarik *et al.*, 2000).

In their comprehensive review of the literature, Bates, Bowden and Barry (2002) draw on research relating to acquired brain damage. In doing so, they emphasize the importance of an ecologically relevant program of rehabilitation in which patients are encouraged to acquire skills relevant to their personal functionality and to develop environmental, behavioral and cognitive processes to accommodate residual areas of deficit. This approach is supported by Baddeley, Kopelman and Wilson (2002), in which memory and orientation aids also play an important role in rehabilitation of ARBD patients. In addition to these longer-term studies, there are some reports demonstrating the benefit of specific cognitive exercises in enhancing performance (Forsberg and Goldman, 1987). Notably, there is some indication that specifically targeted exercises/interventions may have a generic beneficial effect across non-targeted cognitive domains as well (Forsberg and Goldman, 1987).

What limited information there is indicates that care planning and person-centered rehabilitative pathways that draw on established expertise are likely to enhance improvement across social, cognitive and behavioral domains. Whether this expertise/specialization is nested within other services or established within the context of an alcohol treatment service will depend on local service strengths and configurations. A variety of examples exist within the UK and include the provision of services through neuropsychiatric specialists, early-onset dementia services, "stand-alone" services within the context of and accessing the wider services of mental health and social care organizations, and services closely associated with alcohol treatment service provision. A variety of private organizations also exist. They vary in provision and relationship with commissioning agencies and other service providers.

Assessment of ARBD

As mentioned, there is a strong possibility that people presenting to alcohol treatment services may experience varying degrees of intellectual damage (Bates, Bowden and Barry, 2002). A recent cognitive examination of a consecutive series of 188 patients presenting to a detoxification service in the northwest of England indicated that 22 per cent presented with significant cognitive impairment. Cognitive deficits are likely to have a direct impact on prognosis in terms of response to alcohol treatment programs (Bates *et al.*, 2006). Most alcohol treatment services do not formally cater for the cognitive damage experienced by a significant proportion of patients. This may lead to problems in engagement with services, and may be misconstrued as the patient not wanting to use the service (Copersino *et al.*, 2012), not complying or as "in denial" (Rinn *et al.*, 2002). What evidence there is suggests that appropriate cognitive testing and assessing risk of thiamine deficiency should be the norm in the assessment of such patients (NICE, 2011). Therapeutic programs can be appropriately adjusted (Meek, Clark and Solana, 1989; Glass, 1991) to meet individual needs. It is important to note that, provided alcohol abstinence is achieved and nutrition stabilized with appropriate thiamine and vitamin supplementation, then, in most cases, cognitive performance is likely to improve.

From a pragmatic perspective there are four ways of categorizing potential cognitive damage in these patients: the acute effects of intoxication, medium-term cognitive effects, taking three months to recover (stage two), the longer-term effects that may last up to three years (stage three) and permanent effects (relating to stages four and five of rehabilitation). In the absence of more specific guidelines, practical options should be considered.

1. A cognitive examination should be considered early in the withdrawal process and patients at risk of thiamine deficiency should be identified (Thomson, Guerrini and Marshall, 2009) and prescribed parental thiamine.
2. After withdrawal, prior to formal engagement in alcohol education and related treatment, a further examination should be undertaken with view to:
   a. Establishing the level of insight and mental capacity the person has with regard to managing the planned program.
   b. Informing the timing of the program/intervention, bearing in mind that cognitive performance is likely to improve in the context of three months' abstinence, good nutrition and appropriate psychosocial support.
   c. Adjusting interventions and degree of engagement required to suit the individual's personal needs, informed through awareness of cognitive problems.
3. In some cases, the degree of cognitive damage may be so severe that any attempt to engage is compromised; the patient is unable to make relevant, informed decisions and may be a danger to him/herself or others as a consequence of confusion. In these cases, the patient should be considered as suffering from a significant mental disability and the best interest of the patient should be considered in terms of the Mental Capacity Act (England and Wales) or the Adults with Incapacity Act (Scotland) and appropriate referral made for further neurocognitive assessment and management.
4. Likewise, all patients should have a review of their nutritional status and the risk of thiamine deficiency assessed.
   a. When there are one or more signs of Wernicke's Syndrome (WS) the patient should be managed under medical supervision with intravenous thiamine as an in-patient.
   b. When there is a significant risk of thiamine deficiency but no evidence of WS then the patient should be treated with intramuscular thiamine in the context of being aware of the allergic history of the patient (e.g., history of eczema, asthma and allergies to medications and previous treatments).

The impact of impaired cognition in the context of alcohol treatment

In considering the implications of cognitive damage for alcohol educational and treatment programs, there is evidence indicating that the cognitive and behavioral functions outlined in Table 12.1 may be affected, even in relatively mild cases.

A comprehensive knowledge of the individual needs of the patient should inform adaptation of routinely delivered alcohol treatment programs (Fals-Stewart and Lucente, 1994). There are a number of possible adaptations described within the literature, outlined in Table 12.2.

It is likely that problems in concentration, memory, understanding, planning and following complex instructions will influence the individual's engagement with the therapist and team. It may be necessary for the team/therapist to adopt an active engagement strategy to accommodate the needs of cognitively impaired patients. This may involve more frequent visits, more guidance, transport assistance and social support. It is important for the clinician to conceptualize these issues as problem in learning rather than simply assigning them to "motivational issues" (McCrady and Smith, 1986).

TABLE 12.1 Cognitive and behavioral functions that may be affected in individuals presenting to alcohol treatment services

- The ability to concentrate (DeFranco, Tarbox and McLaughlin, 1985).
- Difficulties in learning new information (anterograde amnesia) (Alterman *et al.*, 1989, Mann *et al.*, 1999, Zinn, Stein and Swartzwelder, 2004, Schmidt *et al.*, 2005).
- Problems in reasoning (Beatty *et al.*, 1996, Mann *et al.*, 1999, Zinn, Stein and Swartzwelder, 2004), problem-solving difficulties (Beatty *et al.*, 1996, Mann *et al.*, 1999) and explaining actions and reasons (Beatty *et al.*, 1996).
- The ability to understand complex information and concepts (such as alcohol dependency and implications for behavior) and difficulty in acquiring drink-refusal strategies (Smith and McCrady, 1991).
- The ability to be able to change from one stream of thought to another with normal degrees of flexibility (difficulty in working in groups or following complex discussions) (Beatty *et al.*, 1996; Fox *et al.*, 2000).
- Within the first few weeks of abstinence there is likely to be increased proneness to make impulsive decisions and there is less awareness of the longer-term implications of decisions and actions (Weissenborn and Duka, 2003, Davies *et al.*, 2005, Parks *et al.*, 2010).
- Understanding risks related to actions and decisions (Blume, Schmaling and Marlatt, 2005).
- Reduced organizational skills (Fox *et al.*, 2000, Parks *et al.*, 2010), and planning (Weissenborn and Duka, 2003).
- Poor compliance to treatment programs (Copersino *et al.*, 2012).
- Lower confidence (Bates *et al.*, 2006).
- Breakdown of interpersonal relationships (Patterson *et al.*, 1988).
- Difficulty in remembering and working out the relationship between objects (perceiving and remembering the locations of objects relative to each other and in two- and three-dimensional space), with potential consequences for DIY, constructing things, working with difficult machinery and driving.

TABLE 12.2 Possible adaptations to alcohol treatment for those with cognitive impairment

Adapt treatment for alcohol-use disorders	Focus on supportive or enforced abstinence (McCrady and Smith, 1986). This may be appropriate if the person is too incapacitated to make decisions and may have to be placed in a protective environment.
	Keep drink management strategies very simple and easy to manage.
	In the first few weeks, particular emphasis should be placed on reducing exposure to risk as a consequence of increased likelihood of impulsive decision-making (Weissenborn and Duka, 2003, Davies *et al.*, 2005, Parks *et al.*, 2010).
Memory and learning adaptations	Development of learning texts and materials to assure that one concept is understood and learned before going onto another (McCrady and Smith, 1986).
	Simplification of educational materials (McCrady and Smith, 1986).
	Repetition of information (Kessels, van Loon and Wester, 2007).
	Offering information in a number of ways, including verbal, written and diagrammatic methods, and through multiple sensory modalities (McCrady and Smith, 1986).
	Use memory cues, name tags for staff and prompts (Morgan, McSharry and Sireling, 1990; McCrady and Smith, 1986).
	Diary-keeping may help in terms of cuing memories and informing future planning and activities (Wilson *et al.*, 2012).
Consider timing of interventions, both in commencing and delivering treatment	Delaying the introduction of educational programs until the patient has made sufficient cognitive recovery (McCrady and Smith, 1986).
	Expect the cognitively impaired person to take much longer to benefit from interventions (McCrady and Smith, 1986).
	Providing increased time for individuals within contact sessions (VanDamme and d'Ydewalle, 2008).
Support impaired executive functions	Allow for reduced levels of concentration (DeFranco, Tarbox and McLaughlin, 1985) and difficulties in swapping from topic to topic (Beatty *et al.*, 1996). People may be helped through simplifying subject discussions and educational points within each contact, with an emphasis on focusing on one or two points.
	Support planning by providing a timetable; structure may help (ARBIAS, 2007).
	Working out simple rules to apply when dealing with problems may offer some help (Bardenhagen, Oscar-Berman and Bowden, 2007). This may include problem-solving approaches (D'Zurilla and Goldfried 1971).
Positive reinforcement	Providing some "rewards" relating to appropriate behavior may be beneficial. These may be psychological or social, but should be tailored to the individual and may help recall (Hochhalter and Joseph, 2001).

Example of a specialist ARBD service in the UK

In addressing the management of patients presenting to acute hospital settings, the Wirral services (Wilson *et al.*, 2012) have developed a five-stage rehabilitation program, which provides a relatively structured framework for managing people presenting with severe ARBD. The model was developed from a literature review, drawing on work by a range of specialists within the field, and its utility explored in the context of a consecutive series of patients referred with severe ARBD. The model is flexible enough to be adapted to most service contexts. In acute settings, most patients present in the context of withdrawal, a physical or social crisis associated with excessive drinking (e.g., head trauma, convulsions or encephalopathy).

Stage 1: stabilization

The first stage of the program (stabilization) is devoted to the physical stabilization of the individual. UK guidelines already exist for the management of these conditions. The obvious role of parenteral vitamin supplementation should be emphasized at this stage (NICE, 2010, 2011). The guidelines do not address the psychosocial issues that can reinforce and exacerbate physical health.

Stage 2: assessment and liaison

Having established a causative link between alcohol misuse and the patient's cognitive presentation, the next stage of assessment should include an assessment of capacity in relationship to any of the pertinent aspects of the patient's care plan and associated decisions. This should be considered in the context of appropriate legislation, such as the Mental Capacity Act used in England and Wales, or Adults with Incapacity Act in Scotland. Such an assessment will inform the development of the care plan. During the in-patient stage, all attempts should be made to contact carers and other agencies that have already been working with the patient so as to establish a comprehensive personal history and prepare the ground for future care planning and engagement. Commissioning arrangements should be in place for the relative speedy discharge of the patient from acute hospital settings, as soon as physical stabilization has been completed. This is self-evidently important. In the first instance, the management of confused patients in an acute medical or surgical setting is often problematic for both patients and staff and, second, the patient will be seen to be occupying an acute bed when there is no valid reason (Popoola, Keating and Cassidy, 2008).

During the second stage of rehabilitation, cognition is likely to improve over a few weeks (Cocchi and Chiavarini, 1997a; 1997b). This period is reflected in Oslin's Criteria (Oslin *et al.*, 1998) in which there is a period of approximately two to three months (of abstinence) after which the patient should be assessed in order to evaluate more longstanding cognitive deficits. In this stage, patients may require institutional care; however, in the context of risk assessment and appropriate community support, non-institutional settings may be appropriate. Irrespective of setting, the establishment of a safe, supportive and structured environment is essential. Tasks at this stage are outlined in Table 12.3.

Stage 3: rehabilitation

Once the acute, toxic effects of alcohol on the brain have resolved, it can be expected that residual cognitive impairment during the next (third) stage, will improve gradually over two to three years (in the context of an alcohol-free environment), during which there is notable improvement in associated behavioral disturbance and functionality (Bates, Bowden and Barry, 2002). This improvement is mirrored in changes in structure and function of the brain. However, there is some evidence that concomitant trauma or vascular disease will slow the process (Bartels *et al.*, 2007). Younger people tend to recover more speedily than older patients (Rourke and Grant, 1999). A large number of studies have explored variance in

TABLE 12.3 Tasks to support the establishment of a safe, supportive and structured environment

Assessment	Full assessment of capacity and employment of appropriate legal framework to provide the minimum restrictive environment consistent with the safe management of the patient.
	Introduction of multidisciplinary ongoing assessment and care planning undertaken by teams with specialist knowledge of rehabilitation and the particular needs of those with ARBD (MacRae and Cox, 2003).
Safe environment	Establishment of a calm environment and introduction of daily routine and structure (Kopelman *et al.*, 2009).
Alcohol treatment	Abstinence (Grant, Adams and Reed, 1986; Malloy *et al.*, 1990) and good nutrition (Grant, Adams and Reed, 1986; Malloy *et al.*, 1990).
	Early engagement of alcohol treatment services (MacRae and Cox, 2003).
Social networks	Development (where relevant) of relationships between institutional staff and specialized care team (MacRae and Cox, 2003).
	The introduction of psychosocial support and collaborative relationships (Ylvisaker and Feeney, 1998).
	Early engagement of family and other interested parties already involved with the patient (Ylvisaker and Feeney, 1998).
Early cognitive rehabilitation and psychosocial support	Introduction of memory and orientation cues (Baddeley, Kopelman and Wilson, 2002).
	Mood stabilization (Grant, Adams and Reed, 1986; Malloy *et al.*, 1990) and regularization of sleep pattern (Grant, Adams and Reed, 1986; Malloy *et al.*, 1990).

cognitive improvement across time, with conflicting findings. What little evidence there is indicates that verbal learning improves before other cognitive functions (Parsons and Leber, 1982). Information processing, abstraction and perceptual motor skills may take longer (Yohman, Parsons and Leber, 1985).

As in stage two, there are recommendations relating to both specific and generalized interventions. The rehabilitative approach should be holistic (Prigatano, Glisky and Klonoff, 1996) and not merely focus on cognitive rehabilitation. The main purpose of rehabilitation is to enhance the individual's sense of internal control (Ylvisaker and Feeney, 1998). This involves the introduction of a program of functional rehabilitation (defined as achieving positive psychosocial adaptations by means of collaborative interventions provided in real-world settings) (Ylvisaker and Feeney, 1998). This is facilitated through a milieu-based approach to rehabilitation of the individual (Heinssen, 1996) in which increasing independence in relevant (Giles, 1994) life skills should be purposefully encouraged (Ylvisaker and Feeney, 1998). The environment (whether institutional or domestic) should be facilitative (one in which adaptations can be made to accommodate and optimize the changing cognitive profile of the individual) (Heinssen, 1996; Bates, Bowden and Barry, 2002). The ongoing collaborative (with the patient) assessment should be carried out by an experienced multidisciplinary team in the context of care planning. The patient's decision-making capacity should be assessed in terms of all relevant aspects of life, where it is considered clinically necessary, including exposure to alcohol. The appropriate legal framework should be established which will minimize the restriction for the patient and cater for acceptable levels of risk exposure. Management should be conducted with full collaboration of the patient wherever possible and may include working closely with care staff and family members or friends. Not only does this facilitate continuity, it also enables an easier generalization of skills learned in one environment to other situations, making translation between an institution and more independent living easier (Ylvisaker and Feeney, 1998).

The assessment should furnish targeted, everyday behaviors and skills in which the patient is deficient. Reskilling and the introduction of procedures to facilitate completion of the task will enhance a sense of self-control, independence and confidence (Ylvisaker and Feeney, 1998). In the majority of institutionalized cases it is usual to increase independence and establish the individual in a less dependent environment as they improve over the two to three years of this stage. Three sequential interventions are recommended:

1. Diary keeping (ARBIAS, 2007):
   - To provide memory and reminiscence material.
   - To promote organizational awareness, a sense of predictability and routine.
   - To facilitate patient responsibility and facilitate independence.
   - To facilitate the building of collaborative relationships between caring staff, family and others involved in care.

2. Planning (activity scheduling): a development of the diary in which future activities are planned with the patient. This is at first facilitated, then supervised and eventually the patient is enabled to take responsibility.
    *   To promote planning skills.
    *   To promote predictability.
    *   To reduce periods in which the patient may be vulnerable to relapse.
    *   To provide a vehicle by which increasing independence can be encouraged.
    *   To promote social involvement.
3. Life-skill development and problem-solving (ARBIAS, 2007): this is a procedure by which the patient can be encouraged to become familiar with functional skills which they may have lost or run into problems with. The functional assessment will inform the therapist and patient as to which areas should be focused on. Skills can range from simple to complex, depending on the degree of deficit.
    *   Skill development is designed to improve the independence and sense of control of the patient.
    *   Skill development is a natural progression of the "planning phase", in which potential target skills are identified and rehearsed until an optimal level of independence is reached.
    *   It is collaborative.
    *   It is planned with the patient.
    *   Complex tasks are frequently broken down into stages, with each stage being mastered by the individual prior to moving onto the next stage.
        It is always best to focus on readily achievable skills in the early stages of rehabilitation and capitalize on the improving cognition and behavior through introducing more complex skills as the patient progresses. Skill development may often include generalizing learned skills into less dependent environments as the patient progresses (Ylvisaker and Feeney, 1998).
4. Memory and orientation cues: patients with ARBD can learn and recall new information. This is facilitated by provision of memory cues and encouraging patients not to guess answers (errorless learning; Baddeley, Kopelman and Wilson, 2002). Simple diary-keeping and activity planning can be facilitated by white boards in bedrooms or equivalent so as to facilitate memory and orientation. Updating these and the use of the diary and planner may be facilitating by the carer but with eventual responsibility being taken by the patient.

In the context of psychosocial support, Kadden and colleagues (1989) suggest that interactional group work is beneficial, when compared to CBT (other than in depressed cases). It is certainly necessary to encourage the patient to build informal and formal social networks in order to reduce the likelihood of relapse (Department of Health, 2006).

Stage 4

As cognition reaches an optimal level of improvement, compensatory mechanisms play a role in facilitating further independence. Stage four is characterized by the purposeful acquisition of social, cognitive, behavioral and environmental adaptations (Bates, Bowden and Barry, 2002). It merges closely with stage three and is a critical component of the program. The importance of a facilitative environment (Ylvisaker and Feeney, 1998) is evident. Longstanding environmental adaptations and support provide the optimum situation to achieve the maximum independence in the context of managing risk. Approximately 25 per cent of patients can be expected not to improve enough to enable them to progress out of institutional care. Wilson and colleagues (2012) found that the majority of such patients presented with significant concomitant mental or physical health problems.

Stage 5

The final stage (stage five) of the care planning and rehabilitative process is characterized by integration into a stable social environment and appropriate support structures so as to reduce the likelihood of relapse into alcohol abuse. This phase requires ongoing psychosocial management and is informed by the National Guidelines for the management of people with alcohol-misuse problems (Department of Health, 2006). It should be considered as integral to the care plan (Department of Health, 2006). It includes a number of issues that should be considered:

- Psychosocial therapies: designed to help individuals avoid or cope with high-risk drinking situations.
- Social support: to facilitate lifestyle changes. These may well include maintaining environmental and social adaptations to sustain optimum levels of independence. Examples may include financial help and advocacy, support in maintaining community living arrangements, ongoing institutional care. Social networking is important and re-establishing family connections may be possible; however, many patients will have been socially isolated and may benefit from the development of new networks to support abstinence.
- Structured program of activities: this is a natural extension of the rehabilitative program (diary-keeping, planning and skill development). This is designed to build on the individual's success, identify problems and overcome them through adapting the schedule, reinforce skills and behaviors and prevent relapse.
- Specific alcohol management: ongoing engagement with specialist alcohol treatment services will depend on the relapse vulnerability of the individual and the nature of the local service provision. Any direct engagement must accommodate the residual cognitive and behavioral deficits of the individual. Patients with ARBD frequently find it difficult to engage with generic service provision (Weinstein and Shaffer, 1993). Cognitive dysfunction may contribute to the patient "denying" that alcohol is a problem (Rinn et al., 2002).
- Mood control is often a problem: especially when the patient is confronted with tasks and problems that are too difficult (Fals-Stewart, Shanahan and Brown, 1995). This is not dissimilar to the catastrophic reaction frequently

experienced by patients with stroke or organic brain disease when confronted with frustrating situations (Carota *et al.*, 2001). As the patient gains insight into their circumstances, depression (Wilson *et al.*, 2012) and other problems from the patient's past may well emerge and need appropriate management as both are likely to make the individual vulnerable to relapse into the oblivion of alcohol misuse.

- Ongoing monitoring is essential and should be fully considered as part of the care planning process.

These five stages of management closely reflect the natural history of cognitive, behavioral and social changes experienced by patients with ARBD in the context of abstinence and nutritional stabilization. They have been informed by the literature and their utility has been tested in the context of a study of more than 40 consecutive patients referred to the Wirral service (Wilson *et al.*, 2012). It is difficult to argue that each stage is discrete and separate, as experience will show that patients will develop through these stages at differing rates of progress. Some patients may make a full recovery at the end of stage two, with no evidence of residual cognitive damage, implying that they have not been vitamin deficient. Others may make relatively slow progress; these patients may have psychiatric or physical complications. The five-stage model is summarized in Figure 12.1.

ARBD may present in a variety of service situations. Notably, it can present in the maternity unit as fetal alcohol syndrome, in the context of prison services or in primary care, among others. In this chapter we have presented the literature in relationship to management in the context of acute presentation in general hospital settings and, potentially, the more subtle presentation in the context of alcohol treatment service provision. However, the main aim of this chapter is to present the reader with a framework by which ARBD can be managed and which, in the context of adults, is flexible enough to be applied in a variety of settings. The second aim is to demonstrate that the majority of patients with ARBD will dramatically benefit from abstinence, nutritional support and active and planned care, utilizing fairly basic principles of psychosocial management, care planning and assertive follow-up. Lastly, in the absence of "specialization", there is nothing to stop a local service providing basic care, as it would with any other vulnerable, stigmatized patient with severe mental illness. Developing a service will soon demonstrate that it is potentially cost effective and worth commissioning, even if it is just to reduce hospital admissions and bed days in acute hospital settings (Wilson *et al.*, 2012), irrespective of improving patients' morbidity, mortality and quality of life.

Acknowledgments

The service model described within this chapter is published in the College Report, CR185, "Alcohol and brain damage in adults, with reference to high-risk groups" (Royal College of Psychiatrists, 2014), and is reprinted here with the kind permission of the Royal College of Psychiatrists, UK.

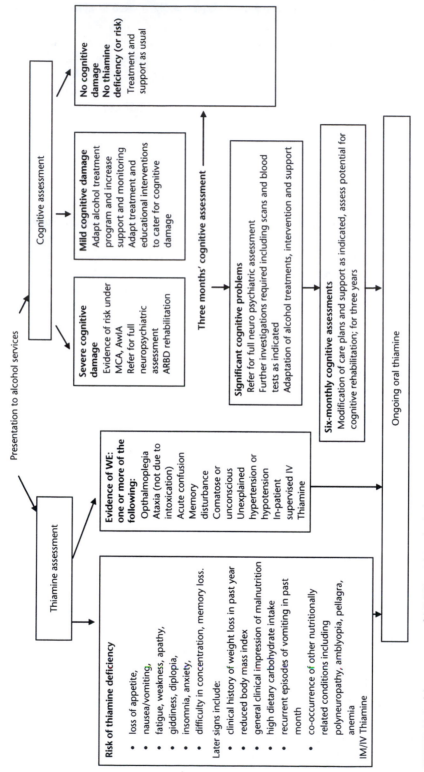

FIGURE 12.1 Management of ARBD within alcohol treatment services.

References

Alterman, A. I., Holahan, J. M., Baughman, T. G. and Michels, S. (1989). Predictors of alcoholics' acquisition of treatment related knowledge. *Journal of Substance Abuse Treatment*, 6, 49–53.

ARBIAS (2011). *Looking Forward: General Information Book on Alcohol Related Brain Impairment* (3rd edn). Bankstown, NSW: ARBIAS.

Baddeley, A. D., Kopelman, M. D. and Wilson, B. A. (2002). *Handbook of Memory Disorders* (2nd edn). Chichester: Wiley.

Bardenhagen, F. J., Oscar-Berman, M. and Bowden, S. C. (2007). Rule knowledge aids performance on spatial and object alternation tasks by alcoholic patients with and without Korsakoff's amnesia. *Neuropsychiatric Diseases and Treatment*, 3(6), 907–18.

Bartels, C., Kunert, H. J., Stawicki, S., Kröner-Herwig, B., Ehrenreich, H. and Krampe, H. (2007). Recovery of hippocampus-related functions in chronic alcoholics during monitored long-term abstinence. *Alcohol and Alcoholism*, 42(2), 92–102.

Bates, M., Bowden, S. and Barry, D. (2002). Neurocognitive impairment associated with alcohol use disorders: implications for treatment. *Experimental and Clinical Psychopharmacology*, 10(3), 193–212.

Bates, M. E., Pawlak, A. P., Tonigan, J. S. and Buckman, J. F. (2006). Cognitive impairment influences drinking outcome by altering therapeutic mechanisms of change. *Psychology of Addictive Behaviors*, 20(3), 241–53.

Beatty, W. W., Hames, K. A., Blanco, C. R., Nixon, S. J. and Tivis, L. J. (1996). Visuospatial perception, construction and memory in alcoholism. *Journal of Studies on Alcohol*, 57(2), 136–43.

Blansjaar, B. A., Takens, H. and Zwinderman, A. H. (1992). The course of alcohol amnestic disorder: a three-year follow-up study of clinical signs and social disabilities. *Acta Psychiatrica Scandinavica*, 86, 240–6.

Blume, A. W., Schmaling, K. B. and Marlatt, G. A., (2005). Memory, executive cognitive function, and readiness to change drinking behavior. *Addictive Behaviours*, 30, 301–14.

Boughy, L. (2007). Alcohol related brain damage: a report of the learning captured from Carenza Care in North Wales. CSIP/Alzheimer's Society Working Group. *http://www.minisitehq. com/businessfiles/6396/Alcoholpercent20Relatedpercent20Brainpercent20Damagepercent20 Reportpercent2024percent20page.pdf*. Accessed 29 June 2014.

Carota, A., Rossetti, A. O., Karapanayiotides, T. and Bogousslavsky, J., (2001). Catastrophic reaction in stroke: a reflex behaviour is aphasic patients. *Neurology*, 57(10), 1902–5.

Cocchi, R. and Chiavarini, M. (1997a). Raven's coloured matrices in female alcoholics before and after detoxification: an investigation on 73 cases. *International Journal of Intellectual Impairment*, 11, 45–9.

Cocchi, R. and Chiavarini, M. (1997b). Raven's coloured matrices in male alcoholics before and after detoxification: a research on 225 subjects. *International Journal of Intellectual Impairment*, 10, 157–60.

Copersino, M. L., Schretlen, D. J., Fitzmaurice, G. M., Sokoloff, J. and Weiss, R. D. (2012). Effects of cognitive impairment on substance abuse treatment attendance: predictive validation of a brief cognitive screening measure. *The American Journal of Drug and Alcohol Abuse*, 38, 246–50.

Davies, S. J. C., Pandit, S. A., Feeney, A., Stevenson, B. J., Kerwin, R. W., Nutt, D. J., Marshall, E. J. and Boddington, S. (2005). Imbalance between neuroexcitatory and neuroinhibitory amino acids causes craving for ethanol. *Addictive Behaviors*, 29, 1325–39.

DeFranco, C., Tarbox, A. R. and McLauglin, E. J. (1985). Cognitive deficits as a function of years of alcohol abuse. *American Journal of Drug and Alcohol Abuse*, 11 (3 and 4), 279–93.

DeLeon, G. (1984). Program-based evaluation research in therapeutic communities. *National Institute on Drug Abuse Research Monograph Series*, 51, 69–87.

DeLeon, G. and Jainhill, N. (1981). Male and female drug abusers: social and psychological status two years after treatment in a therapeutic community. *American Journal of Alcohol Abuse*, 8, 595–600.

Department of Health (2006). *Models of Care for Alcohol Misusers*. London: National Treatment Agency for Alcohol Misuse, Department of Health.

D'Zurilla, T. J. and Goldfried, M. R. (1971). Problem solving and behaviour modification. *Journal of Abnormal Psychology*, 78, 107–26.

Fals-Stewart, W. and Schafer, J. (1992). The relationship between length of stay in drug-free therapeutic communities and neurocognitive functioning. *Journal of Clinical Psychology*, 48(4), 539–43.

Fals-Stewart, W. and Lucente, S. (1994). Treating obsessive compulsive disorder among substance misusers: a guide. *Psychology of Addictive Behaviours*, 8(1), 14–23.

Fals-Stewart, W., Shanahan, T. and Brown, L. (1995). Treating alcoholism and drug abuse: a neuropsychiatric perspective. *Psychotherapy in Private Practice*, 14, 1–21.

Forsberg, L. K. and Goldman, M. S., (1987). Experience-dependent recovery of cognitive deficits in alcoholics: extended transfer of training. *Journal of Abnormal Psychology*, 96, 345–53.

Fox, A. M., Coltheart, M., Solowij, N., Michie, P. T. and Fox, G. A. (2000). Dissociable cognitive impairments in problem drinkers. *Alcohol and Alcoholism*, 35(1), 52–4.

Ganzelves, P. G. J., Geus, B. W. J. and Wester, A. J. (1994). Cognitive and behavioural aspects of Korsakoff's syndrome: the effect of special Korsakoff wards in a general hospital. *Tijdschrift voor Alcohol Drugs en Andere Psychotrope Stoffen*, 20, 20–31.

Giles, G. M. (1994). The status of brain injury rehabilitation. *The American Journal of Occupational Therapy*, 48, 199–205.

Glass, I. (1991). Alcoholic brain damage: what does it mean to patients? *British Journal of Addiction*, 86, 819–21.

Grant, I., Adams, K. M. and Reed, R. (1986). Intermediate-duration (subacute) organic mental disorder of alcoholism. Cited in R. K. Heinssen (1996). The cognitive exoskeleton: environmental interventions in cognitive rehabilitation. In P. W. Corrigan and S. C. Yudofsky (eds), *Cognitive Rehabilitation for Neuropsychiatric Disorders* (pp. 395–423). Washington DC: APA.

Heinssen, R. K. (1996). The cognitive exoskeleton: environmental interventions in cognitive rehabilitation. In P. W. Corrigan and S. C. Yudofsky (eds), *Cognitive Rehabilitation for Neuropsychiatric Disorders* (pp. 395–423). Washington DC: APA.

Hochhalter, A. K. and Joseph, B. (2001). Differential outcomes training facilitates memory in people with Korsakoff and Prader-Willi syndromes. *Integrative Physiological and Behavioral Science*, 36(3), 196–204.

Kadden, R. M., Cooney, N. L., Getter, H. and Litt, M. D. (1989). Matching alcoholics to coping skills or interactional therapies: post-treatment results. *Journal of Consulting and Clinical Psychology*, 57(6), 698–704.

Kessels, R. P. C., van Loon, E. and Wester, A. J. (2007). Route learning in amnesia: a comparison of trial-and-error and errorless learning in patients with the Korsakoff syndrome. *Clinical Rehabilitation*, 21(10), 905–11.

Kopelman, M. D., Thomson, A., Guerrini, I. and Marshall, E. J. (2009). The Korsakoff syndrome: clinical aspects, psychology and treatment. *Alcohol and Alcoholism*, 44, 148–54.

Lennane, K. J. (1986). Management of moderate to severe alcohol related brain damage (Korsakoff's syndrome). *Medical Journal of Australia*, 145, 136–43.

MacRae, R. and Cox, S. (2003). *Meeting the Needs of People with Alcohol Related Brain Damage: A Literature Review on the Existing and Recommended Service Provision and Models of Care*. Stirling, UK: University of Stirling.

Malloy, P., Noel, N., Longabaugh, R. and Beattie, M., (1990). Determinants of neuropsychological impairment in antisocial substance abusers. *Addictive Behaviors*, 15, 431–8.

Mann, K., Gunther, A., Stetter, F. and Ackermann, K. (1999). Rapid recovery from cognitive deficits in abstinent alcoholics: a controlled test-retest study. *Alcohol and Alcoholism*, 23(4), 567–74.

McCrady, B. S. and Smith, D. E. (1986). Implications of cognitive impairment for the treatment of alcoholism. *Alcoholism: Clinical and experimental research*, 10(2), 145–9.

Meek, P. S., Clark, H. W. and Solana, V. L. (1989). Neurocognitive impairment: the unrecognized component of dual diagnosis in substance abuse treatment. *Journal of Psychoactive Drugs*, 21, 153–60.

Mental Welfare Commission for Scotland. (2006). *Investigation into the Care and Treatment of Mr H.* Edinburgh: Mental Welfare Commission.

Morgan, J., McSharry, K. and Sireling, L. (1990). Comparison of a system of staff prompting with a programmable electronic diary in a patient with Korsakoff's syndrome. *International Society of Psychiatry*, 36(3), 225–9.

NICE. (2010). *Alcohol-use Disorders: Diagnosis and Clinical Management of Alcohol-Related Physical Complications*. Guideline 100. London: NICE.

NICE. (2011). *Alcohol-Use Disorders: Diagnosis, Assessment and Management of Harmful Drinking and Alcohol Dependence*. Guideline CG115. London: NICE.

Oslin D., Atkinson R., Smith D. and Hendrie, H. (1998). Alcohol related dementia: proposed clinical criteria. *International Journal of Geriatric Psychiatry*, 13, 203–12.

Parks, M., Greenberg, D., Nickel, M., Dietrich, M. S., Rogers, B. P. and Martin, P. R. (2010). Recruitment of additional brain regions to accomplish simple motor tasks in chronic alcohol dependent patients. *Alcoholism: Clinical and Experimental Research*, 34(6), 1098–109.

Parsons, O. A. and Leber, W. R. (1982). Alcohol, cognitive dysfunction and brain damage. *NIAAA Alcohol Health Monographs*, 2, 213–53.

Patterson, B. W., Parsons, O. A., Schaeffer, K. W. and Errico, A. L. (1988). Interpersonal problem solving in alcoholics. *The Journal of Nervous and Mental Disease*, 176(12), 707–13.

Popoola, A., Keating, A. and Cassidy, E. (2008). Alcohol, cognitive impairment and hard to discharge acute hospital inpatients. *Irish Journal of Medical Science*, 177(2), 141–5.

Price, J., Mitchell, S., Wiltshire, B., Graham, J. and Williams, G. (1988). A follow up study of patients with alcohol related brain damage in the community. *Australian Drug and Alcohol Review*, 7, 83–7.

Prigatano, G. P., Glisky, E. L. and Klonoff, P. S. (1996). Cognitive rehabilitation after traumatic brain injury. In P. W. Corrigan and S. C. Yudofsky (eds), *Cognitive Rehabilitation for Neuropsychiatric Disorders*. Washington DC: APA.

Rinn, W., Desai, N., Rosenblatt, H. and Gastfriend, D. R. (2002). Addiction denial and cognitive dysfunction: a preliminary investigation. *Journal of Neuropsychiatry and Clinical Neurosciences*, 14(1), 52–7.

Rourke, S. B. and Grant, I. (1999). The interactive effects of age and length of abstinence on the recovery of neuropsychological functioning in chronic male alcoholics: a 2-year follow-up study. *International Neuropsychological Society*, 5(3), 234–46.

Royal College of Psychiatrists. (2014). Alcohol and brain damage in adults, with reference to high-risk groups. College Report CR185. Available at http://www.rcpsych.ac.uk/files/pdfversion/CR185.pdf. Accessed 7 May 2014.

Rychtarik, R. G., Connors, G. J., Whitney, R. B., McGillicuddy, N. B., Fitterling, J. M. and Wirtz, P. W. (2000). Treatment settings for persons with alcoholism: evidence for matching clients to inpatient vs outpatient care. *Journal of Consulting and Clinical Psychology*, 68(2), 277–89.

Schmidt, K., Gallo, J., Ferri, C., Sesito, N., Giovannetti, T. and Libon D. (2005). The neuropsychological profile of alcohol related dementia suggests cortical and subcortical pathology. *Dementia and Geriatric Cognitive Disorders*, 20, 286–91.

Smith, D. E. and McCrady, B. S., (1991). Cognitive impairment among alcoholics: impact on drink refusal skill acquisition and treatment outcome. *Addictive Behaviours*, 16, 265–74.

Thomson, A., Guerrini, I. and Marshall, E. (2009). Nutritional issues in gastroenterology: Wernicke's encephalopathy, the role of thiamine. *Practical Gastroenterology*, 75, 21–30.

VanDamme, I. and d'Ydewalle, G. (2008). Elaborative processing in the Korsakoff syndrome: Context versus habit. *Brain Cognition*, 67(2), 212–24.

Weinstein, C. S. and Shaffer, H. J. (1993). Neurocognitive aspects of substance abuse treatment: a psychotherapist's primer. *Psychotherapy: Theory, Research, Practice, Training*, 30(2), 317–33.

Weissenborn, R. and Duka, T. (2003). Acute alcohol effects on cognitive function in social drinkers: their relationship to drinking habits, *Psychopharmacology*, 165, 306–12.

Wilson, K., Halsey, A., Macpherson, H., Billington, J., Hill, S., Johnstone, G., Raju, K. and Abbot, P., (2012). The psycho-social rehabilitation of patients with alcohol-related brain damage in the community. *Alcohol and Alcoholism*, 47(3), 304–11.

Ylvisaker, M. and Feeney, T. J. (1998). *Collaborative Brain Injury Intervention: Positive Everyday Routines*. San Diego, CA: Singular.

Yohman, J. R., Parsons, O. A. and Leber, W. R. (1985). Lack of recovery in male alcoholics' neuropsychological performance one year after treatment. *Alcoholism: Clinical and Experimental Research*, 9(2), 114–17.

Zinn, S., Stein, R. and Swartzwelder, H. S. (2004). Executive functioning early in abstinence from alcohol. *Alcoholism: Clinical and Experimental Research*, 28(9), 1338–46.

INDEX